F. X. Schouppe

Abridged course of religious instruction, apologetic, dogmatic, and moral

F. X. Schouppe

Abridged course of religious instruction, apologetic, dogmatic, and moral

ISBN/EAN: 9783741175978

Manufactured in Europe, USA, Canada, Australia, Japa

Cover: Foto ©Lupo / pixelio.de

Manufactured and distributed by brebook publishing software (www.brebook.com)

F. X. Schouppe

Abridged course of religious instruction, apologetic, dogmatic, and moral

ABRIDGED COURSE

OF

RELIGIOUS INSTRUCTION,

Apologetic, Dogmatic, and Moral:

FOR THE

USE OF CATHOLIC COLLEGES AND SCHOOLS.

BY THE

REV. FATHER F. X. SCHOUPPE,
OF THE SOCIETY OF JESUS.

TRANSLATED FROM THE FRENCH THIRD EDITION.

NEW EDITION,
THOROUGHLY REVISED, WITH THE IMPRIMATUR OF
H.E. CARDINAL MANNING.

LONDON: BURNS AND OATES.
1880.

Nihil obstat.
               Gulielmus Can. Johnson.

Imprimatur.
               HENRICUS EDUARDUS,
                    Card. Archiep. Westmon.

THE TRANSLATOR'S PREFACE.

THE translation follows Father Schouppe's text exactly; nothing has been left out, nothing has been added to the original. Father Schouppe's work was framed on the diocesan Catechism of Malines, in Belgium; and, as might be expected, it contains some instructions which are applicable to Belgium only. The author himself points out what is peculiar to Belgium: *ex.g.* Part III. chap. iii. First Commandment of the Church, I. Nos. 6, 7, p. 326; also Third Commandment of the Church, No. 9, p. 334.

The Malines Catechism differs from the Catechism used in England by enumerating only five Commandments of the Church. The Catechism in England adds a sixth, 'not to marry within certain degrees of kindred, nor to solemnise marriage at the forbidden times;' and inserts, as the fifth, 'to contribute to the support of our pastors.'

The teaching on the two parts of the sixth Commandment of the Church will be found in Part II. chap. xv. Matrimony, Art. I. Nos. 7, 8, pp. 227, 228; and Part III. chap. vii. Art. IV. Matrimony, Nos. 3, 4, pp. 377, 378.

Finally, those who read the *Abridged Course* in English will know that, in England, the contracting of marriage otherwise than before the priest and two witnesses, though *illicit and sinful*, is not necessarily *invalid :* for the Decree of the Council of Trent on clandestine marriages, not having been published in England, is therefore, by virtue of a provision in the Decree itself, not binding upon persons living in this country.

PREFACE.

It cannot be too often repeated that religious instruction is the vital part of education. However noble and precious human science may be, it can only succeed in forming, as it were, a body without life. The knowledge of religion is the vivifying soul. All the profane sciences combined could not prevent youth from straying in this world: the science of faith, which is the true light of human life, can alone guide their steps in the ways of honour and happiness.

This religious science must be solid; it must strike its roots deeply in young hearts, so that it may be able to grow and strengthen as life advances, and resist all the storms that may assail it.

In religious instruction there are two periods or degrees, which may be designated the period of memory and the period of intelligence. The first corresponds to primary teaching, the second to more advanced and higher teaching.

In the primary schools* the text of the diocesan

---

* Under this denomination must be understood, in a wide sense, all those classes composed of children not yet capable of understanding a develoned course of religious instruction.

catechism, which contains elements as precious as they are necessary, should be adhered to. These elements must be impressed on the memory of the children, and the meaning of them made clear by such explanations as they can readily understand. If, after having received this primary education, the children finally leave the schools, they will still take with them the elementary knowledge of Christian doctrine which may afterwards become sufficiently developed in them by hearing the Word of God and reading good books. If, on the other hand, they continue the course of their studies, they will possess the fundamental principles which will serve as a foundation for more complete knowledge. For those more favoured amongst the young who are brought up in the schools of more advanced and higher instruction, the text of the catechism does not suffice: to it must be added the demonstration of faith and a fuller explanation of its dogmas.

The *demonstration* of faith will acquaint the young with the philosophical and historical foundations of our belief, which will put them in possession of solid principles, against which all attacks and sophisms will be vain.

The full explanation of the dogmas of faith will give to the young a better knowledge of their true meaning, and will enable them to view them in their admirable harmony. A multitude of objections and prejudices, arising from ignorance of our mysteries, or a false idea of our dogmas, will thus be removed. This enlightened knowledge will, moreover, cause the Christian religion to be beloved and Jesus Christ and His Church to be cherished. The truths of faith are so beautiful in their nature that they cannot fail to delight the mind when they are seen in their true significance.

To put both this demonstration of faith and a full explanation of its dogmas within the reach of the young is what we have endeavoured to realise in this *Course of Religion.*

The work is composed of three parts, entitled 'Apologetic,' 'Dogmatic,' and 'Moral.'

The first comprises the rational principles of religion, the demonstration of the Christian faith and the true Church of Jesus Christ, as well as the refutation of the principal modern errors.

The second part unfolds the whole series of the dogmas of faith, from the mysteries of God and the creation to the universal judgment, the final term of God's work in this world.

The third part presents an exposition of the Christian virtues and obligations. It treats of laws in general, of the Decalogue and the commandments of the Church, of sins and good works, of the Sacraments and of prayer, of the feasts and of religious ceremonies.

In order to combine clearness and solidity, we adopt a regular and simple method, which appears to us calculated, especially if aided by short explanation *vivâ voce*, to render the logic of the proofs, the true sense of the dogmas, as well as the harmony and the charming beauty of all the virtues of faith, easy to grasp, learn, and comprehend.

CONTENTS.

Part First.

APOLOGETIC.

PRELIMINARY ARTICLES: PAGE
  Art. I. On the End of a Religious Argument . . 2
    II. Three Kinds of Demonstration . . . 4
      1. Indirect Demonstration . . . 4
      2. Summary Demonstration . . . 5

CHAP.
      3. Complete Demonstration . . . 9
I. Truth of the Christian Religion as opposed to Unbelief 10
  Art. I. Grounds of Demonstration 10
    II. Means of Demonstration 26
      1. Miracles 26
      2. Prophecies 27
      3. Authority of the Bible . . . 28
        I. Historical Authority of the New Testament . . . 29
        II. Historical Authority of the Old Testament . . . 33
    III. Facts and Proofs 38
      1. Proof drawn from the Preëminence of Christianity 38
      2. Proof drawn from the Prophecies . 40
      3. Proof drawn from Miracles . 41
II. Truth of the Catholic Religion as opposed to Heresies 48
  Art. I. Nature and Institution of the Church . . 49
    II. First Proof of the Truth of the Catholic Church, the Existence of the Apostolic See 55

CONTENTS.

	PAGE
Art. III. Second Proof of the Truth of the Catholic Church, her four distinctive Marks	56
Unity	57
Holiness	58
Catholicity	59
Apostolicity	60
IV. On the Nature, Constitution, and Authority of the Church	62
V. Accusations brought against the Church	68
1. Intolerance	69
2. The Inquisition	75
3. The Massacre of St. Bartholomew	78
4. The Antagonism between the Church and Science	80
5. Galileo	81
6. The supposed bad Popes	85
7. The Crusades	87
8. The Schism of the East	88
9. The Temporal Power of the Popes, and their Interference with Civil Governments	90
10. Reaction against the Progress of Civilisation	94
11. The Encyclical Letter and the Syllabus, or the Condemnation of Liberalism and modern Liberty	96

Part Second.

DOGMATIC.

CHAP.		
I. Preliminary Dogmas		105
Art. I. The Holy Scriptures		106
II. Tradition		108
III. Doctrinal Authority of the Church		109
II. God and His Attributes		114
Art. I. Quiescent Attributes		115
II. Operative Attributes		117
III. Moral Attributes		118
III. The Blessed Trinity		121
Art. I. Doctrine of the Holy Trinity		121
II. Mystery of the Holy Trinity		123

CONTENTS.

CHAP.		PAGE
IV.	The Creation of the World—the Angels—Man—Original Sin	126
	Art. I. The Creation of the World	126
	II. The Angels	128
	III. Man and Original Sin	131
	1. The Origin and Fall of Man	131
	2. Doctrine respecting Original Sin	134
	3. Mystery of Original Sin	135
	IV. The Immaculate Conception	137
V.	The Incarnation	139
	Art. I. Jesus Christ considered in His History	139
	1. Christ in Prophecy	140
	2. Christ on Earth	144
	3. Christ in Glory	147
	II. Jesus Christ considered in His Person	148
	III. The Work of Jesus Christ	154
	IV. The Worship due to Jesus Christ	156
	V. Effects produced by Jesus Christ on Man	158
VI.	Grace	163
	Art. I. General Remarks on Grace	163
	II. Actual Grace	166
	III. Habitual or sanctifying Grace	169
	IV. Merit	171
VII.	The Sacraments in general	174
	Art. I. True Idea of the Sacraments	174
	II. Constituent Elements and Conditions, or Matter, Form, Ministration, and Subject of the Sacraments in general	177
	III. Effects and Efficacy of the Sacraments—Ceremonies	179
VIII.	Baptism	184
	Art. I. Baptism considered in itself	184
	II. Baptism considered in its Administration	188
IX.	Confirmation	191
	Art. I. Nature, Effects, Administration	191
X.	The Blessed Eucharist considered as a Sacrament	193
	Art. I. Preliminary Notes on the Sacrament of the Eucharist	194
	II. Constituent Parts of the Blessed Eucharist	197
	III. The Eucharist as it regards the Faithful; the Adoration, Administration, Effects, and Sacramental Signs of the Blessed Eucharist	200

CONTENTS.

CHAP.		PAGE
XI. The Blessed Eucharist as a Sacrifice		203
Art. I. Nature of the Eucharistic Sacrifice		203
II. Celebration and Effects of the Mass		208
XII. The Sacrament of Penance		211
Art. I. The Nature of the Sacrament of Penance		211
II. On the Reception of the Sacrament of Penance		214
Appendix: Indulgences		218
XIII. Extreme Unction		220
Art. I. Nature, Effects, and Reception of Extreme Unction		220
XIV. Holy Orders		222
Art. I. Meaning, Degrees, Nature, and Effects of the Sacrament of Holy Orders		222
XV. Matrimony		226
Art. I. Nature, Impediments, Celebration, and Effects of the Sacrament of Matrimony		226
XVI. On the Virtues		229
Art. I. Virtues in general		230
II. The Theological Virtues		235
1. Of the Theological Virtues in general		235
2. Faith		236
3. Hope		240
4. Charity		241
XVII. The Four Last Things		246
Art. I. The Passage from this Life to the next		246
II. Relations between the Living and the Dead		256
III. End of the World		261
XVIII. Recapitulation of Revealed Doctrine		266

Part Third.

MORAL.

I. Laws		273
Art. I. Nature of Laws		273
II. Distinction of Laws		275
Appendix: Conscience		279

CHAP.	PAGE
II. The Decalogue	280
General Meaning of the Decalogue	280
First Commandment: 'I am the Lord thy God. Thou shalt not have strange gods before Me'	283
I. Obligation	283
1. Qualities of Worship	286
2. Acts of Worship	286
3. Worship of the Saints	288
II. Sins against the First Commandment	289
Second Commandment: 'Thou shalt not take the name of the Lord thy God in vain'	291
Third Commandment: 'Remember thou keep holy the Sabbath-day'	293
Fourth Commandment: 'Honour thy father and thy mother'	298
I. The Duties of Children	299
II. The Duties of Parents	302
III. The reciprocal Obligations of other Superiors and Inferiors	306
Fifth Commandment: 'Thou shalt not kill'	311
I. Homicide, or Murder	311
II. Scandal	313
Sixth and Ninth Commandments: 'Thou shalt not commit adultery. Thou shalt not covet thy neighbour's wife'	315
Seventh and Tenth Commandments: 'Thou shalt not steal. Thou shalt not covet thy neighbour's goods'	317
Eighth Commandment: 'Thou shalt not bear false witness against thy neighbour'	319
III. Commandments of the Church	323
First Commandment of the Church: To keep certain appointed days holy, with the obligation of resting from servile work	324
I. Meaning of Holidays or *Feast*-days	324
II. General View of the Liturgical Year	326
Second Commandment of the Church: To hear Mass on all Sundays and holidays of obligation	330
Third Commandment of the Church: To keep the days of fasting and abstinence appointed by the Church	332

		PAGE
	Fourth Commandment of the Church : To confess our sins to our pastors at least once a year	335
	Fifth Commandment of the Church : To receive the Blessed Sacrament at least once a year, and that at Easter or thereabouts	337

CHAP.
IV. Sin 339
    Art. I. The Nature of Sin 339
        II. Distinction of Sins . . . 341
V. Virtues and Good Works 350
    Art. I. The Theological Virtues . . 350
        1. Faith 350
        2. Hope 352
        3. Charity 353
      II. Moral Virtues, Gifts, and Fruits of the Holy Ghost 359
      III. Good Works 363
VI. Christian Perfection : Evangelical Counsels, States of Life, Vocation 365
VII. The Sacraments 366
    Art. I. Confession 367
      II. Holy Communion 373
      III. Holy Orders 375
      IV. Matrimony 377
VIII. Prayer 381
IX. Feasts, Ceremonies, and Religious Practices of the Church 389

ABRIDGED COURSE
OF
RELIGIOUS INSTRUCTION.

INTRODUCTION.

1. THE course of religious instruction is that part of teaching which has for its object religious science. It is of greater importance than any other study, because religion extends its influence not only over the present, but also over the future, life of man. It is the only science which contains a pledge of happiness in this world and in the world to come.

When religious teaching is confined to the first elements of Christian doctrine, and only goes so far as to impress an exact knowledge of them on the memory of children, it is called Catechism, the primary or first course of religious instruction. When it rises to the science, properly so called, or the expounded knowledge of religious truths, it is styled *higher course of religious instruction*.

2. This course, in its full extent, comprises three parts: the *apologetic*, the *dogmatic*, and the *moral*. The *apologetic* shows which is the true religion; the *dogmatic* teaches what the true religion proposes to our belief; the *moral*, what the true religion commands us to practise.

Part First.

APOLOGETIC.

3. THE apologetic part defends the true religion against all adversaries, be they unbelievers or heretics.

4. It comprises two distinct arguments: namely, the truth of the *Christian* religion as opposed to unbelief, and the truth of the *Catholic* religion as opposed to the heresies of the various sects. Two preliminary articles will lead to these arguments.
  I. Preliminary articles.
  II. Chapter i. *Truth of the Christian religion.*
  III. Chapter ii. *Truth of the Catholic religion.*

PRELIMINARY ARTICLES.

First Article: On the End of a Religious Argument.

5. The argument touching the true religion has for its end, (1) to confirm in the truth those who already possess it, and to arm them against error; (2) to confound the ungodly, and to defend the faith against their attacks; (3) to lead to the truth those who are ignorant of it, but seek it in good faith.

6. In order to understand how useful and necessary it is that the true religion should be shown forth, it will suffice to consider, in a general way, the state of the world as regards religious truth. There is in the world a fact

which is apparent to all. It is the existence of the Catholic Church, proclaiming herself to be the pillar of truth, the organ of God, the ark of salvation, the portal which opens to eternal life. For more than eighteen centuries, speaking in the name of God, the Creator of heaven and earth, she says: I alone possess the only true religion. Whoever believes and professes my doctrine shall enter into eternal life; whoever rejects it shall be rejected of God, and hurled into everlasting damnation.

If this solemn affirmation be true, there can be no choice. The teaching of the Church must be received with docility, so as to escape hell and to inherit eternal beatitude. This question, therefore, is plainly of supreme importance. It is not only useful, but it is necessary, to know whether the word of the Church be the expression of the truth. Some persons know it, some are ignorant of it. We, who have received the faith and have been baptised, have the happiness to know it and to believe in it; we are in possession of the truth.

7. But there are some who have not been equally enlightened, and who are not convinced of the truth of Catholicity; they are ignorant of the holy proclamation of the Church, or else they doubt it or deny it, saying, '*The doctrine of the Church is not true.*' To all such it is necessary to present the demonstration of the truth.

8. Let us remark, first of all, that the denial of the Catholic faith by unbelievers is not the expression of a certainty, but of a simple doubt, or of a blind persuasion founded on prejudice and corrupt desires.

They deny the doctrine of the Church because it is distasteful to them, or because, in order to indulge their passions, they wish it to be false. They moreover seek by vain reasoning to persuade themselves that it *is* false; and by the influence that the will can exert over the intelligence, they arrive at a state of doubt, or rather at a sort of persuasion by which they succeed in deceiving themselves. They can go no further with regard to that which is so certain as the Catholic revelation; the mind of the man who rejects it may arrive at doubt, but not at any evidence and certainty of the opposite. He, for example, who would deny the reign and conquests of Alexander might adduce endless reasonings and sophisms, but could never affirm with certainty that Alexander and his conquests are a myth.

9. Instead, therefore, of denying the great affirmation of the Church, unbelievers should be content with demanding proofs, and should apply themselves to a serious examination of this question, *Is the doctrine of the Catholic Church the truth?*

This is in fact the great question, which contains in itself all the strife between Catholicism and its adversaries, the unbelievers of every age and of every variety, *Is the doctrine of the Catholic Church the truth?*

Enlightened by faith, we reply with promptitude, ' *Yes, it is the truth; the pure unchangeable truth.*'

This answer gives our adversaries a right to demand our proofs. We must therefore show forth the truth of the doctrine which the Church proposes as the way of salvation.

Second Article: Three Kinds of Demonstration.

10. There are three kinds of demonstration, or three ways of proving the truth of the Christian faith, which are suited to different degrees of intelligence. The first is an *indirect* demonstration; the second a *direct*, but *summary*, demonstration; the third a *direct and complete* demonstration, which establishes the whole edifice of truth on the ruins of error.

I. Indirect Demonstration.

11. We understand by this indirect demonstration of the true religion a simple reference to the doctors of theology and their writings. In order to appreciate the force and usefulness of these, it is to be remarked that

scientific demonstrations are not the work of every person, but of special men. He who knows a thing to be a fact is not therefore necessarily capable of explaining it. Thus any one may know that an edifice is solidly built, but only the architect may be in a position to explain the causes of its solidity. One may know of the victories of Cyrus, but not be able to prove them, or to remove all the historical difficulties regarding them; such an explanation belongs only to the historical student. One may be perfectly sure of certain truths relating to rights, but at the same time be unable to prove them, not being learned in this particular subject; and if we have opponents who contest these different points, we refer them to particular persons specially qualified to furnish the required proofs and explanations.

It is the same in matters of religion. All the faithful are perfectly aware of the truth of their faith; but only those well versed in religious science, such as priests and theologians, can expound it and answer all objections. It is to such that the mass of the faithful can always refer their opponents. This reference renders all men indirectly capable of demonstrating the truth. Thus every individual among the faithful can answer his opponents in such words as these: 'The truth of the faith which the Church teaches is beyond doubt. I have the happiness of knowing this truth; but if I am not sufficiently learned to furnish all the proofs and explanations that you demand, I know that complete and rigorous demonstrations have been given by the most learned doctors, from the time of the Apostles to our own days. These demonstrations exist, in substance, in all books of theology. Study these books, or apply to the priests and doctors versed in these matters.'

II. Summary Demonstration.

12. This demonstration, which may also be called popular, because it is within reach of every one, is based

upon the great fact of the Resurrection of Jesus Christ. The Apostles themselves gave but little proof of their mission other than this supreme and convincing sign of His divine authority given by Jesus Christ Himself. He said to the stubborn Jews, 'An evil and adulterous generation seeketh a sign; and a sign shall not be given it, but the sign of Jonas the prophet. For as Jonas was in the whale's belly three days and three nights, so shall the Son of Man be in the heart of the earth three days and three nights' (Matt. xii. 39).

The proof[*] drawn from the Resurrection is at once simple and convincing. It only requires, in order to understand it, an upright heart which seeks the truth in good faith, and a reasonable mind which recognises, in miracles and in prophecy, the stamp of divine authority.

It may be argued thus: If Jesus Christ is risen from the dead, His doctrine is divine;[†] and Jesus Christ *is* truly risen; therefore His doctrine is divine.

13. In the *major* of this syllogism we say: *If Christ is risen, His doctrine is divine*—that is, if He is risen, His doctrine is approved, authorised, and declared to be true by God Himself in working such a wonder in its favour. The justness of this conclusion is the more evident because Christ had predicted that He would rise again on the third day in proof of His divine mission.

If His doctrines were false, God must have worked the most astounding prodigy in favour of an impostor. He must have sanctioned falsehood and led mankind into error. This is an impossibility to Him who is the essence of goodness and truth.

---

[*] This demonstration may be seen more amply drawn out in Frayssinous, *Conférences*, tom. ii. confér. 6. Also in Feller, *Catéchisme Philosophique*, tom. ii. p. 323. Above all, in the *Sermon sur la Résurrection*, by Card. Giraud, Archbishop of Cambrai.

[†] The divinity of the *mission* of Jesus Christ must not be confounded with the divinity of His *Person*, which will be considered elsewhere.

The *minor* of the syllogism adds: *Now Jesus Christ is truly risen.* This proposition affirms an historical fact that is proved in a most undeniable manner. The fact of the resurrection of Jesus Christ must indeed be admitted as beyond a doubt if it be attested by numerous obviously truthful witnesses—that is to say, by witnesses who could not have been deceived themselves, who could not have wished to deceive others, who could not have deceived even if they had wished to do so. Now the resurrection of Jesus Christ is attested by such witnesses as these.

(1) These witnesses are, first, the Apostles, who saw their risen Master during forty days, contemplating Him with their eyes, hearing Him with their ears, touching Him with their hands; who, though at first unbelieving, yet afterwards, converted by evidence, devoted their existence to publishing this great event, and, in fact, announced it to the whole world, sanctioning their testimony by miracles, and sealing it with their blood.

(2) Women and disciples of every kind, numbering in all more than 500 ocular witnesses (1 Cor. xv. 6).

(3) Auricular witnesses not less trustworthy, such as innumerable Jews and pagans who, vanquished by the evidence of things, became converted, admitted the Resurrection, and believed in it with the deepest and firmest faith.

(4) The very enemies of Jesus Christ, the chiefs of the Jewish nation, hearing the Apostles declare the Resurrection, did not attempt to arraign them as impostors, and by this conduct themselves gave testimony to the truth. For if there had been imposture, these hostile men would not have failed to confound the impostors. On the one hand, it was their interest and their duty to do so; on the other, they had every means at command for doing so; for, having placed guards at the entrance to the sepulchre, they were likely to know what had become of the body of Christ, and had

but to produce it. If, then, they did not unveil, or seek to unveil, the imposture, it was because there was no imposture. Enemies so powerful and so vigilant, whose interests lay in not being taken unawares, were not likely to be imposed on.

(5) The most avowed enemies of the Christian name, such as Celsus, Porphyry, Hierocles, Julian the Apostate, and others; who, in speaking of the resurrection of Christ have sought to explain it, as well as His other miracles, by the artifice of magic, have never denied the *fact* itself.

(6) All these testimonies are confirmed by the living monument built upon the resurrection of Jesus Christ, namely, the Church and the feast of Easter, the centre of her solemnities. To-day, as in her earliest days, the Church proclaims the resurrection of her Author, saying to all generations: 'I am founded, with my worship and my faith, on the resurrection of Jesus Christ. If He had not risen, I should not exist, the world would not have believed, and would still have been lost in idolatry.'

The witnesses we have enumerated above are of obvious veracity. Taking, for example, merely the Apostles, every unprejudiced mind will allow (1) that they could not have been deceived—their number, their incredulity, the nature of the fact, its continuance during forty days, the multiplicity and variety of the apparitions that attested it, rendered error and hallucination impossible. (2) That they did not wish to deceive; their conscientiousness and their piety, their interest and the prospect of the most terrible consequences of deceit, must have excluded from their minds the very thought of such a crime and of such folly. (3) That they could not have deceived, even if they had wished to do so. In order to succeed in deceiving, they would have had to do two things: (*a*) to take away the body of their Master, who had deceived them; and (*b*) to persuade men that He had come to life again. Both were equally impracticable, on account of the satellites who guarded the tomb, of the impossibility of maintaining secrecy, and of the disinclination of the Jews, and of the world at large, to believe such intelligence, unless imposed upon them by the force of evidence.

We may add, that if we compare this event with every other fact recorded in history, we shall not find another that is established on proofs so numerous and so certain; therefore, if the resurrection of Jesus Christ could be called in question, nothing could be certain in history, and the best authenticated facts would be doubtful, such as the assassination of Cæsar and the conquests of Alexander. The resurrection, then, of Christ is an absolutely incontestable truth. This resurrection is the seal imprinted by God on His religion; this religion is, then, true, and every man must accept it under pain of eternal damnation, acccording to those words of His, '*Qui non crediderit condemnabitur,*—Whosoever believes not, shall be condemned' (Mark xvi. 16).

III. Complete Demonstration.

14. Complete demonstration is that which proves the true religion in a rigorous manner, and in all its parts. It is capable of developments more or less extensive. To keep within the limits of our plan, we shall confine ourselves to presenting the principal proofs, and to the solution of the most frequent objections.*

Complete demonstration embraces a twofold subject,

---

* The plan of this Abridged Course confines us to very narrow limits for the objections. But more lengthened refutations may be found in well-known works, such as Gousset's *Théologie Dogmatique;* Boone's *Manuel de l'Apologiste* and *Motifs de mon Attachement à l'Eglise Catholique;* M. de Ségur's *Réponses aux Objections les plus répandues contre la Religion;* Abbé Berseaux, *La Foi et l'Incrédulité, L'Eglise et le Monde, La Mort et l'Immortalité;* Franco's *Réponses Populaires aux Objections;* Feller's *Catéchisme Philosophique;* Bergier's *De la vraie Religion;* Schouppe's *Elementa Theologiæ Dogm. et Cursus Scripturæ Sacræ.*

the *Christian* religion and the *Catholic* religion. These are, in reality, one and the same religion; but in order to arrive at the truth in an explicit and practical manner, we must make a distinction between them, and explain them separately. By the *Christian* religion in general we understand the doctrine that Jesus Christ preached eighteen centuries ago; and by the *Catholic* religion this same doctrine as it is preserved by the Catholic Church, and distinct from the Christianity of dissenting sects.

CHAPTER I.
TRUTH OF THE CHRISTIAN RELIGION DEMONSTRATED AS OPPOSED TO UNBELIEF.

15. We take the word *unbelievers* in a broad sense, to designate generally all those who are not acquainted with Christian revelation, or who positively refuse to believe in it; such as pagans, Mahometans, Jews, apostate Christians, rationalists, free-thinkers, &c.

16. The demonstration of Christian truth to unbelievers, in order to be complete, must comprise three parts: the grounds of the demonstration, the means of demonstration, and the facts and proofs of which the demonstration consists.

First Article: Grounds of Demonstration.

17. The grounds or bases of Christian demonstration are certain fundamental truths, which are evident to reason, and which it is impossible to deny without shutting one's eyes to its light. They may be reduced to the seven following:

(1) *Certainty*, denied by sceptics.

(2) The *objective existence of bodies*, denied by idealists.

(3) The *personal existence of God*, denied by atheists and pantheists.

(4) The *infinite perfection of God*, His providence, and the free-will of man, denied by fatalists.

(5) The *spirituality of the soul* and its immortality, denied by materialists.

(6) The *natural law* and the force of its obligations, denied by autonomists.

(7) *Religion* and the obligations imposed by it, denied by the impious.

These preliminary truths, obvious to reason, are called *grounds of Christian demonstration*, because it supposes them to exist, and there can be no solid demonstration if they are denied or called in question. They may also be termed common-sense truths, because they are taught by the natural sense common to all reasonable men, and the denial of them would be contrary to this common sense. These *data* of reason are, moreover, amply proved in every course of sound philosophy.* We will confine ourselves to a brief exposition of them.

18. (1) *Certainty.*—Man possesses in his reasonable nature the faculty of recognising truth with a perfect certainty. Those who deny this proposition are called *sceptics*, unreasonable men who reject the light of reason itself, and affirm certainty at the same time that they deny it, for their denial amounts to this, '*It is certain that nothing is certain.*'

The Author of our reasoning nature has given us several means of arriving at true and certain knowledge. Philosophers call them *criteria*, and commonly admit six, namely, evidence, consciousness, exterior sense, authority, analogy, and common sense.

Evidence is the clear perception of the necessity of a judgment, or the affinity of two ideas. Immediate evidence, or the evidence of *intuition*, is distinguished from mediate evidence, or the evidence of *deduction*. Immediate evidence makes known to us truths which are shown by their own light—those primary truths which do not admit

* Such as those of Decker, Liberatore, Tongiorgi, &c.

of demonstration, but on which all other truths are based. Such are analytical judgments, in which the attribute is so inherent to the subject that it is an essential part of it, and only offers the same idea under another form. For example, *two and two make four; the whole is equal to all the parts put together; the whole is greater than its separate parts. There is no effect without a cause.*

Mediate evidence makes known truths which are not apparent of themselves, but which are deduced from the primary truths by means of reasoning or demonstration.

Consciousness gives us the certainty of our existence, and of other facts that take place within us, such as thought, desire, doubt.

Our *exterior senses* make known to us with certainty the exterior and immediate objects which act upon our various sensations; that is, the existence of the bodies that constitute the visible world.

Authority, or *testimony*, under the requisite conditions, gives us a certain knowledge of historical exterior and sensible facts. Of this class are events purely natural, as the death of a man; such also are those facts which are called miraculous, that is, facts which are due to a supernatural cause, but which equally affect the senses, such as the resurrection of a dead person.

Authority is the easy and clear means by which we come to the certain knowledge of the true religion.

Analogy is a criterion which allows a conclusion to be drawn respecting things not known from their similarity to things known. Thus, from the sight of a man and his actions I judge with certainty that he, like myself, is a being gifted with liberty and intelligence. So also, from observing the constant motion of the heavens, I know that the sun which sets to-day will reappear on the horizon to-morrow. Analogy is the basis of foresight and of what is called human experience, and physical science rests on it.

Common sense, which we take here as a criterion, is

a manner of seeing; it is a uniform judgment common to all mankind; in other words it is that general and invincible sentiment of all mankind which is simply the expression of his reasonable nature. It helps us to know universally admitted truths, such as the individual existence of each one of us, that of the objects that surround us, that of the Divinity; also, the difference between good and evil, and the principal points of the natural law.

These several means of knowing the truth suppose an ultimate motive or reason which produces that certainty in the mind which rests in the possession of truth. It is called the *foundation of certainty*. It consists in objective evidence, that is to say, in the evidence of the object itself rendered manifest by the means of some criterion.

19. (2) *Objective and real existence of bodies.*—Those who deny the real and objective existence of bodies are called idealists; they say that there exist in the mind ideas which represent bodies, but that it is not certain that these ideal and *subjective* representations are linked to *objective* realities. These men are refuted by ordinary good sense, and are belied by their own conduct. If, for example, they become the victims of some accident, or of some disagreeable treatment, they do not doubt its reality. The most striking and sensible arguments should be used to convince them, and to make them speedily certain of the objective existence of bodies.

20. (3) *The existence of God.*—We call God the Supreme Being, the Primary Cause of the Universe, the Necessary Self-existent Being, infinitely perfect, and possessing within Himself the plenitude of being. Those who deny the existence of God are called *atheists*.*

---

* To the honour of the human race, it is doubtful whether such persons as veritable atheists really exist. This question can only be elucidated by rightly understanding the meaning of the words 'veritable atheist.' 1. If we understand by them

Those who deny the existence of a personal God, and confound the divine nature with the mass of beings that constitute the universe, are called *pantheists*.

Both are refuted, (1) by the faith of the human race; (2) by the order and the beauty of the universe; (3) by the very existence of the human species; (4) or even by that of any of the living species, by which the earth is inhabited. These are four unanswerable proofs.

21. (1) *The faith of the human race.*—We mean by this the common accord with which all men believe in the existence of God, their worship of Him, and the homage of dependence which they pay Him. This bond of union is as ancient, as universal, and as lasting as the world itself. This belief of the whole world is a most convincing fact: 'Cast your eyes over the face of the earth,' said Plutarch; 'you may there find cities without ramparts, without education, without magistrature; people without fixed habitation, without property, without money; but you will nowhere find a city where the knowledge of God does not exist.'

Cicero and Seneca spoke in the same way, and modern discoveries have verified their words.*

---

an atheist by *conviction*, one convinced by the force of reason of the non-existence of God, it is clear that such atheists cannot exist, because the grounds for such conviction do not exist. 2. If by veritable atheist is understood an atheist by *simple persuasion*, who, from hearing it constantly repeated, deludes himself into the belief that there is no God, in this case also it would seem that the mind of man could not accept so senseless a persuasion. It is only the heart of the fool that would say there is no God. 'The fool has said in his heart,' and not in his intelligence, 'there is no God' (Ps. xiii.) As to *practical* atheists, who live as if there were no God to fear and honour, the fact of their existence is, alas, but too well established. What we have said of atheists will apply also to pantheists.

* Cic. *Tuscul.* lib. i. n. 18; Senec. *Epist.* 117.

This unanimity, this feeling common to all, shows that it is in the nature of man to believe in God, just as it is in the nature of children to entertain feelings of love and gratitude for the authors of their existence. The belief in God therefore springs from nature and from reason; it is the expression of the truth.

22. (2) *The spectacle of the universe*, and the admirable order which prevails, manifest the hand of a Supreme Disposer, who is distinct from His work. The harmony of nature, all the wonders which incessantly strike our eyes, cannot be explained excepting by the action of an intelligent cause, which is God. It is thus that a timepiece proclaims the existence of its maker. To contemplate the universe, and yet deny the God who made it, is to admit effects without cause, the possibility of a palace without an architect. Must not those men be blind who say that the universe is the work of chance, or, what is the same thing, that the world made itself? What would persons so wilfully blind reply if they were told that a house had built itself, that a book or a poem had been written by chance?

23. (3) *The existence of the human race.*—The human race did not make itself. It must, then, have had an author, who existed of Himself, and by the necessity of His essence. It is therefore this Author, existing of Himself, that we call God. We will explain this reasoning. The human race did not make itself; all men in general, and each in particular, must have recognised this fact, and said, No, it is not I who gave myself existence. Humanity, therefore, comes from an author other than itself. Who is this author? I cannot answer that it is a being coming in his turn from another; for the same question is ever recurring. It must, therefore, be one who is self-existing, a necessary being who is the primary and supreme cause of all things—that is, it must be God.

24. (4) *Any of the living species whatever* by which

we are surrounded, if we reflect a little, will in the same manner lead us to the existence of God. Whence, for instance, comes the little bird that sings in the woods? From the egg. And whence the egg? From another bird. And this other bird? From another egg; and the same question may be repeated without possibility of solution or explanation, unless we suppose a primary cause of these living creatures—God, who created them.

25. There is a God, then, in spite of atheism. And this God is not the universe, as the pantheists say; for we have seen that the primary cause and author of the universe is as distinct from the universe as an architect is from the edifice which he has built. The impious system of the pantheists, who found their creed on their assertion that there exists only one substance, and that that substance is God, not only confounds the world with its author, the effect with the cause, but also matter with spirit, the finite with the infinite, and destroys the very idea of God, the Being who is essentially necessary, spiritual, infinitely perfect, and distinct from the visible universe of which He is the primary cause.*

26. (4) *The infinite perfection of God, His Providence, and the liberty of man.*

God *is infinitely perfect;* that is to say, He possesses all perfection in an infinite degree. As proof of this truth, (1) all the perfections which I admire in creatures must be found eminently in God, since He is the primary cause: as also those which are possible—that is to say, those which might exist must be found also in their primary cause; for otherwise they would not be

---

* Pantheism is by its essence an atheistical system—the atheist and atheism become necessarily pantheist; since, if there be no true God, known and recognised, they are forced to declare that the substance of the world is the necessary being, existing of itself in consequence of being God. See Gosehler, *Diction. Encyclop. de la Théologie Cathol.* art. Panthéisme.

possible. The primary cause of all things, who is God, possesses, then, all perfections. He is infinitely perfect. (2) In the second place, God, being by nature necessary and independent, cannot be limited in His perfection; nor could His own nature or a will not His own impose a limit to an absolute and necessary essence like His. He possesses, then, the plenitude of all perfection.

27. *Providence.*—It follows that there is in God the attribute of providence; for, taken as an attribute, providence is a part of wisdom, and must be counted amongst the multitude of God's perfections. It exerts a constant and universal action over all that exists and happens. It is the name we give to the wise and protecting action by which God governs the world and directs all creatures towards an end worthy of Him.

28. *The liberty of man.*—God, in creating the stars, plants, and animals, made them subject to necessity, that is to say, to irresistible functions or instincts by which they of necessity obey the laws of their nature in a mechanical way. He did not act in the same manner towards man. He gave him liberty, that noble attribute which constitutes him master, sole arbiter of his will, that he might direct his actions according to order, obey the laws of his nature, and go forward freely and without constraint towards his end.

We speak here of the essential liberty of man, which is called free-will, and which is opposed to necessity. It may be defined as *the faculty of acting by choice, and of choosing between good and evil.* As the word liberty may be taken in different senses and may lead to confusion, it is important to make a distinction between (1) moral and physical liberty, (2) true and false liberty, (3) natural liberty, or the liberty proceeding from natural right, and civil liberty.

(1) *Physical* liberty is the natural faculty of *willing* and *doing* anything, whether good or evil. Man has full liberty to will; this is the free-will of which we

have been speaking. But as regards the liberty of acting, of executing that which the will determines, he only possesses it in a very limited degree. *Moral* liberty consists, not in the power of acting, but in the *right of acting*, of willing and of doing; it is the faculty of acting by choice in anything which is right and lawful. It will be seen that moral liberty is limited by law and the rules of order; it is restricted to the bounds of that which is lawful. When an action is contrary to order, we may will it and do it physically, but not lawfully or morally. All men are free to work evil and to violate justice, but none have the right to use this freedom.

(2) *True* liberty presupposes order and lawfulness; it is found only within the bounds of that which is right and good. The passions which impel the will towards evil are its enemies. The more a man is master of his passions, the more easily he acts uprightly, and the more he is free and master of himself. *False* liberty is the independence and license which consists in breaking the bounds imposed by order and by law—this is but a wild liberty, proceeding from evil and disorder.

(3) In the objective sense, *civil* liberty must be distinguished from *natural* liberty. The latter is the natural right to do good, to practise virtue, to live according to the maxims of the true religion, to enjoy all the benefits of the Church, to observe the holy laws which Jesus Christ, the Supreme Legislator, has established on earth. *Civil* liberty is that which is granted by the laws of the state, whether in favour of good or of evil.

29. Divine Providence and human liberty are denied by the *fatalists*, who would subject the Sovereign Ruler of the world, as well as man, to the unknown and blind necessity they call *fatality*. Man, they say, is not free. Whether he work good or evil he acts by necessity, and could not do otherwise than he does. These errors are refuted by the laws of all nations, which recognise the

liberty of man; by our consciousness and our common sense, which loudly proclaim it.

30. (5) *The spirituality and immortality of the soul.*—The soul, taken in a broad and general sense, is the vital principle which animates all living creatures, animals as well as men. But this principle in man is distinguished by a particular faculty which elevates the human creature incomparably above all others that live on the earth. Man is gifted with *intelligence*, and is therefore spiritual and immortal; for our soul is not only that which feels in us, but that which thinks—that which makes us know the truth, and love that which is good. Our soul is therefore an *intelligence*—that is to say, a principle of spiritual operations, such as thoughts and judgments.

Now a principle of spiritual operations can be no other than a spiritual substance which is incorruptible and independent, in its existence, of the body to which it is united; so that it does not die with the body, but is immortal, unless its Creator, by a positive act of His will, were to destroy it. This, however, would be contrary to the nature of things, for two reasons: (1) the Author of our nature, having placed in our souls an unconquerable desire of perpetual happiness, has also provided an object, that is to say, a happiness fully commensurate with this desire. Again, this happiness supposes a future and endless life wherein it will be found, since it is not to be found in this transitory life. (2) The great Author of nature, as will be seen later, has engraven in our hearts a law which exacts a sanction of recompense and of chastisement; this sanction also supposes a future life, since it is but rarely bestowed in the present life. This teaching of reason is confirmed by the consent of all nations and the universal belief in the doctrine of a future life.

31. The noble properties of the human soul are denied by the *materialists*, who say that man is only

matter, and does not essentially differ from the brutes or vegetables. They are to be answered thus: first, the essential intelligence of man places a gulf between him and animals devoid of reason. If they are too blind to see this gulf, they may be asked why animals do not speak, and how it is they do not pray. And if they persist in upholding their own relationship with brute-beasts, there is nothing left but, with a feeling of compassion, to abandon to their depravity men who renounce the dignity of human nature.

The error of those who deny the noble *origin* of man, as our faith teaches it, may also be traced to materialism. According to the materialists, man is not created to the image and likeness of God; but he springs from a spontaneous vegetable growth, which little by little became an animal, and by degrees increased in perfection till it developed into man. It will suffice to reply to this mean and revolting hypothesis, that it has been refuted and proved to be impossible by learned men of the first rank, such as Quatrefages.*

---

* See 'Le Darwinisme et l'Origine de l'Homme,' in the *Revue Catholique*, August 1871. As to the opinion regarding *heterogeneity*, or *spontaneous generation*, it is now generally rejected by science. In order to defend it, the ancients founded their theory on the multitude of little animals which appear on substances in a state of putrefaction, and they thought that these creatures were formed at the expense of the elements of such substances. They laid down this principle in consequence: *Corruptio unius, generatio alterius*,—Every creature in dissolution produces another. But the more profound researches of modern times have shown that the production of animals, which is manifested under these circumstances, is due solely to one of the generating processes known to science, and that these animals issue perpetually from germs deposited by creatures of the same kind. Modern science thus opposes this other axiom to the false principle of the ancients: *Omne vivum ex ovo*,—Everything that lives comes from a germ.

The doctrine of spontaneous generation still, however, has its adherents. Unluckily for them, all the experiments they have tried, in order to support this superannuated hypothesis,

32. (6) *The natural law.*—Man has in the depth of his nature a law engraven there by the hand of God. It is that law which says to every one, '*Do good, avoid evil.*' *Honour God. Do not unto others that which you would not have them do unto you. 'Honour thy father and thy mother.*' That is natural law, which

---

have declared against them. The only specious argument which they can urge in its favour is the appearance of living creatures, *sui generis*, in the parenchyma of the organs of divers animals. But it is more than probable that the germs of these creatures have been brought there by means of circulation, as the fine membranes of the capillary vessels would not constitute an insurmountable obstacle to these germs whilst they are of microscopic diminutiveness. The absence of a direct proof of this mode of introduction, due only to our want of the necessary means of observation, cannot be a valid argument in favour of a theory which is in opposition to a universal physiological law. This reason has been accepted by the most distinguished scientific men of our period; but judging, at the same time, that direct proofs are to be found, they have sought them by means of ingenious observations, which have produced results that may be called decisive.

A partisan of the ancient ideas—M. Pouchet, Director of the Museum at Rouen—took certain alterable liquids, such as milk, &c., and placed them in carefully-closed receivers, in which he had either created a vacuum or introduced pure oxygen; or else he had submitted the contents to a temperature of 100 degrees, in order to destroy all living germs which might exist therein. After some days he found the liquids full of germs, which, to his mind, was a proof of spontaneous generation (*Hétérogénie*, Paris, 1859). Another *savant*—M. Pasteur—opposed M. Pouchet, and declared that his experiments had been made under defective conditions, and he himself tried the same experiments, taking however stricter precautions (*Examen des Doctrines de la Génération spontanée*, 1861; *Mémoire sur les Corpuscules organisés*, 1862), and the alterable substances remained indefinitely without producing any organised atoms; an evident proof that life proceeds only from a living germ. The experiments of M. Pasteur appeared so conclusive that, when brought before a commission appointed by the Academy of Sciences, they obtained full sanction from that learned body, who pronounced against the hypothesis of heterogeneity.

may be defined as the *knowledge imprinted in human nature of the moral order, which God ordains shall be followed, and forbids us to disturb.* Those who deny the natural law are called *autonomists.* They say that their will is their law, that there is no essential difference between good and evil, between almsgiving and thieving—that it is a question of custom or of taste, and that everything is indifferent at root, everything is permitted. They may be answered that at least it is not permitted to outrage common sense; and man's common sense does proclaim the existence of a natural law. All men have attached to certain actions an *obligatory* force, coming from the very nature of their objects. The existence of society, domestic, civil, and political, proves this. All society supposes a tie, an *obligation* between the head and the members; a *natural* obligation anterior to any positive law, since law emanates from society, comes after it, and presupposes the obligation of obedience.

Again, is it not the natural law which makes all mankind agree that benevolence is a virtue and murder a crime? What legislator would dare to say that murder and perjury, treason, blasphemy, and ingratitude are lawful things, and may become virtues? Then, again, remorse, which wakes up in a guilty conscience, makes all men feel that there are obligations which none may violate, even could they do so secretly and screened from all human observation.

33. (7) *Religion and the obligations it imposes.*—Religion is the homage which reasonable creatures owe to God. It is defined as the whole duty of man towards God. Taken subjectively, religion is a *virtue* obligatory on all; objectively, it is *a body of theoretical or practical truths* concerning the relations of man towards God.

The act or exercise of religion is called *worship.* It is divided into *interior* and *exterior* worship.

34. There are two kinds of objective religion: *natural*, and *supernatural* or *revealed religion*. The first is that which is learnt by means of the natural light of reason; it consists in certain truths which the Author of nature has imprinted more or less clearly in the heart of man. The second is that which is only learnt by means of a supernatural light, superior to that of reason, namely, the light of revelation. This light is morally necessary to mankind, in order to supply the deficiencies of natural light.

35. Revelation is God's teaching to man, by means of ordinary words, or by other clear and evident signs. Thus, all that God spoke to the patriarchs Himself or by His angels, to the people of Israel by the prophets, to the whole world by His Son Jesus Christ, in order to teach us His law and His mysteries, is revelation.

By the word *revelation* is commonly understood *revealed religion*, and it more particularly designates the Mosaical-Christian religion, which is the only religion divinely revealed.

36. Religion, or the worship of God, is an indispensable duty imposed on man, to neglect which constitutes impiety. This duty, founded on the natural and essential relations between God and man, comprises interior and exterior worship.

To recognise the obligation of *interior* worship, we have only to consult either the first ideas which man forms of God, the universal persuasion of all races, or the dearest and most sacred interests of humanity. (1) God, man's Creator, is Master, Legislator, Father, and Supreme Benefactor. Man is His creature, overwhelmed with His benefits, and essentially subject to His laws. Who does not feel that religious duties spring from these ideas, and that man owes homage to such a Benefactor, to such a Father? (2) History testifies that everywhere and always religion has been considered by men as a duty and a virtue, and impiety as a detestable vice.

(3) Moreover, religion has been regarded in all times and by every people as intimately bound up with the dearest interests of man, with civilisation, the preservation, and the well-being of societies. All legislators have believed in a divine Providence presiding over the government of the universe; and it is on this belief, as on an eternal foundation, that they have raised their institutions and constructed the edifice of society.

The obligation of *exterior* worship is shown (1) by the experience and practice of all nations; (2) by reason, which commands that man should pay homage to God with his whole being, with his body and soul; (3) by natural feeling, which must show itself exteriorly, to proclaim aloud the greatness and the benefits of the Supreme Master of the universe.

37. It follows, then, that *man is bound to know religion.* Since he must perform religious duties, he cannot be permitted to be ignorant of them; he is, then, obliged to acquire the knowledge of them; and if he do not know which is the true religion, he must carefully inquire and search after it. *Revealed religion cannot be excluded from this research,* for the sole reason that it is revealed. For, on the one hand, revelation is possible; to deny its possibility would be to deny the omnipotence and the goodness of God, and to contradict universal belief; and on the other hand, if it has pleased God to reveal a religion—for example, the Christian religion—and to inculcate it on all men, every one is bound to learn it and to practise it with docility.

It has pleased God, as will be proved, to reveal to man a religious law, which is no other than the one above mentioned, namely, the *Christian religion.* This revelation is an historical fact; it is called the *divine fact,* because it has for object God speaking to humanity, the greatest event in the whole history of the human race.

38. The *Christian* religion or revelation, of which we are speaking, takes its name from Jesus of Nazareth,

called Christ, who, at the commencement of the modern era, established it in Judea as an obligatory religion for all the nations of the earth. But it does not, strictly speaking, date from Jesus Christ, since it began with the human race. Having been given, in substance, to the first man, it was faithfully kept and practised by the patriarchs, developed later on by Moses and the other prophets, and finally established by Jesus Christ, who gave to it its later form and its perfection.

Thus the Christian religion presents three distinct phases, called (1) the patriarchal religion, from the time of Adam to that of Moses; (2) the Jewish religion, from the time of Moses to Jesus Christ; (3) the Christian religion from the time of Jesus Christ; this will remain unchanged even to the end of the world.

These three form but one and the same revelation, which has become developed like a mysterious plant; they are all the same divine light; but it has risen over the world slowly and majestically, like the day passing through the gloaming of the aurora before arriving at its perfect brightness.

39. Here occurs the great question which we have to solve. Does the Christian religion proceed really from God? Is it divine—divinely revealed? We affirm *that it is divine*, and we proceed to expound this proposition. We say that the *Christian religion*, founded by Jesus Christ, is divine, and not that *the person* of this admirable Founder is divine, because in this place we abstract from the great dogma of the personal divinity of Jesus Christ, of which we shall treat later on. For the present we regard Christ as a simple Messenger from above, who was authorised by miracles, and who preached a religion in the name of Almighty God. The divinity of *His religion* is allied to the divinity of *His mission*, and what proves the one proves the other also.

We will show, in the first place, that the means of demonstration that we shall use are legitimate.

Second Article: Means of Demonstration.

40. The means of demonstration, the certain proofs by which the Christian religion is shown to be divinely revealed, are miracles and prophecies.

41. In order to prove that miracles and prophecies are legitimate means of demonstration, we shall submit the following questions: (1) What is the true idea of miracles? (2) What is the true idea of prophecies, and how are one and the other certain marks and infallible proofs of true revelation? (3) What authority is there for the Bible, wherein the miracles and prophecies which we give as proofs are related?

I. Miracles.

42. A miracle is a sensible event which takes place contrary to the ordinary laws of nature, by the special intervention of God. A corpse, four days buried and already a prey to corruption, comes out living from his tomb; a violent tempest becomes suddenly appeased; a river returns to its source. These are events which are manifest deviations from the universal and acknowledged laws of the physical world; they are miracles.

Miracles of the *first order* are so called when they surpass the power of any creatures, even that of angels. Miracles of the *second order* are those which surpass the power of man, but not that of angels.

43. To refuse to believe that God can work miracles, would be (1) to refuse Him His omnipotence; (2) to contradict the universal belief of all nations; (3) to deny the best authenticated facts of history.

God works miracles, either by Himself or by His angels. He can work real miracles by Himself, because by His full power He can deviate from the ordinary natural laws of which He is the Author; or He may allow His angels to do so within the sphere of their power.

44. A real *miracle* differs from a *marvel* or a *prodigy* of the devil. A marvel is an illusion produced by cleverness or trickery. A diabolical prodigy is an astounding event which, when God permits, can be produced by the natural strength of the devil. The devil cannot do anything in the visible world without the special permission of God.

45. It is not always easy to discern real from false miracles; but in many cases the divine operation is so manifest, and the hand of God so visible, that it is impossible to mistake it. Such, for instance, is the resurrection of Lazarus, as reported by St. John (chap. xi.).

46. A miracle worked in favour of a doctrine is a divine seal imprinted on that doctrine. It is the mark of God, as the royal seal is the mark of a king to warrant the authenticity of his decrees. A doctrine which is sanctioned by miracles is infallibly true; for if it were false, God would be authorising error, and He who is supreme truth would make Himself a guarantee for falsehood and the accomplice of an imposture. If, then, the Christian revelation is authorised by miracles, it must come from God—it must be divine and true.

II. Prophecies.

47. A prophecy is a certain prediction of a future event, which is merely contingent, the knowledge of which cannot be acquired.

Such, for instance, would be the prophecy of the exact time of a man's birth, the ruin of a flourishing empire, or the establishment of another, foretold several centuries before the occurrence.

Prophecy differs essentially from *conjecture*. A conjectural prediction is neither certain to come to pass, nor is it independent of the natural causes on which it is founded.

48. God alone can prophesy, because He alone knows all things, the future, as well as the present and

the past. The knowledge of the future supposes an infinite intelligence.

49. Prophecy, as it emanates essentially from God, is, like a miracle, a mark of the divine authority, and when made in favour of a doctrine, it imprints on it a divine seal which gives it the infallible character of truth.

50. Hence, as miracles and prophecies are certain proofs of a divine revelation, we may form an argument as follows: If Christianity is authorised by miracles and prophecies, it is truly revealed by God; we know that Christianity *is* authorised by this double sanction, therefore Christianity is truly revealed by God, and is the inevitable truth.

51. The *minor* of this syllogism affirms historical facts, of which we must demonstrate the certainty; and this obliges us in the first place to prove the authority of the Bible.

For if we are asked how we know about miracles worked in favour of the Christian religion, and how we know the ancient prophecies, and whence we derive the assurance of their authenticity, we reply that these are historical facts contained in the Bible. We must, then, prove the historical authority of the Sacred Scriptures, whose authority is unquestionable, and superior to that of any other history.

III. Authority of the Bible.*

52. The Bible is divided into books of the Old and the New Testament. They have a twofold authority: (1) a divine authority; (2) a human and simply historical authority. We shall not treat of the divine authority which they possess, as having been inspired by God, but

---

* See Schouppe, *Cursus Scripturæ Sacræ*, tom. 1. part 1. cap. 1. art. 2, De Librorum Biblicorum Auctoritate, and art. 1, De Libris Biblicis in se spectatis.

shall now regard them from a purely human point of view, as ordinary books of history.

The histories of both the Old and New Testaments have an authority superior to any others; an authority so certain and so amply proved that it is impossible to question it without at the same time rejecting or doubting every record of history, and all historical authority. We would ask our adversaries whether they admit the authority of the books which we possess bearing the names of Tacitus, Plutarch, Thucydides, and others. If they do so, we may add that they cannot challenge the authority of the Bible, which is, as we shall show, far superior to that of profane authors.

We will begin with the New Testament. If this is recognised to be true, its veracity will serve to prove the truth of the Old Testament.

I. Historical Authority of the New Testament.

53. The historical books of the New Testament are the Gospels and the Acts of the Apostles. The perfect authority of these books depends on three conditions—authenticity, integrity, and veracity.

(1) *Authenticity.*—A book is called *authentic* when it is really the work of the author whose name it bears, or to whom it is attributed. Are the books of the New Testament authentic? Were the four Gospels written by the Evangelists, whose names they bear? Does the book of the Acts of the Apostles come from the pen of St. Luke, as is affirmed by Catholics? Our adversaries deny it; they pretend that these books were composed by writers of a later date. We say, on the contrary, that their authenticity cannot admit of a doubt. It is proved by four arguments—prescription or legitimate possession, impossibility of the contrary, marks of authenticity, and testimony.

(*a*) The Universal Church has been in possession of these books ever since their origin, and has always held them to be authentic; and though her cleverest and most furious enemies have tried to prove the contrary, they have never, during the course of so many centuries, been able to do so. Hence this possession of the Church must be considered legitimate and founded on truth.

(*b*) To say that these books have been invented by impostors, and falsely attributed to the Evangelists, is not only gratuitous, but an impossible hypothesis. The invention of them could not have been produced during the lifetime of the Apostles, because these would have protested against them; nor yet after their death—that is to say, after the first century of our era—because these books then already existed, and were spread throughout Christendom like the Christians themselves.

(*c*) The Gospels bear the marks of their authors' hands. The language in which they were composed; the style; the constant allusions to the Scriptures, to the manners and geographical circumstances of the Jews; the facts and words which are reported with a precision of detail which can only be given by an eye-witness—all these things show that their authors were Israelites who were contemporaries and disciples of Jesus.

(*d*) The Gospels and Evangelists are quoted by the earliest fathers, such as St. Justin, St. Irenæus, St. Polycarp, St. Ignatius, St. Clement of Rome, who was a disciple of St. Peter. Moreover, the heretics of the first ages, the pagan philosophers who were hostile to the Church, such as Lucian, Celsus, and Julian the Apostate, admit the authenticity of the Gospels. 'Paul has nowhere dared to give to Jesus the name of God,' says Julian; 'neither have Matthew, Luke, nor Mark; John only has done it in his simplicity.'*

---

* 'Jesum illum neque Paulus Deum dicere ausus est, neque Matthæus, neque Lucas, neque Marcus; sed bonus ille Joannes.' Cf. *Bible vengée*, tom. v.; Bergier, *De la vraie Religion*, tom. viii; Frayssinous, *Confér. de l'Autorité des Evangiles*; Boone, *Manuel de l'Apologiste*.

(2) *Integrity.*—The books of the New Testament have not undergone any substantial interpolation or alteration, (a) because such corruption has always been impossible, and (b) it is positively evident that it never has taken place.

(a) *Impossibility.*—All corruption would have been impossible during the lifetime of the Apostles, and under their eyes. They would have protested against it, and not have suffered it. It was also impossible after their death, as it would be now, because of the dissemination of copies and the vigilance of the Bishops.

(b) It is proved that the New Testament has in fact remained intact; proofs of this are furnished by the writings and commentaries of the Fathers, who quote nearly all the New Testament; by the ancient versions, which are in perfect harmony with the actual text; by the old manuscripts of the New Testament which have come down to us, some of which date from the fourth century, and which present the same text with some unimportant variations.

(3) *Veracity.*—The historians of the New Testament are truthful, veracious, and worthy of belief in the highest degree. We have proof of this in the person of the authors, in the nature of the facts which they report, in the form of their recital, in the confidence which they have inspired from the beginning.

(a) The authors are men who were neither deceived nor deceivers, and who moreover could not, if they would, have deceived. In fact, they were contemporary with, and witnesses of, the events which they relate. Calm of mind and slow of belief, they were men without excitement or enthusiasm; full of religion and probity, they had a horror of imposture, and shed their blood to witness the truth of what they have written.

(b) The history which they write is composed of a series of public and important events, which could easily have been proved to be false, and which contemporaries would have rejected as unworthy impostures if their truthfulness had not been evident. Moreover, these same events are so wonderful, the doctrine and discourses relating to them so sublime, so astonishing, so unheard of until then, that even men of the greatest genius could not have invented them.*

(c) The manner in which the Evangelists relate all these great things bears in itself the stamp of truth. They differ from each other, but do not contradict each other: their candour and simplicity are remarkable. Such is always the testimony of truthful persons who all relate the same events, each one according to his own style.

(d) Is there a single monument of history to which such a degree of veracity has always been attributed? (α) The Gospels, as soon as they appeared, were respected as the faithful expression of the great things of which the first readers had themselves partly been witnesses; (β) it was on the faith of the Evangelists, as on that of the Apostles, that their contemporaries, Jews and Gentiles, embraced the religion of Jesus Christ, though it was new, and only offered to the corrupt society of the times mysteries to believe, a severe morality to practise, and persecutions to undergo. The learned and unlearned received as the pure truth all that is contained in the Gospels, and sealed their belief with their blood.

Therefore the books of the New Testament are of perfect veracity, integrity, and authenticity; therefore they possess the highest degree of authority that can be exacted of history.

* 'Shall we say,' the infidel J. J. Rousseau asks, 'that the history of the Gospel has been invented at pleasure? No people invent thus. It would be more inconceivable that several men had conjointly fabricated this book than that a single person could have furnished the subject. Jewish authors could never have taken such a tone. And the Gospel has in it characters so great, so striking, and so perfectly inimitable, that he who could invent them would be still greater than his heroes' (*Emile*, tom. iii.; vide Feller, n. 248 et sulv.).

II. Historical Authority of the Old Testament.

54. The historical books of the Old Testament, namely, those of Moses, which constitute the Pentateuch, are authentic, are preserved in their integrity, and are truthful. This triple assertion may be proved generally or separately.

General demonstration.—This is furnished by the New Testament. The historians of the New Testament use the writings of the Old Testament, and quote them as books of recognised authenticity, integrity, and veracity; therefore the books were received as such at the period of the Evangelists. This belief, existing amongst Israelites and Christians then as it does now, was founded on truth, because it depended on a constant, unanimous, and public tradition of the Jewish people, a tradition which could not deceive.

In order to appreciate the value of this proof it must be remembered that the books of which we speak were national and sacred. An entire nation—that of the Jews—had accepted them from their very origin, and preserved them, without interruption, with as much religious care and respect as they do to the present day. Hence they cannot have been fictitious nor have undergone alterations. Such an imposture would have been as impossible then as it would be now to falsify the national Charter or Constitution. Therefore they could not have contained anything false or uncertain, for they would not have been accepted with respect by a whole contemporary people, who knew the facts, and who were interested in the highest degree in not being led into error.

Hence the testimony which the New Testament renders to the authority of the Old Testament is the expression of truth.

Separate demonstration: (1) *Authenticity.*—The Pentateuch and the other books of the Old Testament have an undeniable character of authenticity. The nature of the facts related; the precise, and sometimes minute, circumstances of time, place, and persons; the style, the connection between the books, and the events depending one from the other,—everything shows that these volumes were written by the authors to whom they are attributed, and that they date from the period assigned to them by tradition.*

* For evidence of the reality of this proof we have only to open the Bible and read either the books of Moses or the later books, or at any rate certain passages of those. First of all we find in Genesis the history of the creation of the world, of the formation of man, his fall and that of all the human race; the account of the deluge, which destroyed all men excepting one family; there we also see the origin of the different nations, the rise of empires, the foundation of the most ancient cities, the genealogy of the patriarchs, and the subsequent ancestors of the Jewish people recounted with the most precise details. Now, notwithstanding all the researches that have been made up to the present time, this narrative has never been found at fault. It is conformable to the primitive traditions of the most general facts that have been accepted by all nations, some vestiges of which are to be found in the poets, philosophers, and historians of antiquity. Thus the nature of the facts contained in the book of Genesis proves its great antiquity.

Other signs of antiquity are found in the domestic or political manners depicted in Genesis, as also in the custom of raising monuments, which prevailed in the time of the patriarchs. In the primitive ages, when the Scriptures were but little if at all known, the memory of certain events could only be preserved by means of monuments, such as altars, consecrated stones, canticles, symbolical names given to memorable places or to the children whose birth was marked by some extraordinary circumstance. See Genesis, chapters xii. xiii. xiv. xxiv. xxviii.

Finally, the manner in which the four last books of the Pentateuch are written discloses a work contemporary with Moses. Everything tends to show that the writer was eyewitness of the events which he describes. All which concerns the religious ceremonies is related with the smallest details, and with a minute exactness which can only belong to the time of their first institution. Moreover, these four books are more like a journal or a memorandum without order than a

(2) *Integrity.*—No substantial alteration or corruption has taken place before or since the coming of Jesus Christ. (1) None has taken place since Jesus Christ, because the copies possessed by Christians and Jews alike perfectly correspond with each other. (2) None took place before Jesus Christ, because of the religious respect of the Jews for the sacred volumes, the number of copies they possessed, and the traditional knowledge, which preserved the contents of the Scriptures in the memory of the people.

There is but one period during which the integrity of the Bible could have suffered—it is the period of the captivity of the Jews in Babylon; but it is proved that it remained intact during those calamitous times. (1) We see, in the books of Esdras and the Machabees,* that the existing Scriptures were preserved during the captivity. (2) After the return of the tribes to Jerusalem, Esdras collected the sacred volumes with great care, and corrected the copies. (3) The Pentateuch of the Jews is in perfect harmony with that of the Samaritans, who had been their irreconcilable enemies since the reign of Roboam.

(3) *Veracity.*—The historians of the Old Testament are truthful, and the facts which they relate do not admit of doubt, because what we affirm of Moses in particular may be affirmed of all in general—namely, that the historian could neither be deceived nor be a deceiver.

(1) He could not be deceived either about the con-

---

consecutive and methodical history. See Gousset, *Dogmat.*, *Authenticité des Livres Saints;* Glaire, *Intro. aux Livres de l'Anc. et du Nouv. Test.* part i.

* Before Esdras touched the sacred books, the people begged of him not to make the lost Scriptures over again, but to 'bring the book of the law of Moses' (2 Esdras viii. 1). Jeremias, seeing his brethren going into captivity, gave them the law (the sacred writings), that they might not forget the precepts of the Lord (2 Mach. ii. 2).

temporary events which he relates or about those which happened before his time, because they were either notable and public facts, which he saw performed or performed himself, or such as he knew of by certain traditions. As to the events which happened before the existence of man, he knew them by divine revelation. The certainty of his history regarding contemporaneous events, in which the divine intervention is manifest, is a guarantee of the truth of what he relates of the origin of the world. (2) He could not have deceived even had he wished to do so. The impossibility of deception on the part of Moses is shown by his upright character, his probity, by the nature of the things he relates, and by the acceptance of his writings by all the people of Israel, who, if it had not had the evidence of truth, never would have received with such faith and submission a book which was full of onerous duties for them, hard to put in practice.

Hence the veracity, integrity, and authenticity of the books of Moses are established; and, for similar reasons, the other books of the Old Testament are incontestable, and possess historical authenticity in the highest degree.

55. Every effort of impiety has failed up to this time to convict Moses of the slightest error. Innumerable objections have been urged against his books, especially against that of Genesis, in which he relates the history of the creation of the world and the first events of man. These objections, drawn from the sciences—such as geology, astronomy, and chronology—are founded either on uncertain or imperfectly explained scientific facts, or on a false interpretation of the text of the Bible.* Nor do they fail to disappear, together with their unstable grounds, before an enlightened and impartial examination. If at times certain difficulties may have appeared serious, a more attentive study, or a deeper knowledge,

* See later, part ii. chap. iv. 'The Creation.'

has always been forced to acknowledge its own incompetency, and to render adequate homage to the veracity of Moses. It will suffice to quote three illustrious examples. 'Moses,' says Cuvier, 'has left us a cosmogony, the exactitude of which is every day strikingly apparent. Recent geological observations agree perfectly with Genesis in the order of the successive creation of all organised beings.' Ampère, in his *Théorie de la Terre*, writes these words: 'Moses either had a knowledge of the sciences as profound as that of our own day, or else he was inspired.'* The scientific Dumont, who died at Liége in 1857, said, towards the close of his life, 'It is an astonishing thing that, after all the progress of geology, we have to recognise that Moses, at so obscure an epoch, *has spoken of all things with exactness*—even of the different strata and the successive creation of beings.'†

56. Thus all the historical books of both Testaments are of incontestable authority. From this it follows that, if they relate prophecies and miracles in confirmation of the Christian religion, though these belong to the supernatural order, they are no less facts of history which cannot be called in question.

In opening the books as well of the Old‡ as of the New Testament, we find these supernatural events really chronicled in them, which is an indubitable proof of the truth of our belief. 'Let us rejoice,' the celebrated d'Agousseau writes to his son,—'let us rejoice that the

---

* See *Cursus Scripturæ Sacræ*, tom. i. Difficultates Libri Genesis, p. 158 and following.
† *Journal de Bruxelles*, 4th March 1857.
‡ Strictly speaking, the miracles and prophecies of the New Testament will amply testify the truth of the Christian religion. If we also adduce those of the Old Testament it is rather to expose the whole tableau of the Christian revelation, and to show the harmony between the Old and New Testament, than to corroborate the demonstration of facts of the New Testament only.

miracles on which our faith rests are facts as well authenticated as the conquests of Alexander and the death of Cæsar.'

We shall now make a *résumé* of these facts, and present them as proofs of the true religion.

Third Article : Facts and Proofs.

57. *The existence of the Christian religion and its wonderful history* is a fact obvious to the whole world Springing from the Jewish religion, like a flower from its stem, this religion took its rise in Judea in the reign of the Emperor Tiberius. It quickly spread over the whole pagan world, established its centre in Rome, overthrew idolatry, and changed the face of the earth by creating a new society, a new civilisation, which was that of Christianity.

After upwards of eighteen centuries, in spite of numberless persecutions and trials, we see this wonderful religion still existing, ever the same, ever youthful, ever vigorous, ever fruitful.

This is the first uncontested and incontestable fact. The second follows: This same Christian religion is divine; that is, established by God as the true religion, by which humanity must honour its Creator.

The second fact is as incontestable as the first, but it is not unassailable. Unbelievers and the impious contest it relentlessly; therefore we must prove it by some signs which cannot be gainsayed. These signs, or proofs, are very numerous; but we will reduce them to three :

(1) Proof drawn from the preëminence of Christianity over all other religions.

(2) Proof drawn from the prophecies.

(3) Proof drawn from miracles.

I. Proof drawn from the Preëminence of Christianity.

58. When we contemplate all the different religions

which exist on the earth, it becomes evident that they may be reduced to four heads: Paganism, with its offshoots, rationalism and incredulity; Mahometanism, Judaism, and Christianity. Two amongst these religions bear a divine character, and rise above the others— namely, the Judaic and the Christian religions; but the latter, proceeding originally from the Mosaic synagogue, has become elevated far above its origin, and has so eclipsed it by its splendour, that for eighteen centuries it has shone alone to the eyes of the universe like a luminous city built on the summit of a mountain.

It indeed suffices to compare the Christian faith and worship with (1) the superannuated ceremonies of Judaism as it now exists, (2) the manifest errors and the abominations of Mahometanism and Paganism, to recognise at once the preëminence of the religion of Jesus Christ.

Christianity alone is worthy both of God and man. It alone embraces the whole of humanity, and, as a distinguished writer has remarked, with truth, it overrides all time and all ages. It starts from eternity to return thither; it springs from God only to seek Him again, and to repose in Him eternally. Everything in it is truth and holiness. Those who study it and scrutinise its dogmas find therein a marvellous and ever-increasing harmony, beauty, grandeur, and evidence of truthfulness. In fine, all the world may recognise that the purity of its morals, the sublimity of its mysteries, the dignity of its priesthood, the majesty of its worship and of its ceremonies, elevate it so high that, in the eyes of reason, if there exist a true religion on earth, it can only be that of Christianity.

This conclusion is drawn from the following argument: The Christian religion is evidently superior to all others. Now such a religion could not be false; hence the Christian religion could not be other than true.

We will explain the minor of this syllogism, and show

that, by reason of the divine perfection, a religion which is superior to all others could not be false.

If such were the case, man would be the victim of error, and he would be so by the fault of God. God Himself must have delivered this reasonable creature to the invincible spirit of falsehood, which it is absurd to suppose. Here is the proof: In matters of religion man, by his reasoning nature—that is to say, by God Himself, who is the Author of this nature—is obliged to embrace the truth, or, in case of doubt, to accept the most probable doctrine; because, in a matter of such supreme moment, reason demands imperiously that he should take that which is most sure, or at least most probable. The Christian religion, being superior to all the others, is therefore the most probable. Hence man is obliged by God, and even by his own reason, to embrace the Christian religion. From this it is clear that this religion could not be false; for in case of such an hypothesis man would be accepting a false religion by God's own order, which is impossible, seeing that He who is by essence truth and holiness could not lead mankind into error and falsehood.

II. Proof drawn from the Prophecies.

59. The Christian religion is sanctioned by the prophecies. It is marked therefore with the seal of truth. Let us prove the antecedent of this enthymeme:

Christ Jesus and the religion which He founded were announced by prophecies from the very cradle of humanity—that is to say, more than four thousand years before their appearance. On the day when the sin of our first parents delivered the human race over to the slavery of the devil, God promised a Redeemer who would crush the head of the infernal serpent—in other words, who would break the bonds of sin and the devil. God successively announced later that this Redeemer or *Messiah* would be born of the seed of Abraham and Jacob, called also Israel, the father of the Twelve Tribes; then that He would be born of the tribe of Juda, of the royal blood of David, of a Virgin who should give Him birth at Bethlehem, when Judea should be subject to the sway of a stranger, which would happen about five centuries after the reign of Cyrus, king of Persia. All these and many other predictions are found in the books of Genesis, Kings, Psalms, Isaiah, and Daniel.

It may be said in general that the whole of the Old Testament is one great prophecy, which has Christianity for its object. The future law of Christ and His kingdom, meaning His Church, appear therein as the new religion by which Judaism was to be superseded; and as the perfect and universal religion by which God would be honoured by all His people.

We may add that Christ Himself predicted His crucifixion, His resurrection on the third day, His ascension into heaven, and the descent of the Holy Ghost upon His Apostles; also that these latter would establish over all the earth His spiritual kingdom, by which He meant His Church, founded on the primacy of St. Peter; and that the gates of hell, the wickedness of men, and all the powers of darkness would rise up, but could not prevail against it; but, on the contrary, that Jerusalem would be ruined, and her temple razed to the ground. These predictions are all to be found in the Gospels.

The events corresponded to the prophecies; we know from history that they have been verified to the letter, and we ourselves still in part witness their accomplishment.

The Christian religion is, then, stamped with the divine seal of the prophecies; it is, then, the holy and divine religion to which all men must submit.

III. Proof drawn from Miracles.

Christianity has also the sanction of miracles. It is stamped by God, and is obviously divine. To prove the antecedent:

60. It is an historical fact that innumerable miracles accompanied the establishment of the Christian religion; but, notwithstanding the testimony of history, the unbeliever persists in rejecting miracles. We may ask him to explain how and why the universe has embraced the Christian faith; for if the miracles of the Saviour, proved and confirmed by those of the Apostles, be withdrawn, and if all the prodigious facts which are attested by the history of the Church be suppressed, he still will be forced to admit the strangest, greatest, and most incomprehensible miracle of all, namely, that the religion of Jesus Christ, without the aid of miracles, has been able to spread itself over the universe, and remain unchanged up to our own time. It is, then, impossible to deny miracles, for infidelity itself is forced to admit them.

The miracles which have been wrought in favour of the Christian religion may be divided into three classes: (1) miracles of the Old Testament; (2) miracles of the New Testament; (3) miracles of the Gospel.

(1) *Miracles of the Old Testament.*—Striking prodigies, worked in favour of the people of Israel and of the Mosaic religion, are found in the Old Testament—such as the plagues of Egypt, which made even the impious recognise the hand of God; the passage of the Red Sea and the submersion of the Egyptians; the cloud by day and fire by night, that guided the Israelites and regulated their encampments in the desert; the giving of the Law amidst the thunders on Mount Sinai; the sojourn of the people of Israel in the desert, where God fed them with manna which He rained down from heaven, and slaked their thirst with water from the rock—in fine, the conquest of the land of Chanaan, and all the series of marvellous events by which the tribes of Israel established themselves and remained in the Land of Promise.

These miracles, numerous as they are striking,

not only prove the divinity of the law of Moses, but also, though in an indirect way, the divinity of the Christian religion, which had the ancient law for basis. For if the root be planted by the hand of God, the fruit springing therefrom must equally come from God.

Nothing, in fact, is clearer than the connection between the synagogue and the Church. The first is an introduction, a preparation, for the second. The law of Moses, says the Apostle, has been a guide to conduct us to Jesus Christ,—'*Pedagogus noster fuit in Christo*' (Gal. iii. 24). The ancient law, says St. Augustine, carried-in its bosom Christ Jesus, whom one day it was to bring forth,—'*Lex a Christo gravida erat.*'*

Moses, in proclaiming his law, announces another Law-giver who should come after him—a Law-giver *par excellence*, who should be believed: '*Prophetam de gente tua, et de fratribus tuis sicut me suscitabit tibi Dominus Deus tuus: ipsum audies*' (Deut. xviii. 15).†

(2) *Miracles of the New Testament.*—We read in the books of the Gospels, and in the Acts of the Apostles, contained in the New Testament, of the miracles which were wrought by Christ and His Apostles, in testimony of the divine mission of Jesus Christ and the truth of His doctrine. Those which concern our Lord Jesus Christ are such as healing the sick, raising the dead to life, and other wonders, which He works to show His sovereign dominion over all nature. He cures the sick—the lepers, the paralysed, the deaf, the dumb, and the blind; all are restored to perfect health by a word from His mouth, and by a simple act of His all-powerful will. He changes water into wine, multiplies the loaves to feed thousands of men, fills the fishermen's nets with a miraculous draught, quells the winds and the waves of the sea, delivers those possessed by the devil,

---

* August. Serm. xx. De Sanctis.
† See *Elementa Theol. Dogm.* Tract ii. n. 254 seq.; *De Relatione Revelationis Mosaicæ cum Religione Christiana.*

and raises the dead, who are already a prey to corruption, to life again.*

These prodigies are clear and indubitable; Jesus performs them in open daylight, without preparation, before thousands of witnesses, on all sorts of subjects—sometimes even on the absent; so that He leaves no room for the slightest doubt or least suspicion of fraud. In order to be convinced, one has but to read, for instance, of the multiplication of the loaves and fishes (St. John, chap. vi.); the resurrection of Lazarus (St. John, chap. xi.), of which the Pharisees of Jerusalem were witnesses; and the cure of the man born blind (St. John, chap. xi.), who was examined by them before a judicial tribunal. Among the miracles of our Saviour, there is one which surpasses all the others. It shines with a more resplendent lustre, dissipating all darkness and enlightening the whole world. It is His Resurrection—the miracle of miracles—to which we revert in the Apostles' Creed when we say, 'I believe in Jesus Christ, His only Son; . . . the third day He rose again from the dead.'†

Jesus Christ worked miracles without number; but this is not all: He gave to His disciples a similar power, to be used only in His name. St. Peter commenced by the curing of a lame man who lay at the door of the temple. 'In the name of Jesus of Nazareth,' he said to him, 'arise and walk.' At that same instant the lame man arose, perfectly healed; he walked and leaped in sight of all the people. The same Apostle restored health to innumerable sick people, who were brought to him from all parts of Jerusalem. It was sufficient for his shadow to pass over them to deliver them from their infirmities.

* These facts may be seen in every page of the Gospel. See also the *Histoire de la Vie de Jésus-Christ*, by the P. de Ligny; *La Vie de Notre Sauveur*, by l'Abbé Hurdebise.

† The Resurrection of our Lord has been expounded above, p. 5.

What Peter did at Jerusalem the other Apostles did elsewhere, confirming their preaching by miracles wherever they went.

After the death of the Apostles, miracles still continued amongst the Christians, as ecclesiastical history attests, and as we ourselves witness in our own days.

(3) *Miracles of the Gospel.*—By such we mean, not the Evangelical doctrine, which, considered in itself, is a miracle of superhuman wisdom,* but the prodigious effects produced on the world by the preaching of the Gospel. These effects may be reduced to three: (1) the rapid and astonishing growth of the Christian religion, in spite of a thousand obstacles; (2) its preservation unaltered in the midst of persecutions and heresies; (3) the constancy of numerous martyrs under the most cruel torments.

(1). In order to see the supernaturalness of this growth, we must take the Apostles for standpoint, and consider, on the one hand, their enterprise and its impossibilities, and, on the other, their prodigious success. The undertaking (*a*) was to overthrow idolatry, which was established amongst all nations, and sustained by all human power; (*b*) to destroy Judaism, which had been before divinely established, by declaring it to be annulled by Him whom the synagogue had crucified; (*c*) to establish on the ruins of idolatry and of Judaism a new religion, whose incomprehensible dogmas and severe code of morality rendered it difficult of acceptance. The *impossibility* of such an enterprise, humanly speaking, is manifest when the time, the obstacles, and the means are taken into consideration. (*a*) The time chosen for realising this strange conception is the age of Augustus and of Tiberius—an age of science and refinement, of pride and corruption, when Rome, the queen of nations, ruled by her laws and customs, based on the ideal of paganism. (*b*) The obstacles were the passions

* See above, nn. 53-58.

of men, their prejudices and preconceived ideas; the opposition of the synagogue and the formidable power of Rome, armed for the defence of her gods. (c) Of human means, in face of such obstacles, there are none. Twelve poor ignorant fishermen present themselves, armed only with the truth of the doctrine they are come to announce. They present themselves literally, according to the words of their Master, *like lambs in the midst of wolves*, whose prey they could not fail to become.

What was *their success?* They triumphed over the wolves, and changed them into lambs. Jews and pagans became humble Christians, emulous of imitating the Lamb of God, the type of innocence and gentleness. The faith spread so rapidly, not only throughout all the provinces of the Roman empire, but even amongst the Parthians, and also in India, Africa, Spain, Gaul, and among the Germans and Britons, that, at the death of St. John the Apostle, which took place towards the end of the first century, there hardly existed a country which had not received the Christian faith.*

(2) The preservation of Christianity is a no less prodigy than is its establishment, considering that it was in constant warfare with three powerful enemies, which, humanly speaking, it could not have overcome, namely, (a) persecutions, which were meant to stamp it out by force; (b) heresies, which were calculated to annihilate its doctrine; (c) the corruption of morals, calculated to extinguish its spirit of holiness. The gates of hell fought against it in every way, but have never been able to prevail against it.

(3) The martyrs who, ever since the time of St. Stephen down to our own days, have inundated every country with their blood, present a spectacle humanly inexplicable, and in which must be recognised the action of God. To be convinced of the divine intervention, it

* Tert. *Adv. Jud.* n. 7 ; St. August. *In Ps.* xliv. ; St. Chrys. Homil. iii. iv. v. In Epist. 1 Cor.

would suffice, history in hand, to consider, (*a*) the horrors and the duration of their sufferings; (*b*) their calm constancy; (*c*) the frequent prodigies worked in their favour; (*d*) and finally, the number of sufferers, which is computed at about nine millions.*

We have now shown that the Christian religion is stamped with the divine sign of miracles; the conclusion to be drawn is obvious.

61. In collecting together the facts of the preëminence, the prophecies, and the miracles which distinguish the Christian religion, we may say, with Richard de St. Victor: 'If we are mistaken, O my God, Thou hast led us into error; Thou who dost witness to the truth of our faith. For this faith is authenticated by innumerable signs and prodigies, such as Thou alone couldst work.'

62. Such, therefore, is the truth and the stability of the Christian religion that it metaphysically excludes all possibility of error, since such error could come only from God, who is the essence of truth. This conclusion gives rise to another equally practical; for the Christian revelation is presented to the human race, not as a simple theoretical truth, which it suffices to admit, but as a religious law which is absolutely necessary and obligatory. 'Whoever shall believe and be baptised,' says our Lord, 'shall be saved: he who believes not shall be condemned.' It, therefore, must be accepted and put into practice, under pain of eternal damnation. We have proved the fact of the *revelation*, and the truth of the *Christian religion* as opposed to unbelief; we shall now proceed to prove the truth of the *Catholic religion* as opposed to the various heresies.

* See Frayssinous. *Conférences; Foundation of the Christian Religion proved by the Marvels of its Establishment; Questions sur les Martyrs;* also *Elementa Théol. Dogmaticæ*, tom. 1. tract 2; *De Religione Christiana*, nn. 327, 334, 335 seqq.; Boone, *Manuel de l'Apologiste*, part ii.

CHAPTER II.

TRUTH OF THE CATHOLIC RELIGION IN OPPOSITION TO THE HERESIES OF DIVERS SECTS.

1. WE have shown that the Christian religion is the true one. At first sight it would seem that we had already attained our end, and that, the true religion being recognised, it only remains for us to embrace it. But here a new fact presents itself for our consideration. The Christian religion is divided into several confessions or sects, all claiming possession of true Christianity. We must, therefore, distinguish true from false Christianity.

Our arguments will be founded upon principles already proved, namely, (1) on the fact of the divinity of Christianity, to which is attached the divine character of the mission of Christ; (2) on the essential and infallible truth of the words of Christ; (3) on the authenticity of the Scriptures, especially of the Gospels which report His words.

2. In the first place it is certain that the true doctrine of Jesus Christ, which we wish to know, is not lost. The various Christian confessions all claim to possess it; this is impossible, for they are all opposed one to the other; but though it does not belong to all, it undoubtedly must belong to one.

The true religion of Jesus Christ could not have ceased to exist, seeing that the work of its Divine Founder was stable, and that He Himself declared by a solemn prophecy that this faith and this religion should be preserved pure to the end of the world. 'Behold,' He said, 'I am with you all days, even to the consummation of the world' (Matt.). Hence the true faith of Jesus Christ is preserved in the Christian world.

3. Which, then, is this true and pure faith of Jesus Christ? Which communion or branch of Christianity possesses it? We reply that it is the Roman Catholic

Church, and that the faith, the religion, professed by this Church is the true religion of Jesus Christ.

In order rightly to comprehend this assertion and the proofs which we are going to adduce, it must be borne in mind that Christ founded *a Church*, which is nothing else than His religion itself organised into a social body. He gave to this Church a constitution and a determined form. He imprinted on it characteristic signs by which it might be known throughout all ages, and distinguished from all sects. 'In order,' says the Council of the Vatican,* 'that we may satisfy the obligation of embracing the faith, and faithfully persevering therein, God, by His only Son, has instituted a Church, and has provided it with the visible marks of His institution, so that she may be known by all as the guardian of the revealed word, and the mistress who teaches it.'

This Church, which bears the marks of Christ's institution, is the Roman Catholic Church, and we shall proceed to prove this.

4. We shall divide the whole matter into five articles:

I. Nature and Institution of the Church.

II. First demonstration of the true Church.

III. Second demonstration of the true Church.

IV. Particular ideas about the constitution and authority of the Church.

V. Accusations brought against the Church.

First Article: Nature and Institution of the Church.

5. *Nature.*—By the word CHURCH (convocation, assembly) is meant the religious society which was founded by Jesus Christ, when He said to the Apostle Simon Peter, 'Thou art Peter, and upon this rock I will build My Church, and the gates of hell shall not prevail against her' (Matt. xvi. 16).

By these words He established a religious society, of

* Constitution, *Dei Filius*, chap. iii.

which Peter was to be the head; a society or a spiritual state analogous to that of political societies or states, but so perfect that it may be called a model society. This society is the Church, called also 'the Kingdom of Heaven upon earth.' 'The Church,' says Pius IX.,* 'is a real and perfect society, entirely free, enjoying the distinctive perpetual rights which were conferred upon it by its Divine Founder.'

6. In a civil state or kingdom there two orders of citizens: those who command and those who obey. The first are called the governors, the administrators; the second, the people, the subjects. Similarly also, in the Church or kingdom of Jesus Christ, there are two orders of the faithful: those who command and those who obey; or those who teach, and those who are taught. The first are called the clergy—the hierarchy, the priesthood, the pastors; these are the Pope, the bishops, and priests; the second are called the faithful, the sheep or the flock. The first constitute the teaching and governing Church; the second, the Church taught and governed.

7. Every civil state has a fundamental law established from its origin; moreover, it has a form of government proper to itself, either monarchical, aristocratical, or republican. The Church has likewise her fundamental law and her form of government, established from the beginning by Christ Himself, which no human power can alter.

This fundamental law is the Gospel and tradition; that is, all that Jesus Christ has instituted and taught: His doctrine which must be believed; His morals which must be practised; and His Sacraments and Sacrifice, which must be accepted as a means of salvation.

The form of government prevailing in the Church is neither aristocratic nor republican; it is monarchical. In a monarchy there is one sovereign chief, the king;

* Constitut. *Quanta cura*, Dec. 8, 1864, Syllab. xix.

and there are subordinate chiefs or governors of provinces. In like manner in the ecclesiastical monarchy there is a supreme chief, the Pope, the Vicar of Jesus Christ; and governors, or rather, subordinate princes —the bishops in their several dioceses. We say that the Pope, or head of the Church, is the vicar or lieutenant of Jesus Christ; because Christ Himself in heaven is the chief head, properly so called, of the faithful. The Pope is appointed by Christ to govern in His name on earth.

The Church is a monarchy; but a monarchy wisely supported by a subordinate aristocracy; in other words, it is the papacy, aided all over the world by the episcopacy. To understand this more clearly, let us refer to history for the origin and institution of the Church.

8. *Institution of the Church.*—When Jesus Christ wished to establish His Church, which He called the kingdom of heaven on earth, He gathered round Him twelve chosen disciples, to whom He gave the name of *Apostles* (sent). He created them at once priests and bishops, and gave them power to elect other bishops, who should be their successors in the episcopacy, and other priests subordinate to the bishops, who should succeed in the priesthood.

So far the Apostles had all been equals. They had obeyed only Jesus Christ as their head, and formed with Him the infant Church. But Christ was to leave them, and ascend into heaven: He could not remain visibly on earth and govern His Church in person; therefore He established in His place a vicar or vice-regent appointed to govern in His name the kingdom of heaven on earth. His choice fell on Simon Peter, one of the twelve, who thus became the superior of the apostolic college and the visible head of the whole Church; Jesus Christ still remaining its invisible head, seated at the right hand of God the Father in the highest heaven.

These are the words by which Christ first promised

to, and then conferred upon, St. Peter and his successors this supreme authority. Some months before His Passion, the Saviour, finding Himself alone with His Apostles in the plains of Cæsarea and Philippi, asked them what they thought concerning His person, and whom they took Him to be. Peter answered, 'Thou art Christ, the Son of the living God.' At this reply Jesus cast on Peter a look of divine tenderness, and said to him, 'Blessed art thou, Simon Bar-Jona: because flesh and blood hath not revealed it to thee, but My Father, who is in heaven. And I say to thee, that thou art Peter;* and upon this rock I will build My Church, and the gates of hell shall not prevail against it. And I will

---

* As though He said to him, 'Simon, I choose thee to be like Me, a man apart from the rest of men, above the rest, another self. By nature thou art but *Simon*; by grace I make thee *Peter*—the rock, the foundation of My Church. I, the Divine Architect of the Church, give thee solidity of a foundation-stone. It is I who am the principle of thy firmness; thou shalt be united with Me; thou shalt rest on Me, who am not only a rock but the chief foundation. My Church shall lean on Me and on thee. United, and, in a measure, identified with Me, thou shalt share My sufferings, My combats, and My triumphs. The powers of hell, in league against Me, will rise also against My Church and against thee; but they shall ever find in thee an invincible resistance. All their efforts against thee shall be vain, and will but conduce to the triumph of the Church, whose destiny shall be a perpetual alternation of combat and victory, suffering and resurrection.'

As the *rock* or *foundation-stone* marks the sovereignty, and the throne of the ecclesiastical empire given to Simon Peter and his successors in perpetuity, so the *keys* show the power and the attributes of this sovereignty. The keys are the symbol of supreme dominion; and in giving them to Peter, the Son of God confers upon him discretionary power, which is to be unlimited and absolute over the whole Church and over the whole world, as He explains by adding, 'Whatsoever thou shalt bind shall be bound'—words without limit; by virtue of which Peter has power to bind all—will, intelligence, absolutely all: 'Whatsoever thou shalt bind.' Nothing is excepted.

give to thee the keys of the kingdom of heaven. And whatsoever thou shalt bind upon earth it shall be bound also in heaven ; and whatsoever thou shalt loose on earth it shall be loosed also in heaven' (Matt. xvi. 16).

Another time after His resurrection the Saviour, appearing to His disciples on the shores of the Sea of Tiberius, says to Peter, ' Simon, son of John, lovest thou Me more than these?' 'Yea, Lord,' Peter replies; ' Thou knowest that I love Thee.' Then Jesus says to him, ' Feed My lambs.' Again He says, ' Simon, son of John, lovest thou Me?' and Peter answers, ' Thou knowest that I love Thee ;' and Jesus again says, ' Feed My lambs.' A third time He asks him, ' Simon, son of John, lovest thou Me?' Peter, grieved at being asked a third time, ' Lovest thou?' replies, ' Lord, Thou knowest all things; Thou knowest that I love Thee ;' and Jesus says, ' Feed my sheep' (John xxi. 15).

By these divine words the Church was constituted. The faithful formed the flock, the Apostles were the subordinate pastors, and Peter the supreme pastor, invested with unlimited power by Jesus Christ.

9. The Divine Founder, who established His Church in the way we have just shown, gave to it, at the same time, four distinctive marks : He wished it to be *one*, *holy*, *Catholic*, and *Apostolic*. These marks are of the very essence of the Church, and are inseparable from it. They may be seen by all, and are thus the visible signs or notes by which she is known over all the universe, as we shall see later.

10. The work of Christ has to endure and be perpetuated in the world without being shaken by the downfall of human institutions; it has to range over centuries as a perfect empire to the end of time. For Jesus Christ had solemnly declared it by the assurance that the gates of hell should not prevail against His Church, and that He would remain with her all days, ever assisting and aiding her, even to the consummation

of the world. To this perpetuity of existence is added infallibility of doctrine. The Saviour gave to His Church the grace to preserve for ever intact the true faith which He has confided to her. In declaring that the gates of hell should never prevail against His Church (which is essentially a teaching Church), He promises always to preserve her from destruction and her doctrine from error. Hell might indeed prevail if the Church ceased to exist, or if she deviated from the true faith, because then she would no longer be the Church which was founded by Jesus Christ, the society of His true disciples or of true believers. Jesus Christ would then withdraw this perpetual assistance which He promised in these words: 'Go, teach them all things which I have commanded you (to believe and to practise); and behold, I am with you all days, even to the consummation of the world.' As the Church, then, was to last for ever, the Apostles had their successors in the episcopacy as well as in the priesthood—these were the bishops and priests; and Peter also had his successors in the Roman Pontiffs.

11. In founding on St. Peter His spiritual empire, or, which is the same thing, in placing the keys of His Church, the symbols of supreme power, in the hands of Peter and his successors, Jesus Christ made the Prince of the Apostles the founder of a spiritual dynasty. This dynasty of the true Church has been perpetuated uninterruptedly by the 259 successors of Peter, the last of whom is now seated on the pontifical throne under the name of Leo XIII. It forms the trunk of the mystical tree which has since spread its branches over the whole earth.

Some of the branches have separated from the sacred trunk; these are the heretical and schismatical sects: but the trunk itself, united with the root, has remained unchanged, and ever subsists laden with branches and with fruit. It is the succession of the Popes in the

Roman Church, the mother and mistress of all the Churches—the centre of the Universal Church, the true Church of Jesus Christ.

12. The true Church, as we have said, is no other than the Roman Catholic Church; she is the faithful depository of the doctrine of Jesus Christ, as well as of His Sacraments and all the means of salvation which He has bequeathed to humanity. Adversaries rise up against her; these are heretics and schismatics. They allege that the true faith, the true Church of Christ, is not the Roman Catholic Church, but that their particular sect is the true Church of Christ. We must prove, on the contrary, the truth and legitimacy of the Roman faith, or, in other words, that *the Roman Catholic Church is the true Church of Jesus Christ.*

13. The proofs of this assertion are undeniable and clear to all persons of good-will. We shall cite two—the proof drawn from the existence of the Apostolic See, and that of the four marks of the Church.

Second Article: First Proof of the Truth of the Catholic Church, the Existence of the Apostolic See.

14. Amid the bodies which profess Christianity, that one which possesses the apostolic succession is the true Church of Jesus Christ. The Roman Catholic Church possesses the apostolic succession, therefore she is the true Church.

We have in fact already seen that the Divine Founder established the Apostolic See or the Papacy in His Church, of which it was to be the centre and the basis.

Being, then, the centre and the basis of the true Church, the Papacy is inseparable from it, and must ever be preserved therein; therefore, where we find the Papacy, there is also the true Church.

The Papacy or apostolic succession is preserved in the Roman Church. The Prince of the Apostles went to Rome in the reign of the Emperor Claudius, A.D. 42, established his see there, remained there twenty-five years, and died under Nero on the 29th of June of the year 67. In dying, he left the Papal See and the supreme power as a divine inheritance to his successors, SS. Linus, Cletus, Clement, and all the others whose names are known, down to Leo XIII. Rome, and hence the Roman Church, is, then, the depository of the Apostolic See. It is proved by history and loudly proclaimed by monuments and traditions; and, moreover, no sect has ever claimed this incontestable attribute of the Roman Church. She is, then, the true and only Church, established by Jesus Christ; and all sects are but corruptions of the Christian faith, the sacrilegious results of heresy and schism.

15. This argument was proclaimed, from the earliest times, by the formula, which was received as an axiom, '*Ubi Petrus, ibi Ecclesia,*—Where Peter is, there is the Church.' By Peter is here meant the See of Peter, the successor of Peter, or the Roman Pontiff. Every one can comprehend the truth and the force of these words—they admit of no questioning. It is as if one said, 'Where the living trunk is, there the tree also is; where the centre is, there is the circle; where the foundation is found, there is also the edifice; where the throne stands, there exists the empire.' Let us then loudly proclaim this light-diffusing sentence, 'Where Peter is, there is also the Church;' and let us add that which naturally follows, and which is so consoling to the faithful, 'Where the Church is, there is Christ; where Christ is, there is salvation.'

Third Article : Second Proof of the Truth of the Catholic Church, her four distinctive Marks.

16. The Roman Catholic Church is the true Church of Jesus Christ, if the Divine Founder imprinted in His work distinctive marks, and if these marks or signs are found united in the one Roman Catholic Church.

The minor of this syllogism affirms a twofold fact: (1) the divine imprinting of these distinctive marks, and (2) the existence of these marks in the Roman Catholic Church. In order to prove this twofold fact, we must consider the four marks one after the other; and, after having defined in what each one consists, show (1) that Jesus Christ really gave it to His Church as a pledge of authenticity; (2) that this pledge is found in the Roman Church. As the marks of the Church must be visible to the world, we shall, without much reasoning, see them, in fact, shining by their own light in the true Church.*

The four marks of the true Church are her four essential properties, manifesting themselves to the world, unity, holiness, Catholicity, and apostolicity. We make this confession in the Creed which we repeat at Mass, 'I believe in one holy Catholic and Apostolic Church.'

Unity.

17. The unity proper to the Church makes this divinely established society stand out alone on earth, undivided in herself, like an individual person. The Church is one in the sense (1) that there is but one Church founded by Jesus Christ; (2) that this one Church has but one head, one faith, one worship, based on the same Sacraments. The Church or religious society differs thus from civil society, which is not one, but manifold, being divided into a number of kingdoms, which are independent of each other.

Jesus Christ has imprinted on His Church this essential distinctive character of unity. He has chosen a single foundation on which to build, not His Churches, but His Church, like an edifice formed of all the faithful, as of so many living stones, composing one whole. The multitude of faithful, according to the desires of

---

* See Boone, *Motifs de mon Attachement à l'Eglise Catholique*

our Saviour, was to be perfectly united in heart and mind, as He shows by this prayer to His Eternal Father: 'Holy Father, I pray Thee for all those who believe in Me, that all may be one, as Thou, My Father, and I are one; that so the world may believe that Thou hast sent Me' (John xvii. 20, 21).

Is this mark of unity found in the Catholic Church? It suffices to cast one's eyes on the divers people who compose it to see that by their union with their pastors they form but one family, wherein reigns the most admirable unity of head, of faith, and of worship.

Holiness.

18. The mark of holiness consists in the great fruitfulness of the Church in producing holy works. Like to a living and fertile tree, she possesses the virtue of constantly producing various fruits of holy teaching, holy works, and miracles.

Holiness, invisible in itself, manifests its presence by three effects: (1) a teaching and doctrine which is ever pure; (2) exalted virtue and good works ever flourishing in at least some of the members of the Church; (3) the miracles which are continually worked within her pale. Jesus Christ has endowed His Church with the inalienable treasure of holiness, and with the perpetual gift of miracles. 'He has loved His Church,' says the Apostle; and He has 'delivered Himself up for it, that He might sanctify it, cleansing it by the laver of water in the word of life, that He might present it to Himself a glorious Church, not having any spot' (Eph. v. 25). 'I am the vine, you are the branches; he that abideth in Me, and I in him, the same beareth much fruit' (John xv. 5). 'Amen, amen, I say to you, he that believeth in Me, the works that I do, he also shall do, and greater than these shall he do' (John xiv. 12).

Holiness enhanced by miracles is thus inseparable from the Church of Jesus Christ. Now the Catholic

Church in her past history, as in her present state, appears surrounded by an aureola of holiness; and we have but to look into the best-authenticated *Lives of the Saints*,* the acts of the martyrs, the histories of religious orders and of charitable institutions, and the *Annals of the Propagation of the Faith*, in order to recognise this her holiness in the same way as we recognise a tree by its fruits.†

Catholicity.

By the Catholicity of the Church is meant its tendency to extend over the whole earth. Like unto a vine, whose branches spread to a distance, the Church of Jesus Christ is propagated and spread amongst the nations, producing everywhere the same fruits of virtue and good works.

This universality, this diffusion, which is visible to all, is another feature of the true faith. We easily recognise it as a religion made for all mankind, or rather for human nature. It is appropriate to all climates and to all times, emanating from Him who is the Creator, the Redeemer, the common Father of all men, and who desires their salvation, and causes the light of faith to shine over the whole world just as He makes the rays of the sun spread over the universe.

The prophets predicted, and Jesus Christ declared, that His Church should be universal. 'He shall set up a standard unto the nations' (Isaias xi. 12); 'The kingdom of God is like to a grain of mustard-seed, which a man took and cast into his garden, and it grew and became a great tree, and the birds of the air lodged in the branches thereof' (Luke xiii. 19); 'Go ye into the whole world, and preach the Gospel to every creature' (Mark xvi. 15).

* Notably the *Acta Sanctorum* of the Bollandists.
† See Boone, *Motifs de mon Attachement à l'Eglise Catholique*.

Has the Church of Rome this distinguishing mark of Catholicity? Need we answer? Catholicity is so much a part of the Church that it has given to her her glorious title from the very beginning. From the first years of her existence down to our day all Christians who were and are united with and subject to the Roman Church have been, and still are, called *Catholics*. St. Pacien says, 'Christian is my name, Catholic my surname.' And to assure ourselves that it is not an idle word let us look over a map of the world, and consider the most distant countries and the least-known islands in the ocean; let us interrogate the *Annals of the Propagation of the Faith*, or the *Christian Missions*,* and we shall see that there are Catholics everywhere, and that the Roman Church takes root and spreads amongst the most barbarous people in our own days, as in the time of the Apostles.†

Apostolicity.

The Apostolicity of the Church consists in its apostolic foundation. Jesus Christ established His Church upon the Apostles, and made them its foundation and its basis, from which it was never to be separated.

It is founded *on the Apostles*, with Peter for head, and the others as his subordinate colleagues; that is to say, it is founded on the doctrine and by the divine mission of the Apostles, whose doctrine must ever remain in the Church by uninterrupted tradition, and whose mission must be perpetuated by an equally uninterrupted succession. This succession resembles a chain, of which St. Peter is the first link, and the Apostles and their successors the continuation. To this so-called chain, which proceeds from St. Peter and the Apostles, we may suppose others to be attached, representing the bishops of other sees and their successors; and these,

* Marshall, *Christian Missions*.

† See above, Christianity proved by miracles and by the word of the Gospel, chap. i. n. 60 (8).

being thus in communion with the See of Peter, participate in its Apostolicity.

The Gospel plainly shows us that Jesus Christ founded this Church on the Apostles as on a sure foundation, whereon she might stand unshaken to the end of time. 'On this rock,' He said, 'I will build My Church, and the gates of hell shall not prevail against it' (Matt. xvi. 16). And again, 'Go, teach ye all nations, baptising them in the name of the Father, and of the Son, and of the Holy Ghost, teaching them to believe all things whatsoever I have commanded you; and behold, I am with you all days, even to the consummation of the world' (Matt. xxxiii. 26). Where shall we find this mark of Apostolicity if it be not in the Catholic Church? We may search all the different Christian communions in vain till we arrive at the Church that possesses the See of Peter, the Prince of the Apostles, and whose children are united through their bishops and pastors to the Apostolic See, the everlasting depository of the *faith*, and of the *mission* or divine authority of the Apostles.*

19. Hence, the Catholic Church, and it alone, has the divine marks which must distinguish the Church of Jesus Christ. 'The Church,' says the Vatican Council, 'is in herself a great and perpetual argument of faith, and an unalterable proof of her own divine mission, by reason of her prodigious propagation, her eminent sanctity, her inexhaustible fecundity in all sorts of blessings, and because of her Catholic unity, and her unshaken firmness.'†

The Roman Catholic Church is, then, the true Church, and it follows that all men must hearken to her voice and obey her commandments under pain of eternal damnation.‡

---

* Constitution, *Dei Filius*, chap. iii. † Ibid.
‡ See, for fuller explanations, Boone, *Manuel de l'Apologiste* and *Motifs de mon Attachement à l'Eglise Catholique*.

Fourth Article : On the Nature, Constitution, and Authority of the Church.

20. The Church on earth, of which we have been speaking, is but a part or province of the great kingdom whose Founder and Divine Chief is Jesus Christ our Lord. It embraces, besides this Church militant on earth, the Church suffering in purgatory, and the Church triumphant in heaven. The two first are in a transitory state; they are preparing for their union with the Church triumphant, which is settled and immutable, and which, at the end of the world, being fully peopled with saints, will alone endure for all eternity.

21. God, before executing His great work on earth, prepared mankind for it during the space of at least four thousand years. Everything from the time of Adam tended towards this preparation for the Church; the marvellous formation of the Jewish nation, as well as its religion and its synagogue, were, so to speak, a series of temporary scaffoldings aiding the construction of the divine edifice. The figures and prophecies of the Old Law had also the same end and significance.

22. The Church of Jesus Christ was solemnly announced by the prophets; they picture it as a new Jerusalem, whither all nations should repair to praise the Lord; and as a kingdom of justice and of peace that the promised Saviour should found, and that should last till the end of the world. The royal prophet announced that Christ should be king, that He should have all nations for His inheritance and all the universe for His empire (Psalms ii. xxi. lxxi.); also that justice and peace should flourish during His reign until the moon should cease to be (Ps. lxxi.). Christ Himself confirmed these sayings of the prophets by the words He addressed to St. Peter : ' On thee, Peter, will I build My Church, and the gates of hell shall not prevail against it.'

23. The Church is also represented in the Old and New Testaments by numbers of figures and parables, which reveal her wonderful character, and show her under various aspects. The chief figures and parables are, in the Old Testament, the terrestrial Paradise, which is a prototype of the Church, and which contained the tree of life; Eve, the spouse of Adam, called the mother of the living; Noah's ark; the people of Israel, called also the people of God; the Ark of the Covenant; the Promised Land; the city of Jerusalem, Mount Sion, and the Temple of Solomon built thereon.

In the New Testament we find the Church prefigured by the ship in which the Apostles were in company with Jesus Christ, and in the bark of St. Peter; the miraculous draught of fishes; in the seamless garment of our Lord, which could not be divided; and in Jesus Christ Himself. He is the chief representative of the Church, which He has formed to His own Image and Likeness, which must, like Him, be divine, and also human, visible, and invisible; like Him, do good, suffer and bless, die and rise again; and, like Him, enter by the way of the Cross into eternal glory.

The parables relating to the Church are these: the king who made a marriage feast for his son; the great supper; the nets thrown into the sea; the flock, and the sheepfold of the Good Shepherd; the field; the vine; the grain of mustard-seed; the true vine, and its branches.

24. The Church is called by various names, which designate her different characteristics, such as 'the 'House of God;' the 'Great House;' the 'City of God;' the 'New Jerusalem,' in contradistinction to Babylon, the 'City of the World, and of Hell.' She is called also the 'City built upon a Hill;' the 'Kingdom of God;' the 'Kingdom of Heaven;' the 'Kingdom of Jesus Christ,' which is not of this world; the 'True Posterity of Abraham;' the 'Royal and Priestly People;'

the 'Garden, and the Paradise of God;' the 'Fold of Christ;' the 'Spouse of Jesus Christ;' the 'Queen;' the 'Mother of the Faithful;' the 'Body of Christ,' that is to say, His mystical Body, of which the faithful are the members and He the head.

25. The Scriptures, which call the Church on earth the mystical Spouse of Jesus Christ, present her to our view as a moral being, composed of body and soul. The Soul of the Church is the Holy Ghost, who abides in her, and bestows on her life and grace, with faith, hope, charity, and all other good gifts. The body of the Church is composed of a visible chief or head and visible members. The chief or head is the Roman Pontiff, who is the Vicar of Jesus Christ, the invisible Head. The faithful are the members. They are united, and subject to the Roman Pontiff by means of the subordinate pastors.

Holy Baptism makes us members of the Church; and we cease to be such, not by the commission of a mortal sin, but by a public apostasy, or by heresy, by schism, by a sentence of excommunication pronounced against the individual, and after death by the sentence of eternal damnation.

26. The head of the Church, like the head of any civil community, is endowed with power and authority to command his subjects, and to govern the body under his authority. 'Whatsoever thou shalt loose on earth,' said our Saviour, 'shall be loosed also in heaven; all power is given to Me in heaven and on earth; go, then, teach all nations, teaching them to observe all things whatsoever I have commanded you. He that heareth you heareth Me, he that despiseth you despiseth Me.'*

The power of the Church differs from civil power, which, being purely human and resting on natural right,

---

* Matt. xviii. xxviii.; Luke x. Jesus Christ established at the same time both the Church and her authority. See Nature and Institution of the Church, chap. ii. n. 8.

is founded on the natural order established by the Creator. The power of the Church is supernatural in its origin, and divine by positive right, as it was divinely established by the Redeemer.

27. Since the power of the Church is divine, it follows, (1) that it is of an order which is superior to all human power; (2) that it is distinct from, though not opposed to, civil authority, of which it is entirely independent. Ecclesiastical and civil authority, though each in a different way, coming both from God, are not made to war on each other; but, on the contrary, like the two wheels of one chariot, they are meant to sustain each other, and concur in advancing the welfare of human society so as to conduct it safely towards its eternal destiny.

Such is the harmony which, according to the views of God, should reign between the two powers; and it is a grievous and condemned error to say that the Church should be subject to the secular power, or that the Church should be separated from the State, and the State from the Church.*

The mutual relations of the two powers is no obstacle to their reciprocal independence. Each, in its own sphere, is sovereign and independent, excepting, however, the subordination which results from the nature of things and the end proper to each of the two powers. As the body is subject to the soul, and the temporal to the spiritual welfare of man, so the civil power is subject to the religious power, in the sense that those who are invested with civil power are bound to exercise it according to the principles and in the interest of the true religion of Jesus Christ. Governments are bound to protect the Church and her worship, her goods and her ministers; and every law or act of civil administration which is opposed to the discipline or the rights of the Church is an abuse of power and an injustice before God.

* Constitut. Pius IX. Dec. 8, 1864, Syllabus lv.

'The power of kings,' said Pius IX., repeating the words of Popes St. Innocent and St. Felix, 'was instituted, not only for the government of the world, but for the assistance of the Church; and nothing is more glorious or more advantageous to a prince than to leave the Catholic Church in possession of her own rights, and to allow none to interfere with her liberty.*

Infidel or impious princes, though they do not recognise the divine character of the Church, are none the less bound, by virtue of natural right, to respect her as a human society having her own inviolable rights. Moreover, they are obliged to seek instruction in the truth, to acknowledge the divine rights of the Catholic Church, which rest on such good titles, and to submit with docility to her decrees, under pain of eternal damnation.

28. The whole power which Jesus Christ conferred on St. Peter as head of the Church, under the symbol of 'keys,' may be divided into three kinds: the power of teaching, the power of the ministry, and the power of government.

29. *Power of teaching.*—Besides the gift of infallibility in doctrine,† the Church received a mission to teach all nations, but more especially her own children; and in virtue of this power she has the right, not only to define what is true doctrine, to preach and to catechise, but also to watch over the education of the faithful. Hence the bishops have, by divine right, the power to control and inspect every school in their diocese. It is their privilege, and also their duty, to forbid all false teachings, all bad or dangerous schools, and such books and papers as are likely to taint the faith or morals of their people. He who disobeys the bishops in these matters disobeys our Lord Himself.

30. By virtue of her *power of the ministry*, the Church administers all the Sacraments, not excepting marriage, of which she is sole judge, with full power to create

* Constitut. Dec. 8, 1864.   † See above chap. ii. no. 10.

invalidating impediments or to dispense with them...
By the same faculty she grants indulgences, institutes feasts, regulates the ceremonies of the Holy Sacrifice, and all that constitutes public worship. She has a right to have temples for the living and cemeteries for the dead, and to possess property which is necessary or useful to her ministry or the exercise of her worship. It would be not only injustice, but sacrilege, to violate her possessions, because they are consecrated to God and rest on divine right.

31. Three things come under the head of *power of government* possessed by the Church, which is called *jurisdiction;* namely, the religious administration of countries where the faithful dwell, the passing of laws, and the establishment of pains and penalties.

(1) In order to provide for the administration, the Church, or rather the Pope, divides the ecclesiastical empire into dioceses, and the dioceses into parishes. Bishops are nominated for the government of dioceses, and these in their turn ordain priests for the administration of the parishes.

The Pope also approves and institutes religious orders—those communities which are founded on the evangelical counsels of Jesus Christ.

(2) The Church has the right to make laws and precepts which all the faithful are bound to accept. This is the legislative power which the Pope and the Œcumenical Councils exercise over all the faithful: thus were made the commandments of the Church, and also all the canonical legislation. Bishops also can make rules and institute statutes and laws for the government of their dioceses.

(3) The Church has power to impose pains and penalties and censures, such as excommunication and suspension, with which she can punish all refractory subjects. This is *coercive* power. It belongs to the Pope and to the bishops.

32. All this power comes from Jesus Christ, the Man-God, who, possessing the plenitude of power in heaven and on earth, conferred it on His Church, and there preserves it and propagates it like the sap in a tree. This propagation is effected partly by means of the Sacraments, whence the *power of Holy Orders, power of Ordination;* partly also by means of mission or sending, whence *the power of Jurisdiction;* and both one and the other represent the power of Jesus Christ communicated to His ministers. It is, then, the power of Jesus Christ which reigns in the Church, or rather it is Himself who governs the entire Church, even its smallest parishes, by means of the hierarchy, its lawful pastors, its ministers and priests. He has said to each and all, 'He that heareth you, heareth Me; and he that despiseth you, despiseth Me' (Luke x. 16).

Fifth Article : Accusations brought against the Church.

33. If the Church were even a purely human institution, she must still be acknowledged as the most beautiful and venerable institution of the universe. She must be considered a model society, whose organisation appears a masterpiece of wisdom, and all of whose influence and actions tends towards the good of humanity. She has been rightly termed a beneficent society, the civiliser and great benefactress of the people, passing through the course of ages doing good. But in spite of her claims to gratitude and respect, the Church is the butt of hatred and calumny. This is a singular phenomenon whose explanation is to be found, not only in the hostility of human passions, against which the Church wages war, but in the fury of the devil and the powers of darkness. Since the Church is a work of God directly opposed to hell, she must encounter, without ceasing, the attacks of hell; and above all, those directed against her by error and lies. It is the duty of the faithful children of the Church to provide against

these attacks, and to be prepared to defend their mother, and to avenge the truth.

We shall now proceed to treat of some of the accusations most common to our period, the injustice of which we will presently show.

They are designated under these heads: *Intolerance; the Inquisition; the Massacre of St. Bartholomew; Antagonism of the Church to Science; Galileo; Bad Popes; the Crusades; the great Schism of the East; the Temporal Power of the Popes, and their interference with civil governments; Opposition to Progress and Civilisation; the Encyclical Letter and the Syllabus, or the Condemnation of Liberalism and Modern Liberty.*

I. Intolerance.

34. The Church is accused of *intolerance*. This word is sometimes meant to convey the idea of dogmatical or doctrinal intolerance; sometimes the word signifies practical and civil intolerance. In either sense the accusation is unfounded. A few precise definitions will prove this.

(1) What is dogmatic tolerance or intolerance? and in what does the dogmatic intolerance of the Church consist?

35. *Dogmatic tolerance* is another expression for religious indifference, which leaves each one free to choose his own style of worship, as though all religions were equally good, or at the least indifferent.

This tolerance, or rather this *religious indifference*, which is called also *religious indifferentism*, contains a doctrine as absurd as it is impious. It may, in fact, be expressed thus: The Catholic, Protestant, Jewish, Mahometan, worships are, it is true, opposed to each other: the one burns what the other reveres; the one adores Jesus Christ, the other blasphemes Him; the one calls virtue what the other calls crime; nevertheless all are equally true, good, and agreeable to God.

It would be impossible not to admit that such a doctrine can only be called a mockery of God and of His worship, and a practical denial of all religious truth. Dogmatic tolerance is therefore false and impious.

36. *Dogmatic intolerance*, on the contrary, teaches the necessity of one true religion, and it may be thus expressed: In the same way as there is only one God, so there is but one religion by which to worship Him, and this one religion is obligatory on all mankind. It is the doctrine of the Catholic Church contained in these words: '*Out of the Church there is no salvation.*' Is this doctrine reprehensible? It cannot be so if it be true, and we have shown that it is true. It is the doctrine of Jesus Christ Himself, the supreme Lawgiver, who established the universal law, that whosoever should, by faith and baptism, enter the bosom of His Church, should be saved, and whosoever should reject the Church should be condemned. The Church goes no further than to proclaim this divine law, and in this her intolerance consists.

Hence (1) the dogmatic intolerance of the Church is the intolerance of truth which, in its nature unchangeable, can admit of no alliance or compromise with error, which, pure in its nature as the light, rejects the darkness of falsehood, and says, Truth is everything or nothing; (2) the intolerance of the Church is that of God Himself. It is, in other words, the fidelity of the Church in preaching the divine law, and her constant refusal to betray her mission by having any alliance with falsehood.

37. At the same time it is important that this formula, 'Out of the Church there is no salvation,' should be taken in its true sense. It by no means signifies that *whoever is not a Catholic will be damned;* but it means that, as the Catholic religion is obligatory for all men, those who refuse to become acquainted with it, or to embrace it when they know it, become grievously cul-

pable before God, and incur the sentence of eternal damnation. In other words, no man can be saved if, by his own will, he remains *out of the Church*, or does not belong either to the body or *the soul of the Church*. By belonging to the *body* of the Church, we mean being a member of the Catholic Church. Those who belong only to the *soul* of the Church are those heretics who are in good faith observing the law of God as far as they know it. Even a pagan may belong to the Church; for as long as he keeps the natural law, the providence and grace of God will not be wanting to him; and by means of his faith in a God who has redeemed and will reward him, he will be led at least to the baptism of desire, which will assure his justification; and so he will, belonging to the soul of the Church, obtain everlasting salvation.

38. The intolerance of the Church being such as we have explained, we come to see the injustice of making it a subject of reproach. If those who accuse the Church were themselves logical, they would come to join her ranks by a process of simple reasoning which was employed, it is said, by Henry IV., king of France. This Calvinist prince, who wished to return to Catholicity, said to the ministers of his sect, ' According to you it is as easy to be saved by being in the Church as by being a Calvinist. According to the Church she alone can insure salvation. I must, then, choose that which is most certain, and join the Catholic Church.'

(2) *What is practical and civil tolerance or intolerance? and what is the practical intolerance of the Catholic Church?*

39. By *practical* tolerance or intolerance is generally meant external liberty or constraint in matters of religion. The State calls practical tolerance *civil* tolerance, and it may be defined thus: the enactment of laws which permit the free exercise of all religions, or even which afford the same protection to all

sects, whether true or false. Civil *intolerance* is a legal restriction upon the liberty of worship, either in favour of truth or error.

40. This intolerance admits of several degrees: (1) one religion alone may be favoured, the others simply tolerated; or (2) one alone may be allowed, the rest forbidden; or again, (3) one alone may be not only allowed, but enforced under rigorous penalties. When the obligation binds to a false religion, and proscription of the true religion is sanctioned by penalties, it is constraint, violence, and religious persecution.

41. What must be thought of civil tolerance from the point of view of right? *In principle* absolute civil tolerance is bad and unjust, and contrary to both natural and divine right. (1) Truth has a right to be protected against error, as much as virtue against vice and order against disorder. A legislator is, then, bound to protect the true religion, and to repress error, just as much as he is bound to protect order and repress disorder. This obligation springs from natural right quite independently of Christian revelation. But (2) as the Christian revelation is a notorious fact in the world and cannot be eliminated from it, it must be presupposed, and therefore the obligation of which we have just spoken is of divine right. God, who is the Sovereign Legislator, established the Christian law for the whole of humanity; not only each individual man, but nations and societies ought to be Christian; hence also legislation should be Christian, and should respect and protect the Church of Jesus Christ. Can we, then, establish in principle the *separation*, or, we may say, *the divorce, of the Church from the State*, or affirm that the State should be atheist and ignore God, and yet continue to exist, a stranger to all religion? This assertion, so justly condemned by the Church, is contrary alike to divine and natural right and to the persuasion of all mankind. Though the State possesses no

authority in religious matters, it is none the less obliged to further the interests of religion, as being a power charged to protect order and morality.

42. The condemnation of civil tolerance which we have just explained springs immediately from *Catholic truth*, and from the obligation imposed by the Creator on all His creatures to obey the law of Jesus Christ. But as it happens that all men do not obey the Gospel, and that side by side with Catholic truth there exist in the world divers false worships, the principle expressed above must in practice admit of modifications, and the following rules may be established:

(1) When a country is in possession of the truth— that is to say, when it is Catholic—the laws also must be Catholic, and tend to the defence of truth against error.

(2) In a country where there are many religions, but where the Catholic religion predominates, it must be the favoured one. False worships may be tolerated so long as they remain inoffensive.

(3) In a country where there are many religions, and where no one predominates, the law may extend equal protection to all religions, so long as they remain inoffensive.

(4) In a country where many religions exist, and where error predominates, the law cannot prohibit or restrict Catholic truth, even under the pretext that it is dangerous and hurtful to the State; for such could not be the case, seeing that it is divine, inoffensive, and beneficial by its very nature.

(5) In countries entirely infidel, heretical, or pagan, the civil authority has no right to hinder the introduction or propagation of the Catholic faith by means of persuasion. An infidel king, in common with every human being, is bound to acquaint himself, as far as he is able, with the truth, and to further its propagation. Should he act otherwise, believing perhaps that his false religion is the true one, and therefore interdicting the

preaching of the Gospel, he cannot be said to be doing well, but, on the contrary, he is fighting against truth, and doing evil without knowing it, being deceived by a false conscience.

(6) Persecution cannot be lawful in favour either of truth or error. I mean persecution properly so called, that is to say, violence employed against an unoffending religion or error. But if such religion or error becomes, on the contrary, turbulent and hurtful, its acts may be reproved like any other offence, in which case it suffers *punishment*, not persecution. In the same way, if a member of the Church becomes unfaithful, and falls into heresy, or commits some other great crime, such member can be punished by the ecclesiastical authority on whom he depends. The Church has a right not only to censure her subjects, but, if she thinks proper, she can also inflict external penalties, and have recourse to the secular power. In this case also it would be punishment and not persecution that the offender would undergo.*

43. Let us pass from the question of right to that of fact.

What has always been the legislation and the conduct of that Church which has been so much accused of intolerance ?

Faithful to the command of Jesus Christ, the Church has ever been content with *preaching the Gospel ;* that is to say, she has always acted by means of persuasion, without employing any violence. She has never persecuted; but in all times and in all ages, like her Divine Master, she has suffered persecution. With regard to her own rebellious or straying children, when she has judged it expedient to punish them, she has always done it with a maternal hand, in order to bring them back to a sense of duty and to remove scandal. On every page of impartial history this is shown. If, under certain

* Balmez, *Protestantism and Catholicism compared*, chaps. xxxiv. xxv.

circumstances and through an excess of zeal, Christian princes have used harsh and rigorous means to convert unbelievers or sectarians, they have, in doing so, followed their own personal impulses and not the rules of the Church, which cannot therefore be held responsible for their acts. The Inquisition, which was established by the Pope, does not, as we shall hereafter show, prove anything to the contrary.

44. Besides the distinction between *dogmatic* and *civil* intolerance, which we have just been explaining, there is another kind of intolerance, which means almost the same thing. There is intolerance of *doctrines* and *principles*, and intolerance of *persons*. The Church is always full of indulgence for persons. She is only intolerant of evil doctrines and erroneous principles, just as she is intolerant of vice, though full of mercy for the men who are its slaves. She follows the example of Almighty God, who hates sin, but receives sinners with bounty and compassion.

II. The Inquisition.

45. The Inquisition is said loudly to proclaim the intolerance of the Church; it is an historical monument of the violence and cruelty exercised by the Catholic clergy to coerce men's consciences.

The Inquisition has been much talked of; it has been laid to the Church's charge as something monstrous, for which she is accountable. But have these grave accusations any foundation? Is there any proof of the truth of these allegations? Are the facts of the case rightly appreciated or understood? Are not those abuses even which are condemned by the Church considered as the natural fruits of her principles and institutions? What is the truth in all this confusion? The truth is:

46. That what is called the Inquisition consisted of a court of justice, which was at the same time ecclesias-

tical and civil. It was established to take cognisance
of the crime of heresy, and to punish the guilty. The
tribunal of the Inquisition was called the 'Holy Office.'

About the year 1200 it was instituted by Pope
Innocent III. in order to repress the Albigenses
and the Vaudois. As these sects spread together
with their errors a spirit of rebellion against the two
authorities, instruction and persuasion were at first
tried, in order to reclaim them to a sense of duty; but
when these means were found to be ineffectual, the ecclesiastical and the civil powers, being equally menaced,
united against their common enemy; the former lent its
authority to discover crime, and the latter to punish it.
Hence the origin of the Inquisition.

The Roman and Ecclesiastical Inquisition must be
distinguished from what is properly so-called the Spanish
Inquisition.

47. (1) The *Ecclesiastical Inquisition*, regarded from
the point of view of right, was a wise and just institution,* in harmony with the principles by which society

---

* One of the principal obligations imposed upon Popes and
bishops is to combat heresy whenever it makes its appearance,
and this by virtue of the doctrinal and pastoral authority
which they hold from Christ. They are obliged, in the accomplishment of this duty, on the one hand, to discover error, and,
on the other, to prevent its propagation, either by means of
persuasion and gentleness or by means of chastisement. Such
is the end of the Ecclesiastical Inquisition. It is true that, according to the decision of Innocent IV. in 1252, torture might
be employed in the tribunals of the Inquisition, in the same
way as it was generally applied in all the secular tribunals of
the age, but it is also true that the most minute arrangements
were made by the Popes to avoid any possible abuse of power.
Cf. Eymerici, *Directorium Inquisitorum*, Commentar. F. Pegna,
Rom. 1578.

The Inquisition is in its nature good, mild, and preservative;
this is the universal and indelible character of every ecclesiastical institution. This may be seen in Rome and wherever
the Church rules. But if the civil power thinks proper, in
adopting the Inquisition for its own security, to render it more

was then governed; and from the point of view of facts, it was a tribunal of reconciliation rather than of severity. No tribunal ever acted with more gentleness. We have a proof of this in the celebrated trial of the Knights Templars, who requested as a favour to be tried by the Inquisition rather than by any other tribunal.

48. (2) *The Spanish Inquisition.*—The Inquisition established in Spain in the twelfth century was adopted as a state institution by Ferdinand and Isabella in 1481. From that time it was more a royal than an ecclesiastical tribunal, all the members of which, whether priests or laymen, were nominated by the sovereign and withdrawn from the authority of the Church. In the hands of the kings of Spain it was an instrument employed for the triumph of the Christian faith, and at the same time of the Spanish nation, over the conspiracies of the Jews and Moors. The Spanish Inquisition is not, therefore, the work of the Church. The Popes have even disavowed it, by protesting against the usurpation of their rights, and against the severity of some of the inquisitors. We conclude, therefore, that if in Spain abuses had crept in, that is no reason for criminating the Church.

49. Neither is it a reason why the institution in itself should be absolutely condemned. *Thanks to this tribunal, Spain has escaped the horrors of religious warfare, which have deluged Europe with blood, and she has greatly contributed towards saving the interests of Catholicism elsewhere.*

Moreover, these abuses are represented as having been far greater than they were in reality. The Spanish Inquisition did not tear men away from the faith of

---

severe, the Church is not accountable. See Maistre, *Lettres à un Gentilhomme Russe sur l'Inquisition Espagnole*, first letter.

* See Balmes in his above-mentioned work, chaps. xxxvi. and xxxvii.

their fathers like the *English Inquisition* and that which was practised by heretics in other parts; nor did it tyrannise over unbaptised heretics. It exercised its authority over apostates and renegades from the faith, particularly over the Jews and Moors, who, though to all appearances converted, were plotting in secret against the Church and the State. The jurisdiction of the 'Holy Office' was limited to the declaration of the guilt or innocence of the accused, and the penalties which were imposed by another tribunal were according to the criminal code of the country. The number, as well as the rigour, of the chastisements of these so-called 'victims of the Inquisition' has been very greatly exaggerated. The prisons of the Inquisition were more salubrious than any others, and the *auto-da-fé** frequently gave rise to edifying scenes of retractation and of repentance.†

Nothing of what occurred in Spain could compare with the massacres and persecutions of the Catholics by the Protestants of France, Germany, Holland, and, above all, of England. The executions under Henry VIII. may be counted by hundreds, and those under Elizabeth can hardly be numbered. '*This sanguinary queen*,' says Cobbett,‡ 'put to death more persons in one year than the Inquisition did during the whole of its duration.'

III. The Massacre of St. Bartholomew.

50. By this name is signified the massacre of the Huguenots which took place in France on the night preceding the feast of St. Bartholomew, 1572, by the

---

* This word signifies 'act of faith.' The name was given to the public ceremony during which the sentences were pronounced and the penalties endured which were imposed by the Inquisition.

† See Héfelé, *Le Cardinal Ximenès*, trad. Tournai, 1856, chap. xviii.

‡ *Letters on the English Reformation.*

order of Charles IX., under the influence of the advice of his mother, Catherine of Medicis.

51. It is an avowed and now indisputable fact that the Massacre of St. Bartholomew was eminently a political *coup d'état* by which Catherine of Medicis hoped to annihilate the Calvinists, of whom Admiral de Coligny was the soul and the chief.*

It is true that Pope Gregory XIII., misinformed by a first report, and believing that the King of France had just escaped from a conspiracy of the Huguenots, ordered

---

* Shortly before the Massacre of St. Bartholomew Admiral de Coligny, who had narrowly escaped assassination, judged, not without reason, that the blow had been directed by the hand of Catherine. The queen-mother was fully aware of his opinion, and, fearing the consequences of a frustrated crime, and being resolved to avert them, she quickly came to a determination. Being assured of the aid and concurrence of her son, Henry of Anjou, and that of the Dukes of Nevers and of Retz, of Marshal de Tavannes, the Count d'Angoulême, and the Chancellor de Birague, she spoke to the king of a formidable conspiracy of the Huguenots which was ready to break out, and which ought to be prevented by turning against Coligny and his friends the blow which they destined for the king and his most devoted subjects. Cf. Lingard, *History of England*, vol. viii.

Considering this sad event in a broader light, many causes can be discovered. We may trace it to the rebellious teachings in France of the disciples of Luther and Calvin, to the thrice-renewed civil war, and to the incessant plottings of the Reformers. Again, we may ascribe it to the ambition and dark policy of a woman who was as bad a Catholic as she was a cruel queen—Catherine de' Medicis.

Charles IX., justly weary of Coligny's insatiable ambition, of his revolutionary attempts, and the menaces of his partisans, believed, in his weakness, that in complying with the request of his mother he was but administering justice, though under an extraordinary form, which, however, was in his eyes sufficiently justified by the desperate condition to which he was reduced. Gautrelet, *Divinité de l'Eglise Cath. dé"on.* letter 35. Audin, *Hist. de la St. Barthélémy*. Georges Gandi, 'La St. Barthélémy, ses Origines, son vrai Caractère,' &c., in the *Revue des Questions Historiques*, 1866.

a public thanksgiving; but he soon became acquainted with the real nature of the case, and loudly condemned the barbarous action, inspired as it was by an inhuman policy, in which neither he nor the clergy had any part.

The *Te Deum* ordered at first by the Pope was as natural as the letters written by all the European sovereigns to congratulate Louis Philippe on his escape from the murderous attempts of Fieschi and Aliband. Why, then, should it be considered a crime in the Church? And, moreover, we ask once more why the Massacre of St. Bartholomew, the number of whose victims has been so much exaggerated, should be perpetually brought forward, when a veil is thrown over the victims, a thousand times more numerous, of Protestant intolerance in England and elsewhere?

IV. **The Antagonism between the Church and Science.**

52. The Church is said to be an enemy to science. She is founded on faith; she imposes on human intelligence the yoke of faith. Now blind and servile faith is as much opposed to science as darkness is opposed to light.

53. (1) The Church is an enemy only of ignorance and of error. She has always been the promoter of the sciences and arts. All history will attest it. The preservation of letters and arts in the Middle Ages is due to the Church; likewise the founding of universities and other schools throughout Europe, and the impulse given to architecture and to all the liberal arts. Facts so notorious as these ought to silence all accusations.

(2) The Christian's faith is not a *blind* faith. We know that we cannot err in believing; for reason itself commands us to believe God when He speaks.*

The opposition of faith to science is, in fact, a chimera, which disappears when things are seen as they really are.

---

* See further on, part ii. chap. xvi. art. ii. On Faith.

54. What is faith and what is science? Faith, or rather the dogmas of faith are truths revealed by God. Science, or the true teachings of science are truths taught by reason. Truth exists in both, therefore there cannot be opposition, since one truth cannot be opposed to another. These two orders of truth emanate from the same source, which is God. God sees alike scientific and dogmatic truths, and also the relations which bind them together. He teaches us the one by the light of reason, and the other by the light of revelation, that is to say, by His word. No real opposition is therefore possible, even though we may not understand how they can be reconciled.

55. There is, however, a difference to be considered. Faith, or the word of God, cannot be subject to error, whereas reason may be, and indeed is often deceived. This is why, in case of apparent opposition, preference must always be given to faith. Faith is an infallible rule, which prevents reason and science from being misled. Faith is therefore in no way opposed to science, but, on the contrary, she is its safeguard and promoter, because she allows it to cultivate all that belongs to its domain, whilst she still maintains it in the true way and in true progress. In order to be freed from this beneficent guardianship, science has spread and continues to spread monstrous and fatal errors.* This brings us to the subject of Galileo's condemnation.

V. Galileo.

56. It is stated that the astronomer Galileo was persecuted and imprisoned by the Inquisition for having taught, after Copernicus, that the earth moves round the sun; and this is alleged to be a proof of the Church's ignorance, intolerance, and fallibility, and of her opposition to the progress of science.

57. This objection contains a little truth mixed up

* See further on, part ii. chap. xvi. art. ii. On Faith.

with a great deal of falsehood and calumny. Facts have here been strangely misrepresented. We will proceed to show them in their true light.

Galileo, a learned astronomer and distinguished philosopher of Florence, adopted and tried to prove the opinion of Copernicus concerning the rotation of the earth. This was in the beginning of the seventeenth century. His ideas clashed with the peripatetic notions that prevailed at that period,* and troubled the minds of those who were little capable of understanding him. By order of Pope Paul V., his doctrines were examined in Rome in 1616, and were condemned, first by a censure of the Holy Office, and then by a decree of the Congregation of the Index.

The two propositions censured by the theologians of the Holy Office—the first as heretical, the second as erroneous—were, (1) the sun occupies the centre of the universe and has no local movement; (2) the earth is not in the centre of the universe and is not immovable, but turns upon its own axis by a diurnal motion.

Having promised in Rome that he would no longer defend or teach his opinions, Galileo returned peacefully to Florence, and resumed the course of his scientific labours. In 1632 he published his dialogues on the systems of Ptolemy and Copernicus, in which he maintained the proscribed opinions of 1616, and thus drew down upon himself a fresh condemnation by the Holy Office, with the penalty of imprisonment (June 22, 1636). This penalty immediately afterwards was commuted to that of seclusion in the Gardens of Trinità del Monte. Galileo retained his servant, and had full liberty to receive visits, and he very soon obtained leave to return to his country house at Arcetri, a mile from Florence,

* Certain learned men, amongst whom were Tycho Brahé, Lord Bacon, and Descartes, defended the old system of Ptolemy against the new theory, which was itself in an imperfect state.

and he peacefully expired there on the 8th of January 1648.*

Two questions here arise:

58. (1) What is to be said of the persecutions of which Galileo was the victim, of the chains, the dungeon, and the torture which he had to undergo at the hands of the Inquisition? The facts just stated show that all these horrors are but fables and calumny. The truth, which is found in the complete publication of Galileo's interrogations, shows us that his persecution amounted to a menace, and that this menace even was only a formality.

59. (2) Are not the decisions arrived at in Rome in 1616 and 1636 against the earth's motion erroneous? And being so, are they not a serious objection against the doctrinal infallibility of the Church and of the sovereign Pontiff? We admit that the principle of these decisions is erroneous, for the astronomical system condemned by them is now considered to be proved. But as regards the question of doctrinal infallibility, it is quite irrelevant; for the infallibility in doctrine supposes a definition of an œcumenical council, or of the Pope speaking *ex cathedrâ*.† In the case of Galileo such definition never took place; his was simply a sentence passed by some theologians, who, not being representatives of the Church's teaching, were liable to err. It is true that the Pope gave authority to these men to examine the obnoxious doctrine; but it is also quite proved that neither Paul V. nor Urban VIII., whatever may have been their personal convictions, ever uttered or ratified a solemn or public condemnation of the great astronomer's opinions. And the protective providence of God over His Church is manifested in the fact that,

* See Gilbert, *Le Procès de Galilée* (Louvain, Preters, 1869).

† See further on, part ii. chap. i. art. iii. Doctrinal Infallibility.

at a time when the majority of theologians firmly believed the doctrine of Copernicus to be contrary to the Scriptures, the Church never solemnly refuted it. There was only then a sentence* pronounced by fallible theologians; so that the infallibility of the Church and that of the Pope do not enter into the question.

60. It does not follow from this that the Roman Congregations possess no authority, and that their decrees may be disregarded. A congregation instituted to examine questions of doctrine, and to watch over the integrity of the faith, has a legitimate power to interdict certain teachings which, though not false, are rendered dangerous and suspicious by the force of circumstances.

Such a prohibition is a measure dictated by prudence, binding, it is true, in conscience, but in its nature essentially provisionary, and its effects are, not to impede the progress of science, but to insure greater circumspection on the part of the learned, and to guard against possible errors by enforcing a more profound scrutiny of their systems. With regard to the definitive decrees in matters of doctrine, which are called *definitions*, they do not emanate from congregations; they fall under the inalienable prerogative of the Pope and of a Council.

* The system which Galileo patronised was believed to be contrary to the Scriptures, and as, even from a scientific point of view, the question was an undecided one, and gave rise to an animated controversy, this sentence, which was at the same time an interdiction, was meant to prevent natural science from assuming an attitude hostile to the revealed faith, and to preserve this faith from the fluctuations proceeding from individual opinions, so long as the scientific controversy remained in a state of indecision. It was also calculated to be a guarantee for the personal fidelity of Galileo towards the Church, that fidelity owed to her by every Christian, and in which Galileo never failed.

VI. The bad Popes.

61. Again, it is alleged that the Church is not so holy nor so worthy of respect as is supposed. She has fallen into many disorders, and the Holy See itself has been dishonoured by bad Popes.

62. (1) The Church has within her pale both the just and sinners; she labours incessantly for their sanctification, but she only partially succeeds, and all do not respond to her efforts. Though great virtues exist amongst the faithful, disorders and vice exist also; but is the Church responsible for this? Is not the blame entirely due to the weakness and malice of the human heart? Compared with the abominations of paganism, these blots on Christian civilisation are as nothing.

(2) As to the Popes, though they are the Vicars of Jesus Christ, they are not impeccable, for they do not cease to be men; and if they fall, even as did St. Peter himself, their sins are the actions of the men and not of the Pontiffs; nor do these entirely personal* failings in the least impair the sanctity or the authority of the Holy See, which always remains equally worthy of respect and obedience.

63. As a matter of fact, we may ask if there have really been so many bad Popes. Impartial history presents the following account: From the time of Peter down to Pius IX. there have been 258 Pontiffs. This number comprises sixty saints, mostly martyrs, and a multitude of great men, who shone amongst their con-

---

* The distinction must be observed which exists between the authority itself and the person who holds it, between the pontifical authority and the Pontiff himself ; one is susceptible of corruption, but the other is not. Just as the authority of parents and monarchs is ever worthy of respect, though there have been numbers of bad parents and bad kings, so the divinely instituted power of the Popes has not become less holy because it has sometimes passed into the hands of unworthy representatives.

temporaries as did Pius IX. in our own time. Nearly all of them have been men eminent alike for their virtue, their science, and their wisdom. There have, however, been exceptions—such as Stephen VI. and John XII. in the tenth century, Benedict IX. in the eleventh, and Alexander VI. at the end of the fifteenth century. However much we may deplore certain facts affirmed by impartial history, we cannot deny them; but, on the other hand, neither can it be denied that the number of the Popes, who, with more or less reason, have been accused of scandalising the Church by their morals, is comparatively very small indeed, and they almost disappear in the long succession of Pontiffs whose eminent virtues are calculated to eclipse the failings and weaknesses of the less saintly few.

64. We may moreover remark (1) that many of the faults alleged against the Popes have been invented by malice, or else exaggerated and represented in a false light.

(2) That the accused Popes belonged chiefly to an age when the secular power interfered with the Papal election.

(3) That no one of them has decreed anything against the moral or dogmatic purity of the Church's doctrines, or taught or instituted anything with the view of legitimatising his disorders, as the promoters of Protestantism did, for instance, in abolishing monastic vows and the celibacy of the clergy.

In conclusion, we may remark that a succession of 258 princes who, but with few exceptions, have rivalled one another in greatness and virtue, calls forth our admiration as well as our respect. Is not this a phenomenon without parallel in history? Where shall we find another dynasty that can compare with the spiritual dynasty of the Roman Pontiffs?

VII. The Crusades.

65. The enemies of the Church have, with much bitterness, condemned the Crusades, and have sought to impute to the Catholic religion all the real or imaginary evils of which they were the cause. They say that these wars, the offspring of a mistaken religious zeal, resulted, after the loss of two millions of European soldiers, only in ruining the nobility and in transporting enormous sums of money into Asia. It remains to be seen if these statements are true, and if the true character of the Crusades is such as has been described.

66. The Crusades, when rightly estimated, appear to have been just and lawful enterprises, since they were organised in order to protect the Christians of the East from the cruel oppression of the Mahometans, and to defend Europe against the fury of the barbarians, who were threatening a universal invasion.

These gigantic expeditions should be judged of in their entirety, without considering faults and abuses, which accompany all wars. The ill-success of most of the expeditions is to be attributed to the perfidy of the Greeks, and to the disorders which had too commonly crept in amongst the Crusaders. If these wars failed in their original design of delivering the East from the grasp of infidelity, they were, on the other hand, productive of most advantageous results in the West. They preserved Christianity and civilisation from Mussulman invasion; they delivered the people of Europe from evils which they had caused themselves; they put an end to the wars between Christian kings, and they extinguished that civil discord which for two centuries had kept the feudal lords in arms against each other. Moreover, they improved the condition of the people, who became free by taking part in these glorious expeditions; and, in augmenting the influence of the Popes, who were the natural protectors of nations, they provided social order with an efficacious safeguard. It is also incontestible that they reawakened a taste for commerce, science, literature, and the arts,* and that they prepared the way for the outbursts of genius which took place during the reigns of Leo X. and Louis XIV. of France. We may add, that the Crusades were supported by the greatest and most saintly men of their time; that they were solemnly authorised by the Church, protected by the divine assistance, which could not but aid her in such a grave matter, and that they were sanctioned more than once by miracles accompanying their publication.†

VIII. The Schism of the West.

67. In the fourteenth and fifteenth centuries, the period during which the great schism of the West lasted, the Church presented a spectacle of scandalous division. The clergy became demoralised, having lost even the semblance of religion or morality; religious feeling was extinguished in the hearts of the people, and well-meaning souls were thrown into extreme perplexity of conscience. What can be urged in opposition to these views about the schism of the West which are entertained by the Church's enemies?

68. That this schism was an immense misfortune and a hard trial, during which the bark of Peter had more than ever to rely on the divine protection to avoid shipwreck, is true; but looking at it in its true light, this schism, or rather this discord, concerning the legitimate Pope becomes rather a calamity endured by the Church than a scandal of which she was the cause.

69. History tells us that, during a space of more than forty years from the year 1378, there were in the

---

* Notably architecture. The greater number of our edifices in the Gothic style date from the twelfth century, the last epoch of the Crusades.

† See Michaud, *Hist. des Croisades;* Goschler, *Dict. Encyclop. Théol.* art. ' Croisades.'

Church two Sovereign Pontiffs, Urban VI. on one side and Clement VII. on the other, with their respective successors. Pope Clement V., at the beginning of the fourteenth century, transferred the Pontifical See from Rome to Avignon. Soon two parties were formed, the one advocating the Pope's return to Rome, the other his establishment in France; and this gave rise to the election of Clement VII., five months after that of Urban VI., which was declared to have been null. There were then two Popes, both of whom, having been elected by the same cardinals, might seem to be legitimate, and hence there arose a schism amongst Christian nations, some of whom followed Urban, and others Clement; a schism which, though much to be deplored, did not in any way affect the faith. The division of opinion touched the rights of the different Popes, but not the dogma of the primacy of St. Peter and the unity of the Apostolic See. All believed in one visible head of the Church, but under existing circumstances they did not know which was the true Pope. It was quite possible for those on either side to be in good faith and safety of conscience, though they might in ignorance be adherents of the falsely-elected Pope.

70. It must be admitted that this schism was productive of much scandal and many abuses; religion grew weak in many hearts under its baleful influence, but the evil was not so widespread or so excessive as the Church's adversaries declare. At this very period there flourished amongst Christian nations and under the different Popes, many persons who were distinguished alike for their great learning and eminent sanctity.

Though the occupants of the papal throne were blameworthy for their reluctance to sacrifice their own ambition and the interests of their persoual followers to the greater good of the Church, they cannot be said to have been devoid of religion and morals; and history attests that the clergy were not in a state of ignorance and incurable corruption, since their clamour and complaints against the evil are adduced as proofs of its magnitude, nor did God abandon His Church in this extremity of peril. The peace and order of Christendom were soon restored by the universal recognition of Martin V., who was elected Pope at the General Council of Constance in 1417.

IX. The Temporal Power of the Popes, and their Interference with Civil Governments.

71. The Popes are invested with a power which is entirely spiritual; their kingdom is not of this world, according to the words of Christ Himself, yet they are accused of seeking temporal sovereignty and of arrogating to themselves the right of judgment in the civil affairs of princes. They have even gone so far as to depose emperors and free their subjects from their oath of allegiance.

These objections will soon be answered when the confusion of ideas has been cleared away, and the facts have been shown in their true light.

72. (1) *The Temporal Sovereignty of the Popes.*— The papal authority, it is urged, is entirely spiritual. Without doubt it is spiritual and divine; but, though spiritual, it does not exclude temporal means. The ecclesiastical, like the civil, power, being intended for the government of men, must possess also an analogous exterior organisation and means of action. The words of Jesus Christ, 'My kingdom is not of this world,' were a reply to Pilate, who asked our Lord if He was, as the Jews said, a king; and He answered that He was truly a king, but that His title need not alarm the Roman Government, because His kingdom was not like that of the princes of this world. He meant that He had not come to reëstablish amongst the Jews the ancient throne of David, nor to form a kingdom prejudicial to the Romans, who were then the actual masters

of Judea; but that the kingdom He had come to establish was His Church, which He called the Kingdom of Heaven; a real kingdom, though unlike those purely terrestrial, as its tendency, its principal means, and its final term were purely celestial.

Such is the ordinary interpretation of these words. They do not imply, as our adversaries would have it, that the Church is an *entirely spiritual* kingdom, and that she is forbidden to hold temporal possessions; but that the princes of this world have nothing to fear from the Church, whose aim is heaven, and not earthly conquests, though the *use of earthly means* is not denied her. Moreover our Lord does not, as the learned Tolet remarks, say that His kingdom is not *in this world*, but that it is not *of this world*, because it in fact *does exist in this world* amongst mankind, and this necessitates the employment of such earthly means as circumstances may require. The temporal dominion of the Pope is one of these means; and according to the best authenticated interpreters, such as St. Chrysostom (*Panegyric of St. Babylas*) and St. Augustine (*Tract* 15, *in Joan.*), our Saviour, far from declaring that temporal power was not His, only speaks here of the *origin* of His regal power, which He declares He holds, not from this world, but from His Father who is in heaven. The Pope may therefore be at once Head of the Church and sovereign of a temporal state, such as He has been ever since the eighth century, owing to the donations of Pepin, Charlemagne, Lothair, and, later on, the Countess Matilda. This temporal sovereignty does not emanate from the spiritual sovereignty, to which it is not *absolutely necessary*, seeing that during the first ages of the Church it did not exist; but from the eighth century it was the means chosen by Divine Providence to maintain the spiritual authority of the chief of Catholicity in liberty and independence. And in our days, as well as at any previous time, the integrity of the States of the

Church, and the temporal independence of the Popes, is a *morally necessary* condition of the free exercise of their spiritual authority.*

73. (2) *Intervention of the Popes in civil government.* —In order to judge rightly of the intervention of the Popes in the temporal matters of the princes of the Middle Ages, the times and existing constitutions should be taken into consideration; and it will then be seen that the Popes were men of the times, and that they acted as the leaders of society at that epoch were required to act.

European society was entirely Catholic. People and kings recognised the Pope as their spiritual chief, they venerated him as their father, and had recourse to him as the natural arbitrator in all their disputes. This sort of arbitration, becoming more and more frequent, gradually passed into international law, and by the acquiescence of the princes it created in favour of the Popes a supreme suzerainty in the feudal system. Add to this, that the canons of the Councils, according to whose decision the Pope pronounced his sentences, had full authority in the civil legislation. The Pope, on his side, regarded all the faithful as his well-beloved children. Kings, far from being excepted, were the dearest objects of his solicitude, because the welfare of the people depended on them; he instructed them and exhorted them with charity. But if it happened that some prince, deaf to his warnings, continued to oppress the people or trouble the Church by his scandals and crimes, then the Pope threatened with firmness, and often punished him with excommunication.† The authority of the Popes

---

* Address of the bishops to Pius IX. on the day of Pentecost, 1862.

† The Emperors of Germany were those who chiefly called forth these severe measures. They were in constant and serious dispute with the Popes, generally occasioned by the shameful traffic they carried on in regard of ecclesiastical dignities. The

was thus a restraint, which kept the sovereigns in the path of duty, and also a protection to the life and liberties of their subjects. The Popes of the Middle Ages were like what the Popes of all periods had been, and what they still are, the defenders of true liberty against despotism, the protectors of true authority against license, and the advocates of peace in all wars and discord. Did not Pius IX., animated by the same spirit, write a mediatory letter to King William and to Napoleon III. in 1870? And if it had been well received would the murderous wars, which we have since witnessed, ever have taken place?

In dealing with the Emperors of Germany, the Popes have been more authoritative than with other sovereigns, but it was because these princes were exceptionally situated. In resuscitating the Empire of the East the Papacy had established a Christian Empire, subject, in temporal matters, to an elective chief. The election was accompanied by a solemn promise to observe the rules of a certain constitution, the neglect of which should deprive the elected of his rights. The Pope of necessity became his judge in this, and he alone could decide as to his shortcomings; and thus it happened that in passing judgment upon such a chief the Pope released his subjects from their oath of allegiance. The deposition which followed was a legitimate consequence of the Germanic constitution.* Hence the political pro-

---

Roman Pontiffs had allowed them, in acknowledgment of the services they had rendered the Church, the privilege of appointing subjects to the bishoprics; but the emperors turned this privilege to the benefit of their own avarice and ambition, to the great prejudice of ecclesiastical discipline. St. Gregory VII. and his successors, who were zealous defenders of the rights of the Church, vigorously opposed these abuses. See Muzzarelli. *Opusc. Greg. VII.;* Voight, *Hist. de Grég. VII. et son Siècle.*

* See Broeckaert, *Le Fait Divin*, part ii. chap. xiv. ' Rapport des Deux Puissances.' Item, De Maistre, *Du Pape;* Hurter, *Hist. du Pape Innocent III. et de ses Contemporains.*

ceedings of the Papacy in the Middle Ages were founded on law, and were entirely in the interests of the princes and their subjects.

X. Reaction against the Progress of Civilisation.

74. The Church is said to be the enemy of progress and civilisation.

The Church is the enemy only of vice and barbarism, disguised under the semblance of civilisation and progress. She has ever favoured true progress and genuine civilisation; and, enlightened by truth, she distinguishes the one from the other, the true from the false, real progress from that which possesses but the name and the appearance. That which is generally termed progress, the movement towards social perfection and mere material well-being, which flatters avarice and the passions at the expense of morals and the soul's salvation, is, in the eyes of the Church, nothing better than a false and lying progress.

What, then, are we to understand by real progress and civilisation? and what influence does the Church exercise in their regard?

75. (1) Social *progress*, the reverse of social decadence, signifies much the same thing as civilisation and the progress of civilisation. Civilisation is the more or less advanced perfection of social life amongst men, as much with regard to morality and intelligence as to material well-being.

We see, hence, that civilisation has a twofold element, the *moral* and the *material* element, and from this the distinction arises between moral and material civilisation. The first consists in sound morality, the arts, and sciences; and the second comprises riches, mechanical arts, and industry.

Perfect civilisation comprises both the elements, in the same way as human nature consists of two parts, namely, body and soul; and in the same manner as the body is subject to the higher and more noble part of man, which is his soul, so in civilisation the material element is subordinate to the moral element, which is the soul of human society. Where this subordination exists it assures the true happiness of the people for time and for eternity; that is to say, as much happiness as is possible in this world, and perfect happiness in the next.

Where the material element preponderates, it engenders luxury and sensuality, and the spirit of disorder and revolt. The predominance of materialism in our own days is extremely detrimental to morality, and consequently also to the true happiness of the people.

76. (2) The Church desires complete civilisation, embracing both elements. She watches over the preservation, and labours for the progress, of each; but always with wisdom and discretion. Her first care is bestowed on that which is the more precious—sound morals, justice, and right. She wishes the people to enjoy prosperity and abundance, but still more she desires for them justice and virtue. She knows that society will always be sufficiently rich and prosperous if it be only sufficiently moral.

She places in the first rank the maintenance of holy religion, which is the only guardian of true morality; for there cannot be morality without religion, any more than there can be public order without government.

What is the result, we may ask, when this rule of the Church is ignored, when the moral and religious element is eliminated, and a wholly material civilisation is alone preserved? People then possess mechanical arts and riches without the principles of morality and of right by which to turn them to good account. They do not act from a noble motive of duty, but from interest and the desire of pleasure. *Duty* speaks no longer its sublime language to their hearts, for they only understand pleasure, and seek only animal gratifications, for they have become plunged in sensuality. Then when the thirst for enjoyment has become insatiable, will it not be procured at any price?—even at the price of injustice, wars, and revolutions? Are not the recent disasters in France a striking example of this? All the material progress and the advanced state of art helped only to multiply massacres and ravages, for they were pressed into the service of force, which reigns supreme whenever justice and right are no longer heeded.

Such a state of things may be called a *barbarian civilisation*—a state of society in which all the resources of improvement and progress are usurped by the passions of men.

The conclusion to be drawn from all this is plainly that this false civilisation tends to the misery and ruin of society; whereas civilisation, such as the Church understands it, constitutes the happiness of the people, for it alone is true civilisation, true progress.

XI. The Encyclical Letter and the Syllabus, or the Condemnation of Liberalism and modern Liberty.

77. The Church, we are told, is behind the times; she is in opposition to contemporary society; she has declared herself to be the enemy of liberalism and modern liberty. Witness the Encyclical Letter of Gregory XVI.,* and the Syllabus of Pius IX.†

78. We will first speak of what is called liberalism, and next of modern liberty.

(1) The Church is accused of being opposed to liberalism. The Church is the enemy of all that is erroneous, vicious, or fatal to the interests of man. If this be the character of that which the Church condemns‡ as liber-

---

* This is the Encyclical called *Mirari nos*, of the 15th Aug. 1832.

† This is the Syllabus, or eighty condemned propositions annexed to the Encyclical, *Quanta cura*, of Dec. 8, 1864.

‡ The two last propositions condemned by the Syllabus are as follows : ' LXXIX. It is false that the civil liberty of all forms of worship, and that the full power of all openly and

alism, can the Church be blamed for rejecting it, and for being its irreconcilable enemy?

79. We say particularly '*that liberalism which the Church condemns*,' because the abstract term of *liberalism* is too often understood as embracing notions which are entirely heterogeneous. *Liberalism*, as opposed to *Conservatism*, may mean, as in England, that political party and those systems of political economy which are in favour of commerce, industry, and civil liberty. By *liberalism*, again, in contradistinction to *absolutism* is meant that form of government in which the power of the sovereign is limited by a constitution. It is a name specially given to political constitutions which, failing to realise the ideal of Catholic theories, do not prescribe all the good which a perfect political system proposes, nor prohibit all the evil which the positive divine law condemns. This does not prevent such constitutions from being relatively good, and the heads of the Church have often declared that they had no intention of condemning these constitutions, which, though intrinsically imperfect, were legally established.

It would be impossible for us to enumerate all that which, rightly or wrongly, is called *liberalism*. It is only important to know what that liberalism is which is condemned by the Church.

80. Such liberalism is a political system, a social doctrine, or it may be called a moral doctrine applied to the government of states of which the following is the principle or summary formula: *Rationalism*, or, rather, *atheism of the State, consisting in the exclusion from the civil government of all religious influence; above all, that*

---

publicly to manifest all their thoughts and all their opinions, tends to plunge the people more easily into corruption of mind and of morals, and to the propagation of the pestilence of *indifferentism*. LXXX. The Roman Pontiff can and ought to be on good terms, and to coöperate with, progress, liberalism, and modern civilisation.'

H

of the true religion of the Church of Jesus Christ. Or, in other words, *the separation of the State from the Church; absolute independence of the State with regard to the Church,* which means the oppression of the Church by the State. According to this liberalism, the State should act as though the Church did not exist, and, as a consequence, should usurp its rights; just as one proprietor, ignoring the rights of his neighbour, as though they existed not, would, in consequence, be incessantly guilty of injustice in his regard.

The liberal principle may also be described thus : *In all which appertains to civil legislation and administration, man must not take either the Church or Jesus Christ into account.*

These various formulæ contain the avowed principles of the organs of liberalism, or, at the least, are an epitome of their habitual language, which but too closely corresponds with their actions. The *Indépendance Belge* has more than once declared that *liberalism is either war with the Church* or it is nothing. The *Discussion* has said that it *would wage incessant war with the Church,* and that it would *always uphold all her enemies.* This *war with the Church* is not confined to the domain of politics, for this would be neither logical nor possible—it extends to all that touches the Church and Christian revelation. So that liberalism soon touches upon *rationalism and free-thinking.* Hence we have another formula admitted by the liberal press, ' Liberalism is free thought or it is nothing ;' and the declaration of the *Revue de la Belgique,* which is the natural consequence of the said formula, that ' Nothing can be at the same time liberal in politics and Catholic in religion.'

81. (1) The justice of the Church's condemnation of such liberalism as this is not hard to admit; for it is unnecessary to remark that it is *false, impious,* and *disastrous to society.*

(1) It *is false,* being contrary to reason and to the

positive words of Jesus Christ, the Supreme Legislator Reason tells us that human society must be religious and consequently that princes and governments ought to protect the interests of religion. Jesus Christ, in imposing the obligation of baptism on all humanity,* evidently wished that all society should be *Christian ;* and therefore kings and princes should protect the interests of the Christian religion and of the true Church of Jesus Christ.†

Now the spirit of liberalism contradicts this dictate of reason and this word of Christ; therefore liberalism must be *false* in its principle.

(2) Moreover, this principle is *impious*, tending as it does to destroy religion, together with religious feeling in the hearts of the people; it establishes, as a natural right, and as a good thing to be desired, the promiscuousness of worship and the monstrous indifference regarding doctrine, the impiety of which we have already seen.‡

(3) This principle is *disastrous* to society, because a society without religion is a society without morals—without the principles of justice, of order, and of right, It is a prey to the caprices of the strong, to evil passions, revolutions, and all disorders.

We see, then, that the liberalism we have described is as destructive to society as it is impious in itself; and hence it follows that, in combating this great evil, the Church shows herself to be the true protectress of society and of the rights of the people.

82. (2) Before entering upon the subject of modern liberties, which have reference to the liberal principle, we must call to mind what has already been said regarding *civil tolerance.* These liberties, forming part of the

---

* 'Preach the Gospel to every creature. He that believeth and is baptised shall be saved ; but he that believeth not shall be condemned' (Mark xvi. 16).

† See what has already been said on Intolerance.

‡ Page 69, art. v. no. 84.

legal code, as in Belgium, constitute the said tolerance; and it can readily be understood how such a legislation may be permissible on account of exigencies arising out of political circumstances.*

But looking at it from a purely theoretical point of view, the question arises, *What are these so-called modern liberties as to principle and right ?*

83. We boldly affirm that these much-vaunted liberties, as understood by the liberal rationalists, are nothing else than a fearful *license* and impunity granted to *all errors*, and thereby to *all vice*. If liberty there be in this, is it not that of disorder and social corruption?

In fact, these *modern* liberties in reality constitute a law of which the following is the epitome: 'All doctrines, of whatever kind, be they subversive of all morality, order, and religion, are free so long as public tranquillity remains undisturbed. They may be propagated by the press, by teaching, by the theatre, by false religion, by secret and notoriously pernicious societies. The seeds of every disorder may be sown in the minds of the people so long as public order is outwardly respected.'

What can be said of such a law, if not that it is contrary to all reason and to all right, natural and divine, and to the most elementary principles of public order?

84. It is said, in justification of these licentious liberties, that law and government ought to be restricted to the preservation of order and the protection of the property of the subject.

In reply we assert that government is truly limited to the maintenance of order; the civil authority having been instituted by God for the safeguard and defence of *perfect and complete* order in human society.† Now

---

* See in the *Précis Historiques* (March 1, 1869) an article entitled ' Les Principes Catholiques et la Constitution Belge.'

† There is no power but from God; and those that are are

order comprises, not only the right of proprietorship, of tranquillity, and personal inviolability, but also *the right to possess truth and virtue*. If the State is bound to defend the property of the citizen from robbery, and his life from aggressors from within and without, it is equally bound, *according to the measure of a moral possibility*, to protect that which is infinitely more precious, his intellectual and moral welfare, from error and corruption; that is to say, the State must protect the true principles of order and true religious and moral doctrines, and it must defend them from the public scandals of the press, of false teaching, of the theatre, and of all pernicious societies.

Such is natural right when confirmed by the divine; but so-called modern liberties, and that liberalism which patronises them, are in opposition to the natural and divine rights, and to the true principles of public order.

Experience but too unmistakably confirms this conclusion. Such liberties have reigned in France since the end of the last century; every error and impiety and corruption, freely propagated by teaching, by the press, the theatre, and the masonic lodges, have ruined the mind and heart of this noble nation, whilst leaving it an external semblance of prosperity and power. It needed but the shock of the Franco-Prussian war to produce the utter social downfall which we ourselves have witnessed.

Such are the fruits of modern license; such the evils which the Church seeks to avert in combating this license or liberalism* by the publication of the Syllabus.

---

ordained of God. The prince is His minister to thee for good. He is God's minister; 'an avenger to execute wrath upon him that doth evil' (St. Paul to the Romans, chap. xiii.).

* We cannot help here directing attention to the fact that Liberalism is in close connection with Freemasonry, that it adopts the principles and is the servile instrument of this impious sect, which has so often been condemned by the Church.

See Labis, *Liberalism, Freemasonry, and the Catholic Church* (Brussels, Devaux, 1870).

The errors summarised in this document have been justly styled *the articles of the code of the cosmopolitan revolution;* for they are truly revolutionary doctrines expressed in various ways, and calculated to ruin human society root and branch. Would to God that the condemnation which the Church has pronounced were sufficiently powerful to destroy the germs of death and social dissolution!

Part Second.

DOGMATIC.

1. In the first or *Apologetic* part, it has been shown which is the true religion; it remains to be seen what are the dogmas taught by this religion; and this is the object of the second or *Dogmatic* part of our work. The true religion is the Christian religion, established by Jesus Christ; and true and pure Christianity, or the true Church of Jesus Christ, is the Roman Catholic Church.

2. If we wish to know for a certainty which is the true Christian doctrine, such as was preached by Christ and the Apostles, we have only to ask the Church, which is the depository, what she believes and what she teaches. We shall receive for answer the faithful echo of the Apostles' preaching, and of the words of Jesus Christ.

We have fully answered all questions that might arise concerning the truth of the Church's doctrine and the divine origin and revelation of her dogmas. We have now to see what are her dogmas, and what their true meaning and mutual relations to one another; a knowledge which requires not so much proof as teaching and explanation.

The Catholic Church being once acknowledged, demonstrations and proofs, though undoubtedly useful for defending the faith against heresy and impiety, are no longer strictly necessary. They are supplanted by, and comprised in, the infallibility of the Church, which cuts short all controversy concerning dogma: *Solutio omnis controversiæ Ecclesia.*

What, then, is the doctrine of the Catholic Church, and what are her dogmas?

3. The Church answers these questions clearly and precisely by showing the symbol of her faith, the definitions of her Popes and her Councils, and the teachings of her doctors.

4. This symbol or profession of faith, these teachings and definitions, constitute what is called *the doctrine of the Church*, or Catholic doctrine. It is also called the *deposit of faith*, because Jesus Christ confided His doctrine to His Church that she might be its guardian and faithful interpreter, retrenching nothing from, and adding nothing to, it. And the Church preserves it unaltered and unalterable. When necessary she explains that which is obscure, and she defines that which is disputed; but she changes nothing. The revealed truths, which constitute the treasure of faith, are like so many precious stones, of which the Church is the depository. She occasionally places them in a new light, and causes them to shine with a fresh splendour; but she adds no new invention or revelation to the sacred deposit which she received from the Apostles.

5. Catholic doctrine comprises several categories of truths, which, though distinct from one another, are connected together, and form a complete whole, like the various parts of a majestic temple.

They are:

(1) Those regarding the grounds of doctrine, which are called preliminary truths or dogmas.

(2) Those which concern God and His divers attributes.

(3) The mystery of the Blessed Trinity.

(4) The creation of the world, of man, and of the angels.

(5) Original sin.

(6) The Redemption.

(7) Grace.

(8) The Sacraments.
(9) The law of God, sins and virtues.
(10) The last ends of man and of the world.

CHAPTER I.

PRELIMINARY DOGMAS.

6. THE preliminary dogmas are : (1) the divinity of the Christian religion and the Catholic Church ; (2) the rule of Catholic faith. As the first point has already been fully discussed, we will only treat of the second, or the *rule of faith*.

7. There is a double rule of faith. (1) The common or general rule, which consists in the authority of the Church, and which is sufficient to protect and guard the belief of the ordinary faithful. (2) There is also the *scientific* rule of faith, which is more complete, and which is necessary for the proof and the defence of the faith. We are about to treat of this latter rule, which may be thus defined : ' *The Catholic faith comprises all points of doctrine,*[*] *which, being contained in the*

---

[*] By this is meant all points of doctrine which are *articles of faith* in the strictest sense, or those which are not only *certain*, but absolutely *obligatory*, which, if we believe not, our faith is in danger of shipwreck ; and if we do believe, we remain Catholics. Moreover, as Pius IX. wrote to the German *savants*, who were assembled in congress, it is not sufficient for wise and prudent Catholics to accept these solemnly-proposed doctrines ; they must also submit to decisions concerning doctrine which emanate, though in a less solemn manner, from the Sovereign Pontiff or from Roman congregations authorised by him ; nor must they swerve from the doctrine generally taught by theologians and Catholic doctors. 'For,' say the Fathers of the Vatican Council, ' it is not enough to avoid the perversity of heresy, if we do not also carefully shun those errors which more or less nearly approach heresy ; and we warn all Christians that they are in duty bound to observe the con-

Scriptures or in tradition, are proposed by the Church for the belief of the faithful;' or again, in other words, *' The doctrine of the Christian faith is contained in the double treasury of the Scriptures and tradition, and the Church is the infallible interpreter thereof.'** This declaration implicitly comprises several dogmas, which relate to three points: (1) the Holy Scriptures; (2) tradition; (3) the teaching authority of the Church.

First Article: The Holy Scriptures.

8. The Scriptures are no other than the Bible or the biblical books, the authenticity and historical authority of which have been already proved. But we then considered them from a merely human point of view, without speaking of their divine inspiration.

---

stitutions and decrees by which the Holy See has proscribed and condemned the perverse opinions of this kind which are not enumerated here at full length' (Constit. *Dei Filius*, to the end. See *Elementa Théol. Dogm.* Tract. i. n. 146 seq.).

* The infallible authority of the Church, the formal part of the rule of the *Catholic* faith, constitutes the radical difference between our faith and that which is *heterodox*. The adherents of the latter, especially the Protestants, take for rule *the Bible interpreted by individual reason*. This rule, if such it may be called, can be reduced to free examination, individual judgment, and opinion. It is the authority of individual reasoning taking the place of the authority of the Church established by Jesus Christ. Man depends entirely upon his reason, which aids him to explain the Bible as he thinks proper, and soon will lead him to pronounce his 'for' and 'against' upon this revealed work. Under such circumstances the divine and infallible character of the Scriptures vanishes, and nothing remains but human reason abandoned to its own theories and aberrations.

It is thus that Protestants, and in general all heretics who reject the Church's authority, are led, as a consequence, to deny divine revelation, and come to recognise only human reason; or, what amounts to the same thing, they fall into rationalism, free-thinking, and all the errors with which modern impiety is continually deluging the world.

Faith teaches us that these books have a more than human authority—they have a divine authority, that which belongs to the word of God.

9. They truly contain the word of God Himself; their authors were inspired by the Holy Ghost. They worked under His dictation, and He enlightened their understanding, and suggested, at least in substance, what they were to write. A letter, written under the royal dictation, by a king's secretary, and bearing the royal seal, is truly the king's word or the king's letter; so the Scriptures, written under the immediate inspiration of the Holy Ghost, are truly the writings or the word of God. St. Gregory asks, 'What is the volume of the Scriptures?' and he replies with St. Augustine, 'It is a divine letter, a missive from the omnipotent God addressed to His creatures, who live on the earth.'

This divine word contains treasures of wisdom, but it has also its depths and obscurities, wherein ordinary intelligences may get astray. So it must be explained and interpreted to the faithful.

The Church has been constituted its interpreter. It is the Church also that preserves '*the canon of the Scriptures.*'

10. By *canon* of the Scriptures is understood the true catalogue of the inspired books, which are also called, for these reasons, *canonical books*.

11. They are severally distinguished by the learned as *protocanonical* and *deuterocanonical* books, or canonical books of the first and the second order. This distinction does not at all refer to the intrinsic authority of these books, but to a simple historical fact. All possess the same divine character, but the first have always been considered canonical books; whereas the second, less clearly known as such, formerly gave rise to controversies which continued until the Church, later on, solemnly declared them also to be canonical.

The canonical books are seventy-two in number. In

the *Old Testament:* Genesis, Exodus, Leviticus, Numbers, Deuteronomy, Josue, Judges, Ruth, the four Books of Kings, Paralipomenon (two books), Esdras, Nehemias, Tobias, Judith, Esther, Job, the Psalms, Proverbs, Ecclesiastes, the Canticle of Canticles, the Book of Wisdom, Ecclesiasticus, Isaias, Jeremias, Baruch, Ezechiel, Daniel, Osee, Joel, Amos, Abdias, Jonas, Micheas, Nahum, Habacuc, Sophonius, Aggeus, Zacharias, Malachias, and the two Books of the Machabees.

New Testament: The four Gospels, SS. Matthew, Mark, Luke, and John; the Acts of the Apostles, the Epistles (twenty-one in number), and the Apocalypse.

These books of both Testaments make up the sacred Scriptures, and constitute the primary treasury containing revealed truth. The secondary treasury is tradition.

Second Article : Tradition.

12. *Tradition*, or the secondary treasury of faith, is the *unwritten word of God*, as the Scriptures are the *written word of God.* It is, in fact, the supplement to the Scriptures, and may be defined as *the assemblage of those revealed truths which are not written in the sacred books, but which were first taught by the voice of Jesus Christ and the Apostles, and have ever since been preserved in the Church by an uninterrupted transmission,* either in writing or by word of mouth.

We may cite, as examples of traditional dogmas, the canon of the inspired books, the perpetual virginity of the holy Mother of God, the precise number of the Sacraments, &c.

13. Tradition, no less than the Scriptures, has come down to us in all its purity, transmitted, either by constant and universal practice, as the Sacraments have been, or by teaching and the writings of the holy fathers and doctors of the Church.

14. The writings of the fathers and doctors, though not divinely inspired, possess the highest authority, and

merit the most profound respect. Their authors were mostly bishops, as holy as they were learned. They represent the public teaching of the Church from age to age, from the time of the Apostles to our own days. The most celebrated amongst them are St. Ambrose, St. Augustine, St. Jerome, St. Leo, St. Gregory, St. John Chrysostom, St. Basil, St. Athanasius, St. Cyril, St. Bernard, and St. Thomas Aquinas.

Their writings are sometimes called, collectively, *tradition*, because they are the great channel by which divine tradition is transmitted, and because they are the living testimony which the teaching Church has given through all ages to all the truths of faith.

The meaning of the word *tradition*, as applied to the writings of the fathers, must, however, be distinguished from the same term when used in its strict sense to designate all doctrine which is not contained in the Scriptures.

Third Article: Doctrinal Authority of the Church.

15. We have seen that all revealed truth which composes the sacred deposit of the faith is contained in the double treasury of the *Scriptures* and divine *tradition*.

This double treasury had to be preserved from age to age, and the dogmas contained therein had to be taught and explained in their true sense to all generations. For this reason Jesus Christ established His Church to be the faithful guardian and infallible interpreter of His divine doctrine, the pillar and groundwork of truth.

16. In the present discussion, when we speak of the Church, we mean the teaching Church; that is to say, St. Peter and the Apostles at first, and, after them, the Popes and bishops and all the priests who legitimately have instructed, and do instruct, the faithful by means of preaching and teaching. There is, however, a

distinction to be made between bishops and simple priests: the first have the mission not only of preaching, but also of defining true doctrine, and of condemning error; the latter are simply intended to preach to the faithful that which is defined and proposed by the episcopate.

We have seen above* that Jesus Christ bequeathed to His Church the gift of infallibility, which means the grace to be ever secure from all error in faith, or in the teaching of faith. *Infallibility in teaching*, as the term itself indicates, is the attribute of the teaching Church, and the preserving principle of the true faith.

The Saviour desired that throughout the course of ages the faith of His children should remain intact, and that their minds should not vacillate or be carried away by the tide of human opinion; therefore He would give to His Church a lasting and permanent principle of certainty and of light. To accomplish this, it was necessary either that the Son of God should remain in person on the earth, or that He should establish in His stead an oracle, a magistracy which should be infallible like Himself. He chose the latter means, by giving to His teaching Church the prerogative of infallibility, or, in other words, a special assistance from the Holy Ghost which should always guard it from all error in teaching and in faith. 'The spirit of truth shall abide with you, and shall be in you.' 'The Paraclete, the Holy Ghost,' He says, 'whom the Father will send in My name, He will teach you all things, and bring all things to your mind, whatsoever I shall have said to you' (John xiv. 17-21).

By this outpouring of the Holy Ghost the Church is made participator in the infallibility of Jesus Christ Himself, as He declares in these words, 'He that heareth you heareth Me; he that despiseth you despiseth Me' (Luke x. 16). This perpetual teaching of Christ in His

* Part i. chap. ii. art. i. no. 10, p. 53.

Church was prefigured by our Lord's preaching from the bark of Simon Peter, when, seated in the fisherman's boat, He taught the multitude that was assembled on the shores of the lake of Genezareth. He continues to instruct the nations in the Catholic Church, which is the spiritual bark of Peter.

17. There are, besides the words quoted above, others which demonstrate the infallibility of the teaching Church: 'As the Father hath sent Me, so I also send you,' our Lord said to His Apostles (John xx. 21). 'Go ye into the whole world, and preach the Gospel to every creature. He that believeth and is baptised shall be saved; but he that believeth not (your teaching) shall be condemned' (Mark xvi. 15, 16). 'Go, teach all nations; teaching them to observe all things, whatsoever I have commanded you. And behold, I am with you all days, even to the consummation of the world' (Matt. xxviii. 20).

The Divine Founder more especially endowed St. Peter with the privilege of infallibility when He said to him, confiding His whole flock to his care, 'Feed My lambs; feed My sheep.' Shortly before the Good Shepherd had said, 'Simon, Simon, behold Satan hath desired to have you, that he may sift you as wheat (to shake your faith); but I have prayed for thee that thy faith fail not; and thou, being once converted, confirm thy brethren' (Luke xxii. 31).

By these divine and necessarily efficacious words, the Son of God endowed St. Peter personally, and also His whole teaching Church, with the gift of infallibility.

18. In what is the Church infallible, and what is the object of her infallibility?

The Church is infallible, not in purely scientific questions which do not relate to dogmas, but in *matters of faith and morals;* that is to say, in all which concerns matters of religion, such as the definition of articles of faith, the interpretation of the Scriptures, the explanation of the Creed, the decision of controversies, the condemnation of heresies and errors; and also in questions of morals, of general discipline, of liturgy, and the canonisation of saints.

19. Who are the possessors of this privilege of infallibility in the Church, that can interpret the oracles of the Holy Ghost, and decide as positively as our Lord Himself upon questions of doctrine and faith? They are those only who represent the Universal Church; that is, the whole of the teaching Church, namely, the Pope and the body of bishops united to him as their head. But as the bishops may be dispersed over their various dioceses or assembled in council, we will give the following as a complete and distinct definition:

The following are infallible: (1) the Pope, speaking *ex câthedrâ*; (2) the bishops, who, though dispersed, are ever united in communion and faith with the Apostolic See; (3) the bishops assembled in Œcumenical Council, under the authority of the Pope.

It is here to be remarked that, properly speaking, there are not several infallible oracles and supreme tribunals, as though the Pope and the episcopate were separate from and independent of each other; the episcopal body being in reality as inseparable from its chief as the human body is from its head. With such a union there cannot exist two supreme tribunals, but one single tribunal under different conditions, namely, the Pope alone, and the Pope united to his bishops. When the Pope thinks fit, he pronounces without the aid of the bishops; and when he considers it to be necessary or desirable, he convokes a General or Œcumenical Council.

20. The Pope is only truly infallible when he speaks *ex cathedrâ*, or from the throne of St. Peter; that is to say, according to the Vatican Council,* 'When, acting as the pastor and doctor of all Christians, he, by virtue of his supreme apostolic authority, defines a doctrine

* Constit. *Pastor Æternus*, cap. iv.

concerning faith or morals, to be held by the whole Church.'

When the Sovereign Pontiff teaches in a less solemn manner, and without pronouncing strict definitions, his teachings demand the religious acquiescence of the faithful, who could not withhold it without temerity; because the supreme pastor is doctor of the Church even when he has not the intention of exercising his doctrinal authority in all its plenitude.

The unanimous teaching of the bishops dispersed over their dioceses, whether tacitly or expressly authorised by the Pope, is infallible in matters of faith and morals. This unanimity is morally understood, and may exist even should some bishops advance contrary opinions. An individual bishop may be mistaken and may fall into heresy; it is only the moral union or assemblage of bishops, constituting the teaching Church, which enjoys the special assistance of the Holy Ghost and is preserved from error.

21. An *Œcumenical* or General Council is the general assembly of all the bishops of Catholicity, convoked by the Pope and presided over by him or by his legate. This august reunion, representing the teaching Church, is especially assisted by the Holy Ghost, and all its decisions ratified by the Pope are the infallible oracles of supreme truth. All the faithful must submit to them; to refuse to do so would be to incur anathema, to make shipwreck of the faith, and to merit eternal reprobation. There have been, since the time of the Apostles, nineteen Œcumenical Councils. If that held at Jerusalem sixteen years after the Ascension of our Lord, and presided over by St. Peter, be counted, there have been twenty; but this last is generally numbered amongst the particular councils. The most important of the general councils are those of Nice, held in the year 325; Ephesus and Chalcedon in the fifth century; the fourth council of Lateran in 1215; that of Florence in the fifteenth

century; that of Trent, which was held in the sixteenth century against the Protestants, and which was the eighteenth general council. The last or nineteenth general council was that opened in the Basilica of the Vatican, and presided over by Pius IX., on December 8, 1869.

22. How are the infallible oracles of the Church transmitted to the faithful? The teachings of the Popes and the councils are transmitted and communicated to all the faithful, by the bishops and priests, by means of preaching and of the catechism. As long as these means are faithful reproductions of the infallible teaching which comes from above, they in their turn are also incapable of error; and the faithful, in listening to such teaching, cannot be mistaken, for it is to the Church, it is to Jesus Christ, that they listen. ' *Qui vos audit, me audit.*'

CHAPTER II.

GOD AND HIS ATTRIBUTES.

1. THE Catholic doctrine concerning the divine nature and attributes is contained in the following points:

There is one God, the Creator of heaven and earth. God is infinitely perfect. He possesses in Himself, according to our conception, all perfections, all good qualities, in an infinite degree. His nature is the plenitude, the ocean of all that is good and perfect in being, in life, in goodness, in beauty, in wisdom, and in all good things; or rather, He is essentially being, life, truth, beauty, goodness itself. A *good* thing may cease to be good, but *goodness* must always be good, because goodness is its essence, not its quality.

2. These perfections, separately considered, are called *essential attributes or properties*, with which we conceive the divine nature adorned, as the sun is adorned

with its light. They are divided into three classes: *quiescent* attributes, or those which produce no action; *operative*, and *moral*.*

First Article: Quiescent Attributes.

3. The *quiescent* attributes are *unity, simplicity, infinity, eternity, immensity,* and *immutability.* Unity: there is only one God, who occupies the highest place of the immense scale of beings as the supreme, the uncreated cause of all things, infinitely above the world and all creatures. The character of oneness or unity is essential to the divine nature. Were it not so, God would no longer be the Supreme Being.

4. The unity of *nature* in the divinity is not incompatible with the plurality of *persons,* as we shall see in the following chapter.

5. The *simplicity* of the divine nature excludes all the imperfections of that which is material and compound. God is a pure spirit, whose perfections are not, like the faculties of our souls, really distinct from each other. The only distinctions in God are those which we ourselves create, in order to render Him more comprehensible to our minds.

6. The *infinity* of the divine nature, or its infinite perfection, consists in the union and plenitude of every perfection in God. Those which are called *pure,* such as *knowledge,* He possesses *formally,* and in themselves; but not so those which are mixed up with imperfections, such as reason, which requires comparison and deduction before it can understand. God does not possess these latter in themselves, but they form part of others higher and better, which *eminently* or *vir-*

---

* All these attributes are *absolute,* common to the Three Divine Persons; they must not be confounded with those that are termed *relative* attributes — as paternity, filiation, &c., which are personal to one or other of the three different Persons of the Blessed Trinity.

tually contains them much in the same way as a gold coin contains a silver one, and as the genius of the artist contains the work it can produce. So the infinite *knowledge* of God eminently comprises the perfection of reason.

7. God's *eternity* excludes from Him the possibility of beginning, end, or succession. Whilst creatures are perpetually passing with the ceaseless succession of time, God reigns in an eternal present, like a motionless centre in the midst of a circle moving around it. Time is a successive duration, but eternity may be called a simultaneous duration; it is the fulness of duration which God possesses without succession, as immensity is the fulness or plenitude of space, which He fills without movement or progression. *Time* is not a part, but, as it were, a *shadow* of eternity, or, according to the well-known phrase, a changeful image of a changeless eternity.

8. The *immensity* of God is, as it were, the diffusion of this simplicity. By it the divine nature of necessity in its fulness pervades all space. It is, as a learned philosopher has wisely said, a wonderful sphere, the centre of which is everywhere and the circumference nowhere. Of this we have an image, though a very imperfect one, in the human soul, which is so subtly spread over all our being that it exists entire in the whole body, and entire also in every individual member thereof.

The immensity of God produces His substantial *omnipresence*. God is present everywhere in His entirety, without, however, equally manifesting His presence everywhere: for this reason, we say that He is in a special manner present in His temples and in heaven, because He there displays His divine attributes in a more striking manner.

9. His *immutability*. God is immutable in Himself, and exempt from all change or vicissitude. It is true that in His relation with us He may seem to change,

and show Himself sometimes propitious, sometimes angry; but these variations proceed from the creature, who places himself either under the influence of God's love or justice.

Second Article: Operative Attributes.

10. The operative attributes of God, or the principles of His external works in which man participates, are His *knowledge, will,* and *power.*

11. (1) *Knowledge,* to which God's *science* and *wisdom* belong, is His knowledge or clear and intuitive view of all things. It is called the *omniscience* of God.

God sees all things. Past and future as well as the present; that which takes place in open day as well as the most secret intrigues and the most hidden thoughts, —all is clear and unveiled to His sight. He sees things without veil or shadow, such as they are in themselves; nothing could be unknown to God, nor could anything deceive Him.

His knowledge of futurity does not, however, restrict the liberty of man. He sees in the *future* as we see in the *distance.* He sees in futurity those who wilfully damn themselves, as we should see from afar a wretched suicide cast himself over the brink of a precipice. God's knowing interferes no more with the liberty of the act than does our seeing.

(2) The *will* of God is a free, active faculty like the human will, which is its image; but the image differs from the great original because this latter is infinitely perfect.

The will of God, though in itself single and simple, is called by different names, according to the object it affects; thus there is the will of sign, and the will of good pleasure. The will of *sign,* which may also be called the will of rule or direction, is that which dictates precepts and counsels.

The permissive or efficacious will, which causes

things, or allows them, to happen, is called the will of *good pleasure.*

The will of God is ever directed by His infinite wisdom. It is *holy, free,* and *all-powerful.*

(3) *The power of God is infinite;* it is called *omnipotence;* by it nothing is impossible to God, excepting that which implies error or contradiction. He created the universe by a word; and He could, in like manner, create thousands of other worlds. He preserves the existence of creatures, and could annihilate everything by one single act of His divine will. Nothing can resist Him. In a moment He could oppose the progress of all the kings' armies, confound all human wisdom, defeat all the artifices of the wicked, disconcert all the plans and all the efforts of the powers of heaven and earth. He can restore life to the dead, strengthen the weak, enrich the poor and the indigent. Everything is equally easy to Him, both in the order of nature and of grace. He exerts His power as He chooses; that is to say, with perfect liberty, but always according to the views of wisdom and infinite sanctity.

Third Article: Moral Attributes.

12. Those attributes of God which we call *moral* constitute, so to speak, His virtues, which reasonable creatures are bound to imitate. The principal moral attributes are *wisdom, goodness, charity, providence, truth, mercy,* and *justice.*

13. (1) *Wisdom,* considered as a moral perfection, is the perfect conformity of the divine will with the divine intelligence. It is His supreme love of order by which God always works for ends worthy of Himself, and by which He attains His ends by suitable means, equally worthy of His infinite perfections. The wisdom of God, by reason of its sublimity, sometimes cannot be appreciated by creatures. The most signal act of divine wisdom, the redemption of the world by the Cross,

seemed, in the ages of human wisdom, nothing but folly.

(2) *Goodness* is here taken in a relative sense, or inasmuch as God is *good to us*. It does not differ from *benevolence and beneficence*. It is the disposition which urges God to communicate His own happiness to creatures, according to their condition and the counsels of His wisdom.

(3) *The charity and the mercy of God.** The infinite goodness of God towards His reasonable creatures is called also *charity*, inasmuch as God loves us as a father; and *mercy*, inasmuch as He bestows His benefits on the miserable, the unfortunate, and sinners.

(4) By the *holiness* of God we understand, on the one hand, His infinite hatred of iniquity, which, like to the purest light, excludes all shadow of sin; and on the other, His supreme love of justice—a love which includes the possession of every virtue in an infinitely perfect degree.

The holiness of God is also the source of all holiness in creatures.

14. By reason of His goodness, His mercy, and His sanctity, God wishes to save all men; according to St. Paul, God 'will have all men to be saved, and to come to the knowledge of the truth' (1 Tim. xi. 4); and again, ' He that spared not even His own Son, but delivered Him up for us all, how hath He not also, with Him, given us all things!' (Rom. viii. 32.) If some souls are lost in spite of the means of salvation which God gives to all, it is their own fault, and through their own sins. The only cause of reprobation is the rebellious creature, the sinner, and deliberate sin. None can be lost excepting by their own fault.

As regards children who die without baptism, if,

---

* After having considered *mercy* as linked to charity, we will consider it, further on, in its relation to *justice*, so that it may be fully understood.

on account of their stain of original sin, they cannot enter heaven, they, at the same time, do not suffer the torments of hell, which are the chastisement of actual sins, which they have not committed. Their state is one which is in accordance with God's mercy as well as His justice. The general opinion of the doctors and fathers of the Church is, that children who have died without baptism will be exempt from all *pain of the senses*, but that they will be deprived of the *Beatific Vision*. Moreover, St. Thomas teaches that this privation will cause them no pain, but that they rather will enjoy a certain sort of felicity derived from the natural gifts of intelligence and love which they have received from God.

(5) The *providence* of God signifies His wisdom and goodness in the government of the world. It comprises two things: (1) the destination of creatures to their end, which constitutes design, order, and subordination; (2) the fulfilment of this order and design by suitable means. God's providence includes the preservation and subsistence of creatures, the remedy for their miseries, and help in their wants. It embraces all creation down to the smallest insects, but its principal care is man. There is a double providence: that which is *natural*, and that which is *supernatural*, or the order of grace.

(6) *Truth.*—God, who is sovereign truth in Himself, is also the supreme truth in His relations with us. He could neither deceive Himself nor deceive His creatures, either in teaching a doctrine or in making a promise. Truth therefore comprises the infallibility of God and His fidelity to His promises. The first is the foundation of our faith; the second, of our hope.

(7) *The mercy and the justice of God.*—These two perfections, as we take them here, regard sinners.* The first is exercised towards repentant sinners, by pardon

* In a less restricted sense they regard also the just, whom God will crown in His mercy and justice.

and recompense; the second, towards hardened and impenitent sinners, by condemnation and chastisement proportionate in rigour to the malice of their sin.

CHAPTER III.
THE BLESSED TRINITY.

WE have considered the nature and the attributes of God, and seen that the divine nature and the divinity are one—that God is one and single in *nature*. He is not, however, one and single in *person*, for there are Three Divine Persons. This is the dogma and the mystery of the *Most Blessed Trinity*, which is clearly revealed to us in Scripture. 'Baptise,' our Lord says, ' in the name of the Father, and of the Son, and of the Holy Ghost.' The Blessed Trinity is the first, the most sublime, and the most profound of all our mysteries. We will first make an exposition of our faith on this subject; and secondly, suggest certain considerations concerning the mystery itself.

First Article : Doctrine of the Holy Trinity.

1. Faith teaches us that God is a Trinity; that is, that in one and the same divine essence, or divine nature, there are Three Persons, the Father, the Son, and the Holy Ghost. These Three Persons are numerically distinct from each other, but perfectly equal, having all but one and the same nature and substance. They are, in other words, consubstantial.

2. The Three Persons of the Blessed Trinity are eternal, existing from all eternity each in the manner proper to Himself. God the Father exists without birth or origin; God the Son draws His origin from the Father by means of *birth*—He is 'born of the Father;'

and God the Holy Ghost draws His origin by *procession*—He proceeds from the Father and the Son as from a single principle.

3. The attributes of the divine essence are common to the whole Trinity. Power, wisdom, and holiness belong equally to each of the Three Persons; and, in the same way, all the exterior works of the universe—the creation, redemption, and sanctification of the world and of souls—are likewise the common work of the Three Divine Persons. The sacred Scripture, however, attributes power and creation in a more especial manner to the Father, wisdom and redemption to the Son, and to the Holy Ghost holiness and sanctification. This way of speaking is called *appropriation*. It is founded on the personal attributes of the Divine Persons, and is extended moreover to other attributes and other works.

4. The redemption belongs to the Son, not only by appropriation, but also by *personal execution*. The Blessed Trinity willed to save the human race, and the Second Person, God the Son, came down from heaven, and *was made man* by taking to His Divine Person our human nature. In this nature, which He had made His own, He died on the Cross, an expiatory victim for the whole human race. For this reason He is called the *God made man*, the Man-God, the Mediator, the Redeemer, the Author, by His Passion, of our salvation.

5. The Three Divine Persons manifested themselves at the same time at the baptism of Jesus Christ. God the Son was then visible as man, the Holy Ghost appeared in the form of a dove, and the Father announced His presence by the voice which was heard, saying of our Lord, 'This is My beloved Son, in whom I am well pleased.'

6. By the *coming, descent,* or *mission* is signified the relations which the Three Divine Persons have with man on earth. Such relations may be either visible or

invisible. Thus God the Son was sent by His Father to save the world; God the Holy Ghost was sent by the Father and the Son on the day of Pentecost to sanctify the Church; God the Father was not sent, but He *came* to render testimony to Jesus Christ. These are the *visible* missions or comings of the Blessed Trinity. The *invisible* coming, or mission, takes place when the Divine Persons begin to work in our souls in a special manner, which happens when we receive Baptism, Confirmation, the Holy Communion, and the other Sacraments; also in the Mass and in prayer. The Divine Persons at such times descend into well-disposed souls, purifying them, and establishing their abode in them, as in a living temple. This ineffable union of souls with the Blessed Trinity is revealed to us in the words of Christ: 'He who loves Me will keep My word; and the Father will love him, and we will come to Him and take up our abode within Him' (John xiv. 23).

7. The names of the Persons of the Blessed Trinity are expressive of their individual attributes, and are therefore incommunicable. There is but one Father, one Son, and one Holy Ghost. God the Son is called also the *Word*, also *Wisdom*, and the *Substantial Image of the Father;* God the Holy Ghost is called *Charity, Love, the Union of the Father and the Son,* the *Paraclete* or Consoler, the Gift of the Most High, the *Giver of gifts.*

All this doctrine concerning the Blessed Trinity must necessarily have been revealed to us by faith; our own reason being incapable of discovering it, because it contains what is called a *mystery.*

Second Article: Mystery of the Holy Trinity.

8. By a *mystery* is generally meant a truth of whose existence we are certain, but which in itself we cannot understand, excepting in an imperfect manner. Thus, the light of day, the seed which is sown in the earth,

the blade of grass, and the grain of sand which we tread on, all contain inexplicable secrets. They are *mysteries of nature.* There are, in like manner, *mysteries of faith.*

A *mystery of faith* is a revealed truth, which is so much exalted above human intelligence that man could never have soared to its heights unaided by the light of faith; and which, when he is thus enabled to *know,* he still remains incapable of understanding or explaining.

9. A mystery of faith is *above* human reason, without, however, being *contrary* to it. It is a fact of the supernatural order, of which, by faith, we know the existence, though without understanding it; just as in the order of nature we know many facts which we cannot explain. If there is mystery about the creatures that surround us on every side, it is not astonishing that in the supernatural and invisible world, and especially in that which concerns the infinite abyss of the divine nature, there should be depths which we are unable to sound. Reason must submit with docility to the word of God; it would be culpable temerity to try to penetrate into the profound secrets contained therein. The mysteries of faith are like the sun, impenetrable in themselves; they give light and life to those who walk simply in their rays; but they blind the eyes that would audaciously try to scrutinise their splendour.

10. The mystery of the Blessed Trinity consists in the double fact of the plurality of Persons and the unity of nature in God. Here on earth each person has his own body and soul, constituting his own individual and incommunicable nature. In a family, father, mother, and child are three distinct persons, each possessing an individual nature; but in God, the Father, Son, and Holy Ghost, though Three Persons, have only one and the same nature. We cannot see how this is possible, because we do not understand the terms Divine *Nature* and Divine *Persons.* We only know that the *Nature*

is not the *Person;* which is sufficient to show us that there is no contradiction in the declaration that 'the Three Divine Persons have but one and the same divine nature, and are only one God.'

11. The common objection raised by infidelity, that 'the Trinity is a contradiction, and that to admit it is to say that three are one,' has no foundation. We deny, in the first place, the *supposition;* faith does not *say that three are one*, that the number three is the same thing as unity, and that three persons are one person. What faith teaches is that the Three Divine Persons are only one God, because They have only one and the same Divine Nature. This is a mysterious doctrine, it is true, and apparently strange, but it contains no real contradiction.

12. Though this great mystery surpasses the limits of our intelligence, and we are incapable of understanding it in this life, we find, nevertheless, in nature some emblems of the Holy Trinity which facilitate our conception of the dogma and make us feel its propriety. The human soul is a type of the Holy Trinity, endowed as it is with its three distinct faculties of memory, understanding, and will, with which it seems to be blended. Another is the sun, which gives light and heat, and is itself light and heat. The root, the stem, and the branches form but one tree. Three distinct sparks when amalgamated give one and the same light. We say in the Mass that *God the Son is God of God, light of light.* We may add to the foregoing figures of the Blessed Trinity which are spoken of by the fathers that of the triangle, or mysterious union of three angles, symbolising the Trinity. But indeed these imperfect figures or emblems fall very far short of explaining the depths of the mystery. We can only bow our weak intelligence before the Supreme Wisdom, and believe with all our hearts the doctrine of the Holy Trinity, as we believe all the other truths which God reveals to us, and say, 'I believe, my God,

because Thou hast revealed it, and Thy Word is infallible; and in this faith I wish to live and die.'

CHAPTER IV.

THE CREATION OF THE WORLD—THE ANGELS—MAN—ORIGINAL SIN.

1. WE have now learnt what faith teaches us about God, considered in Himself, whether in His nature or in His personality. It remains for us to discuss the doctrine relating to the works of God.

The works of God admit of two distinctions: the creation of the universe, and the providence by which it is governed. We mean, in speaking here of providence, that economy, action, or succession of actions, by which God leads all creatures to their end, and more especially those which hold the first place in the visible world—namely, man, or the human race.

We will first take for consideration the creation of the world; then the angels; and lastly, man and original sin.

First Article: The Creation of the World.

2. God has created—that is, drawn out of nothing—heaven and earth, with all that they contain, either spiritual or corporal. By this is meant all that exists out of God—namely, the earth which we inhabit, the sun, the moon, and all the stars of the firmament, with those millions of globes and suns that occupy the immensity of space; also all living beings, plants, animals, men, and the angels, who are invisible and purely spiritual creatures.

This vast universe has been created by a single word of the Creator, by a simple act of the Divine Will. 'He spoke, and all things were made; He commanded, and they were created' (Ps. cxlviii.).

3. In the first page of Genesis the history of the creation is recorded; but in this recital a distinction ought to be observed between those points which are clear and certain, and those which are disputed or obscure.

The clear and certain points are the following:

(1) In the beginning God created heaven and earth.

(2) God made to His own image and likeness the first man, the sole father of the human race.

(3) God established the law of the Sabbath, in order to consecrate the seventh day to the divine worship; and He did so in memory of the creation, which was a type of the weekly period.

(4) God formed the world as it now exists, with its waters, its plants, and its various species of animals;* and He accomplished this work in the space of six days.

The points which follow are doubtful, and in no way defined by faith:

(1) What must be understood by the *days* of creation? The Hebrew word *iom*, translated as *day*, may signify a period of twenty-four hours, or it may be used to denote an indefinite space of time, or a simple distinction of order, without succession of time.

(2) What was the original state of the universe before the days of creation? Were there plants and animals previous to this, which were subsequently ingulfed in a tremendous overthrow, thus producing the Mosaic chaos?

(3) Did the different words of the Creator, which constitute the distinct acts of creation, produce their effect immediately or gradually? Had all the plants appeared before the creation of the animals? Were

---

* The imaginary theory of Darwin, who endeavours to prove that the different species came in the course of time to be derived from one another, has been refuted by De Quatrefarges, Lecomte, and other learned men. See the *Revue Catholique*, Aug. 1871.

there certain species of plants and animals which subsequently perished and have been superseded by other species?

(4) What are we to understand by the work of the fourth day, when the Scriptures tell us God made the sun and the stars to light the earth? Did the sun and the stars commence their existence then, or did they only begin to light up the world, which had now become capable of receiving their constant influence, they having already been in existence?

These and other questions, which are not defined either by the Bible or by the interpretation of the Church, are left for solution to the investigations of science.*

4. All that faith teaches us about the antiquity of the world is, that it did not always exist, but was created in time, or at the beginning of time. The sacred Scriptures do not begin to reckon years from the creation of the *world*, but from that of *man;* and they count them so as to give us only an uncertain chronology, which varies from 4000 to 5500 years, or even more, from the time which elapsed between the creation of Adam and the coming of Jesus Christ.

5. The end which God had in view in creating the world was His glory, or the manifestation of His divine attributes, and the true happiness of all reasonable creatures.

Second Article: The Angels.

6. The angels hold the highest rank amongst all God's creatures, by reason of the nobility of their nature.

The angels are pure spirits; not like the spirit or soul of man formed to animate a body, though they possess the faculty of appearing to man under borrowed bodies or forms.

* See Schouppe, *Cursus Scripturæ Sacræ*, tom. 1. part. ii. 'Solutio Difficultatum;' Swolfs, *La Création et l' Œuvre des Six Jours* (Brux. Closson).

The angelic nature is very far superior to that of man. The angels are endowed with a natural intelligence, will, power, and beauty far surpassing that which is most perfect in man. One angel exterminated in a single night 105,000 men of the army of King Sennacharib. St. John says, in the Apocalypse xviii. 1, ' I saw another angel come down from heaven, having great power, and the earth was enlightened with his glory.'

The angels originally were all clothed with the light of grace, and destined to enjoy glory and the Beatific Vision, to be the ministers of God and the princes and ornaments of the celestial courts. But, before allowing them to share His glory, God willed that they should undergo a trial as proof of their fidelity.

All were not steadfast under their trial. Great numbers of the angelic host rebelled against their Sovereign Master, and, having fallen into the sin of pride, were precipitated into the fires of hell for all eternity, and became devils. Those who had remained faithful were admitted to the glories of heaven, and they are called the angels of heaven, angels of light, the good, the holy angels.

7. The angels of heaven are many in number. Daniel the prophet, in his divine visions, saw millions and thousands of millions of these glorious spirits around the throne of God. It is supposed that they are much more numerous than the great multitude of the fallen angels.

8. The angels are divided into three hierarchies, and these again are each divided into three choirs. The first hierarchy comprises the Seraphim, Cherubim, and Thrones; the second consists of the Dominations, Principalities, and Powers; and the third is divided into the Virtues, Archangels, and Angels.

9. The name *angel*, meaning *messenger*, is commonly applied in general to all the blessed spirits, without dis-

tinction of hierarchies and choirs. Only three amongst them are known to us under special names: *Gabriel*, the Strength of God; *Michael*, Who is like unto God; and *Raphael*, the Remedy of God.

10. The demons, called also the bad angels and angels of darkness, are not always confined to the limits of hell. Great numbers are permitted to disperse over the world, carrying, however, their torments with them.

The devils, animated constantly with a violent hatred of God and of His work, man, have one wish and one thought, and it is to bring about man's destruction. By means of *temptations* they try to insnare him into sin, and by sin into the bottomless pit of hell. Sometimes also their baneful influence affects even the body, by means of *possession* and sensible troubles and vexations. Their power, however, is limited by Almighty God, and they cannot exercise it over the human body in the visible world without His special permission; nor can they tempt our souls to sin, excepting under certain restrictions and within certain bounds. 'God is faithful,' says the Apostle, 'who will not suffer you to be tempted above that which you are able; but will make also with temptation issue, so that you may be able to bear it' (1 Cor. x. 13). Nevertheless, it is God's will, in time of temptation, that we should implore His aid by prayer.

11. The good angels have the office of praising God in heaven, of being His messengers, His ministers, and the guardians of men on earth.

12. Those blessed spirits are called guardian angels, who, by the mercy of God, are appointed to be the protectors and defenders of men. Faith teaches us that each one of us has a guardian angel attached to his person during the whole course of his life. 'Beware of scandalising one of these little ones,' says our Lord; 'for their angels in heaven always see the face of My Father, who is in heaven' (Matt. xviii. 10). It is, moreover, a generally accepted doctrine, founded on the Scriptures,

that communities—such as the Church, dioceses, and kingdoms—have also their tutelary angels.

The guardian angels defend those of whom they have charge against all the assaults of the demons, and they endeavour to preserve them from all evil of soul and body; but their solicitude tends principally to guard us from sin, and the occasions of sin. If we grieve them by falling, they help us to rise again; and however great be the resistance and indocility of the sinner, his angel guardian never entirely deserts him. If we are docile, our angels keep us in the right path, and help us to become more and more virtuous and holy, suggesting to us good thoughts and holy desires, offering our good actions and our prayers to God, and, above all, assisting us at the hour of death.

After death, if the soul he has been guarding is in a mortal sin, the angel abandons it to the devil; and if it is in the state of grace, he conducts it to purgatory, whence, when entirely purified, he leads it to heaven.

13. The angels constantly enjoy the Beatific Vision, and during their sojourning on earth their beatitude remains ever with them, according to the words of our Lord: 'Their angels look upon the face of My Father, who is in heaven' (Matt. xviii. 10).

Third Article: Man and Original Sin.
I. The Origin and Fall of Man.

14. God, who created pure intelligences for the peopling of heaven, made for the earth's population intelligences united to bodies; or, in other words, He made man.

Having provided the earth with plants and animals, and accomplished the formation of visible nature, God lastly made a creature, destined to be the crowning of His work, namely, man, the chief and king of the visible creation. He made him to His own image and likeness, endowing him with a mortal body and an immortal soul, which was intelligent and free, and capable of knowing, loving, and serving his Creator.

15. The first man was called Adam. God made his body out of clay, and animated it with His breath. Then He created Eve, whom He mysteriously formed from a rib of Adam, because she was to be his spouse and his inseparable companion. Adam and Eve are the first parents of the whole human race; and from them alone are descended every race and variety of man which is spread over the surface of the globe. They were created perfect, with the full use of reason and of speech; and moreover they were endowed with the fulness of precious gifts bearing relation to their sublime destiny.*

16. This destiny was to know, love, bless, and serve God on earth, and to glorify Him eternally in heaven.

It is true that, regarding only the nature of man, it would seem to be adapted especially for earth. He was a terrestrial creature, having a body and intelligence, and his place would seem to be in the visible world, of which he should be, as it were, the pontiff, to praise God in His works, and himself to enjoy the peace of a good conscience, which is the natural fruit of virtue. But, in His mercy, God raised man to a destiny far above his earthly nature. He destined him to be a brother to the angels, and to share heaven together with the blessed spirits; and therefore God enriched man at his origin with most excellent gifts and qualities.

17. The most important of these gifts of God was that of sanctifying grace, called also *original justice*, because it was granted to man from his origin. To this first treasure God added others, namely, integrity or exemption from concupiscence, infused knowledge,

---

* The hypotheses contrary to this dogma have been victoriously refuted by science. See Quatrefarges, *On the Unity of the Human Species.*

immortality, and felicity. All these gifts were gratuitous and superadded to man's nature; and Adam, if he had remained faithful to God, his Benefactor and his Master, would have transmitted them to all his descendants.

Thus enriched with graces and privileges, Adam and Eve were placed in the terrestrial paradise, a garden of delights which God had prepared for them, that they might live there in innocence until the time when, without suffering death, they should be transported to the celestial paradise, their glorious and eternal home. But all these good things were lost to them by their sin.

18. God willed that these creatures of His hand should remain always obedient to Him. He therefore imposed on them a strict command, which was, however, easy to observe, namely, that they should not, under pain of death, eat of the fruit of one particular tree in the garden of paradise. Adam disobeyed, and ate some of the fruit at the solicitation of Eve, who had been led away by the serpent, or rather by the devil, who had assumed the form of that reptile in order to make our first parents fall into sin, and to accomplish their ruin, and that of all their descendants.

Punishment immediately followed the sin. Adam and Eve were turned out of the terrestrial paradise, deprived of all the gratuitous gifts of God, and condemned to live on the earth as in a place of exile until the moment of their death.

This lot was also to be that of all their posterity; for, having lost all the good things with which they had originally been endowed, they could no longer transmit them to their children. They left us instead, alas, together with their sin, all the multiplicity of pains and evils which are the inheritance of sinners, and thus brought about the actual condition of humanity, which is that of a fallen and guilty race. This is the dogma of original sin, the doctrine of which follows.

II. Doctrine respecting Original Sin.

19. All men sinned in Adam their first parent, in this sense, that his sin, together with its consequent evils, are transmitted by means of generation to all his posterity. All men are born, therefore, guilty and children of wrath. They bear in their souls, which were created to the image and likeness of God, a mark of the Evil One, which obscures the image of the Creator. This is *original sin*, so called because man contracts it in his very origin. The Council of Trent defines it thus: 'The sin, in so far as it is renewed by generation in every human being born into the world, is real guilt, inherent in his nature.'

20. The children of Adam inherit, not only his sin, but all the effects of sin. These effects consist in losses and punishments. (1) Man lost by sin all the gratuitous benefits with which his nature was endowed in the persons of our first parents — sanctifying grace, or original justice, as well as the celestial glory of which this grace was the pledge; and in the natural order he forfeited corporal felicity and immortality. (2) He merited positive penalties—the anger and indignation of God and the shameful slavery and tyranny of the devil. Moreover, fallen from his primitive felicity, man has impaired his condition both of body and soul. His body has become subject to death, to sickness and pains, and to all those miseries which nature, transformed into an enemy, ever inflicts on him. His soul also has been attacked and wounded deeply.

The wounds caused by sin in the soul are, according to the doctrine of the Venerable Bede, ignorance in the mind, malice, and inclination to evil in the will; and in the senses, weakness, and what is called concupiscence, or the inclination towards sensual pleasure, honours, and riches. These four wounds, taken collectively, constitute the *fomes peccati*, from which emanates that moral malady which works upon human nature and inclines it to evil.

21. Original sin is remitted by baptism, whose regenerating waters wash away all the guilt contracted in our birth. After this spiritual cleansing no shadow of sin remains; but we are like new-born children of God; we are notwithstanding still liable to concupiscence and to all the miseries of this life. God leaves us these difficulties that we may turn them into subjects of combat and of triumph. Only at the day of corporal regeneration—that is to say, at the glorious resurrection—shall we be entirely delivered from them.

Such is the doctrine revealed by God and taught by the Church regarding original sin. In this doctrine is contained a great mystery.

III. Mystery of Original Sin.

22. We could not, without revelation, know the fact of sin hidden in our nature; nor can we even, knowing it, clearly understand it.

That Adam, the chief of the human race, should have rendered all that race of which he was the originator and representative, guilty and miserable, is a mystery which our reason must accept on the word of God, but which cannot be explained. It cannot be rejected as impossible, nor can anything unjust or contrary to the divine perfections be found in it.

In order to elucidate this doctrine the following parable is sometimes used as an example: A man was raised by his king from the lowest grade of society to the highest rank and nobility. Immense riches and the greatest dignities were also conferred upon him; and, moreover, all these benefits were hereditary and were to be transmitted to his children. But he committed a crime; he was guilty of high treason against his benefactor, and rendered himself deserving of the most severe punishment. Degraded, despoiled of all his goods, and sold as a slave, he died, and left his children overwhelmed with disgrace, and inheritors of his misery and his slavery. The miserable inheritance of these children is a representation of original sin in the descendants of Adam.

The children of Adam, it may be urged, are not only unfortunate, but they are also guilty. How can they be guilty of a sin which they have never committed? From amongst many explanations given by theologians, which are more or less calculated to throw some light on this mystery, we select the following :*

The Council of Trent has defined that the sin of Adam is transmitted to his descendants by the propagation of life. In order to understand this definition a distinction must be observed between that which theologians call *actual* sin and *habitual* sin. Actual sin consists in the *act* by which man transgresses the commandments of God; *habitual* sin is the *state* of him who has violated the divine law. Man, in committing mortal sin, loses sanctifying grace, which is the life of the soul; and thus deprived of life his soul is in a state of death and of sin, which continues until he has recovered sanctifying grace.

So when the Church teaches that the sin of Adam is transmitted to us, she does not mean that the act by which Adam disobeyed God becomes the act of all men; the *actual sin* belongs to Adam alone, and is not communicated to his children. It is only the *habitual sin*, or the deprivation of original justice, which we inherit with our nature.

By reason of Adam's sin we are all born deprived of original justice; and this privation, *so far as it is produced in us by Adam's fault*, constitutes original sin, which is a real stain on the soul, and a sin in all the

* This explanation, like others of the same kind, is only a system of explanation, a theological opinion, and by no means a certain doctrine.

rigorous theological meaning of the word, though it is not a personal actual sin. Hence we are born guilty of a sin which personally we have not committed.

It may be urged, 'Why did God make our fall dependent only on Adam, ordaining that sanctifying grace should be ours only on condition that Adam remained faithful to Him?' We reply that it was just that the happiness of the creature should depend on his fidelity to his Creator. Finally, if the question is pursued to the utmost, and a full explanation of God's actions insisted on, we must remember that human reason cannot account for them. They are a mystery, a divine secret, and, as we said in speaking of the Blessed Trinity, we must simply believe; and submitting our feeble understanding to the teaching of faith, say, 'My God, I believe the doctrine of original sin, because Thou hast revealed it, and Thy word is infallible; and in this faith I will live and die.'

Fourth Article: The Immaculate Conception.

23. Original sin, as we have shown, is contracted in our birth. The children of Adam, in the first moments of their existence, are like stars whose light is extinguished—they are enveloped in the darkness of sin. In uniting itself with the body, so as to constitute human nature, the soul becomes stained with sin, like a precious pearl that has fallen in the mire. Every descendant of guilty man by generation contracts original sin. All his posterity appears in the eye of God marked with a sign of the devil, like a cursed race, and, according to St. Augustine's expression, like a mass of damnation.

There is one admirable exception, one child of light amongst all the children of death, one lily amongst the thorns—the Holy and Immaculate Virgin Mary, the Mother of God. She alone was born in grace; she alone was conceived without the stain of original sin. By an exceptional privilege, called the Immaculate Conception, she was preserved from the universal taint, through the merits of the Redeemer whose Mother she was destined to be.

24. God, who, in His impenetrable designs, had allowed the fall of man, deigned in His mercy to give him a Redeemer, who should deliver him from the slavery of the devil and reinstate him in all his primitive rights.

This Redeemer was promised on the very day of the sin. The Scripture says that God descended into Paradise to impose on man the penalty of death, with which He had threatened him in case of his disobedience. But there was one more guilty even than fallen man—it was the devil, hidden under the form of a serpent. God cursed him, and said, 'I will put enmity between thee and the woman, between thy seed and her seed, and she shall crush thy head.' This woman, who, by *her seed*—that is to say, by her Son—should crush the head and demolish the empire of the devil, was the Virgin Mary. The enmity, the war, between her and the serpent, who, far from overcoming her, is himself utterly vanquished and crushed by her heel, is her triumph over sin, her glorious Immaculate Conception. The same privilege is indicated in the words of God, who, by the mouth of Gabriel, addresses Mary with the title, 'Full of Grace;' words which would fall short of the truth if Mary had been deprived of grace during a single instant of her existence; if she, the true star of the morning, had not from the beginning shone with an ever pure and brilliant light.

In preserving the Blessed Virgin Mary from original sin, God, in His mercy, prepared the way for the redemption of man, for the coming of the Messiah.

CHAPTER V.
THE INCARNATION.

1. THE Incarnation is the mystery of the Son of God made man.

We have seen that by the sin of the first man the whole human race became guilty, and fell from its original state into the slavery of the devil, from whose power it could not escape.

God might have treated sinful man as He did the rebel angels; He might have abandoned him to his fate and delivered him over to the eternal chastisement which he deserved. But He was merciful towards man, and promised him a Redeemer, who should expiate the sin of Adam's race, and reëstablish it in justice and in all its former privileges.

2. The Author of the restoration of the human race was the INCARNATE WORD; that is to say, the Second Person of the Blessed Trinity made man, and called by the name of *Jesus Christ*.

3. God becoming man to save us, such is the great fact taught us by faith, the wonderful dogma of the Incarnation and Redemption. This dogma entirely concerns the Person of Jesus Christ, whom we must endeavour to know according to the infallible teachings of the Church. We will consider Christ (1) in His history; (2) in His Person or His personal constitution; (3) in His works; (4) in the worship due to Him; (5) in His influence on humanity.

First Article : Jesus Christ considered in His History.

4. Considered historically, Jesus Christ is the greatest Person who has ever lived in the world. He stands preëminent; He shines from amongst celebrated men, like the moon amongst the inferior light of the stars, or rather like the sun itself, eclipsing all the other luminaries.

Though a true and real man, Jesus Christ is unlike any other. All men but Himself are born and die, commencing with their birth and completing with their death their appointed destiny. Christ alone existed before His incarnation and lives after His death; of Him only can it be said, '*Jesus Christus heri, et hodie, ipse et in secula,*—Christ yesterday, and to-day, and the same for ever' (Heb. xiii. 8).

Christ is living. He lives always and everywhere, not only in heaven where He ascended, but in the entire world and in the minds and hearts of men. Since His death on Mount Calvary, He has more than ever shown Himself to be the living God, and His living power is specially shown and developed in Christianity; by it He speaks, He teaches, He commands, He forbids, He combats, and He triumphs. All passes away and dies around Him; He alone lives and abides for ever, the Soul and the Head of His Church.

His history, then, is not confined to the thirty-three years which He spent on earth; it extends over all the ages of the world, from Adam to the end of time. Jesus Christ lives in the past by His prophetic existence; He lives in His own contemporary epoch by His mortal life; He lives in the future by His immortal existence.

I. Prophetic Existence of Christ.

5. By the prophetic existence of Christ is meant that which He has in the prophecies announcing His coming, and in the figures which represented Him from the beginning of the world. They are like rays heralding Christ's light, as the dawn announces the sun, or like the shadow which precedes the body, presenting an imperfect likeness of that which has to follow.

6. Christ or the Messiah was first announced in the Garden of Eden, on the day when man fell under the slavery of the devil. God promised, at the same time

THE INCARNATION.

as He punished our first parents, that *a woman born of their race should give birth to a Son, who should crush the serpent's head;* meaning that they should have a Saviour, who would destroy the tyranny of Satan and break the bonds of his thraldom.

Adam gratefully received this magnificent promise, and transmitted it to his descendants.

This first prophecy was pronounced more than 4000 years before the coming of Christ. After that, about 2000 years before our era, God promised to *Abraham* that he should become the father of a great people, and that all the nations of the earth should be blessed and saved by a Son who should come of his race (Gen. xxvi. 4).

In the year 1700* the patriarch *Jacob* predicted that the Saviour of the world, the Expected of nations, should be born of the descendants of the tribe of his son Judah, and that this great event should happen when the royal sceptre which they should wield had passed into the hands of strangers.

In the year 1500 *Moses* announced that the Messiah would be, like him, a Legislator, but a greater than he— a Lawgiver who should give to Israel a lasting and definite law, the accomplishment of the temporary law of Sinai.

In the year 1050 God made known to King David that Christ should be born of his house; that He should be, like him, a King, but a King of glory and holiness, the Head of a spiritual and universal kingdom; that He should save the world by His sufferings and death; that He should be crucified, descend into hell, rise from the dead, and ascend gloriously into heaven, to sit at the right hand of God the Father, whence He should come to judge the world.

In the year 700 *Isaias and the other Prophets* announced that the Saviour should be born miraculously

* That is to say, *about* the year 1700. These dates must be taken approximately.

of a Virgin in Bethlehem of Juda, and that He should be at once God and Man; that He would lead a poor and obscure life, and that He would have a precursor to make this known; that by His doctrine He would instruct men; that He would work miracles on His way, healing the sick, raising the dead to life, teaching the poor; and that finally He would give up His life for the sins of men, and suffer a dolorous Passion for their salvation; that He would establish His Church, or the reign of God in the universe, by His apostolic preaching.

In the year 500 *Daniel* predicted that from the time of the captivity of Babylon seventy weeks of years, or 490 years, should elapse, and that then Christ should be put to death for the salvation of the human race.

7. The figures of Christ are the persons or historical events which, under divers aspects, foreshadow the attributes of the Saviour, His mysteries and His works. The following are the principal:

Adam, the father of the human race according to the flesh, represents Jesus Christ, its Father according to the spirit. Hence the Saviour is called by the Apostle the *Second Adam*.

Abel the just, whose blood, spilt by his brother, cries aloud for vengeance, is a figure of Christ, the eminently Just One, whose Blood, spilt by the Jews His brethren, cries for mercy.

Noah, constructing an ark to save his family from the Deluge, prefigures Christ establishing His Church for the salvation of the faithful.

Melchisedech, priest and king, in offering bread and wine as a sacrifice, is a type of Christ in the Holy Eucharist and the Sacrifice of the Mass.

Isaac, carrying the wood for the sacrifice of which he was himself the destined victim, is an image of Jesus Christ carrying His Cross, on which He was to die a victim for our sins.

Joseph, sold by his brethren, and become the saviour of Egypt, is like Christ, who was sold by Judas and delivered up to His enemies, thus to become the Saviour of the world.

Moses also is a prototype of Christ. He delivers the Israelites from the slavery of Egypt, leading them through the Red Sea, in which their enemies the Egyptians were afterwards swallowed up. He also gives them the law of God, and causes manna to rain down from heaven, and water to spring from a rock, and finally conducts his people through the desert to the Promised Land. Jesus Christ, by His Precious Blood, makes us pass from the slavery of the devil to the promised land of eternal life.

The *Paschal Lamb*, the marks of whose blood on the door-posts of the Israelites averted the blows of the exterminating angel, foreshadows the Lamb of God, whose Divine Blood preserves our souls from death.

The Sacrifices, the Ark of the Covenant, and all the worship of the old law, Aaron the high-priest, the Levites, and all the sacerdotal tribe, are figures and images of what was to follow in the Christian religion, namely, the Priesthood, the Sacrifice of the new law, of Calvary, and of the Eucharist.

The Brazen Serpent, the sight of which healed the wounds of those who had been bitten by the serpents of the desert, is an emblem of Jesus crucified, whose merits and example heal the spiritual wounds of all who believe and hope in Him.

Samson, carrying on his shoulders the gates of Gaza, where he was imprisoned, resembles Jesus Christ rising from the dead, victorious over sin and death, and by His resurrection opening in a manner the prisons of death for the deliverance of men.

David, King of Jerusalem, where he established his throne, tried by persecutions and outrages, triumphant over Goliath and the enemies of his people, is a figure of

Christ, the King and Founder of the kingdom of God or of the Church, the Conqueror of the devil, triumphant also over all the persecutions of His enemies.

Solomon, the peaceful king, full of wisdom, glory, and magnificence, built a temple to the Lord. Christ, the Prince of Peace, the King of wisdom and of glory, built up the living and eternal temple of the Church of God.

Jonas, cast into the sea for the salvation of the vessel, buried in the whale, and cast up again alive on the shore after three days, represents Jesus Christ condemned to death to save us, and rising again to life on the third day.

Elias, taken up into heaven in a fiery chariot in the sight of his disciple Eliseus, prefigures Jesus Christ ascending into heaven from Mount Olivet in the sight of all His disciples.

II. Life of Christ on Earth.

8. The promised Redeemer, for 4000 years the Desired of men, was born in Bethlehem about the year 42 of the reign of the Roman Emperor Augustus, the twenty-fifth year of the reign of Herod the Idumean in Judea, and the sixty-fifth week of Daniel the Prophet.

According to the prophecies, he had for His mother a virgin, the Virgin Mary, of the royal blood of David. He was circumcised according to the Jewish law, and called *Jesus*, meaning *Saviour*, which name was given to Him by God Himself, by the mouth of the angel Gabriel.

He led at first an obscure and humble life, hidden at Nazareth in the cottage of Joseph the carpenter, who was His foster-father, and under whom He worked like a simple artisan, thus giving to the world a great example of obedience, humility, and industry.

At the age of about thirty years Jesus quitted Nazareth, and went to the banks of the Jordan to receive baptism from the hands of His precursor, St. John the

THE INCARNATION.

Baptist, who was an extraordinary man, a great prophet, whose birth was miraculous, and who was listened to by all Israel.

John the Baptist made Jesus Christ known to the people, declaring that the Messiah was come, and that Jesus of Nazareth was He. He proclaimed that He was the Christ, the Son of God, the Lamb of God who taketh away the sins of the world, and that he himself was only the precursor, who went before Him to prepare His ways in their hearts.

At the same time Jesus Christ began to shine with His own splendour. His simple and modest appearance in no way distinguished Him from ordinary men; but the brilliancy of His holiness, His doctrine, and His miracles was resplendent.

The words which came from His mouth bore the impress of superhuman authority and wisdom, such as no man before Him had ever manifested. His life was the perfect example of the doctrine He preached: everything in Him was humility, abnegation, meekness, patience, beneficence, and charity. His miracles were innumerable, and He worked them in favour of all who were in misery. The blind, the deaf, the paralytic, and other sick were cured; the dead were raised to life, and the possessed were delivered from their tormenting devils. All who suffered came to Him: He rejected none; but for their relief He bestowed and worked innumerable miracles, as Isaias and the Prophets had foretold.

It was clear that all the prophecies were fulfilled in His person, and that He was, as John the Baptist declared, the Christ, the promised Saviour-King of Israel.

Jesus preached the coming of the kingdom of God, and, as a requisite condition for entering therein, penance and the remission of sins. In a word, He taught all the doctrine of Christianity as we have it in the Gospel. He was soon followed by a great number of disciples, who wished to hear from His lips the words of eternal life.

L

He chose from amongst His followers the twelve Apostles, whom He attached to His Person in an inseparable way, and instructed with a special care, because He destined them to be the preachers of His doctrine all over the world, and the foundation-stones of His Church. Soon He established His Church. The Apostle St. Peter He made the corner-stone, to him He confided the keys of the kingdom of heaven, to be transmitted by him to his successors.

There existed at that time in Judea a sect called the Pharisees, perverse hypocritical men, who exercised great influence over the people. This sect was composed of the higher classes of the people, and numbered amongst its members most of the doctors of the law, the priests, and the ancients, who were senators, composing the Sanhedrim or great council of the nation. These Pharisees declared against Jesus Christ. Jealous of His popularity, and wounded in their pride by the superiority of His doctrine; embittered by the freedom with which He condemned their errors and unveiled their hypocrisy,—they conceived a great aversion towards Him, which soon deepened into a mortal hatred.

Blinded by their hatred and by the perversity of their hearts, instead of recognising in Jesus the character of Messiah, which shone so clearly through all His works, they persisted in despising His poverty and decrying His virtues and miracles; and finally they seized upon His Person to deliver Him up to death.

Dragged before Caiphas, the high-priest and president of the Sanhedrim, and judicially interrogated by him as to whether He was really the Christ, Jesus declared that He was so. His enemies took His words as imposture and blasphemy, without examination, and condemned Him to death, delivering Him up to Pilate, the Roman governor, to suffer the torment of the cross.

Jesus was then put to death according to the custom of the Romans. After having been cruelly scourged, and submitted to other most painful and ignominious tortures, He was at last nailed to the cross, on which He expired about three o'clock on the afternoon of the Friday, which is supposed by some to have fallen on March 25 of the year 29, or, according to others, in the year 33 of our era, and the eighteenth year of the reign of Tiberius at Rome.

Towards evening of the same day He was laid in a new sepulchre hewn out of a rock; and because He had said publicly that He would rise again three days after His death, the princes of the Jews sealed the entrance to the tomb with the public seal, and caused it to be guarded by soldiers.

But on the third day, the Sunday morning, a little before daybreak, Jesus, in spite of His enemies, rose alive from His tomb, and showed Himself to His disciples, consoling and filling them with joy. He remained forty days among them, completing their instruction and delivering His Sacraments to them, and explaining to them the whole system of His Church, which they were chosen to establish in the world.

On the fortieth day after His resurrection He led them to the Mount of Olives; and there, after promising to send them the Holy Ghost, He raised His hands to bless them, and ascended into heaven in the sight of them all.

III. The Immortal Existence of Jesus Christ.

9. Though the immortal existence of Christ commences really from the moment of His resurrection, we shall take it from the time of His ascension, when He ceased to converse visibly with men.

· Christ, risen from the dead, and living an immortal life in heaven, does not, however, cease to be present on the earth.

Visible in heaven to all the blessed, and sitting in supreme glory at the right hand of the Father, He intercedes for us, and sends the Holy Ghost the Paraclete to

His Church, 'to abide with her for ever.' Such was the decree of God the Father. He wished that His only Son, after accomplishing the redemption of the world, should return to heaven and sit on His right hand, thence to govern the Church throughout all ages. David had so predicted in these words: 'The Lord said to my Lord, Sit Thou at My right hand, until I make Thine enemies Thy footstool' (Ps. cix.).

Jesus Christ, though invisible, is present on the earth (1) *corporally* in the Holy Eucharist; (2) *spiritually* in all His Church, which He assists continually by the Holy Ghost; (3) *morally*, in a representative manner, in the persons of His Vicars, the Roman Pontiffs, the bishops, and other ministers of His Church. In this way, whilst reigning in heaven, He still abides with His own on the earth to the end of the world. 'Behold, I am with you all days, even to the consummation of the world' (Matt. xxviii. 20).

When the end of the world comes, at the great day of universal resurrection, when the dead shall be risen and awaiting their Judge, He will come down from heaven visible, in the splendour of His majesty, and will sit on His throne of justice, to render to all men, sinners and the just, according to their works. The wicked He will condemn to everlasting torments, but to the good He will award the kingdom of heaven. Then, at the head of His elect, the King of Glory will make His entry into the celestial Jerusalem, the city of eternal life.

Second Article: Jesus Christ considered in His Person.

10. After having considered Christ historically as the Redeemer of men, it remains for us to study Him dogmatically—that is to say, with the eye of faith, and in the lessons of faith proposed to us regarding His Person, His mission, the worship which is due to Him, and the wonderful effects produced by Him on the human race.

In the first place, what does faith teach us about the Person of Jesus Christ or His personal constitution?

11. What is the Person of Jesus Christ? Who is this Christ whose history we have been contemplating? Is He a man, a sage, a saint? Is He an angel? Is He God?

He is not an angel. He is at once a God and a man. Jesus Christ is the *Word*, or *God the Son* become incarnate; the Second Person of the Blessed Trinity made man for us. Remaining God as He was from all eternity, the divine Word became also man by means of His birth in time.

12. His birth was miraculous: conceived by the power of the Holy Ghost. He was born of the Virgin Mary, who became His Mother without losing her virginity. She is both Virgin and Mother. In the womb of this Virgin, God the Son took our human nature, by uniting it in His person to the divine nature. In a manner like the son of a king, who over his princely robes wears the dress and badge of slavery, the divine Word clothed Himself with our humanity, which He made His own substance, His second nature.

13. We distinguish three constituent parts in the Person of Jesus Christ, namely, the divine nature, the human nature, and the personality of the Word, which unites the two natures. In other words, Jesus Christ, the Incarnate Word, unites in His one divine personality two natures—that of man and that of God, the divine nature and the human nature. Hence the ordinary mode of expression: in Jesus Christ there are two natures and one only Person, which is divine, namely, the Second Person of the Blessed Trinity.

To understand this doctrine better, we will glance at the contrary heresies, and then consider separately (1) the divinity, (2) the humanity, (3) the union of the two natures, (4) the consequences of this union.

14. As our faith concerning the Person of Jesus

Christ is the basis of the Catholic religion, it has, as a matter of course, been the principal point of attack for the followers of Satan. A crowd of heretics, instigated by the Father of Lies, have risen up against the dogma of the Incarnation, and have attacked each point in turn. The *Arians* denied the divine nature of the Word, and consequently the divinity of Jesus Christ; the *Docetes*, His human nature; the *Nestorians*, the unity of His Person; the *Eutychians*, the distinction of His two natures; the *Monothelites* said there was only one will in Christ; and the *Adoptians* called Christ the *adopted Son*, and not the *only Son*, of God.

15. Denying all these errors, the Catholic Church believes and confesses that in Jesus Christ there are two natures, the divine and the human—distinct from each other, and united together in the single Person of the Word made Flesh.

(1) All the plenitude of the Divinity, says St. Paul, dwells corporally in Jesus Christ (Coloss. ii. 9). Jesus, who appears so poor, is the true God. He is God the Son, equal in everything to His Father. He is the eternal and all-powerful God, the Creator of the world. He is the supreme wisdom, power, goodness, and beauty, and all that is said of God applies also to Him.

The *Divinity* of Jesus Christ is proved (1) by the doctrine of the Church, which has already been shown to be infallible. (2) By the teaching of the Apostles, who preached the following fundamental dogma most clearly: 'The Word was God,' writes St. John; 'the world was made by Him;' 'the Word was made flesh and dwelt amongst us;' 'Jesus, of whom John the Baptist gave testimony' (John i.). (3) By the doctrine of Jesus Christ Himself: 'My Father and I are one; the Father is in Me, and I am in the Father' (John xiv.). 'All power is given to Me in heaven and on earth' (Matt. xxviii.). 'As the Father raises the dead and gives them life, so the Son gives life to whomsoever He pleases' (John v.).

THE INCARNATION.

(2) *Humanity.*—Considered in His human nature, Jesus Christ is truly man, having a body and soul like ours.

His Body, by reason of His free and entire acceptance of our humanity, was, during His mortal life, like ours, subject to sufferings, hunger, cold, and fatigue; to wounds and to death, but not to disease or concupiscence. It possessed no glory, no splendour, nor did a ray of His hidden light pierce through the veil of His Humanity. Once only—at the time of His Transfiguration—the Saviour manifested, as it were, a reflection of it to His disciples, so as to give them some idea of the celestial glory which He promised to the just. After His resurrection His Body became glorious, possessing four heavenly qualities, namely, incorruptibility, subtility, agility, and light, or the beauty of glory.

The Soul of the Son of God, endowed like ours with intelligence and free-will, was susceptible of joy, sorrow, and sadness; but not subject to ignorance, nor to sin. From the first moment of its existence it possessed the perfect use of all its faculties, enriched as it was with all the treasures of wisdom and science, grace and holiness, and, in a word, with all the plenitude of the gifts of the Holy Ghost.

In His mortal life our Saviour always saw God; but He did not taste that joy and glory the intuitive vision produces in the souls of the blessed. It was His will to be deprived of these effects of the beatific vision until the moment of His sacred death upon the cross, when, the work of our redemption being accomplished, His Soul, liberated from His Body as from a darksome prison, became filled with glory and beatitude. In this blessed state He descended into hell—that is to say, into limbo, where the souls of the just of the old law were detained —and there showed Himself in all His splendour and divine beauty. For the Son of God, in showing to the patriarchs His glorious Soul, manifested also to them

His divinity, and gave them in His Person the joys of the beatific vision, thus changing the place of their exile into paradise, as He had promised to the good thief in these words: 'This day thou shalt be with Me in paradise.'

On the third day the glorious Soul of our Saviour reunited itself to His Body, which was lying in the sepulchre, and reanimated it, but with an altogether new life, communicating to it all His glory and His blessed qualities.

(3) *The union of the two natures.*—The human and divine natures are united together in the personality or the Person of the Word, which is called in Greek *hypostasis*, whence we have the expression *hypostatic union*, or personal union. The Person is the point or link that unites the two natures. United to the Person of the Word, the humanity became His own nature in time, as the divinity was essentially His own nature from all eternity.

Thus the Person of the Word, possessing both divinity and humanity, is at once both God and Man; and this God-Man is but one Jesus Christ, in the same way as the soul and the body constitute one man in us.

The hypostatic union is so intimate and indissoluble that death itself could not break it. The Person of the Word remained united to the sacred Body in the tomb, and to the sacred Soul in limbo.

(4) *Consequences of the hypostatic union.*—These consequences are the *theandric actions* of Jesus Christ —the double filiation, the dignity, the excellence, and all the graces and treasures of His Person.

Jesus Christ, the Man-God, having two natures, acted sometimes by one, sometimes by the other, and sometimes by both natures combined, according to the works He performed. For instance, when He ate or slept He acted by His human nature, for these were human actions; when He pardoned sinners He performed a divine act. The act of healing the sick was in part divine, in part human: the touching was a human act, the curing was a divine act.

As the Person of Jesus Christ comprises two natures, both really His own, all the actions produced and the properties possessed by both may be truly attributed to Him. In considering the Person of Christ, we may say of Him He is God and He is Man; He is mortal and He is immortal. In Him a God is Man, and a Man is God; in Him a God suffers, a God dies for men.

Jesus Christ has moreover a double filiation: a divine filiation, as born of the Father, and a human filiation, as born of the Virgin Mary. Therefore we must say of Him, Jesus Christ is the true Son of God, and at the same time the true Son of the Virgin Mary; and reciprocally Mary is truly the Mother of God, since Jesus, her Son, is true God, and one with the Father. We confess this in the Creed: 'I believe in Jesus Christ His only Son, born of the Virgin Mary.'

The further consequences of the hypostatic union are:

(1) The Person of Jesus Christ possesses an *infinite dignity*, because it is divine.

(2) All that Jesus Christ does, all that He possesses, whether as God or as Man, must be attributed to God the Son; for it is always God the Son who acts and who possesses. Thus His words, His sufferings, His Blood, are the words and sufferings and Blood of the Son of God; consequently *all these things are divine.*

(3) All the actions of Jesus Christ are infinite in dignity, because they are the actions of a God; they are divine actions, and therefore they are *of infinite value* and *of infinite merit.*

(4) All the actions of Jesus Christ are infinitely holy, because, being the actions of a God, they are incapable

of being tainted by the slightest shadow of sin. This is what is meant by the *impeccability* of Jesus Christ.

(5) All things belonging to Jesus Christ, even in His human nature, as His Flesh and Blood, are of an infinite dignity, are divine, and, as such, *adorable*, for the Flesh and the Blood are those of a God.

(6) Jesus Christ, being the only Son of God, *was infinitely acceptable to His Heavenly Father.*

(7) He was filled in His humanity with all the gifts of God—that is to say, *with the plenitule of grace and of knowledge*—the plenitude, as St. John says, from which we should all draw.

Third Article: The Work of Jesus Christ.

16. The work of Jesus Christ, the great work which He had to accomplish on earth, was the Redemption—the restoration of humanity fallen by sin, or its reconciliation with God, offended by sin. He had therefore entirely to destroy sin and its effects, to deliver prevaricating man from the evils that weighed upon him, and to restore to him all the blessings that he had lost.

This was a work of mediation between sinful man and the God offended by his sins. Christ is called therefore the Mediator, or the representative of humanity, interposing between us and God in order to reconcile us to God.

17. In order fully to accomplish the work of our redemption, Christ had to pay the price to God, and to apply to each one of us the benefit. He had on the one hand to offer a worthy sacrifice to God, and on the other to teach men the true doctrine, and bring them under obedience to His Father in one kingdom—*the kingdom of God.* Hence the reason why Jesus Christ had the triple character of Priest, Prophet, and King. He was Priest in order to offer a sacrifice; Prophet so that He might instruct; and King that He might found and govern the kingdom of God, which is the Church. These

three characters are expressed by the name *Christ*, which signifies *anointed;* because the Son of God, sent by His Father, had received from Him the mission and the divine *anointing* of Priest, Prophet, and King. We have only to speak of the Sacrifice.

18. He offered it on the altar of the cross, where He was both Priest and Victim, immolating Himself to His Heavenly Father for the salvation of the world.

His sacrifice was of an infinite price by reason of the infinite dignity of the Offerer and of the Victim. It was satisfactory, and at the same time meritorious, containing infinite satisfaction and infinite merit. It sufficed therefore, on the one hand, to expiate all sins, and on the other to merit all those privileges of grace and of glory which man had lost.

As all the actions of Christ were of infinite value in the eyes of God, He could, by a single tear, or by one drop of His Blood, have saved us all; but God the Father willed that our redemption should be effected by the death of the cross; and therefore all the other actions of Jesus Christ contributed only to the great end, in conjunction with His death and the effusion of His precious Blood.

19. Jesus Christ, dying upon the cross, was the representative of guilty and fallen humanity. He had taken our place; He was, as the prophet says, charged with our iniquities, and laden with all our sins on His cross. He suffered the penalty of them in our stead, and satisfied for us the divine justice of an offended God.

20. He merited also, (1) *for Himself*, His glorious resurrection, the glory of His name, the adoration of the universe, though it was already due to Him as the Son of God; (2) *for us*, justification, eternal life, and all the gifts of grace that precede or follow justification.

In order that the satisfaction and the merits of our Redeemer may be applied to us, and that we may really obtain the pardon of the sins for which He has satisfied, and the eternal life which He has purchased for us, certain conditions must be complied with on our part. We must believe with all our heart, sincerely repent of our sins, practise good works, and partake in the sufferings of Jesus Christ.

Fourth Article : The Worship due to Jesus Christ.

21. Jesus Christ, being at once the great King and benefactor of the human race, has a right to our homage and our gratitude. Man is bound to worship Him as much on account of His Person as His benefits.

22. (1) On account of *His Person*, we owe Him the supreme worship of *latria* or adoration, as He is true God and the Second Person of the Blessed Trinity.

This adoration must be given to everything belonging to Him, because all in Him is divine and adorable. We must, therefore, not only adore His divinity, but His humanity also. His Flesh, because it is the Flesh of a God; His Blood, because it is the Blood of a God; His Heart, because it is the Heart of a God. A child honours his father's person in this manner when he kisses his hand, because it is the hand of his father.

23. (2) On account of *His benefits* the human race owes eternal gratitude to Jesus Christ. We show this gratitude (1) by honouring with a special worship the blessed Wounds and the sacred Heart of our Saviour; (2) by celebrating His glorious titles, which form a compendium of His greatness and His benefits. In worshipping the Wounds of Jesus Christ we adore His divine members, wounded for our salvation; in worshipping His sacred Heart we adore that divine Heart wounded by the spear, and still more so by His love for us. This act of adoration contains at the same time an act of gratitude: by the special worship rendered to the Wounds of our Lord and to His sacred Heart, we intend to thank Him for all the benefits which they represent.

24. As the names and titles of our Saviour bring

to mind the greatness and the mysteries of His Person, whether it be the sublime function He fulfilled, or His works and benefits, they comprise all the glory of Jesus Christ; and to recognise and celebrate these titles is to glorify and render Him thanks. The principal of these are:

(1) *Names which relate to His person and His nature.*—He is called God, Son of God, Son of Man, Man-God, Emmanuel, or God with us.

(2) *Names which relate to His properties.*—Our Saviour is called Lamb, because of His gentleness; Lion, because of His strength; Star, because of His light; Flower, because of His beauty; Branch and Root, because of His vital influence; Mountain, because of His elevation; Stone or Rock, because of His firmness; Door, because He opens heaven; Way, because He leads to heaven; Light, on account of His doctrine; Vine, because of His far-spreading and His fruitfulness; Spouse, on account of His love for the Church.

(3) *Names which relate to His office and His supreme functions.*—From this point of view the Man-God is called Messiah or Christ, Jesus, Mediator, Priest, Prophet, King, Saviour, Doctor and Master, Pontiff, Angel, Apostle, Lawgiver, Pastor, Supreme and Sovereign Lord, Judge of the living and the dead, Head of the Church, of angels, and of men.

This last title indicates that the Man-God is the head of the universal society formed by all reasonable creatures—angels and men, the only exception being the reprobate. These latter are totally separated from Him, though under the dominion of His justice and His power.

Jesus Christ is the head of creatures, as a king is the head of his people and a father of his family. He governs and influences them, as the head governs and influences the body and all its members. This intimate and vivifying influence consists especially in grace, of which Jesus Christ is the author and source: divine grace is diffused through Him into His mystical members, like sap in the vine, like life in an animated body. This divine influence of grace will form the subject of the following chapter.

Fifth Article : Effects produced by Jesus Christ on Man.

25. The mystery of the Incarnation has produced on man two great effects—an effect of glory and an effect of felicity.

The Son of God, by becoming the Son of Man and a member of the great human family, has raised man, His brother, to the highest degree of glory and happiness, to the glory and happiness of the *children of God.* The Man-God is the glory and happiness of man.

(1) *Glory of man.* — By appearing in the world Christ, like a divine star, has illuminated the whole of the human race, and has communicated to it the splendour of His divinity. 'The Son of God,' say the Fathers, 'became man, that man might become God;' that is to say, that man might participate in the sanctity and glory of God.

This glory belongs to the human race in general, and to each one of us in particular.

26. (1) It is the glory of the *human race* to have produced Christ, and to possess Him. When a member of a family especially distinguishes himself his glory is reflected upon his brethren, and the house that has produced a hero is rendered for ever illustrious by the name and deeds of this member. Now the great human family has produced a divine member; it counts a God among its children; we count a God among our brethren —namely, Christ—born like us of the race of Adam; truly our brother, our flesh and blood, but at the same time the only Son of God. O, what a parentage! What a brotherhood! What a glory for man!

The splendour of this glory is reflected on the very earth itself, the dwelling-place of man here below. If an obscure hamlet becomes famous by being the birthplace of a great man, how great must have been the glory shed over our earth, on which Christ was born! The earth has produced not a great man, but a Man-God; and this divine fruit constitutes its greatest glory. *Terra dedit fructum suum.* The earth has been sanctified and glorified by the dwelling thereon of the Man-God, and the traces of His divine footsteps.

The earth, therefore, and human nature shine in the sight of God the Father with all the splendour of His only Son. This only Son, the object of His divine complacency, has united Himself to the human family by the most intimate union : as the Scripture expresses it, He has espoused human nature. For this reason the Heavenly Father no longer looks upon our earth and our race except as in their union with His Son. In His sight the earth is the cherished abode of His Son; and He regards mankind as a multitude of brethren united to their elder Brother, who is no other than that beloved Son in whom He is well pleased: *Ut sit ipse primogenitus in multis fratribus* (Rom. viii. 29).

(2) Men, considered individually, are raised to the highest possible dignity, to the dignity of the children of God. 'The Word was made flesh,' says St. John, and He has given to men, His brethren, 'the power to be made the children of God.' And again, in his first Epistle (iii. 1), he says: 'Behold what manner of charity the Father hath bestowed upon us, that we should be called and should be the sons of God.'

This is the mystery of divine adoption. The only Son of God having become Son of Man and our Brother, His Heavenly Father has in consequence adopted us for children.

This adoption, merited for us by our Saviour on the Cross, takes place at baptism, which for that reason is called the Sacrament of Regeneration. In it we are born again spiritually as the adopted children of God. In baptism we are begotten of God according to the Spirit, as we had been begotten of the old Adam according to the flesh.

Regeneration by water and the Holy Ghost produces a twofold effect on those who are spiritually born anew: it imprints on their souls the image of God the Father, as also a resemblance to Jesus Christ their Brother; and it also bestows on them a right to the heavenly inheritance. This image of God and resemblance to Jesus Christ consists in the baptismal character and sanctifying grace, which St. Peter calls a participation in the divine nature.

This grace, light, beauty—this spiritual life—contains the germs of every virtue. It is altogether interior and hidden in the soul, as seed is in the earth. 'Dearly beloved,' again writes the beloved disciple, 'we are now the sons of God, and it hath not yet appeared what we shall be.' We shall one day partake of His glory and beauty; but now all is hidden beneath the dark veil of our mortality.

Externally Jesus Christ was poor and like other men; within Him there dwelt all the majesty of a God. He 'dwelt amongst us,' says the Evangelist, 'and we saw His glory, the glory of the only begotten of the Father.'

After the same manner should a Christian, the brother of Jesus Christ and adopted son of God, make manifest his nobility of birth to the eyes of the world. His conduct, his works, and his virtues ought to be those of a child of God, and a copy of the conduct, works, and virtues of Christ, the only Son of God.

To the character of child of God is attached the right of inheritance. 'As the adopted sons of God,' says St. Paul, 'we are heirs of God,' our Father, 'and co-heirs with Jesus Christ,' our brother. Whosoever shall conduct himself as a worthy son of God will enter into possession of his inheritance. He will receive a portion of it even in this life, and will enjoy it in its plenitude in the next.

This inheritance constitutes the happiness that Christ has communicated to mankind.

27. (2) *Happiness of man.*—Christ is our happiness by His *person* and by His *possessions*. We are happy because we possess Him Himself, and because we share all His riches.

28. (a) *Possession of Jesus Christ.*—Christ, the divine Emmanuel, belongs to us, and we possess Him.

(1) He belongs to us, because He has been given to us. Christ is a gift bestowed on man, an ineffable gift of divine love: 'God so loved the world as to bestow His only Son upon it.'

He belongs to us by birth, as a child born in a family belongs to that family, and is bound to his brothers by indissoluble ties. He is, moreover, to us what a father is to his children, a king to his subjects, a friend to his friends, a husband to his wife, what a guide, a protector is to him whom he has undertaken to guide and protect.

(2) We possess Christ. We possess Him everywhere and in every way. We possess Him in heaven, where He is our advocate with the Father. We possess Him on earth in the person of His Vicar the Roman Pontiff; in the person of His bishops, of His priests; in the person of the poor and of every individual member of the Church, which is His mystical body. We possess Him in His divine nature, by which He is present everywhere as God. We possess Him in His human nature, with which He dwells in the midst of us as man, in the adorable Eucharist. O, what a presence is that! His delight is to be with the children of men, His well-beloved brothers. O, what a happiness for us in this valley of tears to possess such a Father, such a Friend, such a Protector, such a Consoler! With Him our

M

hearts know neither sadness nor fear; and we can say with the prophet-king, 'If I should walk in the midst of the shadows of death, I will fear no evil, for Thou art with me' (Ps. xxii.).

29. (b) *Participation in the riches of Jesus Christ.*—Jesus Christ recognises us as His brothers and co-heirs, and communicates to us all the goods that constitute His inheritance, (1) during life; (2) at the moment of death; and (3) at the day of the future resurrection.

(1) *During life* He bestows on us the riches of grace: His holy word, which is the light of our souls; His divine Sacraments, which are their nourishment; and the hierarchy of His Church for their safeguard and direction. These exercise the most important influence over the happiness of man, even in the natural order: for whenever Christianity is allowed free action, it promotes real individual, family, and social happiness. Nevertheless, great as are these various effects of grace, they do not alter the condition of our fallen nature, and we still remain subject to the miseries of this mortal life.

(2) *The moment of death* is that of the beginning of glory; the soul of the just man, disengaged from its bonds, is freed from the darkness of its earthly prison-house, and enters into eternal life. There it is transformed in glory, and appears as a bride of exquisite beauty in the presence of the Eternal Bridegroom.

'When the veil shall be withdrawn,' says St. John, 'and the Lord shall show us His face, we shall be like unto Him, for we shall see Him as He is.' In this manner the soul will participate in the good things with which the glorious soul of Jesus Christ is endowed; and the human body will also participate in the good things bestowed on His glorious body.

(3) *At the great day of Resurrection* our blessed souls will receive this fulness of beatitude when they are again united to their glorified bodies. Then will the

grand promise of Christ be fulfilled: 'I am the resurrection and the life. Whosoever believeth in Me shall live. I will raise him up at the last day.... Then shall the just shine as stars in the kingdom of their Heavenly Father.' Then will the children of God appear, in all the beauty, both spiritual and corporal, of their divine origin. Then will all that remained in them of the old Adam be effaced; the corruptible shall put on incorruptibility, and the mortal body shall put on immortality; death shall be totally absorbed by life: *Ut absorbeatur quod mortale est a vita* (2 Cor. v. 4).

Then will the Son of God, who made Himself poor and preached poverty in order to enrich us, load us with true riches, and clothe us with His own glory; He will give to our now abject bodies so new an appearance, that they will become like to His own glorious body: *Qui reformabit corpus humilitatis nostræ, configuratum corpori claritatis suæ* (Phil. iii. 21).

Then all the elect will shine like innumerable stars, each with his own splendour; and at their head will shine Jesus Christ, the King of Glory, who will introduce them into the kingdom of His Father, to put them in possession of all His treasures, all His glory, all His joys and never-ending delights. This will be the perfect felicity of man glorified by Christ.

CHAPTER VI.
GRACE.
First Article: General Remarks on Grace.

1. GRACE is the fruit of the Passion of Jesus Christ. He has merited it for us by His precious Blood; and it may be said to flow from His sacred Wounds as from so many inexhaustible fountains.

2. It is a gift that comes from God, the sole Author of grace, and is specially attributed to the Holy Ghost, who is called the Dispenser of graces and of all good gifts.

3. By grace, man fallen by sin is raised again; he recovers all that sin had deprived him of, and is reëstablished in the supernatural order.

4. The supernatural order comprises two things, viz. a *supernatural end* and the *right means* of attaining that end.

(1) The *supernatural end* of man is beatitude or heavenly glory, which consists in the Beatific Vision of God in heaven. This end is called *supernatural*, because it is above human nature and all created nature. Man, by his nature, has no more right to aspire to so sublime a destiny than a slave born in a hut has to claim the privileges of the sons of a king in their father's palace.

Having a nature made for earth, man has no right to occupy any other abode than that of earth, there to praise and serve his Creator; but God, by an ineffable mercy, drawing him from his low condition, calls him to dwell with the pure spirits in heaven, in order that he may there, as a child of adoption, enjoy the plenitude of all the riches of His house.

(2) This is the supernatural end; the *means* of it must also be *supernatural*, and this means is *grace;* by grace man becomes worthy of glory.

We must understand that, to be admitted to supernatural glory, man must put on a supernatural form—that is to say, a new form, and, so to speak, a new nature: 'He must put off the old man,' as the Apostle says, ' and put on the new.' Just as a poor man, called to dwell with a king in his palace, would be required to change his garments and his manners, the human creature, called by the divine bounty to share His heavenly dwelling-place, must undergo a transformation which changes him into a heavenly creature, worthy of the abode of holiness and the presence of God.

This transformation must be complete, and renovate the whole man—his soul, his body, and his works. His soul, his body, and his works must all become ennobled; must pass from darkness to light, and shine with a divine beauty which is the participation in the splendour of God Himself.

Now all these effects of renovation, of transformation, are worked in man by grace. Grace elevates, purifies, and perfects him; it causes him to become altogether heavenly and fit to enjoy the glory of heaven. Grace is the means that prepares for glory, that conducts to glory; it may even be said that it produces glory, as a seed produces its flower; hence the well-known expression, *Grace is the seed of glory.*

But the question here arises, What is this wonderful agent called *grace?* What idea are we to form of it in accordance with the teachings of the Catholic faith?

5. Grace, in general, is a supernatural and gratuitous gift granted by God, through the merits of Christ, to His reasonable creatures for their eternal salvation.

6. We distinguish *exterior graces* from *interior graces.* The former are the gifts of God existing externally to ourselves, as the Incarnation, the doctrine of Jesus Christ, sermons, spiritual books, good example; the latter are the spiritual gifts which God bestows interiorly on our souls, as faith, hope, charity, &c. It is of interior grace we are about to treat.

7. With regard to the nature of grace, we may say in general that it is a spiritual principle, which is, in the world of souls, what light, heat, sap, and life are in the world of bodies and visible nature. As the hidden life in a seed is the principle of its development and the fruits it will produce, as the life diffused through the members of an animated body is the principle of its

beauty and fecundity, so grace, spread throughout the body of the Church and in its members—that is to say, in our souls—is the invisible principle of their activity, vitality, and spiritual beauty.

8. To understand this doctrine clearly, we must distinguish: (1) actual grace; (2) habitual or sanctifying grace; (3) merit. The first prepares the way for sanctifying grace, or contributes to its increase; sanctifying grace is properly the supernatural life of the soul; merit is the fruit of grace as well sanctifying as actual.

Second Article : Actual Grace.

9. Regarding actual grace five questions may be put: (1) What is meant by actual grace? (2) How far is it necessary? (3) What effects does it produce? (4) How is it distributed? (5) How may we obtain it?

(1) *Actual grace.*—We mean by actual grace an interior *supernatural help*, which the Holy Ghost gives us to accomplish the works of salvation. Widely differing from exterior graces, such as sermons and other means of salvation that fall under the senses, actual grace is purely interior, spiritual, and invisible: it is like a ray from the Holy Spirit, penetrating the soul and affecting it in all its faculties.

The principal effects produced by it in the soul are these four: (1) it enlightens the understanding; (2) it inflames the will; (3) it increases the strength of the soul; (4) it raises our actions to a superhuman dignity. Because of these effects it is called, sometimes the *light* of the Holy Ghost, sometimes *inspiration* or *unction*, or, again, *virtue* from on high, or divine *assistance* which fortifies and elevates the soul.

Grace shines as light on the understanding, showing it the truth, the duty to be fulfilled, the good to be done; as unction it causes good to be appreciated; as help and strength it aids in the doing of good; as elevating power it ennobles the action of the creature, and invests it with the lustre of a divine action, worthy to be regarded by God. A writer having only common ink can only write in ordinary characters; but give him liquid gold and the writing he produces will shine with the brilliancy of gold. In like manner it is that man, provided with the grace of the Holy Spirit, and corresponding with that grace, produces works that are of heavenly value and brilliancy.

(2) *Necessity of actual grace.*—The interior grace of the Holy Ghost is absolutely necessary to man to enable him to perform the works of salvation; without the interior help of grace he is incapable of doing anything good for heaven, or of taking a single step in the way of salvation. If a bird cannot soar into the air without wings, still less can man ascend to the ineffable heights of salvation—in other words, to God Himself—without grace.

Although by the simple powers of nature man, fallen by sin, is still capable of distinguishing good from evil, and of leading a good life in conformity with the dictates of the natural law within certain limits, he nevertheless requires the help of God to know that natural law, to observe all its precepts, and to overcome all the temptations that incline him to violate it.

All men have need of grace: sinners that they may rise from their sins, and the just that they may persevere in good.

Final perseverance is a grace apart, a grace of especial value and necessity; but God does not refuse it to those who humbly pray for it.

3. *Efficacy of grace.*—The grace of God is all-powerful. Without it, and left to ourselves, we are weakness itself; but by its help we can do all things. 'I can do all things,' says St. Paul, 'in Him who strengthens me' (Phil. iv. 13). Without the hand of God, who sustains him by grace, man is like a tottering child, that can neither walk nor stand without the help

of its mother's hand. And on the other side, with the help of this same grace, if they will only correspond with it, the greatest sinners can return to God, break the chains of their evil habits, tear themselves away from the occasions of sin, and regain the friendship of God by a sincere conversion. The just also, fortified by grace, triumph over all temptations, all persecutions, all obstacles in the way of good, and practise the eminent virtues we admire in the saints and martyrs.

Notwithstanding its power, grace leaves man perfectly free: he may, if he chooses, accept it and render it fruitful by his coöperation; or he may, if he chooses, reject it and render it sterile.

(4) *Distribution of grace.*—Grace is a *gift of God* perfectly *gratuitous* in itself, and so excellent, that no created being can merit it by his own works. But our Lord Jesus Christ has merited it for us by His Blood; and in consideration of His infinite merits, the divine mercy bestows on all men at least a sufficient degree of grace for their salvation: 'For God,' says the Apostle, 'will have all men to be saved, and to come to the knowledge of the truth' (Tim. ii. 4). The greatest sinners, even those most hardened in their guilt, receive graces, from time to time, to lead them back to God. At the same time it is true that God distributes this precious gift unequally, granting more grace to some, and less to others, according to the inscrutable designs of His wisdom and mercy.

The goodness of God prevents souls, gratuitously granting to all a first grace, by which they may produce good works and thus obtain further graces. Generally speaking, the first grace given is the grace to pray, in order to obtain more abundant help. It is like money given in alms to a poor hungry beggar; with this money he must buy the bread he wants to support him. We see by this the necessity of prayer, even independently of the precept given by our Lord.

(5) *Means of obtaining grace.*—The means by which to obtain further graces are prayer, the Sacraments, and good works of every kind. By employing these means we receive powerful helps to observe the commandments of God, to overcome all temptations and all obstacles. Therefore no man will be lost for want of grace, but purely through his own fault :* it is in the power of all to obtain graces from God, and to gain eternal life by coöperating with them.

Third Article : Sanctifying Grace.

10. The doctrine concerning sanctifying grace may be reduced to four questions : (1) What is sanctifying grace? (2) What are its effects? (3) How may it be acquired or lost? (4) By what signs can its presence be recognised in the soul?

(1) *Definition.*—Sanctifying grace is a supernatural gift which, dwelling in our souls, renders us just, holy, agreeable to God, and capable of meriting eternal life. This divine gift is a quality, an *abiding* influence divinely diffused in the soul, united to it and inherent to it as life is to the body that it animates. This grace renders man just and holy in the eyes of God, as his corporal life constitutes him a living being in the eyes of man.

Sanctifying grace, commonly designated in Scripture by the word *life*, is in reality the supernatural life of the soul ; a real life like that of the body, but invisible and latent like the life hidden in a seed. It is also called *light, seed, pledge, seal or mark of the Holy Spirit, unction, fountain, charity.*

Sanctifying grace is called charity, because it is inseparable from charity, as the sun is from its own light.

Other virtues besides charity always accompany

* See p. 119, no. 14.

sanctifying grace; for, together with it, the three theological virtues, the cardinal and other moral virtues, as well as the gifts of the Holy Ghost, are all diffused in the soul.

(2) *Effects of sanctifying grace.*—(1) It makes us innocent by effacing sin from our souls. Grace casts out sin, as light dispels darkness, as a resurrection to life chases away death. (2) It renders us just, holy, and the friends of God. The soul adorned by grace is beloved by God with an ineffable love; the Blessed Trinity takes possession of it and dwells therein. (3) It makes us partakers of the divine nature, and as like unto God as the creature can be to the Creator here below. (4) It enables us to bring forth the works of heaven, works that merit eternal life. (5) It makes us become children of God by adoption, heirs of God and co-heirs with Jesus Christ.

(3) Sanctifying grace *may be acquired*, (1) by baptism and the other Sacraments received with due dispositions; (2) by an act of perfect charity.

It *is lost* by mortal sin. That grave violation of the law of God which we call mortal sin is like a deep wound that destroys the life of grace in the soul, and makes it appear in the eyes of God like a hideous corpse impressed with the likeness of the devil.

It *is preserved* by the faithful observance of the law of God, by the avoidance of mortal sin.

It is *augmented* and increased by prayer, the Sacraments, and all good works. It is capable of continual increase during this life: 'The path of the just, as a shining light, goeth forwards, and increaseth even to perfect day' (Prov. iv. 18).

(4) *By what signs can its presence be recognised in the soul?*—Sanctifying grace, being an entirely spiritual and invisible gift, a divine treasure concealed in man as in a vessel of clay, is not made evidently manifest, as life is in a living body, or as light in crystal. At the

same time, however, there are signs by which we may have a moral assurance of being in the grace of God, namely:

(1) If we love to think of God. 'Where thy treasure is, there is thy heart also' (St. Matt. vi. 21).

(2) If we have a love for the word of God, for His worship, and for holy things. 'He that is of God heareth the words of God' (John viii. 47).

(3) If we are faithful in observing the commandments of God. 'He that hath My commandments and keepeth them, he it is that loveth Me' (John xiv. 21).

(4) If we have a sincere love for our neighbour, and practise the works of mercy towards the poor. 'By this shall all men know that you are My disciples, if you have love one for another' (John xiii. 35).

(5) If we have zeal for souls, and an esteem and appreciation of spiritual and imperishable things, and if we love whatever relates to God and to eternal life. 'If you be risen with Christ, seek the things that are above, not the things that are upon the earth' (Coloss. iii. 1, 2).

(6) If we venerate the Church and her ministers in the spirit of faith and love. 'I am the Good Shepherd; and I know Mine, and Mine know Me' (John x. 14).

(7) Lastly, if we have within ourselves the testimony of a good conscience. 'If our heart do not reprehend us, we have confidence towards God' (1 John iii. 21).

'For the Spirit Himself giveth testimony to our spirit, that we are the sons of God' (Rom. viii. 16).

Fourth Article: Merit.

11. Merit is the fruit of grace, in this sense, that grace renders us capable of producing works that are meritorious in the sight of God. Man, when in the state of grace, according to the words of our Lord, is like a branch of the vine-tree united to the vine itself. This branch bears abundant fruit, because it draws its

life-giving sap, which is the principle of its productiveness, from the parent stem. Grace is this spiritual sap, the principle of merit.

12. (1) What is meant by merit? (2) What is the object of merit? (3) What conditions are required for gaining merit?

(1) What we here mean by a meritorious work is a good work done by the help of grace, with reference to God, and worthy in His eyes of an eternal reward.

There is a distinction to be made between the merit of *right, de condigno*, and the merit of *fitness, de congruo*. The former signifies a strict right to reward; the latter, a certain suitableness worthy of consideration, but not a claim of strict justice. It might be designated *merit of mercy*, because it is founded chiefly on the mercy of God.

We distinguish also the merit of the *just* man, who is in the state of grace, and that of the *sinner*, who is in the state of mortal sin. The former can merit in strict justice, as a servant working for his master merits; the latter can only merit as being a suitable object for the exercise of God's mercy, in the same way as a poor man humbly begging alms may deserve to receive them.

(2) The just man, by his works, merits an increase of sanctifying grace, and at the same time an increase of glory for eternity. These two rewards are linked together: every degree of grace in this life has a corresponding degree of glory for the next.

The *sinner*, by his prayers, penances, and good works, can merit the grace to break away from sin and return to God by a sincere conversion.

All can merit from the divine mercy actual grace, and all the helps necessary to avoid sin, to advance in good, and to persevere to the blessed consummation of a happy death.

Besides merit, properly so called, of which we have spoken, there are *satisfaction* and *impetration*, which often accompany merit or the meritorious value in the one work. *Satisfaction* is a penal work, which God accepts in place of heavier penalties due to sin. *Impetration* is the constraining power of prayer before God; a most mighty power, because of the promise of Jesus Christ, saying to all, 'Ask, and you shall receive.'

(3) For all merit there must be the help of actual grace; but this condition, which depends on God, is never wanting. For this reason we only speak here of the conditions on the part of man.

Now, (1) for the *merit of fitness*, it is sufficient to do any good work *with an intention of faith*—that is, with reference to God and our own salvation.

(2) For merit, properly so called, or the *merit of right*—that is to say, in order to merit an increase of grace and of eternal glory—we must be in the state of grace, and offer our good works to God with a holy intention.

A work so offered, be it only a draught of water given to a poor man, is accepted by God as if bestowed on Himself, and receives a divine reward.

The greatness of merit depends (1) on the person or on the dignity and holiness of him who acts. Thus the merit of Jesus Christ is infinite, because the dignity of His person is infinite. The merit of the just man is beyond comparison greater than that of the sinner, because he is adorned with sanctifying grace, which gives him the dignity of the child and friend of God.

(2) It depends on the excellence or the difficulty of the work. Thus a large alms is more meritorious than a small one given by the same person; but the widow's mite is of more value in the sight of our Lord than gold offered by the rich. So, again, an act of charity is more meritorious than an act of faith or hope.

(3) It depends on the perfection, the purity of intention, the fervour, and above all, on the charity of the

person who acts. Fervour and charity give such a value to good works that they change them, as it were, into gold and precious stones for the kingdom of heaven.

The time destined for merit is the present life, during which the sinner can merit* his salvation, and the just man can grow in merit, rising higher and higher in holiness and glory, according to that saying of our Saviour, 'Lay up to yourselves treasures in heaven.'

CHAPTER VII.

THE SACRAMENTS IN GENERAL.

1. GRACE, which we have just been considering, is the life of the Church—a divine life, flowing through the veins and diffused throughout all the members of the mystical body of Christ, and having its source in the Wounds and the opened Heart of our Redeemer. But it is necessary that there should be channels by which it must be conveyed from this divine source to our souls; and these mysterious channels are the Sacraments.

2. We will examine (1) what is the true idea of the Sacraments, and (2) their effects and their efficacy.

First Article: True Idea of the Sacraments.

3. The word *sacrament* signifies a *holy thing*, because the thing it designates is holy in itself and in its effects: it produces holiness in the soul.

4. A sacrament is defined as being *an outward sign of inward grace, instituted by Jesus Christ for the sanctification of souls.*

An *outward sign*—that is, a symbolic rite, such as

---

* There is question here of the merit of *fitness*. See p. 172.

an ablution or an anointing, which indicates and represents to the eyes an *inward grace*, which is the spiritual effect produced in the soul by this corporal sign.

A sign *instituted by Jesus Christ*. He alone has the power of attaching to any rite whatsoever the divine gift of grace.

The Son of God was pleased to adopt these material means (1) in order to offer a sensible object to the devotion of the faithful, and to raise them, by means of visible things, to things invisible; (2) in order to render the profession of the Christian religion public and solemn. He did not delegate the institution of the Sacraments to His Church; He instituted them Himself, and bequeathed them to the Church as substantial rites, of which she was to be the depositary, the guardian, and dispenser, with power to surround them with ceremonies, but in no way to change them in their substance.

A sign instituted *to sanctify our souls*, or, what is the same thing, *to confer grace upon us*—this is the end and effect of the Sacraments. They give, they confer grace—habitual grace and actual grace, which are necessary to the faithful individually, and to the whole body of the Church.

They *confer* grace and produce it in the soul; and this is what distinguishes them from simple benedictions, prayers, and other religious ceremonies. All these things can obtain grace by way of supplication, or merit it by way of good works; but they do not confer it, producing it by their own intrinsic power.

5. This productive virtue of grace also distinguishes our Sacraments from the religious rites of the Old Law—such as circumcision and legal ablutions, which also are called *sacraments*. These sacraments, incorrectly so termed, did not bestow grace; but they prefigured it for the future: they were figurative, not vivifying, signs. They nevertheless obtained justification as being good works, in virtue of the faith and devotion of those who

practised them. They were the shadows of the Sacraments of the New Law.

Jesus Christ instituted as Sacraments Baptism, Confirmation, the Holy Eucharist, Penance, Extreme Unction, Holy Orders, and Matrimony.

6. These seven Sacraments seem to have been indicated in the Old Law, (1) by the golden candlestick, shown in a vision to the prophet Zachary, which was surmounted by seven lamps, fed with oil from seven channels. And the seven Sacraments are in fact like seven channels through which the oil of grace is incessantly flowing. (2) By the seven pillars, of which the Holy Spirit speaks when He tells us that Wisdom built herself a house, and made seven pillars to support it. The seven Sacraments answer to them; for they are as it were the pillars of the Church, on which the whole structure of her public worship is brought to bear. This is why we say with reason that the Sacraments form the basis of Christian worship.

7. It is not difficult to discern the most profound wisdom in the number and choice of the Sacraments. The five first concern private or individual good, the two last the public good of the Church. The seven contain what is necessary and sufficient for the life, preservation, and spiritual prosperity as well of the whole body of the Church as of each individual member composing it.

To understand this, we may remark that the spiritual order resembles the order of nature, and follows a course analogous to it. Thus in the natural order man must be born, grow strong, and be nourished. If he falls sick, he needs medical treatment to escape death, and afterwards strengthening remedies to repair the injury caused by his sickness. Human society requires government to maintain it in order and prosperity; it requires also matrimony to perpetuate it.

In a similar manner, in the supernatural order, there is a birth, which is Baptism; the strength of manhood, which is Confirmation; nourishment, which is the Blessed Eucharist; a medicinal remedy against death, which is Penance; a balm for healing the wounds and destroying the remains of sin, which is Extreme Unction. Moreover there is an infallible principle of order and government, which is found in the Sacrament of Holy Orders; and, lastly, a holy propagation of the faithful, which belongs to the Sacrament of Matrimony.

8. The Sacraments differ from each other, (1) in point of dignity (one of them, namely, the Blessed Eucharist, is more august than any of the others); (2) in point of necessity; (3) as regards the dispositions required in those who receive them.

9. They are divided (1) into Sacraments of the *living* and Sacraments of the *dead*. The former can only be received by those who are *living*, with the life of grace; the latter can be received by those who are dead to grace —that is to say, by those who are in the state of mortal sin. (2) Into Sacraments *which imprint a character*, and which can be received only once; and Sacraments which *do not imprint a character*, and which may be received many times. (3) Into Sacraments *necessary as necessary means*, Sacraments *necessary by necessity of precept*, and Sacraments of *free choice*.

Second Article: Constituent Elements and Conditions, or Matter, Form, Ministration, and Subject of the Sacraments in general.

10. 'The Sacraments,' says Pope Eugenius IV., 'are perfected by the concurrence of three elements: the thing, which is the matter; the words, which are the form; and the person of the minister, who confers the Sacrament with the intention of doing what the Church does.' We may say, in other words, that three things are requisite for the existence or making up of a Sacrament—matter, form, and the minister who joins the matter and form together.

11. Rightly to understand this, we must observe that,

in the distinction of the three constituent elements, we liken the Sacraments to the compounds of nature, in which we distinguish matter, form, and the union of one with the other.

Thus in man there is a matter which is the body, a form which is the soul; and, besides, there is the union of the soul with the body—that vital and essential union which determines the existence of man. And it is by analogy that in the Sacrament, which is a moral compound, we likewise distinguish matter, form, and the union of both, effected by a lawful minister.

(1) *Matter.*—In a Sacrament, the matter is the thing or part which signifies grace in an indistinct manner. For example, the bread and wine in the Blessed Eucharist, the water in Baptism, or its being poured upon the head of the catechumen.

(2) *Form.*—The form consists in the sacramental words, or that part of the rite which signifies grace in a distinct manner. For example, in Baptism, 'I baptise thee in the name of the Father, and of the Son, and of the Holy Ghost.'

(3) *Union.*—The union of the form and the matter takes place through the act of the minister, who pronounces the words over the matter duly present.

12. The form united to the matter by a lawful minister properly constitutes the rite or sacramental sign instituted by Jesus Christ. For example, in Baptism, water poured over the head of the catechumen by the minister, who, at the same time, pronounces the sacramental formula, is the Sacrament regarded in its most simple state, in its strict essence. This form, matter, and minister are three elements chosen by the Son of God, and are unchangeable, and essential for the validity of the Sacrament. Any change or substantial defect in these points would render the Sacrament null, because it would no longer be the rite instituted by Jesus Christ.

Besides the substance and essence there are, in the Sacraments, accessory parts; these are the ceremonies, of which we shall treat later.

13. The minister of the Sacrament is the person authorised by Jesus Christ to accomplish or confer the Sacrament.

Each Sacrament has its proper minister, sometimes a bishop, sometimes a priest, or occasionally a layman.

The minister must have the intention of doing what the Church does—that is, of performing the rite used by the Church. So far as the validity of the Sacrament is concerned, this is the only condition required on the part of the minister; holiness, uprightness, and even faith itself are not necessary for the valid administration of the Sacraments.

It is without doubt true, that, being a holy thing, a Sacrament ought to be administered by one in the state of grace; for if in the state of mortal sin, the minister would incur the guilt of sacrilege by performing this function. Nevertheless this would not affect the validity of the Sacrament. It would remain the same; just as the royal seal will always impress the image of the king upon wax, whether the seal be of gold or baser metal; and as a key will open just the same, whether the hand that turns the lock be spotless or defiled.

14. As a seal requires wax to receive its impression, so do the Sacraments, in order to produce their effect, require a *subject*, a human person to receive them. Here the Blessed Eucharist is an exception; this Sacrament exists in itself, independently of the communion in which it is received by the faithful.

Third Article: Effects and Efficacy of the Sacraments—Ceremonies.

15. What are the effects of the Sacraments, and how do they produce these effects in the soul?

(1) *The effects* of the Sacraments are three in number: sanctifying grace, actual graces, and character.

16. (1) All the Sacraments confer sanctifying grace; some of them the first grace, others the second. We call the *first* sanctifying grace that which is given to souls still stained by mortal sin, because it changes their state from that of sin to that of holiness. We call that *second* sanctifying grace, or *augmentation of grace*, which further sanctifies souls already sanctified, and which is added to the grace they already possess, to increase their spiritual treasure. The Sacraments of the dead are instituted to produce the first sanctifying grace; those of the living to produce the second, or the increase of grace.

(2) All the Sacraments also bestow *actual graces* proper to the end of each; or rather, they give the right, founded on sanctifying grace, to receive actual graces corresponding to the end of the Sacrament that has been received, whenever we stand in need of them. Thus the actual graces of Baptism are the helps which the baptised person will need to enable him to preserve his baptismal innocence and lead a Christian life.

17. (3) Three of the Sacraments imprint on the soul a *character*, an indelible spiritual mark, which renders their second reception impossible. This character, says the Council of Trent, has two effects: by one of them we are rendered capable of receiving or doing certain things in the order of religion; the other serves to distinguish those who have received the Sacraments that imprint a character. These Sacraments are Baptism, Confirmation, and Holy Orders.

Baptism is a *spiritual birth*, in which is received the character, the distinctive mark of being a child of God by adoption, and a member of the great Christian family, with the right to participate in all the blessings which the Church communicates to her children.

Confirmation is *a putting on of spiritual armour;*

in it we receive a military character, the distinctive mark of the soldiers of Jesus Christ. This character gives strength to fight and suffer for the faith; it also renders the person confirmed more fit to receive the other Sacraments.

Holy Orders is a *spiritual consecration*, by which he who is ordained receives the sacerdotal character, the distinctive mark of the ministers of the Church. This character raises those who receive it above the ordinary faithful, as leaders are raised above the common soldiers, as shepherds above a flock; it bestows on them a resemblance to Jesus Christ, the great High-Priest or Pontiff by nature; associates them to His sacerdotal dignity, and to all the power that was given to him in heaven and on earth.

18. (2) *Efficacy of the Sacraments, or manner in which the Sacraments produce their effects.*—The Sacraments produce their effects by their own power, independently of the disposition of the minister, but dependently on those of the subject who receives them.

19. *Power and virtue proper to the Sacraments.*— They act by their own power, or, as we may say, they produce their effects by virtue of the *act done*, and not by virtue of him who does it. In other words, the Sacraments act in a necessary manner, as natural agents do; for instance, fire, water, and the like.

A Sacrament is not a mere prayer, the effect of which depends on the devotion of him who prays. It constitutes in the spiritual order a cause that bears analogy to causes in the natural order. Therefore it always produces its effect by whatever minister it may be conferred; as fire always consumes wood by whatever hand they are brought into contact; as a seal always leaves its impression on soft wax by whatever hand it be pressed upon it; as seed enriches cultivated land by whatever hand it be scattered there. So, whether the minister of the Sacrament be good or bad, whether he be a saint or an imitator of the perfidious apostle who betrayed his divine Master, the baptism he confers, the absolution he gives, the Mass which he celebrates, will always be equally valid. If he exercises his functions unworthily, woe indeed is his, but his alone; the Sacrament suffers not in the least, and its effect is not thereby diminished.

The reason of all this is that the visible minister is only the secondary minister, an instrument of Jesus Christ, who is the invisible and principal minister. He it is who baptises by the hand of the man, who confirms by the hand of the bishop, who consecrates, who absolves, by the mouth of the priest; it is Christ Himself, always holy, always full of grace and truth, who gives to the Sacrament its full efficacy.

20. (2) *Dispositions of the subject.*—But although on the part of the Sacrament the effect is infallible and necessary, on the part of the subject it depends on fitness and disposition.

As wax must be soft to receive an impression, wood dry to take fire, the land prepared to receive the seed, so must he who receives a Sacrament be duly prepared and disposed in order to obtain its effects.

21. There are two kinds of dispositions to be distinguished: those necessary for the validity of the Sacrament, and those for the fruit or production of grace. In the case of adults, the first are, (1) the intention; (2) the baptismal character, for the Sacraments that follow baptism. The second dispositions are not the same for all the Sacraments; we shall take them into account when treating of each Sacrament in particular.

22. As the dispositions of the subject can vary, and be either good or defective, so, consequently, the nature of the sacramental reception varies: it may be valid, null, fruitful, or informal.

The reception is *valid* when the subject (1) is capable of receiving the Sacrament, and (2) when he has the intention or *wish* to receive it. Thus all unbaptised persons who *wish* to be baptised always receive baptism validly.

The reception is *null* when the subject is not capable, or has not the intention of receiving the Sacrament. For instance, if an infidel were to be baptised against his will, or a child already validly baptised were to be rebaptised, the baptism would be null. He who receives absolution without repentance, or without a sincere confession, renders the Sacrament of Penance null. Not because he is incapable or lacks the intention, but because he subtracts from that Sacrament the matter proper to it, which is repentance and sincere accusation. The reception is *fruitful* when it is not only valid, but efficacious as well; that is, when it produces all its fruits in the soul. This is what takes place every time the subject (1) is capable of receiving the Sacrament, and intends to receive it; (2) and has all the dispositions required by the Sacrament he receives. Thus baptism is fruitful in an adult when, besides the wish to receive baptism, he has faith, sufficient instruction, and repents of his sins.

The reception is *informal* when it is valid but unfruitful. Thus an adult receiving baptism without faith or sorrow for his sins would be validly baptised, but would not receive sanctifying grace. In such a case, the baptismal character would be stamped upon the soul, but, like seed falling upon dry land, it could not produce its fruit of sanctification. The same is to be said of Confirmation and Holy Orders. These three Sacraments can *revive*—that is, they can produce the rest of their effects later on, if the obstacle is removed, and the subject puts himself into the required dispositions. According to the established opinion of the doctors, Extreme Unction and Matrimony are in this respect like the three Sacraments which imprint a character; those who have received them in mortal sin can afterwards receive their salutary effects by means of a sincere conversion.

Ceremonies are to the Sacraments what the gold or silver setting of a diamond is to the jewel incased in it.

They are sacred and symbolical ornaments with which the Sacraments are invested, (1) that they may be administered with greater dignity and respect; (2) that the faithful may better understand their effects and mysteries.

All the ceremonies prescribed are necessary from the necessity of precept, but not essentially necessary for their validity; a Sacrament would produce all its effects without them.

CHAPTER VIII.

BAPTISM.

First Article: Baptism considered in itself.

1. THE word *baptism* signifies *immersion*, and points to the manner of baptising most in use in the primitive Church, namely, by immersion.

We distinguish three kinds of baptism—the baptism of *blood* or martyrdom, the baptism of *desire*, and baptism by *water*, which last named is the Sacrament we are about to consider. Any one of these three baptisms will suffice to purify the soul from sin and to open the gates of heaven to it; but baptism by water alone is a Sacrament, and it alone imprints the baptismal character on the soul.

2. Baptism is the first and most necessary of the Sacraments, that which, by external ablution and the invocation of the Blessed Trinity, effects the spiritual regeneration of man, and cleanses him from all his sins.

It is called the *first* of the Sacraments, because no person can receive any of the others without having previously been baptised; the most *necessary*, because no man can enter the kingdom of heaven if he has not received baptism, even if deprived of it without any fault of his own. This necessity is called the *necessity as means*.

In the case of adults, baptism by water may be supplied for by the baptism of blood or of desire.

3. The matter of baptism is real and natural water, with which the *ablution* is performed by pouring it on the head of the baptised person. The baptism would be equally valid if the catechumen were sprinkled with, or entirely plunged in the baptismal waters, as in the primitive ages; this is called baptism by *aspersion* and by *immersion*.

The form or formula of baptism is the invocation of the Blessed Trinity, as follows: 'I baptise thee in the name of the Father, and of the Son, and of the Holy Ghost.' These words must be pronounced by the minister at the same time as the water is poured.

The minister of baptism is a priest consecrated for this office; but in case of necessity any layman or woman may baptise, even though a heretic or an infidel.*

4. The general effect of baptism is spiritual regeneration. Man is born a second time in this Sacrament and receives a new life, the life of the children of God; and for this reason baptism is also called the *Sacrament of Regeneration*.

The particular effects of baptism are three in number: (1) The remission of all sin, both original and actual, and also of all the punishments due to sin.

(2) The infusion of sanctifying grace, accompanied by the three theological virtues—faith, hope, and charity, as well as the other virtues and gifts of the Holy Ghost. (3) The impression of the character by which the baptised person becomes the adopted Son of God and His

---

* Baptism administered by infidels or heretics is valid; provided, as has been already said, they have the intention of doing what the Church does. It is true that heretics returning to Catholicism are often rebaptised, but the baptism is conditional only; because, generally speaking, it is doubtful whether the convert was baptised in his former sect with the conditions of matter and form necessary for validity.

heir, a member of Jesus Christ and of His holy Church. The character of child of God consists in resemblance to the only Son of God, our Lord Jesus Christ.

5. With regard to the total remission of punishment, it must be remarked that baptism does not remove the punishments of original sin *during this life*. It leaves the baptised person subject to death and to all the miseries consequent upon original sin, which miseries, after baptism, are called *penalties*. God wills that these miseries shall remain with us as a memorial of our fall, and that they shall serve us during this life as occasions of combat, merit, and triumph. By the virtue of baptism we shall be totally delivered from them on the day of the glorious resurrection.

6. All these effects are signified by the sacramental sign. The baptismal ablution, whether it be effected by infusion, aspersion, or immersion, indicates, (1) that the soul is interiorly cleansed from all its stains; (2) that the baptised person is born again and rises to a new life, like to that of Jesus Christ after His resurrection. The waters of baptism, into which the baptised are supposed to go down, and from which they emerge and reappear to light, represent a twofold grave and a twofold resurrection: (1) the tomb of our Lord Jesus Christ, who went down into it in the most pitiable state, and came out from it in a glorious state, rising again to an entirely new life; (2) the mystical grave of the old man, the man of sin, who disappears there to give place to the new man, formed to the likeness of Christ, rising from the blessed waters regenerated and adorned with graces and virtues. (3) The ablution indicates, moreover, that baptism gives the grace to lead a Christian life and to subdue the passions; for as water refreshes the body, so does the grace of baptism moderate the heat of concupiscence, and help the baptised to keep the rebellious flesh under submission to the spirit. (4) Lastly, the sacred rite indicates that the person baptised

becomes a child of God, and receives the character of divine adoption. For the baptismal regeneration is effected in the name of the Blessed Trinity, which shows that the Three Divine Persons—that is, God Himself, by the action of His minister—confer a new life on their creature, and stamp him with the august character of child by adoption.

7. It was fitting that this great Sacrament of the New Law should have been prefigured in the Old. Among the many types in which we recognise it are the Ark of Noah; the waters of the Red Sea, in which the Egyptians found their grave and the Israelites their salvation; the waters of the Jordan, into which Naaman was plunged, covered with leprosy, and from which he stepped forth with skin as pure and clean as that of a child; circumcision, which marked the Israelites with the sacred character of the children of Abraham. We may see in all these mysterious facts a foreshadowing of the salutary ablution of baptism and its effects on the soul.

But none of the above figures approach the reality so closely as did the baptism of St. John the Baptist. His baptism of penance was not the Sacrament of the New Law, but it was the most striking image of it, and above all when our Lord Jesus Himself was baptised. Then the heavens opened, the Holy Ghost descended in the form of a dove, and the voice of the Heavenly Father was heard proclaiming, 'This is My beloved Son, in whom I am well pleased.'

These facts represent in the most lively manner what takes place visibly and invisibly at the baptism instituted by Jesus Christ.

8. It was in receiving baptism at the hands of St. John that Jesus Christ preluded the institution of the baptism of the New Law. He then, say the Fathers, by contact with His divine flesh, communicated to the waters the virtue to sanctify our souls; and shortly after

that time He instituted His Sacrament. This at least is the opinion of the Doctors of the Church, founded on the Gospel, in which we see our Lord administering baptism by the hands of His disciples, whilst St. John the Baptist was yet living. It was not, however, till after His resurrection that the Saviour solemnly promulgated the law of baptism and extended it to the whole world. 'Go,' said He to His Apostles; 'teach ye all nations, baptising them in the name of the Father, and of the Son, and of the Holy Ghost. He that believeth and is baptised shall be saved; but he that believeth not shall be condemned' (Matthew and Mark, last chapters).

Second Article : Baptism considered in its Administration.

9. Two things relate to the administration of the Sacrament of Baptism: the subject to be baptised, and the manner in which the baptism must be conferred on him.

10. (1) *Subject.*—The subject of baptism is the adult or the child. The *adult* must bring with him certain dispositions, namely, the desire to receive baptism; faith, accompanied by proper instruction; repentance of his actual sins; and the resolution to lead a Christian life.

The *child* brings no obstacle to baptism, and on account of the necessity of this Sacrament the divine mercy dispenses him from any positive disposition of which he is incapable.

This necessity is so absolute, that children dying without baptism, though innocent of all actual sin, are excluded for ever from heaven, on account of the original stain which they bear upon their souls. Therefore our Lord has permitted them to be baptised as soon as they are born, and has given the utmost facility to the administration of so indispensable a Sacrament.

11. (2) *Administration.*—The administration of baptism may be either *simple* or *solemn.* The former takes place in cases of necessity; the latter in ordinary cases.

In *case of necessity* any person may baptise. It suffices for him to have the intention of giving the baptism according to the rite of the Church; to take natural water and pour it on the head or forehead of the child, whilst he pronounces the words, 'I baptise thee in the name of the Father, and of the Son, and of the Holy Ghost.'

In *ordinary cases* baptism must be administered solemnly—that is, by a priest in the church, with baptismal water, and with all the ceremonies prescribed by the Church.

12. The ceremonies observed in baptising are many and beautiful. Some precede, some accompany, and others follow the baptismal ablution. The chief of them are as follows:

(1) *Preliminary ceremonies.*—In the first place, the catechumen is stopped at the church-door, to signify that baptism is to open it for his admission. A saint's name is given to him, because he is about to be inscribed in the number of the saints and children of God. The priest breathes in his face, to signify that he will be purified from the unclean spirit by the virtue of the Holy Ghost, who comes to breathe a new life into him. He is signed with the sign of the cross on the forehead and breast, in order that, being made a Christian, he may carry the sign of his crucified Master with love and courage. Blessed salt is put into his mouth—the symbol of incorruptibility and wisdom—to teach him that he must preserve himself from the corruption of sin, and live according to the wisdom and faith of Jesus Christ. His ears and nostrils are touched with spittle, to point out to him that he must henceforward listen to the voice of God, and love the good odour of Christian piety.

(2) *Accompanying ceremonies.* — Having been admitted into the church and reached the font or place where he is to be baptised, the catechumen renounces Satan, and all his works, and all his pomps, and gives himself over to Jesus Christ, by asking for baptism.

He renounces *Satan*, namely, the service of the prince of darkness; *all his works*, namely, sin; and *all his pomps*, namely, the vanities of the world and the occasions of sin. These are the promises or *vows of baptism*. In baptism there is a kind of contract entered into between God and man. God grants to man all the advantages of His adopted children; and man, on his side, engages to live as a true Christian, according to the precepts of faith and the example of Jesus Christ. The godfathers and godmothers contract these engagements on behalf of the infants for whom they stand sponsors, they being unable to do it for themselves. And the sponsors thereby become guarantees for the promises of their godchildren, and are bound afterwards to watch over their Christian education.

The catechumen then makes his profession of faith by reciting the *Credo*. He is anointed with holy oil on the breast and shoulders (this oil is called the *oil of catechumens*), that he may be strong and valiant in the service of Christ, and lovingly bear the sweet yoke of his divine Master.

Next comes the sacramental ablution, which is given by pouring the blessed water over the head of the child in the form of a cross three separate times, to signify the death of our Lord and His resurrection on the third day.

(3) *Ceremonies which follow the ablution.*—Again the person baptised is anointed; but this time it is with *chrism* on the top of his head, which signifies that he has become a *Christian*—that is, the anointed of the Lord—and that he has received the invisible unction of the Holy Spirit, by which he is made partaker in the royal Priesthood of Jesus Christ. He is then clothed with a white garment, the symbol of baptismal innocence, which he is to preserve unstained till death, then to present it to Jesus Christ as he has received it in baptism. A lighted taper is put in his hand, to teach him that he must not only preserve faith, hope, and charity in his

heart, but that he must moreover openly profess these virtues, and practise them by his works. Finally, the priest dismisses him with these words, 'N., go in peace; and the Lord be with you.'

CHAPTER IX.

CONFIRMATION.

Nature, Effects, Administration.

1. CONFIRMATION takes the second place in the order of the Sacraments, because formerly it was the custom to administer it immediately after baptism, of which it is the completion. Baptism bestows spiritual life; Confirmation strengthens it. Baptism brings forth children of God; Confirmation gives them spiritual growth, and changes them into strong men and soldiers of Jesus Christ.

2. The precise time when Confirmation was instituted is a matter of uncertainty. According to some of the Doctors of the Church, it was at the Last Supper; and according to the more probable opinion of others, it was after the Resurrection—at the time when our Lord spoke of the kingdom of heaven, announced the coming of the Holy Ghost, and, as St. Leo says, established great Sacraments and revealed great mysteries.

3. Confirmation is defined as a Sacrament in which, by the imposition of hands, the unction of chrism, and sacred words, those who have been baptised receive the strength of the Holy Ghost steadfastly to confess the faith which they have received in baptism.

4. The matter of Confirmation is the *holy chrism*, which is a mixture of the oil of olives and balsam, blessed by the bishop. There are three kinds of holy oils of which use is made in different Sacraments, and which are blessed by the bishop on Maundy Thursday—the

oil of catechumens, the oil of the sick, and the holy chrism, the matter of the Sacrament of Confirmation.

The unction of chrism must be given by the hand of a bishop, the ordinary minister of the Sacrament of Confirmation. For this reason this Sacrament is sometimes called the *imposition of the episcopal hand*, the Sacrament of *Unction*.

The form consists in the words pronounced by the bishop, either while extending his hands over those who are to be confirmed, or whilst he is anointing them on the forehead. The words that accompany the anointing are: 'I sign thee with the sign of the cross, and I confirm thee with the chrism of salvation, in the name of the Father, and of the Son, and of the Holy Ghost;' or also those used in the Greek Church: 'I imprint on thee the mark of the gift of the Holy Ghost.'

5. The effects of Confirmation are, (1) The increase of sanctifying grace, of the Christian virtues, and of the seven gifts of the Holy Ghost, which, and especially the gift of strength, are communicated to those who are confirmed, in a more eminent degree than at baptism. (2) Actual grace, consisting in the strength which the Holy Ghost will give them, when needed, to be firm in the confession of the faith, in heart, word, and deed; to overcome human respect and temptations against the faith; to triumph over all the enemies of salvation, the world, the flesh, and the devil; to bear patiently all the trials they may have to endure on account of their faith. (3) The indelible character imprinted on the soul, which is more glorious and noble in the sight of God than all the insignia of earthly dignities.

6. In order to receive the plenitude of these fruits, the aspirant to Confirmation must know and desire them, and must purify his heart from all sin.

7. The precious effects of Confirmation are signified by the sacramental sign and the ceremonies. (1) The oil and anointing represent grace; for in the same manner

as oil feeds the flame, and gives strength to the athlete, so does the grace of the Holy Ghost nourish the light of faith and fortify the soldier of Jesus Christ. (3) The anointing is given in the form of a cross and upon the forehead, to signify that it confers strength never to be ashamed of the cross of Christ. (4) The bishop imposes his hands on the person confirmed, to show that the Holy Ghost comes down upon him and takes possession of his soul. (5) He gives him a slight slap, to let him understand that he must suffer all persecutions and all adversities for the name of Jesus Christ.

CHAPTER X.

THE BLESSED EUCHARIST CONSIDERED AS A SACRAMENT.

1. OF all the Sacraments instituted by our Lord the Blessed Eucharist is the holiest, the most august, and the most admirable. What the sun is in the world, what the heart is in man, the Blessed Eucharist is in the Church of Jesus Christ.

It is the resplendent and divine centre of Catholic worship to which all the other Sacraments refer. It is like the altar of a temple, to which all the other parts of the edifice are subordinate, and which is the point of attraction for all worshippers. So the Blessed Eucharist appears as the central mystery towards which all the religious ceremonies of the Church converge.

The Blessed Eucharist also contains the vital principle of Christianity. It is the soul which animates everything, which nourishes the life of faith and charity in our hearts. It is the soul of all our feasts, of all our offices, of all religious ceremonials.

It is called with reason the greatest, most wonderful, and most divine of all our mysteries: an abridgment of all the other mysteries of the Christian faith, according to these words: 'The Lord hath established a memorial of His wonderful works; He hath given food to them that fear Him' (Ps. cx.).

2. The mystery of the Eucharist has a twofold character. It is at once a Sacrament and a Sacrifice. It is a Sacrament when received by the faithful in the Holy Communion or exposed for their adoration, and a Sacrifice when offered to God in the Holy Mass. The Eucharist as a Sacrifice will be the subject of the following chapter; in the present one we shall consider it as a Sacrament. In order to give a clear exposition of the whole doctrine we will consider, (1) the preliminary ideas concerning the Blessed Sacrament, (2) its constituent elements, (3) its reception and its effects.

First Article: Preliminary Notes on the Sacrament of the Eucharist.

3. The name *Eucharist* signifies *thanksgiving*. This Sacrament is so called because, in instituting it, our Saviour returned thanks to His Father; and because we ourselves are enabled by it to render thanks to God, which are worthy of His acceptance, for the inestimable benefit of our redemption. It is called also by various other names, which all indicate its nature and its different properties: The *Host* or the Holy Victim, the Holy *Communion*, the Holy *Viaticum* or *Bread* of the Traveller, the Holy *Table*, the Sacred *Banquet*, the *Bread of Angels* descended from heaven, the Most *Holy Sacrament*, the *Sacrament of the Altar*, the *Sacrament of Love—of Charity*.

4. The Holy Eucharist is defined as *the Sacrament of the Body and Blood of Jesus Christ*; or, in other words, it is the Sacrament which contains really and substantially, under the appearance of bread and wine, the living Body and Blood of Jesus Christ; that is, Jesus Christ Himself in His entirety, in His humanity,

and in His Divinity, as He sits in heaven at the right hand of His Father.

5. This Sacrament differs from the others in several ways: (1) The other Sacraments have the power to confer grace, but this contains the Author and Source of grace. (2) The others consist in a transitory action, but this in a permanent and substantial thing. (3) The others have only the one character of Sacraments, but the Eucharist has the twofold character of Sacrament and Sacrifice.

It may be added that the Holy Eucharist is also distinguished among the other Sacraments by the magnificence of the figures by which it was foretold, and by the solemnity of its institution.

6. The principal figures of the Holy Eucharist are the following: (1) *The Tree of Life*, planted in the garden of Paradise, whose fruits bestowed immortality. (2) *The bread and wine* offered in sacrifice by Melchisedech, the priest-king. (3) *The Paschal Lamb*, whose blood protected the Israelites in Egypt from death, and whose flesh had to be eaten with unleavened bread. (4) *The Manna*, or the bread which God rained down from heaven to feed the Israelites in the desert. (5) *The Loaves of Proposition* which the priests placed before the Lord in the tabernacle, and which could only be eaten by men who had been purified and sanctified according to the law. (6) The bread baked in the ashes which Elias received from the hand of an angel, which so strengthened him that he walked for forty days and forty nights till he reached the holy mountain of Horeb. (7) *The water changed into wine* at the marriage feast of Cana, and the *bread multiplied by our Saviour* to feed the people who had followed Him into the desert.

7. The Son of God, after having given a telling image of the Blessed Eucharist in the multiplication of the loaves, that miraculous bread which He twice distributed to the people by the hands of the Apostles, the

future pastors of the Church, announced to His hearers that He would give them a more excellent bread than that which they had eaten, a living bread, the true bread from heaven, of which the manna was but a figure. He told them that this bread would be His own Flesh and Blood, and that by eating His Flesh and drinking His Blood they should possess eternal life. This promise, which was then scarcely comprehended, was to be fulfilled and understood at the Last Supper. On the eve of His Passion our Lord went with His disciples to a large and handsome room in Jerusalem, where the Paschal Supper was already prepared. On the table was the lamb, which was immolated according to the law; also bread and wine for the repast. After the eating of the mysterious lamb, Jesus washed the feet of His disciples; and then, being seated with them at table, He took the bread in His sacred hands, and lifting His eyes to heaven He gave thanks to His Father, blessed the bread, broke it, and gave it to His disciples, saying, 'Take ye, and eat; for this is My Body, which shall be delivered for you. Do this in remembrance of Me.' Then taking the chalice, He blessed it also and gave it to His disciples, saying, 'Take, and drink ye all of this; for this is My Blood of the New Testament, which shall be shed for you and for many unto the remission of sins. Do this in remembrance of Me.' This institution plainly contains the proof of the dogma of the real presence of Jesus Christ in the Eucharist, a dogma which is moreover clearly taught by the traditions of all ages.*

8. The design which our Lord had in instituting this Sacrament is multifarious. He wished to leave us, (1) a living monument of His Passion, whereby to perpetuate its salutary remembrance; (2) a testimony of His ineffable love; (3) food for our souls and a preservative against sin; (4) a pledge of future glory; (5) a living image of His Church, that mystical body of which

* See further on, p. 198, no. 12.

He is the Head; (6) a pure and perfect sacrifice infinitely agreeable to His Father; (7) a great consolation in the exile of this life, that we might have Him always really present in the midst of us.

Second Article: Constituent Parts of the Blessed Eucharist.

In order to show with clearness the parts or elements which constitute the Blessed Eucharist, we must consider this Sacrament from a twofold point of view: (1) as it exists; (2) in the act of its production.

9. (1) As it exists the Eucharist comprises two parts: the sacramental species and the real presence of Jesus Christ in those species.

10. (*a*) The *species* or appearances are the external parts of the Eucharist, or all that falls under the senses —the colour, the form, the odour, and the taste of bread and wine. These are what are called the *appearances*, or the simple *accidents* of bread and wine; because they do not contain their proper substance, which is that of bread and wine, but a substance naturally foreign to them—the Body and Blood of Jesus Christ.

In fact, after the consecration, there remains not an atom of bread or wine; these substances have given place to those of the Body and the Blood of Jesus Christ. But there are still the *accidents* of bread and wine, which are miraculously preserved to veil the real presence of our Lord.

The changing of bread and wine into the Body and Blood of Christ is effected in the Mass by the words of consecration, and is called *Transubstantiation*, or the changing of substance.

11. (*b*) The dogma of the *real presence* may be stated as follows: There are, under the species of bread and wine, the true Body and the true Blood of Jesus Christ, and not merely a figure or symbol representing them. Although, according to the sacramental

words, there is only the Body of Christ under the form of bread, and His Blood only under the form of wine, we nevertheless possess Christ wholly and entirely as much under the one form as under the other, and even in each particle of the species when divided; because, Jesus Christ, being actually living and immortal, is wholly and entirely where His Body is, and wholly and entirely where His Blood is, since His Body and Blood are inseparable from His Person. Before the Sacred Host is broken, and as long as it is whole, Jesus Christ fills it entirely with His presence, in much the same manner as our souls fill our bodies and all our members. When the Host is divided He fills each particle equally with His presence, much in the same way as a light reflected in a mirror is reproduced in each fragment of it when the mirror comes to be broken.

It is not, therefore, the Body of Jesus Christ which is multiplied, but it is His presence. There are not several Jesus Christs, but the one divine Person is present in several Hosts in different places and all over the earth in a much more perfect manner than that in which the sun, though but one, gives his light to all the inhabitants of the globe. The presence of the sun in different countries is only a virtual presence, the sun remaining in the firmament; but the presence of Jesus Christ is a *real presence* descending on the holy altars, to dwell in the Sacrament as truly as He sits at the right hand of the Father in the highest heavens.

12. This real presence of Jesus Christ is a supernatural effect, and a mystery of the love and omnipotence of God; a most wonderful effect, but one which, considering the almighty power of its Author, ought not to amaze us. He created heaven and earth. In His hands He holds the substance and accidents of all things. Could it therefore be difficult to Him to destroy the substance of a particle of bread and to place a human body under its appearances? The word of the

Son of God ought to be sufficient for us. 'Take,' He said, 'and eat; this is My Body.' The Apostles believed this mystery; they wrote it in the Gospels, in their Epistles, and they taught it everywhere, and since their death the Church has continued to teach and to believe it as well as all the other mysteries of our divine religion down to our own day. I believe, Lord Jesus, in Thy real presence in the holy Eucharist. I believe with gratitude and love, and in this faith I will live and die.

13. The consequence that flows from this truth of our faith is that we owe to the Divine Eucharist the worship due to Jesus Christ, seeing that, because veiled under the sacramental species, the Son of God is not the less worthy of our homage. We therefore owe to the Blessed Eucharist the adoration, the respect, the devotion, and the love of our hearts; and these sentiments ought not only to be manifested by our devotion in the churches, but also by zeal for the Holy Places themselves, for the propriety and magnificence of churches, altars, and sacred vessels, and, in a word, for everything that concerns the adorable mystery.

14. (2) In the *Production* of the Holy Eucharist, which takes place during Mass, and which is called the *Consecration*, there are the matter, the form, and the minister.

15. The necessary *matter* is wheaten bread and the wine of the grape. It is not essential for the validity that the bread be leavened or unleavened; nevertheless, that which the Church prescribes in this respect should be faithfully attended to.

The *form* consists in the words of consecration, which are the same as Jesus Christ pronounced in consecrating the bread and wine, namely, 'This is My Body. . . . This is My Blood.' These words have the divine virtue of effecting the prodigy of transubstantiation.

The *minister* is the priest, who pronounces these

divine words at the altar* in the middle of the Holy Sacrifice of the Mass. He pronounces them in the name of Jesus Christ, whose Person he represents; or rather, it is Jesus Christ Himself who pronounces them by his mouth; for the priest does not say, 'This is the Body of Jesus Christ,' but, 'This is My Body.'

Hardly has he said the word before he bends his knee to adore the Host, which he holds in his hands; then he raises it, that the faithful may see and adore it, together with the angels; for this Host is Jesus Christ in person descended from heaven, and adored by the angels, who accompany Him. The heavenly court, as the holy Fathers say, comes down, with its King, upon the earth.

Third Article : The Eucharist as it regards the Faithful ; the Adoration, Administration, Effects, and Sacramental Signs of the Blessed Eucharist.

16. The Blessed Eucharist is preserved in the churches for the adoration of the faithful, and for distribution to them at the holy table. Solemn adoration principally takes place during the *prayer of the forty hours*, and at the *processions* and *Benediction* of the Blessed Sacrament.

The administration† of the Blessed Eucharist is the office of the priest, whose hands, anointed with oil, are consecrated to touch the adorable and virginal Body of Jesus Christ. He administers this Sacrament in the church when he gives Holy Communion, and also in the houses to which he takes the Viaticum for the sick.

---

* There is a difference between the minister of the *Consecration* and the minister of the *Dispensation*, of whom we shall speak in the next article. This article regards only the former.

† The priest is the *ordinary* minister charged with dispensing the Holy Eucharist, with giving the Holy Communion to the faithful. In case of necessity, however, a simple deacon may fulfil this function. because he is the *extraordinary* minister of the dispensation of the Eucharist.

Before giving Holy Communion the priest elevates the Host, saying, 'Behold the Lamb of God; behold Him who takes away the sins of the world.' When placing the sacred Host on the tongue of the communicant, he says: 'May the Body of our Lord Jesus Christ preserve thy soul to life everlasting.'

17. The Eucharist was instituted to be received by the faithful at the holy table. This is Holy Communion. There is a distinction between the Communion under both kinds and the Communion under only one kind. Both one and the other produce the same effect, but the Church, for wise reasons, has ordained that Communion, excepting that of the priest at the Mass, should only be administered under one kind, that of bread.

When the faithful have received Holy Communion, Jesus Christ, with His humanity and His divinity, dwells in them so long as the species of bread preserves its nature. When the sacred species is consumed, the Body of Jesus Christ also has disappeared, but the divine Host remains in the soul by His divinity; for He says: 'He that eateth My Body and drinketh My Blood abideth in Me, and I in him.'

18. Communion is the most sublime act that a Christian can perform, and every one ought to know when and in what manner he should perform it.

(1) As regards the *time* when we ought to communicate, we must distinguish the First Communion, the annual or Paschal Communion, the Communion of devotion, frequent Communion, and lastly, the Communion as Viaticum.*

(2) With respect to the *manner* of communicating and the requisite conditions for body and soul, the essential thing is to be in a state of grace. Moreover, the sacramental fast must be observed, and the preparation before and thanksgiving after Communion ought to be

---

* See 'Moral' Part, chap. iii. 'Fifth Commandment of the Church,' and chap. vii. 'The Sacraments.'

fervently made. The more perfect the dispositions, the more abundant will be the fruits of the Sacrament.

19. Its fruits are inestimable. The Eucharist generally produces in the soul all the effects which the most nourishing food produces in the body. It preserves it from death, renews its strength, heals its lighter wounds, causes it to grow in virtue, and to taste sweetness and joy.

The particular effects of Holy Communion are the following:

(1) The increase of sanctifying grace and virtue, especially the virtue of charity, which intimately unites the soul with Jesus Christ, and in a manner transforms us into Him. (2) It bestows those actual graces which preserve the life of the soul, moderate the heat of the passions, and lead us to the practice of all the virtues, especially that of charity. (3) It gives spiritual peace and joy. (4) It remits venial sin; and (5) it preserves us from future sins. (6) It is a pledge of immortality and of the glorious resurrection, the germs of which it implants in us.

Many of these effects are produced gradually, and by little and little. The Eucharist, after the manner of corporal bread, must be continually received at longer or shorter intervals; and this is what is called the *frequentation of the holy table.*

20. The effects which we have enumerated are signified by the Sacrament, considered in itself and in its reception.

Bread, which is composed of many grains ground under the mill-stone, and *wine*, which is the juice of many grapes crushed in the wine-press, for the food and nourishment of man, signify, (1) the real presence of the Body and Blood of the same Jesus Christ who was immolated for us in His Passion; (2) the spiritual nourishment which our souls receive in Holy Communion; (3) the charity which unites all the faithful to form one body—the mystical body of Jesus Christ.

It is the Holy Eucharist which is the furnace of that charity, and the bond of that union.

Transubstantiation, or the changing of bread and wine into the Body and Blood of Jesus Christ, is symbolical of the spiritual change effected in the Christian, who, by virtue of the Eucharist, is transformed into another Jesus Christ.

The sacred banquet of *Communion* represents the banquet of the everlasting nuptials in the glory of heaven.

The *Sacred Host*, which, under the appearance of inanimate bread, contains the Author of life, shows how the life of grace lies hidden in our souls. It is also the image of the children of God, hidden here below under the obscurity of the mortal body.

21. Such is the Blessed Eucharist considered as a Sacrament, and instituted for the sanctification of men. It remains for us to consider it as it is a Sacrifice, and relates directly to the worship of God.

CHAPTER XI.

THE BLESSED EUCHARIST AS A SACRIFICE.

First Article: Nature of the Eucharistic Sacrifice.

22. THE word *sacrifice* signifies a *holy action*, and designates in general every offering made to God for His honour. There are two kinds of sacrifice, *interior* and *exterior*. The first consists in a religious act, by which we offer our hearts and our good works to God. This is not properly speaking a sacrifice. The sacrifice, properly so called, of which we have to speak, is the *exterior* sacrifice. *Exterior* sacrifice, the great act of religion, is thus defined: 'The oblation made to God of a sensible thing as an acknowledgment of His sovereign dominion over all creatures.' Or, more fully explained,

'it is the oblation made to God alone by a lawful minister, of a visible and sensible thing, accompanied by the destruction or the changing of the thing offered, and by particular rites for the purpose of acknowledging the sovereign dominion of God over all creatures, and of rendering to His divine majesty all the homage due to Him.'

It will be seen by this definition, that the following things are necessary to constitute a sacrifice: (1) an offering or oblation, (2) a sensible thing, (3) a change in the state or being of that thing, (4) a minister deputed especially to that end, (5) a particular rite, (6) a religious end. The minister of the sacrifice is called the *priest ;* the thing offered, when it is a living object, is termed the *victim ;* the change which it undergoes, the *immolation ;* the religious aim, *the end of the sacrifice.*

23. Sacrifice is called the great, the principal, the solemn *act of religion*, because it constitutes the essence of the worship which man ought to render to God. Therefore we find that sacrifices are as ancient as religion itself—that is, they commenced with the commencement of the world.

24. According to the common teaching of the Doctors, founded on the Scriptures, our first parents, after their fall, learnt from the mouth of God that, by the future merits of the Redeemer, they should obtain mercy, and that in this faith and this hope they might offer to their Creator prayers, gifts, and sacrifices, which would be agreeable to Him. God willed that they should immolate animals in His honour, in order that in sacrificing them they might remember that they had themselves deserved death, and that these victims were substituted in their stead. By offering sacrifices they also recognised God as the absolute master of life and death, and acknowledged that sin could only be washed away by blood, but by blood of which that of the animals sacrificed was but the figure. Our first parents transmitted these precious doctrines to their children. Hence, we

see the sacrifices offered by Cain and Abel, by Noah and his descendants.

The primitive revelation regarding sacrifices, preserved by mankind up to the Deluge, was spread, after the dispersion of the human race, over the whole world. From this time we trace the presence of altars and sacrifices everywhere, even amongst idolaters.

25. All the ancient sacrifices were shadows or figures of the sacrifice of the New Law. The most striking of those figurative sacrifices are those of Abel, of Noah, of Melchisedech, and of Abraham; also the Paschal Lamb, and divers sacrifices and oblations of the law of Moses.

26. Moses, under the direction of God, prescribed that the Israelites should offer sacrifices for four different ends. According to these ends, they are designated by the following names: the *latreutic, eucharistic, propitiatory,* and *impetratory* sacrifices. The first, offered to acknowledge the sovereign dominion of God, was called *Holocaust;* the second, offered in thanksgiving for His benefits, was called *peace offering;* the third, to implore mercy and pardon, was called *sin offering;* and the fourth, to beg fresh benefits and favours, this was also a *peace offering.* The sacrifice of the New Law takes the place, and embraces in the most perfect manner all the figurative sacrifices of the Old Law.

27. We call the sacrifice of the New Law the one and only Sacrifice of Jesus Christ, in which the divine Mediator is Himself both Priest and Victim.

This divine Sacrifice is one in its substance and twofold in the mode of offering, namely, the *bloody and unbloody* Sacrifice. The first is that which Jesus Christ offered on the altar of the Cross; the second, that which He first offered at the Last Supper, and continues to offer each day by the hands of His ministers, the priests of the Church. This is the *Holy Sacrifice of the Mass,* the unbloody continuation throughout all ages and generations of the bloody Sacrifice which was offered on Mount Calvary. It may be defined as 'the sacrifice of the Body and Blood of Jesus Christ under the species of bread and wine, offered by the ministry of the priest to acknowledge the sovereign dominion of God.'

28. Jesus Christ instituted the Holy Mass at the Last Supper, at the same time as the Sacrament of the Eucharist. The table in the cenacle was the first altar on which our Lord celebrated the first Mass and administered the first Communion, and it was there that He raised His Apostles to the dignity of priests of the New Law, by saying to them, 'Do this in memory of Me;' that is to say, 'Celebrate as I am doing the Sacrifice of the Mass in memory of My Passion.'

29. The Mass being a true sacrifice, it possesses also all the requisite conditions. (1) It is a *visible oblation*, since the victim offered is no other than the Sacred Host, or the Body and Blood of Christ under the visible species of bread and wine. (2) It is offered *to God alone* and never to the Saints; a commemoration only of the Saints is made, to obtain their protection and to thank God for the graces He has bestowed on them. (3) The Mass is offered *by a lawful minister*, the priest. The high-priest is Jesus Christ, who is invisible, being concealed in the person of the secondary and visible priest, His minister at the altar. (4) There is, if not a real, at least a mystical *destruction* of the victim; since Jesus Christ on the altar is, as it were, in a state of death, and His Body and Blood are consecrated separately; so that by virtue of the words of consecration, the Body is separated from His Blood. In reality, however, as Jesus Christ is living and incapable of undergoing a second death, He is present in His entirety where His Blood is, and present also in His entirety where His Body is. The Mass comprises three principal parts: the Offertory, the Consecration, and the Communion. The essence of the sacrifice is in the consecration; or, according to an-

other opinion, it consists in the consecration and the priest's communion.

30. Mass, or the *Sacrifice* of the Eucharist, differs from the *Sacrament*, in that the Sacrament is permanent and lasts as long as the species remain; whereas the sacrifice is transitory and finishes with the act which constitutes it.

Though the Mass celebrated by the priest is the same as the first Mass celebrated by Jesus Christ at the Last Supper, it differs from it in some accidental circumstances. (1) In the cenacle Jesus offered Himself with His own hands, but on the altar He offers Himself by the hands of the priest and His minister; (2) there He pronounced with His own lips, here He pronounces by the mouth of the priest, the words of consecration; (3) there He offered His yet mortal humanity, here it is His glorious and immortal humanity which is offered; (4) the sacrifice at the Last Supper represented the death of Jesus Christ as to come, but the sacrifice of the altar represents it as past; (5) our Lord in the cenacle made use of few ceremonies, those of the Mass are more numerous.

The Sacrifice of the Mass is the same in substance as that of Calvary, but it differs from it in the manner of offering. It is the same in substance, because there is the same Victim and the same High-priest: Jesus Christ, visible on Calvary, invisible and hidden in the minister at the altar—Jesus Christ, a visible Victim on Calvary, invisible and veiled under the Sacrament of the Altar. It differs in the mode of immolation; for (1) on Calvary Jesus was immolated in a bloody manner; on the altar He is immolated in an unbloody and mystical manner by the separation of the two species, which, consecrated separately, represent the Blood of Jesus spilt and separated from His Body. In the Mass Jesus Christ is, in the eye of His Father, what He was on the Cross; His Wounds and His Blood cry for mercy. (2)

On the Cross Jesus Christ offered Himself without the ministry of another priest; on the altar He is still the principal sacrificer, but uses the ministry of a secondary priest. (3) On the Cross He was immolated under His own proper form; on the altar He offers Himself visibly under the forms of bread and wine. (4) The sacrifice of the Cross was offered as the price of our redemption; that of the altar is offered as the means of applying that redemption to our souls. (5) The sacrifice of the Cross was offered only once; that of the Mass is offered every day, and will be so till the end of time.

Second Article: Celebration and Effects of the Mass.

31. The Sacrifice of the Mass is a public act, the most solemn act of the whole Catholic worship, performed in the name of all the faithful, who must assist at, and take part in it. The very appearance of a Catholic church shows that the celebration of the Mass is the principal act of worship; for the altar is always there as the central and most prominent point.

32. The priest is delegated by the Church to offer to the Divine Majesty the homage of all the faithful. The people also offer the Sacrifice; but it is by the hands of the priest, and they participate in it by uniting their minds and hearts with those of the priest.

33. As the Mass is the greatest act of public worship, it is becoming that it should be celebrated with an imposing accompaniment of sacred and august ceremonies, which are called *the liturgy;* the sublime drama which represents visibly the invisible mysteries of the altar. They may be divided into three parts: the preparation for the Sacrifice, the Sacrifice itself, and the thanksgiving after the Sacrifice.

(1) The preparation or the *preparatory part* extends to the offertory of the Mass, and is composed of prayers, instructions, and lectures taken from the Gospels, the Epistles, and other holy books.

(2) The *action of the Sacrifice* commences at the Offertory, and lasts till the Communion. It comprises, besides the prayers, various ceremonies, which precede, accompany, and follow the consecration.

(3) The *thanksgiving* begins after the Communion, and lasts to the end of the last Gospel. It consists of prayers addressed to God, to thank Him for the Sacrifice which has just been offered, and to beg of Him to produce all its fruits in our souls. This outpouring of graces is signified by the blessing of the priest. The whole is terminated by the recitation of the Gospel of St. John, so well calculated to impress us with the grandeur of the Victim which has been immolated.

34. Without entering into details concerning the signification of the ceremonies accompanying the celebration of the Mass, it may be said of them in general that they serve to show two things, namely, the Passion of our Saviour, the mystery of which is here renewed; and the dispositions with which we ought to assist at it. The altar, which is approached by steps, represents Mount Calvary. The crucifix placed at the top of the altar shows us Jesus Christ dying on His Cross. The lighted tapers are symbolical of the faith and devotion with which the faithful ought to assist at it. The sacred vestments, marked with the sign of the Cross, indicate that the priest is the minister and visible image of Jesus Christ crucified, who is the principal and invisible High-priest. The inclinations and genuflections are acts of adoration and signs of respect. The multiplied signs of the Cross, made by the priest over the Host and the chalice, tell us repeatedly that we are offering to the Heavenly Father the Divine Victim of the Cross, and that we must unite ourselves to it by the love of the Cross, of patience, and of Christian penance.

35. As far as regards the Victim offered, and the Sacrifice of the Mass itself, it is of infinite value; but

in the application of this value to the faithful, which is called the fruits of the Mass, it is not infinite.

The Mass produces four effects, corresponding with the four ends of the Sacrifice. It renders to God the supreme homage which is due to Him, which is the latreutic effect; it offers to Him worthy acts of thanksgiving, which is the eucharistic effect; it procures for us the remission of our sins and the punishment due to them—this is the propitiatory effect; and lastly, it obtains for us fresh benefits, and this is the impetratory effect of the Sacrifice.

36. The two first of these effects of the Sacrifice relate to God; the two last, namely, propitiation and impetration, relate to the faithful, and constitute the *fruit* of the Sacrifice.

The Sacrifice of the Mass remits *sin* by obtaining for the sinner the spirit of penance, which effaces sin. It remits to the just the temporal *punishment* due to sin in a direct manner, according to the measure of their dispositions. This remission of punishment is called also the *satisfactory effect* of the Sacrifice.

The Holy Mass obtains all sorts of graces, not only spiritual, but also temporal. The purely temporal graces, however, such as health, or the success of an enterprise, and the rest are only granted so far as they may conduce to the soul's salvation.

37. The Sacrifice of the Mass works its effects by its own power, and independently of the holiness of the priest; but the fruits which are gathered by the faithful are proportioned to their individual dispositions of faith, confidence, and fervour, as well as to their more or less efficacious concurrence in the celebration of the Sacrifice.

38. According as this concurrence is more or less perfect, three degrees of participation in the fruits of the Mass may be noted: (1) the *general* fruits, which are bestowed on the faithful, but especially on those

present; (2) the *special* fruits accrue to the celebrant; (3) the *principal* fruit is the fruit of *intention*, which is derived by the person who caused the Mass to be celebrated, or for whom it is offered.

39. The Sacrifice of the Mass may be offered for all the faithful, living or dead. When it is offered for a departed soul, a part of the satisfactions of Jesus Christ are laid at the feet of God for that soul; and God applies them according to the measure of His justice and His mercy.

CHAPTER XII.
THE SACRAMENT OF PENANCE.

First Article: The Nature of the Sacrament of Penance.

1. THE word *penance* is used to designate sometimes a virtue, sometimes a Sacrament.

The *virtue* of penance is a supernatural disposition which makes the sinner detest his sins and punish himself in order to offer reparation for the injury he has done to God. Acts of penance may be *interior* or *exterior*. The *interior* acts are called contrition or repentance; the *exterior* acts are corporal pains and punishments which are borne in satisfaction for sins committed. The virtue of penance has always been necessary to obtain the pardon of sins. *Without penance there is no pardon*, and, for those guilty of mortal sin, *without penance there is no salvation*. The virtue of penance essentially differs from the Sacrament of Penance, yet it is a part of the latter, because the interior act of the virtue of penance—that is to say, contrition—must form part of the Sacrament.

The *Sacrament* of Penance is that Sacrament by which the sins committed after baptism are remitted, by the absolution of the priest, to those who confess their sins with sorrow.

2. The sins of the penitent and his three acts, contrition, confession, and satisfaction, constitute the matter of the Sacrament. The sins are the *passive* matter, or that which has to be destroyed; but the acts of the penitent are the *active* matter, which concurs with the absolution in destroying the sins; just as the action of him who throws wood on the fire concurs with the flames in burning it.

The form of the Sacrament of Penance is the absolution pronounced by the priest in these words, by the authority of our Lord Jesus Christ: 'I absolve thee from thy sins in the name of the Father, and of the Son, and of the Holy Ghost. Amen.'

The minister of the Sacrament is the priest endowed with the double power of Holy Orders and jurisdiction.

3. Jesus Christ instituted the Sacrament of Penance on the day of His Resurrection, because this Sacrament effects the resurrection of souls dead by sin. He had promised it some months previously when, speaking to His disciples of the conversion of sinners, He expressed Himself in these words: 'Amen, I say to you, whatsoever you shall bind on earth shall be bound also in heaven; and whatever you shall loose on earth shall be loosed also in heaven' (Matthew xviii. 13). This promise He fulfilled on Easter-day, when He appeared to the assembled Apostles, and preached to them, saying, 'Receive the Holy Ghost; whose sins you shall forgive, they are forgiven; and whose sins you shall retain, they are retained.'

4. By these words our Lord conferred on the priests of His Church the power to remit, by the Sacrament of Penance, all sins, however great or numerous they might be. This power is inherent to the sacerdotal character. It is called *the power of Orders*, because it is given to priests at their ordination. Nevertheless, before using this power they have to obtain a second power, called *the power of jurisdiction*, which is

conferred by episcopal approbation, without which the power of Holy Orders is like a sword in its scabbard. The priest cannot make any use of it, excepting in case of the dying.

A priest can only validly remit the sins of the faithful over whom his jurisdiction extends: just as civil judges can only give judgment in that part of the country which is assigned to them.

The double power of Orders and of jurisdiction is called the *power of the keys*.

The power to remit sins is judicial. The priests are made judges of the sins, and also of the dispositions of the sinner. If they consider him worthy of pardon, they absolve him, and their absolution is just as efficacious as would be that of Jesus Christ Himself, whose place they hold.

5. Thus we see that the Sacrament of Penance takes the form of a trial; it is a *tribunal*, but a tribunal of mercy and of reconciliation. In it the priest is the *judge*, and the penitent is at one and the same time the *accuser* and *accused;* the *cause* is the sins; and the *sentence* consists in the absolution, together with the penance that the confessor imposes.

This judgment constitutes the sacramental *sign*. It signifies the grace conferred, that of the remission of sins. But as the sins are stains on the soul, spiritual wounds and maladies, the sacred tribunal is called also a *sacred bath* for the purification of souls, and a *spiritual medicine* for the cure of their deepest wounds. It was under the latter aspect that our Saviour depicted the Sacrament of Penance in the parable of the Good Samaritan. The good and charitable man who bound up the wounds of the dying traveller represents Jesus Christ, who, in the person of the confessor, heals the wounds of souls, and pours into them the oil and wine of sacramental grace.

Second Article: On the Reception of the Sacrament of Penance.

6. For the proper reception of the Sacrament of Penance we must (1) beg of God the grace to make a good confession, to know our sins, and to be sorry for them; (2) examine our conscience; (3) excite ourselves to a true contrition; (4) confess our sins; (5) accomplish the penance imposed by the confessor.

The three last named of these acts, namely, *contrition, confession,* and *satisfaction,* form part of the Sacrament of which they constitute the matter. Contrition and confession are essential for its validity, satisfaction, or the performance of the sacramental penance, as an integral, but not an essential part; if it were omitted the Sacrament would be none the less valid, though it cannot be omitted without sin.

7. (1) *Contrition.*—Contrition is a heartfelt sorrow for, and a detestation of, the sins we have committed, accompanied with a firm purpose of amendment for the future. It includes two elements, namely, (1) sorrow for, and a detestation of, the past; and (2) a firm purpose of amendment for the nature.

Contrition must possess four necessary qualities; that is, it must be interior, supernatural, sovereign, and universal.

8. There are two kinds of contrition. Imperfect contrition, which is called also *attrition,* and perfect contrition. *Imperfect contrition,* so called because its motives are not perfect, is that which springs from the consideration of the hideousness and the number of our sins; from the fear of hell, which we have deserved; and the thought of heaven, which we have lost. This contrition is good in itself, and sufficient for the validity of the Sacrament. *Perfect contrition,* so called because the motives are perfect, is that which proceeds from *charity;*

that is to say, from that sublime virtue by which we love God for His own sake and for His sovereign goodness. Thus, when I consider with the eyes of faith that my God, my Heavenly Father, is the supreme God; that He is infinitely amiable, infinitely worthy of my love; when for these reasons I sincerely repent of having offended Him, of having displeased Him by my sins, I make an act of perfect contrition. This contrition, joined to the resolution or the desire to receive the Sacrament of Penance, is sufficient at once to reconcile the soul to God, even before the reception of the Sacrament.

9. (2) *Confession.*—By confession we mean the declaration which we make of our sins to a priest in the sacred tribunal of penance. It must be humble, sincere, and entire.

Sacramental confession, which we are considering here as part of the Sacrament of Penance, is of divine institution. Jesus Christ implicitly prescribes it in constituting priests judges in the matter of sin, by giving them power to remit or retain sins according to their discretion. It follows that if a confessor is to *judge*, he must be acquainted with the *case*. This he cannot be unless the penitent makes his conscience known to him, which he does by confession. Confession, then, is of divine precept.

We see also from historical records that it has always existed in the Church. It was in full vigour in the time of Innocent III., who, in order to correct the negligence of certain Christians in this respect, made the decree of annual confession at the fourth Council of the Lateran in 1215. Before that period confession was practised by the faithful, and it is mentioned by the holy Fathers during all ages, going back to the time of the apostles. Thus in the fifth century we have St. Leo and St. Chrysostom, who, amongst many others, speak of sacramental confession. In the fourth century we have St. Ambrose and St. Basil; in the third, Origen and St. Cyprian; in the second, Tertullian and St. Irenæus; and in the first, St. Clement, Pope and disciple of St. Peter, who, in his second epistle to the Corinthians, tells the faithful 'that they must take advantage of the present time to repent of their sins; for,' he adds, 'once out of this life, we can no longer go to confession or do penance in the next world.'*

Confession is therefore a divine institution and law, which, established at the same time as the Sacrament of Penance, has been promulgated by the Apostles, and faithfully preserved in the Church. Moreover, none but God could impose a law of this nature on man; no human power could have introduced it.

10. Confession is made under the most inviolable secrecy, which is called the *seal of confession*. The natural as well as the ecclesiastical and divine laws impose so rigorous an obligation on the confessor, that no human power can dispense him from it, or allow him to infringe it. What he learns from the avowal of the penitent does not belong to him. It is the secret of God, whose place he holds in the sacred tribunal.

11. (3) *Satisfaction.*—Satisfaction, *generally speaking*, is the reparation of the injury done to God by sin, and of wrong done to our neighbour. This reparation *as a matter of justice* is indispensable for the remission of sins; and if at the time it be impossible, the will at least to make it when possible is necessary. That is why it is said, 'Without reparation no pardon.' As a *part of the Sacrament of Penance*, the satisfaction is the penitential work imposed by the confessor; it is called *sacramentul penance*. The penitent is obliged to accept it, and to accomplish it faithfully.

12. To the acts of the penitent must be added the

* See the *Elementa Theol. Dogm.* tom. ii. *De Sacramento Penitentiæ*, and other theological works; item, Gyr, *Manuel de la Science de la Religion*, ii.

priest's absolution. The *absolution* is a judicial sentence which constitutes the form of the Sacrament and effects the remission of sins. The priest can only give it to those whom he judges worthy to receive it; and if he do not consider the penitent sufficiently worthy, he is bound to refuse it. In the case of its being pronounced over an unworthy person, the absolution is invalid. Moreover, the priest is personally responsible before God for the use of his power; and if he betray his ministry, in assuming the power to remit sins which ought to be retained, he draws down the most terrible chastisements upon his own head.

13. The reception of the Sacrament of Penance is a *divine precept* which concerns all who, after baptism, are guilty of mortal sin. It is of the strictest obligation, there being no other means by which they can be reconciled to God. Confession, therefore, is called the *second plank after shipwreck;* that is to say, a means of salvation as necessary after the second shipwreck as baptism was after the first. An actual or implicit wish to confess, joined to perfect contrition, is necessary as a necessary means for those who cannot go to confession.

Besides the *divine* precept, there is a commandment of the Church, issued, as we have before said, by Innocent III., in the year 1215, obliging all the faithful to go to confession at least once a year.

14. In order to understand the effects of the Sacrament of Penance we should know those of sin which it is instituted to destroy. The effects of sin are four in number: (1) the *culpa* or *guilt*, or the stain of the soul, a stain which excludes sanctifying grace when the sin is mortal; (2) the *penalty* incurred either for time or for eternity; (3) the *loss* of merit; (4) the *traces* or remains of sin, the trouble of soul, bad habits, and other hurtful tendencies which are the consequences of sin.

The Sacrament of Penance, which tends to repair sin and its ravages in the soul, produces the following effects: (1) the remission both of the *guilt* and of the *eternal punishment* of sin (the temporal punishment is not ordinarily entirely remitted); (2) the restitution of merits and (3) of sanctifying grace; (4) the bestowal of actual medicinal graces; (5) peace of conscience and interior serenity and consolation.

15. The Sacrament does not entirely and at once destroy the remains of sin and the traces it leaves; but it weakens them and effaces them little by little; like those medicinal appliances which heal by degrees our corporal wounds and infirmities. Hence the reason why this spiritual remedy should be repeated and frequently used; this is called *frequenting the Sacrament of Penance*. The penitent receives these benefits according as his dispositions are more or less perfect.

16. *Censures*, such as an interdict or excommunication, are also remitted by the power of the keys, either in the Sacrament, or apart from the Sacrament.

Appendix: Indulgences.

17. *The remission of temporal punishment granted in virtue of the power of the keys, apart from the Sacrament, is called an Indulgence.*

It has been seen that, after the remission of the guilt of sin, there still generally remains a debt of temporal punishment due to the divine justice, which must be paid either in this life or in purgatory. In this life we may make satisfaction, (1) by our good deeds and by private penance offered to God in union with the merits of Jesus Christ; (2) by the satisfactory deeds of others when they are transferred to us. This transfer is especially effected by indulgences, which apply to the faithful the superabundant satisfactions of the Saints, of the Blessed Virgin, and of our Lord Jesus Christ.

18. The superabundant satisfactions of the Saints, and the infinite satisfactions of Jesus Christ, constitute the *treasure of indulgences*, the dispensing of which is

confided to the head of the Church, and forms a part of the power of the keys. It is properly called the power of granting indulgences.

This power belongs (1) to the Sovereign Pontiff, who alone has the right to grant indulgences throughout the whole Church; (2) to the bishops, who may grant partial indulgences in their dioceses.

19. There are several kinds of indulgences: such as the plenary indulgence, partial indulgence, and indulgence applicable to the souls in purgatory; also the indulgence of the jubilee.

(1) The *plenary* indulgence is the remission, granted to those who gain this indulgence, of all the temporal punishment of which they are deserving in the eyes of God.

(2) The *partial* indulgence consists in the remission of a certain number of days or years, by which is meant days and years of public or canonical penance, such as used formerly to be imposed on sinners according to the ancient discipline of the Church. Thus an indulgence of forty days or of seven years is the remission of as much temporal punishment as would be cancelled by God by our performance of forty days or seven years of canonical penance.

(3) *By indulgences applicable to the souls in purgatory* is meant those which we are authorised by the Church to lay before the throne of God, that He may deign to apply them to the suffering souls. This is what is called *application by way of suffrage*. Such satisfaction, presented to God in the name of holy Church, is always accepted; and God applies it either to the particular soul that He intends to aid, or to others upon whom He wishes to bestow this favour, or else to all in general.

(4) *Jubilee.* There is amongst plenary indulgences one more solemn than the rest, called the indulgence of the jubilee. It is granted regularly every twenty-five

years; and besides this, every new Pope ordinarily publishes a jubilee on the occasion of his accession to the pontifical throne.

The word *jubilee* is borrowed from the Old Law, which established the *year of jubilee*, or remission every fifty years. This holy year brought with it three privileges: (1) all debts were cancelled; (2) slaves were set free and regained their liberty; (3) patrimony and inheritance, which had been alienated or sold, were returned gratuitously to the rightful heirs. The jubilee year was for three reasons called the *year of remission*. The jubilee of the New Law, by reason of the graces which accompany it, produces the same effects in the spiritual order in a still more excellent manner. By this virtue the debts of our souls are cancelled, we are released from servitude, and our inheritance is restored.

20. Two things are necessary in order to gain a jubilee or any other indulgence : (1) to fulfil exactly all the conditions or good works prescribed; (2) to be free from all grievous sins—that is to say, to be in a state of grace, at least when the last condition is fulfilled.

The use of indulgences is singularly beneficial to the faithful; they not only help to pay the debts due to the divine justice, but they moreover powerfully help to nourish their souls with faith, hope, piety, and fervour.

CHAPTER XIII.

EXTREME UNCTION.

Nature, Effects, and Reception of Extreme Unction.

1. EXTREME UNCTION, so called because it is the last anointing of the Christian, is the supplement or completion of the Sacrament of Penance, as Confirmation is that of Baptism. *It is a Sacrament conferred by the holy*

anointing and the prayers of the priest for the spiritual and corporal relief of the sick.

2. The matter is the oil of olives blessed by the bishop on Maundy Thursday. The minister is the priest who anoints with the holy oil those organs which are the principal instruments of sin, namely, the eyes, the ears, the nostrils, the mouth, the hands, and the feet.

The form consists in the prayers said by the priest during the anointing. These prayers are the following: ' Through this holy unction, and through His most tender mercy, may the Lord pardon thee whatever sins thou hast committed by seeing, by hearing, by smelling, by speech, by touch, by walking.'

Extreme Unction is only administered to adults who are dangerously ill. It is not at all necessary that life be despaired of; it is enough that the illness be serious in its nature.

3. Extreme Unction produces two kinds of effects, having reference, one to the soul and the other to the body.

(1) Extreme Unction affects the soul thus: it remits venial sins and even mortal sins when the sick person has no longer the strength to go to confession, provided in the heart there is attrition or imperfect contrition. (2) It completes the purification of the soul by destroying the remains of sin. (3) It fortifies the sick person, and helps him to bear his sufferings with patience, to resist the attacks of the devil at the last moment, and to make with Christian resignation the sacrifice of his life to God.

(2) Extreme Unction affects the body by the alleviation of suffering and malady. It even sometimes restores health, if God judge it expedient for salvation.

All these effects are indicated by the sacramental sign, particularly by the properties of the oil used in the holy anointing. Natural oil heals, calms, and strengthens the members of those who fight. It is the means of giving light and dissipating darkness. Thus it is the image of the holy oil, which produces analogous effects on the sick person.

The sacramental oil must be blessed; and the anointing is accompanied with prayers, to show that it is not by its natural virtue, but by the power of the Holy Ghost, that it heals the soul and body of the sick person.

4. To obtain the precious effects of Extreme Unction, the sick person must have holy dispositions, and above all he must not postpone the reception of the Sacrament too long. Promptitude in employing this divine remedy is very necessary and important, especially to obtain bodily relief and cure. The holy oil produces its effect on the body after the manner of natural remedies. Like a valuable medicinal remedy, this Sacrament seconds nature, in which there remains a certain vigour; whereas it is ineffectual if that nature be already too much enfeebled, and life itself almost extinct. Many sick persons succumb because they defer this salutary Sacrament to the last, whereas it is not an uncommon thing to see those cured who hasten to receive it.

CHAPTER XIV.

HOLY ORDERS.

Meaning, Degrees, Nature, Effects of the Sacrament of Holy Orders.

1. THE word *orders*, as applied to the ecclesiastical hierarchy, has two significations. (1) It designates the *permanent state* of the ministers of the Church, which is the hierarchy, and its various degrees, the *clergy*, or the *clerical order*, divinely established and distinct from the *lay order*, which is composed of the ordinary faithful (2) The *rites*, or consecrating action by which the ordinary faithful are raised successively to the various de-

grees of the hierarchical order, and which is called *ordination*. It is in the latter sense that we are about to treat of Orders, as the means chosen by Jesus Christ to perpetuate in His Church the sacerdotal character which He gave to His Apostles at the Last Supper.

2. Holy Orders, called also the *imposition of hands*, is a Sacrament instituted by Jesus Christ to confer on those who receive it ecclesiastical powers, and the grace to use them with dignity worthily and fruitfully.

3. The Sacrament of Holy Orders comprises seven degrees or partial orders, which are divided into *minor* and *major orders*. The major orders are those of priest, deacon, and sub-deacon; the minor orders are those of acolyte, exorcist, reader, and door-keeper.

4. (1) *The priesthood.*—The priesthood is divided into two degrees, the episcopate and the priesthood.

The episcopate, which is the plenitude of the priesthood, confers on all those who receive it the power to administer all the Sacraments, and the grace to govern the Church well. Bishops are by divine right superior to simple priests. They are at the head of the sacred hierarchy as princes of the Church, judges in matters of faith, and successors of the Apostles, inasmuch as these were pastors of the Church. The priesthood confers the power to perform, under authority and episcopal direction, the same functions as bishops, with the exception of a few, such as the administration of Holy Orders and of Confirmation.*

(2) *Orders of deacon and sub-deacon.*—The order of deacon confers the power to serve the priest at the solemn celebration of the sacred mysteries, and that of sub-deacon the right of serving the deacon at the altar.

5. *The four minor orders* refer also, though in a less intimate manner, to the holy Sacrifice of the Mass.

* A simple priest may, however, be delegated by the Pope to administer the Sacrament of Confirmation in an exceptional case of need.

6. Though there are seven different orders, there is only one Sacrament of Holy Orders, which is more or less fully received according to the degree conferred, in the same manner as in a state there is only one power, in which the different functionaries participate according to their several degrees. The altar where the Holy Eucharist is offered, and which is attained by means of several steps, is a figure of the Sacrament of Holy Orders, the steps of the altar representing the six inferior degrees of orders, which lead to the supreme order of priesthood.

7. The degrees of bishop, priest, deacon, and the other sacred ministers constitute the *hierarchy of Holy Orders*. Besides this, there is another subordination, which is called the *hierarchy of jurisdiction*, formed by the Pope and Cardinals, the patriarchs and primates, archbishops and bishops. The *cardinalate* is a *dignity* superior to that of the bishops, though cardinals need not necessarily be bishops. They constitute a kind of venerable senate, whose mission it is to assist the Pope by their counsels in grave matters, and, on the decease of a Pope, to elect his successor.

8. Bishops, priests, and other clerics who belong to the religious orders established in the Church are called *regular clergy;* those who do not belong to those orders are called *secular clergy*.

9. The bishop is the minister of the Sacrament of Holy Orders, and to the episcopal character the power of conferring the priesthood essentially belongs.

The matter of Holy Orders in general consists in the tradition of the instruments or attributes of each degree, such as the book of the Epistles or Gospels. The deaconate and priesthood require, besides the tradition of the instruments, the imposition of the hands of the bishop.

The various words pronounced by the bishop in imposing his hands or bestowing the attributes constitute the form of the Sacrament.

10. The effects of Holy Orders are three in number: the indelible character, to which the power is attached; sanctifying grace; and actual graces for the worthy fulfilment of the sacred functions.

These effects are indicated by the sacramental sign—that is to say, by the words, by the instruments or symbols of power, as well as by the imposition of hands. Formerly, in the assemblies of the people, the head of the community placed his hand on the heads of those whom he meant to elevate to the magistracy.

In order to perform the greater part of his functions, the priest requires, besides the *power of Orders* inherent to his priestly character, the *power of jurisdiction*, which is conferred upon him by a legitimate mission.

11. Though every man who has been baptised may be capable of receiving Holy Orders, three conditions are necessary for his admittance to the priesthood—namely, a divine vocation, knowledge, and virtue.

12. *The tonsure.*—Before rising to the superior orders, it is necessary to pass through the inferior degrees, and, first of all, to receive the clerical tonsure.

The *tonsure* is not an order, but a preliminary ceremony by which the candidate for the sanctuary is distinguished from the laity, consecrated to God, and incorporated with the clergy.

13. The clergy of the New Law were prefigured in the Old by the priesthood of Aaron and his descendants, and also by the Levites, or inferior ministers of the Mosaic Law. All, priests and Levites, alike belonged to the tribe of Levi, which God had chosen to be entirely consecrated to the service of His temple and altars. The Christian clergy likewise form a holy tribe, but elevated above that of the Levites in proportion to the more august functions which they have to perform.

CHAPTER XV.
MATRIMONY.

Nature, Impediments, Celebration, and Effects of the Sacrament of Matrimony.

1. MARRIAGE, which has existed in all times and amongst all nations, has, in the Church of Jesus Christ, the character of a Sacrament.

Marriage was instituted by the Creator at the beginning of the world, when He joined our first parents together as spouses. From that time till the coming of Jesus Christ marriage was a sacred and indissoluble contract, but in itself a *purely natural* contract. Our Lord rendered it *supernatural* by elevating it to the dignity of a Sacrament of the New Law.

2. The Divine Author of our holy religion, wishing to sanctify those who marry, took the natural contract of marriage, and, without adding any other rite, declared it to be a Sacrament, and consequently gave it as such into the hands of the Church, with the power and commission to regulate that which concerns it, and to administer it in a holy manner, like the Sacrament of Baptism and all the other Sacraments.

3. By virtue of this divine institution the *marriage of Christians* is a Sacrament, and will ever remain so. Any matrimonial contract between Christians not having the character of a Sacrament would not be a real marriage, nor even a valid contract. The purely *natural* contract no longer exists, except amongst infidels—that is to say, the unbaptised.

4. In order to understand this fully, two important remarks are necessary. (1) Marriage consists essentially in a *contract* formed between two persons, and is called *the contract of marriage;* (2) what is commonly called *civil marriage* differs essentially from the ecclesiastical marriage, which alone is real marriage, the former having nothing but the name.*

* With regard to England, see Translator's Preface.

5. Civil marriage is a simple legal *formality* by virtue of which the affianced are considered as man and wife in the eyes of the law, and they enjoy the rights which the law accords to married persons and their legitimate children. This purely nominal marriage in no way constitutes the affianced *man and wife* before God,* and if they did not also contract the ecclesiastical marriage their living together would be a sin.

Ecclesiastical marriage, the true and only marriage amongst those who have been baptised,* is *one of the seven Sacraments*. It may be defined as the legitimate contract between Christian man and wife, adopted as a sacramental rite by Jesus Christ to represent the union between Him and His Church, and to confer on the contracting parties the grace to fulfil the duties of husbands or wives, and those of Christian parents.

6. The Sacrament consists entirely in the lawful contract. The expressed consent and the mutual acceptance of the two parties before the priest are the form and the matter which constitute the Sacrament of Marriage, as the ablution and the accompanying words constitute the form of Baptism.

We say the *lawful* contract, to show that it must only be entered into by persons capable of contracting it, labouring under none of the conditions of incapacity which are called *impediments*.

7. There are two kinds of impediments, namely, *prohibitive* impediments, which render a marriage *illicit;* and *diriment* impediments, which render it *null* by incapacitating the parties from forming the contract. (1) The prohibitive impediments are, for example, the prohibition of the Church to contract marriage with certain persons, such as heretics ; and also to solemnise it at certain times, such as Lent and Advent. (2) Amongst diriment impediments the principal are *natural relationship*, or *consanguinity*, whether in a direct line extending to all the degrees, or in a collateral line extending

* With regard to England, see Translator's Preface.

to the fourth inclusively. Also the *relationship of alliance*, or *affinity*, which would annul the marriage of a widower with the relations of his deceased wife, or that of a widow with the relations of her husband, also to the fourth degree.*

8. Persons who are bound by a diriment impediment cannot contract marriage without having obtained a dispensation from the ecclesiastical authority. The Church only can grant such dispensation. Jesus Christ, in confiding the matrimonial contract to His Church as a Sacrament, gave her at the same time the power to establish impediments, and to dispense from them, in the interests of the Sacrament and of the faithful.

9. Christian marriage, considered as a contract, has two great properties: unity and indissolubility. It joins the two contracting parties by ties of the most sacred fidelity, and establishes them in a settled state which is called the state of marriage. Matrimonial union, once consummated, is indissoluble, and only ceases with the death of one of the two parties. No human power can break the sacred engagement of marriage that a fresh union may be contracted.

10. What is called *civil divorce* leaves the matrimonial tie in full force, and whilst the two persons are alive a new marriage is impossible. If attempted it would only be a detestable adultery.

---

* Here it is question of canonical degrees, which are not counted entirely like those of the civil law. According to the Canon Law, (1) in direct line there are as many degrees as there are persons, without counting the original progenitor; (2) in collateral line, two persons are removed by as many degrees from each other as they are from the common stock; and if they are unequally removed therefrom, they are only considered relations according to the degree of the farther removed of the two. In the civil courts, the same rules are not followed with regard to the collateral line. The courts count the degrees by the number of persons who are all descendants from the same parent stock; hence, brothers and sisters are of

Marriage, considered as a Sacrament, has two effects: it confers grace and imposes duties. (1) It produces an increase of sanctifying grace at the same time that it bestows actual graces and powerful aid on those who receive it, to enable them to fulfil all their duties, bear all their trials, and constantly practise all the virtues proper to Christian spouses and parents. (2) The duties it imposes are: (1) Fidelity, love, and mutual support. (2) The care of governing the family well. The husband is the head. It is to him that the principal authority belongs. The wife owes him submission and obedience; but at the same time, not being his slave, but his companion, she shares his dignity, his rights, and his honours. (3) The great duty of the education of children. Children belong to God, who has created them and adopted them in holy baptism, but has confided them to their parents as a precious and sacred trust, which they must return without stain or corruption. But the safeguard of this treasure, the only means of insuring the virtue and the happiness of the children, is to give them a substantially moral and Christian education.

CHAPTER XVI.

ON THE VIRTUES.

1. THE doctrine we have been discussing relates to grace, and to the means of salvation given to man by the mercy of God. Man, on his side, must make use of these means, correspond with grace, and thus produce good works, which will make him worthy of salvation.

These good works are acts of the virtues which we must practise according to the law of God and by the grace of God.

---

the second degree, cousins german of the fourth degree of kindred, and so on.

To practise these virtues it is necessary to know them well and to study them from the teachings of faith, joined to those of sound reason.

We will sum up this doctrine in two articles:
Article I. The Virtues in general.
Article II. The Theological Virtues.

First Article: Virtues in general.

2. The word *virtue*, in a broad acceptation, means *strength;* here we take it in its moral acceptation, as strength of the soul, or a good moral quality in man. In this sense virtue may be defined as *a disposition, or an inclination, of the soul which leads men to do good actions, and which renders him good who is endowed with it.*

Virtue is the opposite of *vice,* which consists in a bad habit or inclination of the soul, which leads man to commit bad and blameworthy actions, and renders him bad who is under its dominion.

3. In virtue two elements may be distinguished, namely, (1) the *disposition* of the soul, or the virtue itself, and the *act* of virtue; (2) the *subject* of the virtue and its *object.*

4. (1) The *disposition* of soul—which is, properly speaking, the virtue—is a state of being (*habitus*), a quality, a faculty, or an abiding power; the act is only the transitory exercise of it. A virtuous disposition not only renders us capable of performing virtuous acts, but it also inclines us to produce them; and, being permanent, it remains after the production of such acts. It is easy to recognise the analogy between the *disposition* which constitutes virtue and that which constitutes a science or an art. Consider, for example, the art of music: it is a disposition or faculty by which the musician produces harmonious sounds, and which remains with him after the musical performance is over. In the same way a virtue—for instance, the virtue of faith—causes

the production of acts of faith, and still remains in the soul after those acts have been produced, soon again to become active, and repeat its own acts indefinitely. Virtue, again, may be compared to a *tree*, and acts of virtue to the fruit it produces.

5. An act of virtue, however, does not always necessarily suppose the corresponding virtue; and the virtue itself may sometimes exist without producing acts on all occasions. Thus, to show patience in some particular case is not a proof of the possession of the virtue itself; and if occasionally impatience should be shown instead, it is not a proof that the virtue is wholly wanting in the individual, but only that it has failed in an isolated instance.

6. (2) The person who possesses a virtue, or, more strictly speaking, the soul and the powers of the soul which are its seat, are called the *subject* of the virtue. Thus, the subject of the theological virtues is the Christian who possesses them, and above all his soul where they reign together with grace. Thus, again, the subject of faith is the understanding, and that of charity the will.

The *object* of a virtue is the thing on which it is exercised. Thus the object of faith is the truths which are believed; that of hope, the good which is expected and desired; that of charity, Almighty God, the sovereign good, who is beloved.

This theory may be explained by saying the subject answers to *who?* and the object to *what?* To the object is linked the *motive* of the virtue, which answers to the question *why?*

7. Virtue constitutes the perfection proper to man, and renders him good and perfect in the eyes of his Creator. Man is made to practise virtue as a tree to bear fruits, and the sun to spread its rays. Virtue is the fruit which the reasonable creature ought to produce; it constitutes his glory and beauty, whereas, without virtue man is a barren tree, a rayless sun.

It follows, then, that the perfection of the human

creature, in the eyes of God, and his true glory, consist neither in riches nor science, nor in any exterior advantage, but in virtue; and that man is more or less perfect according to the greater or smaller number of his virtues.

8. Virtues are divided, (1) according to their object, into theological and moral virtues; (2) according to their origin, into infused and acquired virtues, or into supernatural virtues, and natural or human virtues.

9. (1) The *theological* virtues have God Himself for their object; they relate immediately to Him, and direct our morals only mediately by the influence they exert over our thoughts, feelings, views, and actions. They are three in number, namely, faith, hope, and charity.

The *moral* virtues have for their object the regulation of our lives, and they only refer to God in an indirect manner. They are very numerous, and form four groups, so to speak, that are linked to the four *cardinal* virtues —prudence, justice, fortitude, and temperance.

10. (2) A virtue is said to be *infused* when the Holy Ghost bestows it on man, and infuses it into the soul, together with sanctifying grace.

A virtue is called *acquired* when man gains it by his own efforts and by the frequent repetition of the acts it prescribes.

Those virtues are called *supernatural* which are practised with the help of grace from motives of faith, which relate to God and our eternal salvation.

A virtue is *natural* and *human* when it is practised by man according to the simple lights of reason, and for a purely natural and earthly end.

11. Virtues are connected one with the other, like the different branches of one tree, so that one leads by degrees to the others; if one in particular be cultivated, all the others profit thereby; and when one is possessed in perfection, all the others are possessed to a certain degree. A similar bond exists between vices. Vice is

a malignant gangrene which, having attacked one member, very soon spreads to the others.

The three theological virtues are connected in a very particular manner. Faith is the foundation of the two others, because we cannot either hope in God or love Him without first knowing Him by faith. Hope and charity cannot, then, exist here below without faith; but faith and hope can exist without charity, though only in an imperfect degree.

12. All the virtues together constitute that which is the perfection of man, namely, holiness. Their brilliant assemblage resembles that of the flowers which form a garden, or that of the stars which form a firmament, the features which go to make up a portrait, or the members which form a living body. As found in the Christian, they reflect in his soul the image of Jesus Christ; they constitute the interior man, the new and spiritual man created by the grace of our Saviour.

13. It will, then, be understood that the virtues are not without a certain order, nor are they gathered together confusedly, like pieces of gold or silver thrown haphazard into a treasury. They are, on the contrary, coördinate, and dependent one on the other from different points of view.

Order of generation.—Faith is, as it were, the generating principle of hope and of charity. Charity in turn becomes the mother of the other virtues, because it commands the practice of them.

Order of dignity.—The three theological virtues, having God for their direct object, hold the first rank. The most august of the three, and the queen of all the others, is charity, after which come hope, and then faith. Prudence holds the first rank amongst the moral virtues, and next to it justice, with the virtue of religion which accompanies it; then fortitude, and lastly, temperance.

Order of influence.—There are two virtues which

principally influence the others. They may be compared to the two poles on which the whole sphere of virtues moves. They are humility and charity. Humility abases itself, charity rises aloft. The one is like the basis upon which all the virtues rest securely, and the other, like the head which commands the exercise of them.

Besides humility and charity, several other virtues, such as obedience, mortification, and conformity to the will of God, have a preponderating importance. They are called fundamental, solid, or capital virtues.

Order of the practical acquisition of virtues.—In the practical acquisition of Christian virtues it may be said in general that the first is humility, to which faith is linked; the second is confidence in God, to which are joined the spirit of penance, prayer, mortification, and the other moral virtues; the third is charity, the practical love of God and our neighbour, with all the accompanying virtues.

This order is indicated by Origen and St. Augustine when they say that the spiritual temple of God in the soul is founded on faith, supported by hope, and crowned by charity.

14. It remains to be seen how virtues are acquired, how they grow, become weakened, or are lost.

They are acquired either by divine infusion or by exercise. All the supernatural virtues, and the gifts of the Holy Ghost, are received by *infusion;* God infuses them into the soul, and augments them by sanctifying grace. The infused virtues, however, are ordinarily given as a germ which requires man's coöperation for its development; that is the practice of virtue. Natural virtues are acquired by *exercise*, and they are also preserved and strengthened by exercise and practice.

The infused virtues become less active and energetic by negligence in practising them, and they are lost by acts of the vices opposed to them; thus faith is lost by the sin of infidelity, hope by despair, and charity by the commission of any mortal sin.

Acquired virtues languish, and are sometimes totally lost, by a lengthened negligence in practising them.

After this life is over, no virtue can remain to those who are miserable enough to be condemned; but the elect will retain in heaven all the virtues which are in accordance with their beatified state, such as charity, the gifts of the Holy Ghost, and certain moral virtues, such as gratitude. But faith, hope, penance, and others will vanish in the light of glory. In purgatory, however, the theological and nearly all the moral virtues still exist.

15. The end of virtue is the perfection of man, being, as he is, a reasonable creature, raised to the dignity of a child of God. They perfect him wholly, and sanctify him in his intelligence, in his will, in all his senses and exterior works. They bestow on him all the greatness and riches, nobility and beauty, of which he is susceptible. They model him after the Type of human perfection, the Man-God, our Lord Jesus Christ; they render him truly the child of God, like unto the only Son of God made man; and they make him worthy to live with Him in the abode of His glory. Heaven is the final term and recompense of virtue.

Second Article : The Theological Virtues.

I. Of the Theological Virtues in general.

16. We have seen that there are three *theological* or divine virtues—faith, hope, and charity. Faith is the engendering principle of the two others; hope is born of faith; and charity, of faith and hope.

Charity is the most excellent of the three; it is their soul and life. Without charity, faith and hope are dead, and incapable of meriting eternal life.

17. *Essential and common characteristics.* — The

theological virtues have characteristics which are essential, and, consequently, common to them all. (1) They are the most noble, elevated, and efficacious of all the virtues. No moral virtue can compare with them; none has so much influence over man; none can so raise his intelligence, sentiments, actions; and none so much contributes to his present and future happiness. (2.) All three are necessary to eternal salvation; without them all the moral virtues put together could not be of any avail. (3) All three proceed from the same principle —namely, from God Himself, who plants them in the soul. (4) They have all the same object also—God Himself, to whom they attain directly and immediately in three different ways. (5) All three tend towards the same end — the sanctification of man, his eternal salvation, and the glory of God.

The man who possesses these three virtues possesses all the others, at least in a certain degree.

II. Faith.*

18. The virtue of faith is a gift of God and a divine light, by which we firmly believe, because of His supreme truthfulness, whatever God has revealed, and the Church proposes; or revealed by Him, as being so.

This definition points out the nature of faith, its action, motive, and material object.

19. Faith is by its nature (1) a *gift of God;* that is to say, a gratuitous benefit of the pure mercy of God. (2) It is a *light*—an interior and supernatural light—like unto but superior to the light of reason. There are three sorts of light: corporal light, which enables us to see created things; intellectual light, or reason, which makes known to us the truths of the natural order; and the light of faith, which makes known to us supernatural truths.

* See *L'Instruction Synodale* of the Bishop of Poictiers on the Constitution, *Dei Filius.*

By faith man comes to know his eternal destiny, which is salvation, and also the way and the means to obtain it. Without faith man walks in darkness, because his reason alone does not suffice for his guidance.

20. Though faith is a sure light which expels all error from our intelligence, it does not at the same time chase away all darkness; for though faith makes us certain of truth, it does not show us the truth itself, but only shows it *in a witness*. This is why it is compared to a mirror, which shows an object in an unmistakable manner, but only indirectly and by reflection. It is also sometimes represented as a veil, which, whilst it covers a person, allows us to see that person, though in an imperfect manner.

21. An act of faith consists in believing firmly; that is to say, in giving to revealed truths the full consent of our intellect, without even a shadow of doubt; such a consent as is due to the testimony and word of God.

22. The motive—which is called also the formal object of faith, the *wherefore* of our faith—is the supreme veracity of God who speaks, which excludes all possibility of error.

This formal object contains two distinct elements:

(1) That God has said a thing; (2) that His word is infallible. Both are made known to us by the light of reason, by history, and by the evident testimony of the Church, and also by the light and help of grace.

23. Faith, then, is not a blind or imprudent act, but one that is eminently reasonable. 'I believe the mysteries of religion,' says Monseigneur de Ségur, 'as I believe the mysteries of nature, because I know that they exist. I know that the mysteries of nature exist, because undeniable testimony convinces me—that of my senses and my common sense. I know that the mysteries of religion exist, because still more undeniable witnesses convince me—Jesus Christ and His Church. My reason serves to examine, to weigh, the value of their evidence.

But having once examined the facts, which prove the truth, divinity, and infallibility of these witnesses, by the light of philosophy, criticism, and common sense, my reason has finished its work: faith must then come in. Reason has led me to truth; it speaks, and I have but to listen, to open my soul, to believe, and to adore. My faith then is supremely reasonable.'

24. This does not mean that, before believing, the faithful ought first to examine the grounds of faith. Those who, being born in the Catholic Church, have been brought up as Christians, possess faith, and are as certain of their faith as one is certain of enjoying the light when day breaks. It is not, then, necessary for them, in order to believe, to examine the facts which prove the truth of the Church's testimony; and if they do examine them, it is only to enable them to see more clearly what they already knew, to arm themselves against error, or in order to defend the truth.

Those adults, however, who are not of the faithful, or who have had the misfortune to lose their faith, are obliged to become instructed. In considering such facts as the resurrection of Jesus Christ, and others which are called motives of credibility, it will be easily recognised that God has truly spoken, and that the Church is the depositary of His word. Then reason itself will make it a duty to believe, and the necessary grace will not be refused to those who pray for it.

25. The material object of faith—*what* we believe—comprises in general all that God has revealed, or has made known to men, in speaking to them by angels and prophets, or by His only Son, our Lord Jesus Christ. These teachings are all contained in the double treasure of Scripture and tradition.

26. As it is not possible that every one should understand the Scriptures and tradition, God has established His Church, to expound the revealed truths in an infallible, succinct, and popular manner.

The Church does this by the symbol of faith, the definitions of Councils, the Catechism, and by sermons.

27. Faith is divided into that which is interior and exterior, implicit and explicit, living and dead. (1) Faith is said to be *interior*, as it exists in the heart and mind; *exterior*, when it is professed by words and signs. (2) It is *implicit* when we believe in a general manner the truths which are unknown to us in particular, and *explicit* when the truths which we believe are distinctly known to us. (3) Faith is *dead* when it is not animated by sanctifying grace, and *living* when it is animated by grace and charity, and so rendered fruitful in good works.

That is called a *lively faith* which sees truths in a distinct and enlightened manner, in opposition to a *weak faith*, which only sees them indistinctly and afar off.

28. Faith and science are two means of knowing the truth. Both come from God, and both concur in giving man the knowledge useful and necessary for this life and the next. No antagonism,* therefore, exists between faith and science; but there are two differences, one of which concerns the object, and the other the certainty. (1) Regarding the object, science only considers the truths of the natural order; but faith embraces all the truths which God has been pleased to reveal, even those which are the most inaccessible to reason. (2) As regards certainty, faith can be subject to no error, no fluctuation; it is an immovable rock. Science, on the contrary, is not essentially beyond error and change. It is often mistaken in its assertions, often produces systems and hypotheses which mutually upset each other, and follow in succession. For this reason, science must always respect the unchangable truths of faith. It will thus, by confining itself to its proper object, escape many errors, and survey the vast field of nature which

* See above, 'Accusations against the Church, Antagonism between the Church and Science,' p. 80.

God has given up to its investigations in a more enlightened manner and with greater success.

29. Faith is absolutely necessary for salvation. The Council of Trent calls it 'the beginning of the salvation of man, the foundation and root of all justification.' 'Without faith,' says St. Paul, 'it is impossible to please God.' And our Saviour declared to mankind that 'he who believes not shall be condemned' (Mark xvi. 16).

The faithful are not obliged to *know* all the truths of faith. It is enough that they believe generally, by an act of *implicit* faith, all that God has revealed to His Church. There are, however, certain truths which must be believed with an *explicit* faith, and which the faithful are consequently obliged to know in particular. Amongst these points of faith there are some the knowledge of which is necessary only *by precept*, and others which must be known *as necessary means;* that is to say, of absolute necessity for salvation. These latter are the four following: the existence of God, the remunerative and avenging justice of God, the Blessed Trinity, and the Incarnation of God the Son. We must add that a solidly probable opinion holds that explicit faith in the two last points is not absolutely necessary.

III. Hope.

30. Hope is a gift of God, and an infused virtue which leads us to expect of Him, through the divine promises and the merits of our Lord, eternal life, and the means of attaining it.

31. The material object of hope, *what* we must hope for, comprises (1) eternal life, or God Himself, because He is our Sovereign Good, and He will make us partakers of eternal life by the Beatific Vision. (2) The means of salvation, namely, the graces and supernatural, and even the natural, helps which we need, in order to obtain supreme happiness.

The motive, called also the groundwork of hope, is

fourfold, namely, (1) the merits of Jesus Christ; (2) the infinite mercy of God; (3) His omnipotence; (4) and, above all, His fidelity to His promises. God, in view of the merits of Jesus Christ, solemnly promised eternal life to all mankind, on condition that they observed the law of the Gospel, and especially the precept of prayer. We see that the divine promise is conditional.

32. Two qualities are essential to hope, namely, firmness and fear. (1) It must be firm and unshaken as it regards God, because God cannot fail in His promises; (2) humble and mixed with fear as it regards man, because he may be wanting in the conditions on which the fulfilment of his hope depends. Hope is compared by the Apostle to a firm and sure anchor, which keeps the bark of our souls safe on the sea of this world, the anchor remaining still whilst the bark is in constant agitation.

The firmness essential to hope is called *confidence in God*. It may be more or less perfect, more or less tranquil and unshaken. We also call, by the word *confidence*, a filial trust in Providence amidst all the events of life.

33. Hope is more perfect in proportion as it is more confident and efficacious. Efficaciousness consists in the efforts and coöperation of man in attaining the object of his hope.

34. The hope which is not accompanied by charity is called *dead;* and that which charity animates and vivifies is called *living* hope.

35. *Effects.* Hope raises the soul by its desires; it gives energy and leads it to pray and to fulfil the other conditions necessary to obtain that which we hope for.

IV. Charity.

36. Charity is the most august, the most divine of all virtues. It is that which shines amongst the others

like a sun amongst the stars of heaven. It is the virtue *par excellence*, the most sublime participation in the holiness of God, who is charity by essence. 'God,' says St. John, 'is charity; and he that abideth in charity abideth in God, and God in him' (1 John iv. 16).

37. Charity is an infused virtue, a gift of God and a spiritual fire which, penetrating our hearts, makes us love God above all things for His own sake, and our neighbour as ourselves for the love of God.

38. Charity is called (1) *a gift of God* by reason of its inestimable price, and of its essentially divine origin. God alone can enrich His creatures with it; (2) *a spiritual fire*, because it produces effects resembling those of material fire; it warms the heart and inflames it with love, a spiritual love, a love pure and heavenly, and much superior to natural and earthly love.

39. There are two kinds of love, the love of *selfishness* and that of *benevolence*.

(1) The first is an interested love, by which one loves a person less for himself than for his goods, or the advantages we expect from him. Thus a mercenary servant loves his master for the sake of the salary he receives from him. This is also called the *love of hope;* and though it really springs from, and is reduced to, a love of self, yet when it relates to the goods which are eternal, it is holy and agreeable to God, but less perfect than the *love of charity*, which is a love of benevolence.

(2) The love of benevolence, *disinterested* in its nature, loves a person for himself, and not for his benefits. Forgetting self, it cares but for the beloved, and wishes for and furthers his welfare. Such is the love of a child for its mother, of a mother for her child. It is called also the love of friendship, because, if it be mutual, it constitutes friendship.

Charity is a love of mutual benevolence, a real friendship between God and His creature.

40. The material object of charity is God and our

neighbour—God loved for Himself, and our neighbour for God. Hence we have charity towards God and charity towards our neighbour.

There are not, however, two, but one single virtue of charity, which embraces a double object: on the one hand, God in Himself; and on the other, God still, but in His children, who are our neighbours. Charity is like a tree of life having two branches, which both draw their life from the same divine sap.

The motive or formal object of charity is God, considered in Himself as infinitely amiable and infinitely worthy of all love. Being essentially amiability, wisdom, goodness, perfection itself, God is the true object of love for which our hearts were made, as our eyes were made for the light.

41. There is *perfect* charity, which suffices of itself to justify the sinner; and *imperfect* charity, which does not suffice for this end. The latter, improperly called charity, consists in a love of benevolence by which we love God for Himself, but not *above all things*. Perfect charity loves God above all things; this is charity properly so called. It is the essentially sovereign love.

42. This sovereignty, this supremacy of the love of God above every other love must not be judged by the intensity of its acts; and still less by the ardour or sensible emotion which sometimes accompanies it, but by the superiority of its *preference*. To love God sovereignly and *above all things* is to love Him preferably to all things, and to all that could be seriously displeasing to Him. In other words, we love God sovereignly and above all things when we are disposed, with the help of His holy grace, to lose and to suffer all things rather than offend Him by one mortal sin.

So that true charity, sovereign and perfect charity, essentially excludes mortal sin.

43. It admits of three degrees of purity and perfection. The first simply excludes mortal sin; the second

venial sin; the third seeks all that can be most pleasing to God, and His good pleasure in all things.

44. Charity produces wonderful effects, (1) on the other virtues, (2) on the soul that possesses it.

(1) With regard to the virtues, charity is the mother, the queen, the life, and the splendour of all the others.

(a) As their *mother*, it produces the others, preserves and nourishes them. Whoever possesses charity by that fact alone possesses to some extent all other virtues. It is the fulfilment of the divine law.

There are amongst the virtues which surround charity as their mother some more closely linked with it, namely, those which are called the *eight beatitudes*— poverty of spirit, meekness, holy mourning, hunger and thirst after justice, mercy and cleanness of heart, peacemaking, the love of the cross, or patience under persecution.

Charity is also the mother of all good works, whether towards God or our neighbour. Those which regard our neighbour are called *works of mercy*, and are divided into corporal and spiritual works of mercy. These latter, which have for their object the spiritual good of our neighbour, are called also *works of zeal*. Zeal, which is justly termed the purest flame of charity, is an active ardour for the glory of God and the salvation of souls.

(b) As their *queen*, charity commands the other virtues, and puts them in practice.

(c) As their *life*, it animates the other virtues as the soul animates the body and all its members: it binds together also the moral virtues; it perfects them and renders them meritorious.

(d) As their *splendour*, it ennobles all virtues and communicates to them a beauty, refulgence, and additional value, as the sun by his light embellishes all nature and gives to every flower its perfection of beauty.

45. (2) In regard to the soul which possesses it, charity is a principle (1) of joy, (2) of strength, (3) of fer-

tility, (4) of riches and merit; for it changes all actions into gold and jewels for heaven.

Moreover charity makes the soul resemble God, as the heat which penetrates iron renders it by degrees incandescent and like fire itself. Charity is the essential disposition of the Heart of God, of the Heart of our Lord Jesus Christ; so that this sublime virtue communicates to men's hearts the disposition and all the sentiments of God Himself and of our Lord Jesus Christ.

It is the property of love, says St. Augustine, to transform us in some measure into the object of our affection. He who loves earth becomes earthly; he who loves the flesh becomes carnal; he who loves heaven becomes heavenly; and he who loves God becomes all divine and almost God Himself.

Charity may be called a beginning of the life of paradise. Once lighted in the soul, this divine fire never dies if sin comes not to extinguish it. When on departing this life, and being ushered into the presence of its Beloved, the loving soul shall find herself face to face with her all-amiable God, her love will be inflamed to the highest degree, will transport her into the arms of God, and transform her into Himself by an ineffable union. She will be, as the Apostle says, one spirit with the Lord: 'Qui adhæret Domino, unus spiritus est' (1 Cor. vi. 17).

46. The precept of charity is the first and principal of all the precepts. Our Lord says, 'Thou shalt love the Lord thy God with thy whole heart, and with thy whole soul, and with all thy strength: this is the greatest and the first commandment. And the second is like to this: Thou shalt love thy neighbour as thyself. On these two commandments dependeth the whole Law and the prophets.'[1]

The perfect model and source of all charity is the

* Luke x. 27; Matt. xxii. 40.

Sacred Heart of the only Son of God, our Saviour Jesus Christ, whose Heart is inflamed with the purest charity, which communicates its ardour to all who approach Him.

CHAPTER XVII.
THE FOUR LAST THINGS.

1. WE have seen, according to Christian doctrine, how God, after having first created and then redeemed humanity, conducts it by means of grace to the term of glory. It remains for us to consider how He leads man to his last end, and establishes him there for ever; and this is the object of this chapter on *the last things*.

2. We understand by *last things* the last events which must come to pass to each man in particular, as well as all in general and to the whole world. The doctrine concerning them may be divided into three articles: (1) the passage from this life to the next; (2) the relations between the living and the dead; (3) the end of time.

First Article: The Passage from this Life to the next.

3. Man, having arrived at the term of his existence, passes from this world to the next; this passage is made at the time of our death.

Death is the separation of the soul from the body. The soul, being immortal, passes to a new life, which is assigned to it by the Creator according to its merit. The body remains here and decomposes. It becomes corrupted and changes at last into dust, which is assimilated and becomes confounded with earth.

Faith teaches us, (1) that all men must die once; (2) that the hour of death is uncertain; (3) that death terminates the period given to men for the acquiring of merit, and fixes irrevocably their eternal lot, according to the merit of their works; (4) that death is the punishment of original sin; (5) that Jesus Christ, by His death, has vanquished death and has merited for us our resurrection.

4. *All men*, we have said, must die once; so that before the day of judgment all will have suffered death. This doctrine, according to the word of St. Paul, 'It is appointed for all men once to die,' is in no way opposed to the Apostles' Creed, where we say that Christ will come to judge the living and the dead; for by the living is understood the elect, or rather those who will be alive at the end of the world, and who will die only to rise again immediately and be present at the judgment.

5. Faith presents death to us as the *punishment of sin*. It is true that the nature of man is mortal, independently of sin; but God, by His grace, had rendered it immortal in the person of Adam, who was to transmit immortality and justice to all his descendants. Adam, by his sin, lost the privilege of immortality; and God punished him, together with all his descendants, with death. Hence, in dying, we suffer the penalty of sin.

6. There are two judgments, the particular and the universal. The latter will take place at the end of the world, after the general resurrection; the particular judgment immediately after the death of each one of us. When man comes to die, his soul, freed from his body, and subsisting with all its faculties in its spiritual nature, will appear before the tribunal of Jesus Christ, to be judged according to the words of the Apostle, 'After death, the judgment.'

The sentence pronounced is immediately put into execution, and the soul is placed according to its merits.

7. There are four different abodes or dwelling-places for souls that have left this life: limbo, purgatory, hell, and heaven or paradise. Limbo was deserted when heaven was opened by Jesus Christ; purgatory will last only till the end of the world; so that, after the general judgment, only hell and heaven will remain.

8. Limbo is the place where the souls of the just

were detained before the coming of Jesus Christ. It was a place of rest, of peace and consolation, where the souls of the patriarchs and the other saints awaited the coming of the Redeemer.

In Scripture limbo is sometimes called *Abraham's bosom*, more frequently *hell;* it was there that the soul of our Lord went after His death, as we say in the Creed, 'He descended into hell.' Our Lord descended there to announce to His captive saints the deliverance they were expecting. His presence and the manifestation of His divinity changed it into a paradise, as He gave the good thief to understand: 'This day thou shalt be with Me in paradise.'

Revelation has not made known to us the situation of limbo, any more than that of purgatory and hell. According to an opinion commonly received by the Doctors, these different places of sojourn occupy the vast regions of the interior of the earth. Some also are of opinion that limbo, since the Ascension of our Saviour, has become the abode of those who have died with the single stain of original sin upon their souls.

9. Faith teaches us on the subject of hell, (1) that there is a hell—that is, a place of suffering prepared for sinners; (2) that the souls of those who die in mortal sin are sent there immediately after death; (3) that the pains of hell are eternal. These, our Lord said, in speaking of the reprobate, shall go into eternal punishment, and the just into eternal life. Again He said that the rich man died and was buried in hell; and elsewhere He calls hell the fire that is never extinguished, where there will be weeping and gnashing of teeth, and where the gnawing worm shall not die. Jesus Christ repeats in the Gospel as often as fifteen times that there is a hell.

10. The reprobate suffer a double kind of anguish, called the pain of loss and the pain of sense. The first consists in the privation of the sight of God, the Supreme

Good, and the last end of man's existence. This privation is accompanied by the most sovereign anguish. The second pain consists in the suffering caused by the avenging flames, as well as all the other torments, which are part of hell, including the horrible society of the reprobate.

Though the nature of the fire of hell is not defined by faith, nevertheless the language of Scripture and of the Fathers of the Church leaves no doubt that it is a material fire, but endowed, by the power of God, with especial properties, in order to be the instrument of His justice. It acts directly on the lost souls, and makes them experience, without the medium of their bodies, sensible sufferings which, naturally speaking, they could only suffer through the organs of the senses. This is what our Lord wishes to bring before us in the parable of the wicked rich man, when He shows us the soul of the unhappy wretch in hell, and puts into his mouth the words: 'Abraham, have mercy on me; and send Lazarus that he may dip the tip of his finger in water to cool my tongue, for I am tormented in this flame.'

Hell surpasses in horror all that can be said of it. There one hour of torments far surpasses the rigour of a hundred years spent on earth in the most austere penance.

11. The nature of the pains is the same for all the reprobate, but their intensity differs; for each one suffers in proportion to his sins. The nature even of the sufferings corresponds to the nature of the sins which have provoked them. They are tormented, the Scripture says, by those things by which they have sinned.* 'As much as she hath glorified herself and lived in delicacies, so much torment and sorrow give ye to her.'†

12. As to the reprobate considered in themselves, they retain their natural faculties, memory, understand-

* Sap. xi. 17.   † Apoc. xviii. 7.

ing, and will; and after the resurrection they will possess their bodies with all their members and senses, but only that they may expiate the abuse of them of which they have been guilty.

Their memory will keep the remembrance of their sins, and they will have them unceasingly before their eyes as the cause of their misfortune. From them they will derive frightful remorse, and the gnawing worm of conscience spoken of by Jesus Christ. They will recollect also the miserable pleasures of this life, for which they have bartered their immortal souls. Their understanding will know the blessings and goods of paradise that they might so easily have obtained, like many others; and they will ever think of them with inexpressible regret.

Their will, irrevocably given to evil, will have only perverse and criminal tendencies, though their malice cannot further aggravate their chastisement, because they no longer possess the necessary liberty to do evil; but their evil will will form part of their suffering, as the good will of the elect will be part of their happiness.

13. What adds to the torments of hell all the horrors of despair is their eternity, their interminable eternity. No dogma is more forcibly affirmed in Scripture and tradition than the eternity of suffering. At the last day Jesus Christ will pronounce this sentence against the reprobate: 'Depart from Me, ye cursed, into everlasting fire; and these shall go into everlasting punishment, but the just into life everlasting' (Matt. xxv. 41-46). 'It is better for thee,' He says again, 'to enter into life maimed than, having two hands, to go into hell, into unquenchable fire, where the worm dieth not, and the fire is not extinguished' (Mark ix. 42, 43). 'Those,' says St. Paul, 'who obey not the Gospel of our Lord Jesus Christ shall suffer eternal punishment in destruction,—*Pœnas dabunt in interitu*

æternas' (2. Thess. i. 9). The eternity of the pains of hell is not opposed to divine justice. For as an eternal recompense is in no way contrary to the remunerative justice of God, so an eternal chastisement is not contrary to His avenging justice. For God only inflicts this punishment on those who die in mortal sin, which they have committed of their own free will. By committing mortal sin the sinner renounces God, and makes creatures his last end, consenting, for their sake, to become the enemy of God, and to be separated from Him for ever. If he die in this disposition of will, at enmity with God, he must remain so eternally, because the time for conversion and grace is past. He will therefore remain the enemy of God for all eternity, and will be for ever treated as such; in other words, he will himself be the cause of his eternal punishment. This unhappy state of the reprobate is no more unjust than the fate of a man would be who, having voluntarily deprived himself of sight, would remain blind for ever, supposing he could live for ever.

14. Faith teaches us that there is a purgatory, and that the souls who are detained there can be helped by the prayers of the faithful, and above all by the Sacrifice of the Mass. 'It is a holy and wholesome thought to pray for the dead, that they may be loosed from their sins,' says the Scripture.

Purgatory is the name given to that place of expiation where souls, who have died in a state of grace, but who still owe something to the divine justice, suffer the amount of temporal punishment due to their sins.

15. There are two kinds of pain in purgatory: the pain of loss and the pain of sense. The first consists in the delay or the privation for a time of the Beatific Vision. As to the pains of sense, their nature is not defined by faith; but the common opinion of the Doctors of the Church is that they consist in fire and other sufferings.

These pains are most intense; they surpass all the pains of this present life, without, however, attaining to the horror of the sufferings of hell; they are softened by the consolations of hope, and differ in intensity according to the merits of each soul.

The duration of this expiation is uncertain, and is likewise proportioned to merit. The opinion that it may be prolonged during many years is founded on the practice of the Church, which celebrates anniversaries of the departed for an indefinite period.

16. The holy souls in purgatory in the midst of their sufferings retain the sweet certainty of salvation. They are safe from sin, and they suffer with the most unalterable patience and most perfect resignation. Though incapable of helping themselves by their prayers, they can pray for those who help them.

The *suffrages* by which we can relieve the holy souls are prayer, fasting, almsdeeds and other good works, the application of indulgences, and above all the Holy Sacrifice of the Mass.

17. The name of heaven is sometimes confounded with the happiness enjoyed in heaven. There is a distinction between these two things. Heaven is properly a place, and the felicity of heaven a state.

By heaven is meant that place where man is destined to enjoy supreme happiness. It is with reason called *the House of God*—His glorious house, where the blessed live as the children of their Heavenly Father. It is called also *Paradise*, the *Holy City*, the *eternal Tabernacle*, the *New Jerusalem*, the *throne of God*, and the *true Country* as opposed to the exile of this world.

18. We do not know anything definite as regards the situation of heaven; but the Scriptures, which habitually oppose hell to heaven, use the expressions, *ascend* into heaven; *descend* into hell; and thus present to us the abode of the blessed as situated in the

highest regions. Hence we have the opinion of the Doctors, who place it beyond the vast firmament of the visible heavens.

The nature of the heavenly house must be in harmony with the nature of its inmates—God, the angels, and the just. The nature of heaven, then, must be such that it can serve as an abode not only for pure spirits, but also for corporeal creatures; for men who will be furnished with glorified bodies after the general resurrection.

The beauty and immensity of heaven can neither be conceived nor expressed. All that we can say of it is, that its magnificence must be worthy of its monarch, and of the saintly population who reign there with Him. 'There only,' says the prophet, 'God is magnificent,—*Solummodo ibi magnificus est Dominus noster.*'

19. *Happiness* consists in the enjoyment of all good, and the freedom from all evil. This exists nowhere on earth, and man can only attain it after the present life. The happiness for which we were created is called beatitude. St. Thomas defines beatitude as *the supreme good which fully satisfies the reasonable desires of the human heart*. It is found in God, and in Him only, since He alone is the Supreme Good.

There are distinctions to be observed in this beatitude. (1) *Natural beatitude*, that which the goods of nature could give if man were not raised by grace to the supernatural order; and there is also *supernatural* beatitude, which can only be attained by the help of grace. (2) There is also *imperfect* supernatural beatitude, which can be enjoyed by Christians here below; and *perfect* supernatural beatitude, which belongs only to the future life. (3) The beatitude of the future life, considered in blessed souls before the resurrection, is called *incomplete*, in comparison with that which they will enter into after the glorious resurrection, and which will be *complete* for the soul and for the body.

20. These distinctions suffice to show that the beatitude of heaven is a *supernatural beatitude,—perfect, excluding all that is evil, comprising all that is good both for the soul and the body.*

21. The beatitude of the soul, which is termed *essential* beatitude, will be the principle of the body's beatitude; at the day of resurrection it will be diffused throughout the corporeal substance, as the lustre of a flame is throughout the crystal that covers it. This beatitude consists in the possession and enjoyment of God by the Beatific Vision.

The loving contemplation of the divine essence is what is meant by the beatific or intuitive vision of God. The elect are admitted into the presence of God like beloved children to that of a father who opens to them all his treasures. They see God face to face in all His beauty, in all His magnificence and amiability. In seeing Him, they love Him with all their affections; and in loving Him, they possess Him with all His goods; they are united to Him, rendered like Him as far as a creature can be like his Creator. 'We shall be like unto Him,' says St. John, 'because we shall see Him as He is.' In the ardour of this ineffable love the creature is transformed into God, and is, as it were, deified. God communicates Himself to him as far as He is susceptible of such communication.

Human intelligence, being incapable by its nature of seeing the splendour of the divine essence, requires to be elevated to a state superior to its natural condition, and to receive new strength and light to enable it to contemplate the divine and uncreated world, as it formerly contemplated the created universe. This new light with which the intelligence is endowed is called the *light of glory.*

22. Enlightened by the light of glory, the souls of the blessed see God Himself and all things in Him. They see the mystery of the Blessed Trinity, and all the

other mysteries; they see also the world and creatures, so far as they are interested in them. Thus the saints, glorified in heaven, see the homage and the honours paid to them on earth; the pastors of the Church see their flocks; parents their children, and children their parents; in fine, all see and know what regards them and what is agreeable to them.

23. Though the blessedness of heaven in its nature and object is the same for all the saints, there are, however, various degrees of the possession of this happiness; each one participates therein according to his personal merits. All the blessed see and possess God, but each one in the measure of his capacity; all these measures, though unequal, are filled, and all hearts are fully satisfied. Those who are in an inferior degree of glory are not the less perfectly happy: the sight of a degree superior to their own causes them no pain, because each one rejoices in the happiness of the other, and in the good pleasure of God. All the elect form a body, of which each member is content with its function; a family wherein envy and arrogance are unknown, in which all the children are united amongst themselves with their father by the bonds of sweetest charity.

24. Essential beatitude, which we have been explaining, is called also *salvation, glory, crown of glory, eternal inheritance, everlasting nuptials, eternal repose, eternal recompense,* and *eternal life.*

Eternity, the sweet assurance of being happy for ever and ever, forms the completion of celestial beatitude.

25. Besides the beatitude of essential glory there are, in heaven, accidental glories, which are called *crowns,* which are granted to the saints who have gained certain special and signal victories. There are three distinctions: the Crown of the Martyrs, who have vanquished the world; that of the Doctors, who have vanquished the demon, the father of error and lies; that

of the Virgins, who have vanquished the flesh and its voluptuousness.

Another accidental happiness, and common to all, consists in the enjoyment of the society of angels, and of all the other inhabitants of the heavenly city.

Second Article : Relations between the Living and the Dead.

26. The relations between the living and the dead are founded on the dogma of the Communion of Saints. We call the *Communion of Saints* that union which exists for time and eternity between all the members of the Church gathered into one body, of which Jesus Christ is the head; also that each participates in a certain manner in the spiritual goods of the others.

Let us here remember what has been said elsewhere, that the Church of Jesus Christ, considered in all its extent, comprises three branches or three partial churches : the Church *militant*, the Church *suffering*, and the Church *triumphant*. The first is composed of the faithful who are on the earth, the second of the souls in purgatory, the third of the blessed in heaven. These three parts form together but one complete Church, one single society, one mystical body, one spiritual family, with Jesus Christ for head, of which all the members are animated with the same spirit, bound by the ties of the same charity, and united by a reciprocal influence, which is called the *Communion of Saints*.

It is called the *Communion of Saints*, and not the communion of Christians, (1) because the name of *saints* is given in Scripture to all the faithful; (2) because all have been sanctified by baptism; (3) because all are called to a state of perfect sanctity, and a great number have already attained it.

It has been said in the definition that the communion of saints exists both during *time and eternity*; because neither the union of the members of the Church between themselves, nor the union with Jesus Christ their head, is broken by death.

27. The members of the Church militant on earth hold communion among themselves with the souls in purgatory and with the saints in heaven.

(1) *They hold communion among themselves* (1) by the profession of the same faith and the same hope; (2) by the participation in the same worship and the same Sacraments; (3) by the dependence on the same visible head, who is the Pope; (4) by the community of spiritual goods.

The spiritual goods of the Church, such as the holy Sacrifice of the Mass, prayers, and good works, are in common amongst the faithful without, however, detracting from the merits of him who does the good works. The faithful participate in the goods of the whole body; but all do not participate in them equally. Each one receives according to the measure of his faith and charity. The Christian who is in a state of mortal sin, being like a paralysed member, receives the least part; and notoriously excommunicated persons, heretics, and schismatics, being members who are separated from the Church, are entirely deprived of the communion of saints.

(2) The faithful on earth communicate with the *souls in purgatory* by the brotherly love which they feel for them; by the help which they procure for them; and, reciprocally, by the gratitude of the holy souls towards those who help them, and their prayers to God for their benefactors.

(3) They communicate with the *saints in heaven* by the honours which they render them, and, reciprocally, by the benefit of the intercession which the saints make for them.

28. Faith teaches us that the saints in heaven make intercession for us at the throne of God; and that it is a holy and praiseworthy practice to honour and invoke

them, and to venerate their relics and images. This is what is called the *homage due to the saints*.

By the *saints*, we understand the Blessed Virgin Mary, the Mother of God, the holy angels, and all the blessed whom the Church has placed on her altars.

29. We have already spoken, in the chapter on the Incarnation, of the worship of Jesus Christ, to whom we render, by reason of His divinity, the supreme worship due to God alone. The homage or worship rendered to the saints is altogether different. They being creatures we honour them as such, by a worship which is inferior to the worship rendered to the Creator. In order to understand all that has reference to this matter, it is necessary to have an exact idea of homage or worship and the different kinds of worship.

By *worship* in general we mean the honour rendered to a person or thing because of his or its dignity or merit. We call the *object* of worship *that which* is honoured; the *motive* of worship *that for which* honour is rendered.

There are two distinctions to be observed here: (1) *natural* or civil and *religious* worship. The first, founded on a natural dignity, is that which is due, for example, to parents from their children and from subjects to their kings. It is generally called *honour* and *respect*. *Religious worship* has for its motive the supernatural dignity and excellence of its object. It is this worship that we render to God and His saints, to the Church and to her Sacraments and ministers.

(2) Religious worship is divided into *supreme* and *inferior* worship. The first is rendered to God by reason of His divine and uncreated excellence; the second to certain creatures by reason of a supernatural dignity or excellence which they have received from Him. The first is called the worship of *latria* (adoration), and the second that of *dulia* (homage).

Amongst the creatures enriched by the benedictions of God, Mary, the holy Virgin Mother, shines forth with a lustre and a splendour beyond any of the others. By reason of her entirely exceptional dignity an especial homage is due to her, which is called the homage of *hyperdulia*, that is, superior homage.

The inferior homage rendered to the saints redounds to the honour of God, who is the Principle and Author of the holiness which we venerate in them.

(3) We also distinguish *absolute* worship and *relative* worship. The first is rendered directly to a person because of his own intrinsic excellence. Such is the worship rendered to God, to Jesus Christ, to the Holy Eucharist, and to the saints in heaven. The second is rendered to an object, not because of its own virtue or excellence, but because of its relation to a person whom we honour. Such is the worship rendered by the Church to relics and holy images. This worship, then, resembling the respect which is given to the likeness of kings or the portrait of a father or mother, does not stop at the immediate object, but it refers to, and is connected with, the person represented by the object; and, properly speaking, it is rendered to that person, though in an indirect manner.

After these explanations, it will be easy to understand what is the nature of the worship which the Church renders to the saints, to relics, and to images.

30. We honour the angels, the saints, and especially the Blessed Virgin Mother of God, as the servants and friends of God, who are enriched by the gifts of His mercy; and at the same time we implore their intercession with the Divine Majesty on our behalf. This is an *absolute* though *subordinate* worship. The Sacrifice of the Mass, which is celebrated on their feast-days, is not offered to the saints, but to God, to thank Him for all He has done in their favour, to give glory to those whom He has glorified, and to implore their intercession.

This worship is virtually referred to God Himself, whom we glorify in His saints.

31. We mean by *relics* the bodies of saints, their bones, or some part of their bodies, as well as all the objects which have belonged to them, and which they have touched. The Church venerates these sacred remains, not because it sees in them inherent virtues, but because the bodies of the saints have been the instruments of their virtues, the temples of the Holy Ghost, and will one day be glorified in heaven. It is the same thing with the objects that they have touched, or which, having served as instruments of their martyrdom, have been in a measure sanctified by that touch or use.

The worship rendered to relics rising to, and terminating in, the person whose relics are venerated, is a *relative* worship of the same degree as the absolute worship due to that person. Thus the relics of the true Cross and the other instruments of the Passion, likewise garments of Jesus Christ, are honoured by the worship of *relative latria*, and the relics of the saints by the worship of *relative dulia*.

The worship rendered to *holy images* and the prayers which are said before them, addressed, not to the images, but to the persons whom they represent, constitute, in the same manner, a *relative* worship, of the supreme degree of latria if the image of Jesus Christ or of the Cross be the object of veneration; of hyperdulia if the veneration is directed to the image of the Blessed Virgin; and it is a veneration of simple dulia if homage is rendered to the relics of the other saints.

32. The angels and saints hear our prayers and see the honour we pay them as if they were present. Not that they are really present; but, enjoying the sight of God, they see and hear things in the most perfect manner in His divine essence, as the words of our Lord in the Gospel show: 'There is joy before the angels of God over one sinner doing penance.'

Third Article: End of the World.

33. By the end of the world we mean the last events, which will put an end to the then actual state of the world, and will fix for ever the doom, happy or unhappy, of all reasonable creatures.

The end of time will come with the second Advent of Jesus Christ, when He comes in His glory to judge the living and the dead. All the doctrine relating to this matter may be summed up in three principal points: (1) the second coming of Jesus Christ and the signs which will precede it; (2) the resurrection of the dead; (3) the general judgment.

34. (1) *The second coming of Jesus Christ.*—Jesus Christ came into the world to save it at the time of His birth in Bethlehem; this was His first coming. He will come again to judge the world; this will be His second coming. The first Advent was only marked by humility and mercy; but the second will be proclaimed amid the splendour of glory and justice which belongs to the King of the universe, to the Judge of the living and the dead.

Jesus Christ has plainly announced to us His coming, but not the time at which it will happen; this is a secret which it has pleased Him to reserve to Himself. He has, however, indicated foreshadowing signs, which will announce the approach of the great day.

(*a*) The Gospel will be preached in the entire universe.

(*b*) Charity will become cold amongst Christians, and faith itself will appear lost in the world.

(*c*) The Jews will be converted to Jesus Christ.

(*d*) There will be great wars, famines, pestilence, earthquakes, and troubling of the sea; the sun, moon, and stars will be darkened, and will not give their light, and will not follow their accustomed course. All the order of nature will be troubled, and will announce impending destruction.

(*e*) A man will appear of the utmost perversity, who will be called Antichrist, that is, opposed to Jesus Christ. He will seduce the people, and will create terrible persecutions, and will produce an almost universal apostasy. His reign, according to Scripture, will last about three years and a half.

(*f*) The prophet Elias and the patriarch Enoch will return to the earth to oppose Antichrist, to enlighten the Jews, and to sustain the faith of Christians. These two powerful antagonists will be put to death by Antichrist, who will himself be confounded and overthrown by the power of Jesus Christ.

(*g*) Then there will come a fire which will destroy all things on earth; and this is what is meant by the *final conflagration*.

35. (2) *The resurrection of the dead.*—This dogma teaches us (1) that at the last day all men, the just as well as sinners, will rise again in their bodies; (2) that every one will be clothed with his own flesh, and the body which formerly belonged to him; (3) that the condition and qualities of the risen bodies will differ according to the state of the souls; for the good will rise to eternal life, and the wicked to eternal condemnation; and the difference of destiny will be shown in the bodies of all. The reprobate will be horrible to behold, like the demons and hell which they are in future to inhabit. The elect, on the other hand, will rise glorious and radiant from their dust, like to the angels, whose brethren they have become; like unto God Himself, whose true children they are.

36. The resurrection of the dead is clearly expressed in the Scriptures. Its likelihood and propriety are, besides, easily understood; for the body of a man, having served as the instrument of his vices or his virtues, should share the fate of the soul; and as it was

the entire man who was sinful or virtuous, so must the entire man be either punished, rewarded, or recompensed.

The possibility of the resurrection is not less evident than the all-powerfulness of God, who operates it. Is not He who made the body when it had no previous existence, and who drew the entire world out of nothing, capable also of remaking our bodies, and reproducing them from their ashes? Moreover, God will only work again in the general resurrection the miracle of the resurrection of Jesus Christ, and that of numbers of other particular resurrections mentioned in history.

37. When all mankind shall be dead, and the surface of the earth purified by fire, Jesus Christ, says the Gospel, 'will send His angels with a trumpet and a great noise,' meaning that angels will be sent to raise up their voices and proclaim the commands of Jesus Christ.

The great noise of the angels will resound like a trumpet from one end of the universe to the other, and will send forth these or like words, 'Arise, ye dead, and come to judgment!'

At this divine command all souls will quit heaven or purgatory or hell, and will again take possession of their bodies. The dead, who have risen from the different parts of the universe, will be all mingled together at first, the just with the sinners. But soon the angels, those ministers of the Supreme Judge, will separate one from the other, and will cause them to assemble in the place of judgment.

38. (3) *The judgment, and the place where it will be.*—The place in which the last scene of the world's history will be enacted is not defined by faith. It is therefore not certain that it will be in the Valley of Jehosaphat, situated near Jerusalem, the place which once witnessed the mystery of the redemption of man, and would thus also bear witness to the mystery of

God's justice. Nevertheless, the place chosen by God as the theatre of judgment will be truly called Jehosaphat, which means *the Lord Judge.*

39. When the great assembly, comprising the whole of the human race, shall be in solemn waiting, there will appear in the air the sign of the Cross, the glorious standard which will precede the King of the universe. Then the Son of God Himself, in the sight of the whole human race, will descend from heaven in a luminous cloud with great power and majesty.

Innumerable legions of angels in visible forms will accompany Him; and all the just, clothed in their glorified bodies, will advance to meet and escort Him.

Christ will sit on His throne to judge the living and the dead, the just and sinners. At His side will be the Apostles, seated also on twelve thrones, to judge together with their Lord rebellious men and angels.

The Judge will cause the elect to stand at His right hand and the reprobate at His left. Then, says the Scriptures, 'the books will be opened;' words which signify that consciences shall be laid bare. The conscience of each one, all the hidden recesses of his heart, his actions, and his entire life, will be exposed like a living picture, not only to his own eyes, but to those of the whole universe. 'Nothing is hidden now,' says the Saviour, 'which will not be revealed at the great day.'

Jesus Christ will then pronounce the supreme sentence. He will say to the elect, ' Come, ye blessed of My Father, possess ye the kingdom which is prepared for you from the foundation of the world.' Then, turning to the reprobate, He will address to them these overwhelming words : ' Depart, ye cursed, into everlasting fire, which was prepared for the devil and his angels.'

Immediately after this double sentence, hell will open and swallow up the bodies and souls of the multitude of the damned, and will then close on them for ever.

40. The elect will remain, forming the glorious Church of Jesus Christ, ready to ascend with their King and Father to the kingdom of heaven; for they will for ever after be worthy to inhabit that blessed region, both in body and soul, in company with Jesus Christ and His angels, since by their glorious resurrection they have become celestial beings like to the blessed spirits themselves.

41. The bodies of the elect will be endowed with four glorious qualities—impassibility, subtility, agility, and light.

Impassibility will render them invulnerable, and inaccessible to suffering and death.

Subtility will render them able to obey the soul most perfectly in all kinds of actions and movements without being hindered by any obstacle. They will, as Jesus Christ did after His resurrection, pass through material substances, and will in a manner be spiritualised.

Agility will help them to transport themselves to any distance in an almost imperceptible moment.

Light will give them an incomparable beauty, and will make them shine like the sun.

'Then,' says our Lord, 'the just will shine like the sun in the kingdom of My Father.'

This glory, however, will be proportioned to each one's merit. 'As star differs from star,' says St. Paul, 'so will it be with the bodies which have risen to glory.'

42. The bodies of the blessed, being immortal and incorruptible, will no longer require nourishment, but they will taste for ever the joys of the senses in all that is most pure and holy. For if it be just that the reprobate suffer in their senses for their abuse of them, it is also just that the saints be recompensed in their senses for having submitted them to the mortification of Jesus Christ. Their hearing then will be charmed by the most harmonious melodies; their sight ravished by ineffable beauties, namely, those of Jesus Christ and His

Blessed Mother, and all the blessed; also by the glories of nature, which they will be enabled to contemplate throughout the whole extent of creation.

43. Clothed in these glorious bodies, the blessed, united with the angels, will form a countless multitude, and will ascend into heaven in the retinue of Jesus Christ, and enter with Him into the heavenly Jerusalem. Such will be the holy Church of God, brought by the divine mercy to supreme perfection, its final state, its eternal triumph.

44. The Doctors consider that the world and the material creation will not be destroyed after the end of time; but purified, renewed, and rendered as it were participator in the resurrection of the just. This is the meaning given to these words of St. Peter, 'We look for new heavens and a new earth, according to His promises, in which justice dwelleth' (2 Peter iii. 13).

CHAPTER XVIII.

RECAPITULATION OF REVEALED DOCTRINE.

1. In casting a retrospective glance over the whole doctrine of faith we see that it embraces all truth, the beginning and the end of all things. Revelation is truly the veil lifted—it unfolds everything to us, both the visible and invisible universe; or rather it shows us in a distinct manner the two immense objects which constitute the universality of beings—God and His Work, the Creator and His creatures.

2. (1) *God.*—God, one in nature, three in persons, is ineffable majesty containing in Himself all the treasures of life and wisdom, power and beauty, goodness and charity. The ocean of all good, the abyss of all perfections, infinitely admirable, infinitely amiable, God is the

true and worthy end of all intelligences and of all hearts.

(2) *The works of God.*—This great God has produced a work worthy of His goodness and wisdom, namely, the universe, the sum of all creatures, whose existence unfolds with the succession of ages.

3. The cause and end of this work was the wisdom of God and His diffusive goodness, whose tendency it is to pour itself out in benefits as the sun pours forth its light.

This infinitely bountiful Being wished to communicate His perfections to other beings. He wished to produce creatures to whom He could manifest all His magnificence and His treasures in such a manner as to render them participators thereof. This participation in the treasures of God is what we call glory, the glorification of the creature, his beatitude.

4. For such an end as this, it was necessary that there should be creatures capable of knowing and of loving; of knowing the wonders of God, and of loving His goodness. It was necessary that there should be intelligent creatures, made to the image of God. The Creator made two kinds of such beings: angels to glorify the spiritual world, and men to glorify the material world.

5. The angels were meant to occupy the first rank in glory, and to form, as it were, the throne and crown of the Divine Majesty. God bestowed on them, together with their natural life, the supernatural life of grace, by means of which they should, after a short trial, arrive at glory.

But in this trial, instead of conforming to the views of God, a great number of these sublime spirits abused their liberty and committed sin. They separated themselves from God, and by that act deprived themselves of grace. The iniquity of the creature provoked the justice of the Creator; justice was done; and the guilty were banished to hell, a frightful abode corresponding to the monstrous state into which those unhappy spirits had placed themselves by their sin. The other angels, on the contrary, who remained faithful under trial, were admitted to the region of glory which was destined for them.

6. Man also was called to share the glory of God in heaven; but, like the angels, man also had first to prove his fidelity on earth.

The Creator, having made the first man to His image and likeness, gave him a double life, the natural life proper to an earthly creature, and the supernatural life of grace proper to an inhabitant of heaven.

Living by this life of grace, he was made so that he might grow on earth in virtue and sanctity till the time when, without suffering death, he should be translated into heaven, and pass from the terrestrial to the heavenly paradise. Adam was destined to be the father of a numerous posterity, who were to be the inheritors of his privileges. Together with corporal life, he had to transmit to his children the spiritual life of grace, and to become the head of an innumerable multitude of just and of saints.

7. Unhappily, the head of the human race committed sin, and by sin he destroyed the life of grace in his soul. Deprived of this life himself, he could no longer transmit it to his descendants, who thenceforth would have been for ever disinherited, if God Himself had not intervened in all His power and mercy. Adam had committed *spiritual suicide;* for in committing sin he had taken his own life, and by the same blow he had brought death to all his race.

What would have happened if Adam had put himself to death corporally before he had any children? Would he not, in his own person, have killed the whole human race? Having become nothing but a dead body, he could not have given corporal life to those who were to have been born of him; neither could he have repaired so great an evil; for though he could take away his life, he could not take it back again. The human race, then, would have remained in eternal death, if God, the Author of life, had not intervened to resuscitate Adam.

In the same way, by committing the spiritual suicide of sin, the head of the human race dealt the same blow of spiritual death to the whole of the human race. His children could still be born according to the flesh, and receive corporal life from him, but not the spiritual life of grace, which was dried up at its source.

8. The plan of Almighty God was frustrated by the malice of His creature, and the work of God in the visible world ruined at its foundation. The evil was irreparable; neither Adam nor any other creature could apply a remedy. The Author of life, He who gave it at the first, God alone, could restore it.

Will God restore life? Man, by rejecting the life of grace, and plunging himself in death by sin, has offered a serious injury to his Creator. Will not his Creator abandon him to his unhappy lot? No; God, who is all love and mercy, will not reject our guilty race. He will save it. But as God is also infinitely *just*, He exacts reparation. This does not mean that God could not have pardoned man gratuitously; but it pleased Him to combine justice and mercy, and to demand from man reparation for the sin of which he had been guilty.

9. Who will make this reparation? Which amongst the children of man is capable of doing so? What man can render unto God a homage which can compensate for the injury done to His infinite majesty? A man of infinite dignity is needed for such an office; in other words, a Man-God alone can suffice: God must become man, and work the ineffable mystery of the *Incarnation*.

And behold, the love of God is nothing daunted by

such a condition. 'God so loved the world,' says St. John, 'as to bestow His only Son upon it.' God the Son will become man to save us; and thus, in order to satisfy His justice, God will exhaust the treasures of His love and mercy.

God the Son will become man; the Second Person of the Blessed Trinity will take our human nature, and whilst still remaining God, like His Father, He will become man like us, one of the children of the great family of Adam, and incorporated with our race.

Then there will be a God amongst men, a man who can answer for His brethren, a Man-God who can converse with God, repair the sin of His adopted race, and redeem that life which was lost by sin.

Then the spiritual life of grace will be restored to the human race. The Man-God, the Christ, the new Adam, will become the head and father of the whole human race, *according to the Spirit;* that is to say, as far as regards the spiritual life of grace, and also that of glory.

10. The new Adam is incomparably superior to the first man, who was the physical head of our race. Jesus Christ became its spiritual and moral head; in other words, the Father according to the Spirit, and the King of the great human family.

(1) Christ is the Father of mankind according to the Spirit. The old Adam gave to all mankind the life of the body; a life, however, mixed up with death and misery; but Christ gives to all, not only the spiritual life of grace, but also corporal life in all its perfection; for 'He is the resurrection and the life.'

On the cross we were begotten of Christ; in baptism He made us live again the life of grace; and in the resurrection at the last day He will cause us to be born, even in our bodies, to a glorious life. This is the reason of His being called 'the Father of the world to come, the Father of a numerous race.' *Si posuerit pro peccato animam suam, videbit semen longævum* (Isaias liii. 10). He won this life for us by His death of expiation; and He has conferred it on all generations by the seven Sacraments, which are its seven divine channels; and by His Church, which is the dispenser of them unto the end of the world.

(2) He is the moral head, or king, to govern and judge mankind, to distribute the gifts of life to us, according to the divine laws of mercy and justice.

Thus the work of God in the visible world, destroyed by the first Adam, is restored by the second in the most admirable manner, like a temple which rises from its ruins much more magnificent than it was before its fall.

11. Christ, then, atoned for sin and redeemed the human race with His blood. He holds the salvation of men in His hands; but, respecting their liberty, He wishes that they should freely retain it, and fulfil certain conditions, which are as light as they are equitable and just.

Presenting Himself to men, His brothers, He offers them life, and the abundance of life; He gives them the power to become the children of God, if only they believe in His name. 'I am,' He says, 'the resurrection and the life. He that believeth in Me shall never die. He that believeth and is baptised shall be saved.' On this there is a division amongst mankind. Some men accept the offer, and join themselves to Christ as their head; others refuse it, and oppose Him like rebels and enemies.

Thus we have mankind divided into two camps: on one side are those who adhere to Christ, namely, His disciples and His Church; on the other are ranged those who reject Him, namely, the powers of hell and their followers. Christ and His Church remain invincible in the midst of their attacks, offering life to all generations, until the end shall arrive and the number of the elect be filled up.

12. Then the day of justice will come, for justice must be done; and those who have not accepted mercy shall pay the entire debt due to justice.

In that great day the Man-God, or, as He calls Himself, the Son of Man, will descend from heaven in all His majesty, as head and chief of the human race, to judge the living and the dead, the good and the wicked.

The wicked will be punished and thrown into the eternal prisons of death, which they have chosen and deserved; but the just will receive the plenitude of life, and will enter with their King into the kingdom of glory, which was destined for them from the creation of the world.

The elect, with Christ their chief, will constitute glorified humanity, and they will be rendered eternal participators in the life and the heavenly treasures, and, as St. Peter says, in the very nature of God. *Divinæ consortes naturæ.* This is in a measure the apotheosis of human nature.

Part Third.

MORAL.

1. HAVING shown in the first part of this work the truth of our holy religion, and in the second her dogmatic doctrine, it remains for us to explain her moral doctrine, which will form the subject of the third part.

We shall divide the subject into nine chapters: (1) on laws; (2) the commandments of God; (3) the commandments of the Church; (4) sins and vices; (5) virtues and good works; (6) perfection and the evangelical counsels; (7) the Sacraments; (8) prayer; (9) the feasts, ceremonies, and pious practices of the Church.

CHAPTER I.

LAWS.

First Article: Nature of Laws.

2. *Law*, in the general acceptation of the term, is a rule imposed upon creatures, that they may attain their end by the proper exercise of their faculties. From this we understand that a law is but the expression of the will of the Creator, or, which comes to the same thing, the expression of the order which He has established in the universe.

In this general acceptation distinction is first to be made between the *physical* and the *moral law*. The first is that which regulates the formation of creatures, their development, and their necessary operations; the second is that which directs the free actions of man.

3. Moral law may be defined as a rule that is *obligatory, general, just, and permanent, and promulgated in the interest of a society, by him who has the right to govern it.* This definition distinctly shows the essential properties of a law, or the conditions requisite for every true law. It must be obligatory, just, general, stable, useful, legitimately imposed, duly promulgated. Let us see how each of these conditions is to be understood.

(1) *The obligation.*—A law properly so called is not merely a directive rule, but an obligatory prescription, the violation of which constitutes a fault.

(2) *Its justice.*—As a law must be the expression of the will of God, it cannot imply injustice. An unjust command is not a law, but an abuse of power and an act of tyranny.

(3) *Its generality.*—A law must equally oblige all the members of the body to which it has reference, otherwise it would cease to be just, not being conformable to distributive justice.

(4) *Its stability.*—A law is not a transitory measure; the legislator may die, but the law does not die.

(5) *Its utility.*—The end of a law is the common good; hence every law ought to be useful to the community.

(6) *Its legitimacy.*—In order to be founded on right and to possess obligatory force, a law must emanate from a legitimate superior invested with legislative power. This superior is God Himself or those who hold His place, and are invested with His power, namely, the heads of human society, civil as well as ecclesiastical. All, as the Apostle says, are in the order established by God, and there is no power but from God.

Their commands therefore, as far as they are just, are the expression of the will of God, to which those who are inferiors must submit. 'Let every soul be subject to higher powers' (Rom. xiii. 1).

(7) *Its promulgation.*—In order to be binding, a law must be announced to the community by a proper promulgation. Promulgation differs from intimation and from conscience. *Intimation* is the particular knowledge of a command or a law given to an individual. *Conscience* is the judgment or interior voice which pronounces sentence on a particular act, declaring it conformable or contrary to the law; but *promulgation* is the public act by which a law is announced to a community.

4. Law differs in two points from a simple precept. (1) A precept is addressed to particular persons, but law concerns a society. (2) A precept is transitory, but law remains, being established for ever, or at least for a long period.

Second Article: Distinction of Laws.

5. Moral law, inasmuch as it is the expression of the divine law, is divided into eternal law and temporal law. By *eternal* law is meant the whole of the decisions of the divine will, by which God eternally accomplishes all good in Himself. *Temporal* law comprises all the expressions of the divine will which have been given to man, and which must be fulfilled by him in time.

Temporal law in its turn is divided into *divine* law, properly so called, and *human* law. The first emanates directly from God; the second from human superiors invested with power by God. We will consider them separately.

6. (1) *Divine law.*—Divine law is *natural* or *positive*, according as it emanates necessarily or freely from the Creator. There is but one *natural* law, but there are two positive laws, namely, the *Mosaic* law, which

was promulgated by Moses, and the *evangelical* law, which was given by Jesus Christ.

7. By *natural law* is meant the moral order which must be observed by man that he may arrive at his *natural* destination. This order consists in the whole of the natural duties of man towards God, himself, and his neighbour. The natural law is communicated to man simultaneously with his creation; it is graven on his reasonable nature. 'It is only,' as St. Thomas says, 'like the reflection of divine light within us, a participation by an intelligent creature in the eternal laws.'

Natural law admits of no change or dispensation; for, being founded on human nature, it is, like it, invariable. It is, however, susceptible of perfection; indeed it required the positive divine laws to perfect it. The natural law is in itself imperfect, and only regards the natural destinies of man; but as man, by grace, has been elevated to a supernatural end and destiny, it was necessary that a higher law, relating to a higher end, should be joined to the natural law. This second law, which does not abolish but perfects natural law, has therefore been given to man in the form of the mosaic law and the evangelical law.

8. The *Mosaic law* comprises, besides dogmatic doctrine, three distinct parts: (1) the moral part, which is only the clear and definite expression of the natural law, the general rules of which are contained in the Decalogue; (2) the ritual or ceremonial, which regulated the divine worship of the Jewish people; (3) the civil or judicial part, which concerned the national policy.

9. The *evangelical law* is composed, (1) of dogmatic truths, which must be believed; (2) of precepts, which are obligatory on all; (3) of counsels, which all are not bound to follow. The precepts relate to the morals of the faithful and to the divine worship; the counsels relate to perfection, and concern those whom God calls to a state of life specially consecrated to His service.

The evangelical law being formed for all men and all ages, our Lord did not establish civil or political laws as Moses did. For men can be Christians and loyal citizens always and everywhere, whatever be the form of government under which they live.

Though the Gospel includes several precepts that are only of positive right, and which depend solely upon the will of God, it is, properly speaking, not susceptible of any dispensation. The Church, whose mission it is to interpret the divine law, cannot derogate from it in any point. She only possesses this power with regard to her own laws, which are called ecclesiastical laws.

10. (2) *Human laws.*—Human laws may be either *ecclesiastical* or *civil*.

11. By ecclesiastical laws we mean those which emanate from the Sovereign Pontiff and the bishops for the government of the Church. It is a matter of faith that the Church can establish laws, properly so called, which cannot be violated without guilt before God. For (1) the legislative power was positively conferred upon the Church by her Divine Founder: 'Whatsoever you shall bind on earth shall be bound also in heaven;' and 'if he will not hear the Church let him be unto thee as a heathen and a publican' (Matt. xvii.). (2) By virtue of the natural right, the Church possesses legislative power independently of the positive divine right. Being a perfect and independent society, it has the right of self-government and that of ordaining what is necessary for its preservation or conducive to its end.

By virtue of this power the Church can establish laws and commandments, watch over their observance, and punish transgressions by excommunication, and the refusal of the Sacraments and Christian burial.

The universal legislative power for the whole of Christendom belongs to the Pope and to the bishops in their respective dioceses, and to the councils or assemblies of bishops for the entire Church or for that part of the Church which they represent.

The object of the ecclesiastical laws is, (1) to maintain order and peace throughout the body of the Church by a stable and prudent administration; (2) to prevent abuses; (3) to facilitate to the faithful the observance of the divine law and the practice of all that Jesus Christ has prescribed and taught.

The laws of the Church are numerous; some of them regard hierarchical superiors, and others the clergy and religious orders; while others, again, have reference to the Sacraments, worship, and Church property; and lastly, some concern the whole body of the faithful. The principal of these last are those called *the Commandments of the Church.*

12. Civil laws proceed from the temporal power. They are established by those who govern the state, to maintain order, discipline, and public tranquillity, and to define the respective rights of citizens. The civil laws are binding in conscience so long as they are conformable to the constitution of the state, and also are not contrary to justice, religion, or the rights of the Catholic Church.

13. All men are bound by the precepts of the natural law as well as by that of the Gospel. Human laws, however, are only binding on those who are subjects of the legislator who enacts them, and then only after they have attained the use of reason.

14. Human precepts are not binding in case of the want of power to observe them; that is to say, when there exists a physical or moral impossibility of fulfilling them. But no incompetency or fear can exempt from the observance of the natural law, as far as it is prohibitive. Thus perjury, blasphemy, and impurity are always forbidden, and never can admit of excuse or dispensation.

15. Human laws are susceptible of dispensation,

which means an act by which the lawgiver, in particular circumstances, exempts a subject from the observance of a law, though that law itself remains in full vigour. The power of dispensing belongs to the Sovereign Pontiff for all ecclesiastical laws, vows, oaths, and obstacles to marriage, and to bishops for all that concerns their statutes and the rules of their dioceses. Parish priests and their curates can also dispense their parishioners from fasting and abstinence or the observance of Sundays and holidays of obligation.

Appendix : Conscience.

16. The interior application of laws to particular actions is made, as has already been said, by the voice of *conscience.* Conscience is defined as a practical judgment, which pronounces sentence on the goodness or malice, the lawfulness or unlawfulness, of an act which must be either done or avoided in the particular circumstances in which the individual is placed.

17. We are never allowed to act contrary to the voice or dictate of conscience; but we must not, we even cannot, always follow its inspirations. We can only regard our conscience as a rule of conduct when we can prudently judge it to be *right,* or, which comes to the same thing, when it is *prudently formed.*

A *right* conscience is one whose judgment is conformable to truth and the correct interpretation of the law; it is erroneous or *false* when it represents to us an action as good which is really bad, or a really good action as one that is bad. Errors of conscience are like the ignorance from which they spring, and they may be either vincible or invincible. Error is *vincible* when he who acts, having certain doubts as to the goodness or badness of his act, and as to the obligation of examining whether that act is really good or bad, nevertheless neglects to take the necessary means of discovering the truth. Error is *invincible* when there is no doubt about it in the mind, and no suspicion regarding the nature of an act either during its performance or on consideration of the cause of the act.

18. This being established, the principles which should rule our actions will be the following: (1) When the conscience is right we must follow it in all things, either in performing what it commands or in abstaining from that which it condemns. 2. When the conscience is *invincibly erroneous* we may and ought to obey it. 3. When the conscience is *vincibly* erroneous—that is, confused with doubts and suspicions as to the lawfulness or unlawfulness of the action it permits—we must not act according to the voice of such a conscience, but we must rectify it by examination, consultation, and employing the ordinary means to become enlightened according to the individual circumstances. He whose conscience is perplexed—that is, placed between two actions which appear bad—must, as far as he can, take counsel of prudent men; and when he cannot consult such and is still under the necessity of acting, he must choose what appears the lesser evil, and in so acting he will not commit sin.

In order to form the conscience prudently, we must (1) become acquainted with the divine laws, according to our state and condition; (2) we must follow the advice and direction of an enlightened confessor.

CHAPTER II.

THE DECALOGUE.

General Meaning of the Decalogue.

1. JUST as the *Apostles' Creed* is the compendium of all we must believe, so the *Decalogue*, or ten command-

ments of God, is the abridgment of all we must do to be saved. 'If thou wilt enter into eternal life,' says our Lord, 'keep the commandments' (Matt. xix. 17).

The word *decalogue* signifies *word*, or *law composed of ten articles*, which are called the ten commandments. It is the law imposed by God on His reasonable creatures.

This law, which was in the beginning engraved on human nature itself by the Creator, was later on more clearly promulgated to the people of Israel by the ministry of Moses, and finally ratified in the fulness of time by Jesus Christ, who perfected it and confided it to the Church to be proposed for the observance of all the faithful. The law of Moses was promulgated on Mount Sinai, midst thunder and lightning, with terrible majesty. The Christian ratification took place first on the Mount of the Beatitudes, and afterwards on Mount Sion, at the descent of the Holy Ghost, amid the effusions of divine charity.

3. The ten commandments are the expression of practical truth, of order, and of that justice according to which it is the duty of every man to live on earth. The justice of the commandments of God and the obligation to observe them are founded (1) on the will of God, which is the rule of all moral good; (2) on our nature and on our relations with God and our fellow-creatures; (3) on the obvious interests of each man in particular and of all mankind in general.

4. The ten commandments are binding on all men, without exception, and no power can dispense from any one of them. If, then, they are binding on all, they are impossible to none; and it is in our power to observe even the most difficult with the help of the grace which God offers to us, and which He is ready to give to all who humbly implore it of Him. God does not command impossibilities; but, as the Council of Trent says (sess. vi.), '*In commanding, He recommends us to do what*

we can; to ask for that which we cannot accomplish; and lastly, He helps us that we may be able to do it.'

Moreover, the commandments are not only not impossible with the aid of grace, they are even not difficult; above all, when we give ourselves up to their observance from youth in the spirit of love. The love of God consists in practising His commandments; 'and His commandments are not heavy' (1 John v. 3).

5. The motives which should engage us to keep this holy law are, on the one hand, the will of God, and on the other, our own happiness; for God, in order to sanction His laws, has decreed that our own happiness should absolutely depend on our fidelity in observing them.

6. The Supreme Legislator promises an eternal recompense to those who keep His Commandments; and He threatens with eternal chastisement those who transgress them. He has willed also that His holy law should be a principle of true happiness for men, even in this world, according to these words, 'Justice exalteth a nation; but sin maketh nations miserable' (Prov. xiv. 34).

7. The ten commandments are generally expressed in the following terms:

I. I am the Lord thy God, who brought thee out of the land of Israel, and out of the house of bondage. Thou shalt not have strange gods before Me. Thou shalt not make to thyself any graven thing, neither of the things that are in heaven, or on the earth, or in the waters under the earth. Thou shalt not adore them, nor serve them.

II. Thou shalt not take the name of the Lord thy God in vain.

III. Remember thou keep holy the Sabbath day.

IV. Honour thy father and thy mother.

V. Thou shalt not kill.

VI. Thou shalt not commit adultery.

VII. Thou shalt not steal.

VIII. Thou shalt not bear false witness against thy neighbour.

IX. Thou shalt not covet thy neighbour's wife.

X. Thou shalt not covet thy neighbour's goods.

The faithful are obliged to know the commandments by heart, and it would be good for them to recite them every day. Moreover, they should study and understand them.

8. Before beginning to explain each commandment in particular, let us remark in general that the *Decalogue* is the development of the great law of charity, which comprises, as Jesus Christ expressly teaches, two distinct precepts, *Thou shalt love the Lord thy God with thy whole heart, and thy neighbour as thyself.* It was because of this twofold fundamental precept that God engraved the Decalogue on two tablets of stone, on the first of which were inscribed the duties towards God, and on the second those towards ourselves and our neighbour.

All the commandments, in whatever form they be expressed, are at once both preceptive and prohibitive; that is to say, each commandment contains a command and a prohibition, a particular duty which is prescribed, and a particular sin which is forbidden.

First Commandment:
'I am the Lord thy God. Thou shalt not have strange gods before Me.'

I. Obligation.

1. The first commandment ordains that we should know the true God and render to Him that supreme homage which is due to Him. It was given to the people of Israel in these terms, ' I am the Lord thy God, who brought thee out of the land of Egypt and out of the house of bondage. Thou shalt not have strange gods before Me. Thou shalt not adore them nor serve them ;

for I am the Lord thy God, showing mercy to them that love me (Exod. xx. 2). This declaration comprises, (1) faith, hope, and charity, which are the three theological virtues, and (2) religion, which occupies the first rank amongst the moral virtues.

The first commandment plainly prescribes the worship of God, or the virtue of religion; but it is not so plain at first sight that it also prescribes the three theological virtues. In order, however, to understand this, it will suffice to consider, (1) that these virtues are contained in the precept of worship, for it is impossible to worship God perfectly without loving Him, and love supposes faith and hope; (2) that these three virtues are involved in the precept of knowing the true God expressed in these words, 'I am the Lord thy God ... who show mercy to those who love Me;' for by virtue of these words, I must not only acknowledge and believe that there is one God, Creator of heaven and earth, but, moreover, that the one God is *my* God, my first principle, my last end, my sovereign good; that He answers to all the wants of my intelligence, because He is the eternal truth; all the desires of my heart, because He is infinitely good towards me; all the aspirations of my love, because He is infinitely good and amiable in Himself: in a word, I must acknowledge Him as my supreme end, and as the grand object to which all my being must tend by faith, by hope, and by charity. Jesus Christ speaks of this perfect and loving knowledge of God when He says, 'This is eternal life; that they may know the only true God' (John xvii. 3).

2. We must therefore, by virtue of the first commandment, (1) know the true God, (2) believe in Him, (3) hope in Him, (4) love Him with all our heart, (5) render Him the supreme worship which is due to Him.

(1) Above all we must open the eyes of our intelligence to know the living personal God, the Creator and Master of the universe, the only true God whom all

nature proclaims, whom the light of reason as well as that of faith shows us by evidence.*

(2) We must believe in God, and by our faith render homage to His supreme truth. Faith† is a supernatural virtue, by which we believe firmly on the infallible word of God all that is divinely revealed and proposed as such by the Church.

(3) We must hope in God, so as to render homage to His goodness towards us. Hope is a supernatural virtue, by which we expect from God eternal salvation and the means to attain it, because He has promised them through the merits of Jesus Christ; and He is infinitely good, powerful and faithful to His promises.

(4) We must love God so as to honour His perfection and His infinite amiability. Charity, the most excellent of the supernatural virtues, makes us love God above all things for His own sake, and our neighbour as ourselves for the love of God. The first commandment prescribes the love of God apart from the love of our neighbour, which latter forms the subject of the precept of the second table.

(5) We must render to God the supreme worship which is due to Him. This is really the virtue of *religion*, which is defined as a moral virtue, by which we render to God a worship worthy of Him. Worship, to be really worthy of God, must be animated by the theological virtues, faith, hope, and charity, which are, so to speak, the soul of the virtue of religion. What, then, must worship be? What are the acts by which we must practise it, and what must we understand by the worship of the saints?

* See the 'Apologetic' Part, chap. i. first article, 'The Existence of God,' p. 14.

† See the 'Dogmatic' Part, chap. xvi. second article, and also chap. v. second article, 'Of the Theological Virtues.'

1. Qualities of Worship.

3. Worship must be interior and exterior, direct and indirect.

4. *Interior worship* consists in acts of faith, respect, love, and other acts which are produced by the heart. *Exterior worship* consists in vocal prayers, sacred song, and the offices of the Church. It is called also *public worship*, because it is rendered to God, not by isolated individuals, but by the community at large, by human society.

Purely interior worship is not sufficient; for man owes also to God an exterior and public worship, (1) because, as he belongs entirely to God, he owes Him the homage of his whole being; (2) because exterior acts serve to raise his mind and heart to God; (3) because exterior worship gathers men as children round their father; (4) because, since the beginning of the world, God has always prescribed an exterior and public worship.*

5. *Direct worship* is that by which we honour God in Himself. *Indirect* worship is that by which we honour the saints in the way which will be explained later on.

2. Acts of Worship.

6. The principal acts by which we must practise religion and worship are, adoration, sacrifice, the oblation of ourselves, prayer, and the participation in the public worship of the Church.

Adoration consists in venerating God as the Creator of all things, as the Supreme Master whom all the universe must serve; and in submitting ourselves entirely to His sovereign dominion.

Sacrifice is the oblation and immolation of a victim to honour the supreme majesty of God and obtain His favours.

---

* See the 'Apologetic' Part, chap. i.

The oblation of ourselves consists in offering our bodies and souls, also all that we are and all that we possess, to God, and in doing all our actions for His greater glory, according to the words of St. Paul, ' Whether you eat or drink, or whatever else you do, do it all for the glory of God.'

7. *Prayer* is the communing with God, or, as others express it, an elevation of the soul to God, to offer Him our praises, our petitions, and all the feelings of our heart. Prayer is necessary for our salvation, not only by necessity of precept, but also by necessity of means for adults, in the sense that prayer is the ordinary means by which they must obtain the necessary helps to salvation.*

8. The precept of prayer, though always obligatory, is not binding at every instant of the day; but it obliges us to pray, (1) as soon as we have attained the age of reason; (2) when we are strongly tempted; (3) when we have fallen into mortal sin; (4) when we are in danger of death; (5) from time to time during life; (6) in time of public calamities.

Theologians teach that absolutely to neglect all prayer during the space of a month would constitute a grave violation of the precept of prayer.† But a true Christian, without asking what is of grave and strict obligation, makes a frequent use of this holy exercise, and has his prayers regulated for every day.

We should never omit our morning or evening prayers, and those before and after meals, which are customary amongst the faithful. A person who, without any reason, would pass a day without saying a prayer, invoking God or the Blessed Virgin, or his angel guardian or the saints, could hardly be counted free

---

* See later, chapter ' On Prayer.'

† Gousset. As Mgr. Gousset has collected in his *Moral Theology* the doctrine of all the best authors, we have taken him for our principal guide in the explanation of the Decalogue.

from venial sin; but to miss or neglect the duty of morning and evening prayer, frequently and for days together, without supplying the omission during the day by another prayer, would be to expose oneself to the danger of losing every sentiment of piety, and of soon falling into some grave sin. Besides, as it is not necessary that these prayers should be long, they are possible to every one. Devotion requires that they should be said kneeling; but those who cannot conveniently pray in this posture are readily exempted from it.

9. *The participation in the public worship of the Church* consists in frequenting the Sacraments, in assisting at the Sacrifice of the Mass, as well as at the other offices and solemnities which are celebrated in the churches.

8. Worship of the Saints.

10. We honour God, though in an indirect manner, by the honour we render to *the saints;* that is to say, to the Blessed Virgin, the saints, the martyrs, and other blessed souls who are recognised as saints by the Church. These honours consist in offering prayers, praises, and supplications to them, and in celebrating their feasts and honouring their memory.

11. The worship of the saints differs essentially from the worship of God.* The worship of God is *supreme*, and rendered to the infinite excellence of the Divine Majesty; whereas the worship of the saints is *inferior*, and rendered to the creatures whom the Creator has crowned with grace and glory. This worship, rendered directly to the saints, refers indirectly to God, who is the Author of all sanctity. The worship rendered to God is called *latria* (adoration); that which is rendered to the saints is called *dulia* (homage); that which is rendered to the Blessed Virgin is called *hyperdulia* (superior homage), because of her supereminent dignity as Mother of God.

* See 'Dogmatic,' chap. xvii. second article, 'Last Things.'

12. The worship of the saints is not only just and lawful, but it possesses also most precious advantages; for (1) this worship is consecrated by the general practice of the Church, a practice which is founded upon tradition and the Scriptures; (2) it is agreeable to God, who beholds Himself glorified in His saints, and honoured by the honour rendered to His servants; (3) it procures for the faithful powerful intercessors in heaven, and stimulates them to imitate their virtues on earth.

13. We honour the saints in two ways: (1) directly, in themselves; (2) in their relics, images. Such, besides, is the practice of the universal Church, a holy and salutary practice, which is authorised by the Scriptures and the most venerable tradition.

We honour *the relics of the saints*, (1) because they are precious memorials of our best friends; (2) because the bodies of the saints, having been instruments of virtue and members of Jesus Christ, will rise again in glory; (3) because it has pleased God to glorify these sacred remains by miracles.

We honour the images of Jesus Christ and the saints because they excite devotion, fix our attention during prayer, remind us of salutary truths, and place the most beautiful examples before our eyes.

14. The worship rendered to holy images and relics is a *relative* worship, which ascends to and reaches the persons whose relics are venerated. This relative worship is in the supreme degree of *latria*, when Jesus Christ or the relics of His holy Passion are worshipped; of *dulia*, when we venerate the relics of the saints; and of *hyperdulia*, when we honour the images of the Blessed Virgin.

II. Sins against the First Commandment.

15. The first commandment forbids all sins contrary to faith, hope, charity, and the virtue of religion.* It for-

* See further on, chap. v. first article, 'Sins against the Theological Virtues.'

bids (1) to refuse belief to what the Church teaches, to wilfully doubt in matters of faith, to neglect instruction, to expose ourselves to lose our faith by bad books, to be ashamed of our faith through cowardly human respect; (2) to despair or to presume in the matter of salvation; (3) to give our hearts to creatures with prejudice to the law of God, to neglect to make acts of the love of God, to hate God, to fight against God or His Church. (4) The sins contrary to the virtue of religion may be reduced to two principal ones—superstition and irreligion—which are opposed to this virtue, one by excess and the other by default.

16. (1) The principal sins which relate to superstition are idolatry, divination, and magic. It is not only forbidden to adore demons or false gods, but also to consult fortune-tellers, to conjure up spirits, to have pretended communications with the souls of the dead, or to seek evil or marvellous effects from magic by the intervention of the devil. It is superstitious to interrogate a table, or any other article of furniture, as if it were endowed with intelligence. As to animal magnetism or mesmerism, whatever it may have been in its origin, it has since been allied to superstition and licentiousness to such an extent that it has been condemned by Rome, and has been forbidden as a culpable and dangerous abuse.*

17. (2) Amongst the sins of irreligion we distinguish four principal ones: heresy, apostasy, impiety, and sacrilege. *Heresy* consists in obstinately denying a dogma of faith proposed by the Church. *Apostasy* is the renouncing of the Catholic faith to adhere to a sect of any kind, even that of the freethinkers. *Impiety* is the sin of those who outrage or blaspheme God and His Church. By *sacrilege* is meant the profanation of a holy thing. It is called *personal*, *real*, or *local*, according as it is directed against a person, a thing, or a place consecrated to divine worship. It is a sacrilege to

* 'Ency. of the Holy Office,' August 4 1856.

profane the Sacraments, a cemetery, or the goods belonging to a church. Those who usurp or confiscate the goods, revenues, rights of the Church, or pious foundations, are sentenced to excommunication by the holy Council of Trent, and can only be absolved by the Sovereign Pontiff himself.

Second Commandment:
'Thou shalt not take the name of the Lord thy God in vain.'

1. The second commandment ordains that we must revere the holy name of the Lord, always speak of God and holy things with profound respect; we testify this respect by pronouncing or invoking His holy name, or that of His Divine Son our Lord Jesus Christ, with sentiments of piety and veneration.

Such is the precept indirectly expressed in this commandment, the *direct* expression of which is a prohibition. It forbids all acts contrary to the respect we owe to the holy name of God; above all, blasphemy, perjury, and the violation of vows.

2. (1) To *blaspheme* is to utter words injurious to God, to speak or disseminate writings against God. It is not necessary, to constitute blasphemy, that the discourse uttered should be directly against God; it is enough if it be against the saints or holy things, such as the Church of Jesus Christ, her Sacraments, her ministers, and whatever relates to our holy religion. The injury then reverts to God, the Author of these holy institutions and of all holiness.

3. There are distinctions in blasphemy. (1) There is the simple blasphemy, which means a gross oath; and there is the blasphemy of a connected discourse, or conversation in which blasphemous ideas are often brought forward under a seductive and polished form. (2) There are also the spoken and the written blasphemy; (3) the blasphemy of malediction and that of derision or of sacrilegious jesting. Impious *imprecations*, by which

the vengeance of God is invoked on our own heads or on others, may also be classed under the head of blasphemies.

Real blasphemy must not be confounded with strong language and those popular unseemly blasphemous phrases, which resemble and approach to it.

Blasphemy, properly so called, is always a mortal sin. The Scripture says: 'He that blasphemeth the name of the Lord, dying, let him die' (Leviticus xxiv. 16). Words approaching to blasphemy, without being mortal sins, are unfit for the mouth of a Christian.

4. Besides those who formally utter blasphemy, there are others who render themselves gravely culpable in this respect, namely, those who provoke or applaud it; those who, being bound to prevent, tolerate it; those who publish impious and blasphemous newspapers, reviews, pamphlets, or other productions; those who read them with pleasure, and even those who, without reading them, favour their publication, or support them by their subscriptions.

5. (2) Perjury is a false oath, or the abuse of the religious act which is called an oath or swearing.

To swear is to call on God to witness the truth of what we say or promise. This act is good and holy in itself. To call upon God to witness is to profess that God is the supreme truth, and that He knows all things.

6. Three conditions, however, are always necessary to make an oath lawful in practice: truth, justice, and judgment; which means that it is necessary not only that the matter of the oath be true, and that it involves no sin, but also that there be a just reason for affirming it by oath. It is a mortal sin to affirm in this way a lie, a calumny, a criminal project, &c. To swear lightly and for slight reasons is disrespectful to the Divine Majesty, and exposes him who does so to falling into the sin of perjury.

7. Promises made on oath must be fulfilled, if the thing promised is neither bad nor forbidden. It is not allowed to fulfil an oath which promises the accomplishment of a bad action. A sin has been committed by taking the oath, but a second would be committed by its fulfilment, because we can never be obliged to offend God.

8. (3) We sin against the second commandment by breaking vows. By a vow is meant a promise made to God, with deliberation and an intention that it should be binding, to accomplish some greater good. By a *greater good* we mean a thing which is good in itself, and which it is more meritorious to perform than to omit. A vow must not be confounded with a good resolution, which latter does not include the *will* to bind oneself under pain of sin.

9. A *solemn* vow is that which is taken in religious orders approved by the Church, at the time of profession; and a *simple* vow is one that is made under other circumstances.

10. A vow is a useful and holy thing so long as in making it we are guided by discretion and prudence. If it relates to an important thing which we wish to promise to God, it is wise to pray a great deal before taking the vow, and to ask the advice of one's confessor.

11. The Church, by virtue of the power of binding and loosing, which she has received from Jesus Christ, may for any just reason dispense from vows, or commute them to other good works. She can also dispense from a promissory oath. This power belongs to the Pope and the bishops, who exercise it either themselves or by their delegates.

Third Commandment:
'Remember thou keep holy the Sabbath-day.'

1. The third commandment of God ordains that we should sanctify the Sunday, or the day of the Lord, and it forbids us to profane it.

2. The natural law prescribed the sanctification of a day from time to time, by consecrating it to the worship of the Lord, but it did not fix any particular day. The Mosaic revelation specifies the sanctification of the *Sabbath*, and the Christian decalogue that of the *Sunday*.

The Sabbath was established in the Old Testament in memory of the repose of God after the six days of Creation, and also of the benefit which He had conferred upon the people of Israel by delivering them from the slavery of Egypt (Deut. v. 14, 15). The law of the Sabbath seems to have existed before the time of Moses, and probably goes back to the origin of the human race.

The Apostles substituted Sunday for the Sabbath, in perpetual remembrance of the great mystery of the resurrection of Jesus Christ and of the descent of the Holy Ghost. These mysteries, which comprehend a spiritual deliverance and a new creation more excellent than the first, were accomplished, not on the seventh day of the week, but on the eighth, which is also the first day of a new week. Our Lord Himself sanctified this day, to a certain degree, with His disciples, by appearing in the midst of them in the cenacle on two successive Sundays.

Therefore the disciples most justly regarded this day as sacred, and called it *Sunday, Dominica dies*, or *the day of the Lord*, and commanded all the faithful to sanctify it.

3. It is right and just that we should give one day to the Lord after giving six to the cares of the world. The sanctification of the Sunday is a public profession of our faith, and a necessary aliment to the life of our souls.

The sanctification of the Sunday comprises two distinct obligations, that of rest and that of divine worship. In other words, to sanctify the day of the Lord we must, (1) abstain from servile works; and (2) apply ourselves to religious exercises.

4. (1) Work is prohibited on Sunday because it would hinder the religious exercises which God exacts on that day, and because, continued without interruption, it would be prejudicial even to the bodily well-being of man. God has ordained this holy rest in the interests of both soul and body.

5. The law of rest prohibits *servile* works, but not those which are called *liberal* or *ordinary*.

By servile works are meant those which exercise the body principally, and which are especially for its use. Such are mechanical works, trades and various manufactures, agricultural pursuits, and manual labour; work also done with the needle or other implements, even when it is not done to gain money. Those who work are not the only persons guilty of sin, but those also who force others, or allow their inferiors to work. Their sin is as great as if they worked themselves, and they render themselves guilty besides of the sins of others, and the scandal caused by them.

Besides servile works, *law proceedings*, which are accompanied with noise and contention, such as trying a case, summoning witnesses, and hearing them, &c., are equally forbidden by the Church, which is the interpreter of the law of God.

The Church also forbids public buying and selling, the displaying of goods, noisy traffic in open shops, transactions and contracts, and markets and fairs. This prohibition is modified according to the manners and customs of different places.

It is pretty generally admitted that it is allowable to sell articles of which country people have to lay in a supply for a week or several weeks at a time, such as eatables, clothing, and other articles of consumption.

6. *Ordinary* works are those which relate to daily necessities, and to the cares of the household. They are

not prohibited any more than are journeys, so long as their accomplishment does not expose us to the danger of missing Mass without reason.

7. The *liberal* works, which are in a similar way allowed, are those which depend more on the activity of the mind than on that of the body, and which tend directly to the cultivation of the intelligence, such as reading, writing, teaching, drawing, study, and all that belongs to the liberal arts. The professors of arts or sciences may work or give lessons. Architects, painters, sculptors, and embroiderers may trace designs, projects, and plans of work on paper.

8. The *rest* of Sunday is obligatory from one midnight to the next. A person working without reason or necessity for a considerable time (for example, for several consecutive or non-consecutive hours) would be guilty of mortal sin.

9. There are, however, reasons which may dispense with the obligation to rest: (1) dispensation, which may be granted by the bishop or parish priest, when there is sufficient ground; (2) necessity; for instance, in case of fire or inundation; (3) piety, which excuses certain servile works performed for divine worship; (4) charity, which allows us to work for the sick and the poor when they are under pressing necessity.

10. (2) Besides the obligation of rest there is that of performing *religious exercises*. The first and principal of the good works which we must perform on the Lord's day is to assist at the holy Sacrifice of the Mass. The faithful, who have arrived at the use of reason, are obliged to hear Mass on Sundays and feasts of obligation. We are obliged to hear an entire Mass, under pain of mortal sin; so that if we arrive much too late, say after the Offertory, we are obliged to hear another Mass. We must also assist at Mass in a Christian spirit, that is with respect and devotion. It does not suffice to be present bodily if our minds are

occupied with anything rather than the service of God.*

Mass is prescribed for Sundays and holidays of obligation, because, being the renewal of the Sacrifice of the Cross, it constitutes the most holy and salutary of actions, and is the one best calculated to honour the Divine Majesty.

11. Besides hearing Mass, it is proper to assist as far as possible at the other divine offices; at sermons or instructions; also to frequent the Sacraments, and to occupy ourselves with acts of piety and charity proper to each one's state. We are not, however, obliged to consecrate the whole day to acts of piety and charity, but are allowed to employ a part of it in lawful and Christian recreation.

12. The precept of hearing Mass ceases to be of obligation when it is morally or physically impossible for us to fulfil it. Thus the following persons are dispensed from hearing Mass on Sundays: the sick; the convalescent, who cannot get out without the danger of a relapse; those who have to attend to the sick; those who cannot be replaced in taking care of the house or young children; shepherds who cannot leave their flocks; those who, on account of the great distance from church, can only get there with much difficulty. Persons who are in mourning are also excused during all the period of their remaining in the house, according to the custom of the place they live in. And lastly, servants, children, and wives, when their masters, parents, or husbands insist on their working during the time of Mass, are dispensed when their refusal to obey would result in serious inconvenience.

13. The Sunday is profaned not only by forbidden work, but more especially by other sins, and by dangerous and sinful amusements.

* See further on, the way to hear Mass well (Second Commandment of the Church).

Just as Almighty God often bestows His special benedictions on families and nations who are faithful to the observance of Sunday, so does He threaten with the most severe chastisements those who profane the holy day. The profanation of the Sunday is a great crime in the eyes of God, a disgrace to religion, and a scandal to one's neighbour. Its results are most fatal; for it produces forgetfulness of God and duty, the demoralisation of the people, and the ruin of Christianity in souls. There can exist no religion without the observance of the Sunday, because without it there is no longer any instruction or any religious observance.

Fourth Commandment:
'Honour thy father and thy mother.'

1. 'The fourth commandment,' says the Apostle St. Paul, 'is the first commandment with a promise' (Eph. vi. 2). This promise of a long and happy life being, however, conditional on the welfare of the children, is not always fulfilled here below. Sometimes God is pleased to reserve all the recompense for eternity.

This commandment is also the first of the second table of the law; that is, the first of those which concern our neighbour. It contains the reciprocal duties of parents and children, as well as those of all other superiors and inferiors.

2. If we look at the letter of the precept, it would seem at first sight to speak only of duties towards our father and mother. It has, however, a much wider meaning. The words 'Honour thy father and thy mother' signify 'Honour thy parents and all thy superiors;' for according to the original language of the Scriptures the name of *father* includes not only those to whom we owe our life, but also those who, according to the dispositions of Divine Providence, are our superiors in the spiritual and in the temporal order. Moreover, since these superiors must be honoured by their inferiors,

it follows that on their part, by a natural reciprocity, they are obliged to merit such honours by fulfilling their duties towards their children and inferiors.

3. We will speak, (1) of the duties of children; (2) of the duties of parents; (3) of the reciprocal duties of other superiors and inferiors.

I. The Duties of Children.

4. 'Honour,' says the sacred text, 'thy father and thy mother.' To honour our parents is to love them, to respect them, to obey them; love, respect, and obedience constitute *filial piety*, or the whole duties of the child towards the parent. Under the word 'parents,' grandfathers, grandmothers, and other ancestors are also included, who have a right to the love and respect of their grandchildren.

(1) To love our parents is to have for them a sincere, grateful, and constant affection, whatever they may be in themselves, and to give them proofs of it during their life, at their death, and after their death. Nothing can dispense us from filial love: if our parents be poor and infirm we must cherish them all the more; and if even they be wicked and vicious we should still love them, hating only their vices and misconduct. Filial love makes it a duty for us to assist our parents in their temporal needs, and above all to see that they do not die without the helps of our holy religion. It would only be cruelty to give way to false delicacy, to the cowardly fear of causing pain to the sick, to neglect calling for a priest in time to prepare a father or mother for the awful passage into eternity. We must pray for them also during their life, pray ourselves and obtain the prayers of others for them after their death, and faithfully fulfil their last requests.

Fraternal love imposes similar, though less stringent, obligations between brothers and sisters.

5. (2) We must have for our parents a true interior

and exterior respect, regarding them as taking the place of God, showing them esteem and honour, speaking to them with deference and civility, receiving their corrections, bearing with, excusing, and hiding their faults. It is moreover a holy and Christian practice to ask the blessing of our parents.

6. (3) To obey our parents is to do what they command; but to obey them in a Christian spirit is to do it with zeal and promptitude, having in view Almighty God, whose will it is that we should obey our parents as we would obey Him Himself. Faith, in fact, teaches us that our parents and superiors are invested with the authority of God, and that to obey them in all that is just and right is to obey God Himself.

Children owe this Christian obedience to their parents in all that is not contrary to the law of God; they owe it particularly, as St. Thomas says, in all that concerns their education, their training in morality, in those things which concern family government and order.

7. We sin against filial *love* when we cherish in our hearts aversion or hatred towards our parents; when we curse them or wish them evil; when we make them angry, grieve them, fill them with bitterness, or neglect to pray for them.

8. We sin against *respect* when we despise them, give them cross looks, speak to them harshly, or answer them insolently; when we scoff at their advice, or mimic them so as to turn them into ridicule; also when we indulge in projects to their injury or menace them. To lift a threatening hand against father or mother, even without striking them, is a mortal sin.

It is also undutiful towards our parents to take pleasure in thinking of their faults; to tell those faults to others, who were ignorant of them before; or to exaggerate them; in a word, to injure their reputation in any way. In this case there is a double sin—a sin against justice and a sin against filial piety.

Lastly, those persons are blameworthy who, having become rich or elevated in rank themselves, refuse, through pride or vanity, to acknowledge their parents publicly, to visit them, and receive them at their homes, because they are poor or uneducated.

9. We sin against filial *obedience* when we refuse to do what our parents command, or when we murmur at having to do it. The sin of disobedience may be mortal or venial, according to the degree of resistance or obstinacy accompanying it, and according as the command is more or less important. We sin when, in spite of the advice of our parents, we frequent the company of bad people, or suspicious houses, taverns, dances, shows, or nocturnal amusements; when, despite our parents' orders, we neglect to hear Mass on feast-days, to approach the Sacrament of Penance, and to assist at the parochial instructions. We sin, again, when we do not perform what is commanded by our parents for the interest of the family, or when, without legitimate cause, we quit the paternal roof against their will. A person who forms a particular friendship with a view to marriage without the knowledge of his parents is also wanting in deference to parental authority.

10. To disobey our parents is a special sin which we must mention in confession. Thus, for example, he who, notwithstanding the orders of his parents, does not hear Mass on Sundays, must accuse himself, not only of this omission, but also of having disobeyed his parents.

11. If, however, a parent is unhappy enough to give a command contrary to the law of God, to justice, or morality, a child must refuse obedience; it would not then be disobeying a parent, but obeying Almighty God. Moreover, when a child, having arrived at a certain age, has to choose a state of life, as such choice is of very great importance in the affairs of salvation, he must ask God's grace to know His will in this respect in order that he may make his choice according to it. But

besides consulting God by prayer and a prudent director in the tribunal of Penance, Christian children must also, generally speaking, consult their father and mother on such a serious subject, and especially when it is a case of choosing a state in the world.

II. The Duties of Parents.

12. Parents must love their children, and show them this love by procuring for them the blessings of maintenance, education, and a suitable establishment in life.

13. (1) They must love their children in a Christian manner; that is, for God's sake, with a love mingled with respect, regarding them as a sacred charge confided to them by the Lord, desiring and seeking their real welfare both of body and soul. This is why it is important, above all, to procure for them the grace of baptism.

14. (2) We understand by *maintenance* whatever regards corporal well-being and the necessities of life. Parents are obliged to take great care to preserve the life and health of their children, and also the perfect formation of their members; they must provide nourishment and suitable clothing for them according to their condition.

15. (3) Education consists in the formation of the man *as man*, that is, as a reasonable moral creature who is endowed with an immortal soul. It comprises two parts—the formation of the mind or *instruction;* and that of the heart, which consists in good habits.

16. Education must be Christian, that is, based upon Christian doctrine and morality. The reason of this is, (1) that, by virtue of the positive law of Jesus Christ, all men are obliged to live according to His holy doctrine; and (2) that an education which is not Christian is not a true education, but only a false and bad training; for (3) if we consider the *intellectual part* of education, which is *instruction*, as soon as it becomes purely

profane and separated from religious teaching it cannot be otherwise than false and incomplete. It must be incomplete, because human instruction comprises not only the knowledge which relates to the body and to the present life, but also that which regards the soul and the future life of man. Now of these two parts, a purely secular education includes only the first and least important. It must, moreover, be false, because it gives to man a false tendency, making him direct his actions and his career to the goods of this world, instead of those immortal goods which are the principal end of his existence. If we consider what *moral training* is, we shall find that it cannot exist without religion, which alone can subdue the passions of the human heart and make a man virtuous. An exclusively secular education may make a man skilful in natural sciences, in industry, and politics; but however skilful he may become by such training, he will never be anything but a vicious man.

17. Christian education is begun in the family, and is generally completed in schools. Domestic education must be the basis of scholastic or public education. The duties of parents with regard to education comprise instruction, vigilance, correction, and good example.

18. (1) Parents, after having procured for their children the blessing of holy baptism, are bound to give them that Christian instruction which the baptismal character demands; for this reason, they must teach them, as soon as they are capable of learning them, the first truths of religion: the sign of the cross, the Lord's Prayer, and all that a Christian is bound to know. They must also train them early to practices of piety and virtue, by making them say their morning and night prayers, and by accustoming them to go to church and attend the parochial catechism; to observe the laws of abstinence, and to go to confession from time to time; also by removing them from all danger to their souls and from all the snares laid for their innocence, such as bad

servants, bad companions, bad games, bad reading, bad schools, &c.

19. (2) It is, moreover, the strict duty of parents carefully to watch over their children's conduct; to warn them when they do wrong; to reprehend, correct, and even punish them if there is no other means of making them respect parental authority. If, however, punishment is necessary, it must be just and reasonable. Mildness must be mingled with severity; that firmness and prudent energy must be observed which keeps the happy medium between violence and weakness.

20. (3) Parents must add good example to their vigilance, advice, and teaching, otherwise all the rest will be useless; for children should see the instructions of their parents exemplified in their own piety, words, and actions.

21. (4) Parents must interest themselves in the future of their children by applying them to work and to studies, in order to fit them for a suitable and honest career in after life. In the choice of this state they must aid them, if necessary, by their advice, in consulting not merely human preferences and interest, but the order and vocation of God, which they must strive to know. To this end they must study the inclination and aptitude of the child, and pray to God, taking counsel also of wise, enlightened, and disinterested persons. By acting thus they will provide for the future of their children in a Christian manner, without prejudice to the rights of God and of those of the children themselves. It would be abusing their authority to try to force a child to enter into the married state, or into religion, or into the priesthood. It would be going against God to oppose the inclination of a child and a vocation approved by a prudent confessor.

22. Parents sin against *parental love* by fostering an aversion or hatred for their children, by uttering imprecations and maledictions with regard to them, by ill-

treating them, speaking of their faults before strangers. They sin, again, when they have an excessive and ill-regulated affection for their children, which leads them to bring them up softly, to allow them everything they desire, and hinders them from correcting their faults; also they sin when their love is not equal for all their children, but is shown to an unjust degree towards one or several to the exclusion of the others, which is an ordinary cause of jealousy and discord in families.

23. Parents neglect their duty with regard to the *bodily* well-being of their children when they expose them to accidents which might kill them, maim them, or deform them. All negligence that leads to a serious injury to the life, health, or proper development of the child is a mortal sin. It is a sin also when by sloth, or unnecessary expenses, or gambling, parents deprive their children of the means of proper subsistence, and also when they destroy their future prospects by neglecting to form them for a social position.

24. Parents neglect the *spiritual* good of their children if they are the cause of their being deprived of baptism, and if they do not make it their first care to see to the Christian education of those who, by baptism, have been made the disciples of Jesus Christ.

25. When parents wish to lay on others the responsibility of the care or education of their children, they must choose persons who, in all respects, are worthy of their confidence. They are guilty of mortal sin if they confide them to teachers who are destitute of faith, religion, or morality, and who are capable of perverting the young by their principles or bad example, or by their mere indifference.

26. Parents sin when they give scandal to their children by their own negligence in matters of religion, or by their impiety, blasphemies, falsehoods, calumnies, by cursing any one, or by any other act which is contrary to charity, justice, holiness, or evangelical morality

They would be still more guilty if they took them to dangerous amusements, and if they commanded them to do things which are forbidden by the laws of religion, of the Church, or of justice. In such a case there would be a double sin—one against parental love, and the other against the virtue outraged by the sinful action.

III. The reciprocal Obligations of other Superiors and Inferiors.

27. Besides parents there are three other kinds of superiors, namely, those who take the place of our parents, those who are our superiors in the spiritual order, and those who are our superiors in the temporal order.

(1) The superiors who take the place of our parents are tutors and instructors.

28. The obligations of *guardians* towards their wards, as regards both temporal and spiritual things, are much the same as those of fathers and mothers towards their children. It is the duty of a guardian to provide for the young person confided to his care a suitable education, to watch over his conduct, and to warn and correct him. And reciprocally, the duties of wards towards their guardians are much the same as those of children towards their parents, with the exception, however, of the duty of assistance.

29. *Teachers*, schoolmasters, and all charged with the education and instruction of youth, being the persons in whom parents have placed their confidence, and to whom they have delegated their parental authority, are bound to labour constantly for the advancement of their pupils in piety, virtue, and science. They render themselves seriously guilty, either by leaving them to themselves without watching over their conduct and making them fulfil their religious duties, or by neglecting to provide against anything that might be injurious to their

health, or by leaving within their reach books dangerous to their faith or morals, or, in fine, by giving them bad example. The duties of pupils with regard to their masters are similar to those of children towards their parents, at least as far as regards respect and obedience.

30. (2) *Superiors in the spiritual order* are the ecclesiastical authorities—the Pope, the bishops, and the priests charged with the guidance of souls. They have great obligations to fulfil towards the people confided to their care. The principal of these are—to teach, to exhort, to administer the Sacraments, to fight against scandals, to visit the sick, and to help the dying, even at the peril of their own lives. The duties of the faithful towards their pastors are—to respect them, and to obey them as they would Jesus Christ in things that relate to the spiritual order; and, if it be necessary, to provide for their subsistence. All the ministers of religion have a right to our respect; but we must honour in a special manner the Sovereign Pontiff, who is our common father, the pastor of pastors, the Vicar of Jesus Christ; the bishop, who is the pastor of the whole diocese; the parish-priest, who is the pastor of the parish; the confessor, who is the father of all those whom he directs in the way of salvation. We sin against the respect due to a priest by raillery, by back-biting, and by calumny. If it should happen that his character is so much injured as to render him unable to fulfil the duties of his ministry with advantage to souls, this would be a grave sin against justice and religion.

31. (3) *Superiors in the temporal order* are sovereigns, legislators, magistrates, and masters.

Sovereigns, legislators, and magistrates have equally duties to fulfil towards the people. What a father of a family is to his children a head of the State should be in a certain degree to his subjects, namely, a protector and a guide, holding the place of God. The people belong to God, who confides them to the care of princes, like sheep to their shepherds.

A prince is 'God's minister for good,' says the Apostle (Rom. xiii. 4); the civil power is established by God for the good of the State, as paternal authority is for the good of the family.

Such is the end which the Apostle, in accordance with right reason, assigns to civil power, which is given to a prince in the interest of the people to procure the public good; in other words, to promote order and suppress disorder. *Order* is justice, peace, property, virtue, religion; and these are what a prince must protect. *Disorder* is injustice, theft, all violation of right, all wrongs caused to citizens, not only in their temporal goods, but also in those of their souls, by public scandals, by the corruption of mind, heart, principles, and morals.

32. From these explanations it is easy to understand what are the obligations of *princes* and *magistrates*. Ministers of Divine Providence for the good of the people, they are obliged to devote themselves to the general good and to the maintenance of public order, the defence of their country; to protect the interests of individuals, to administer justice, to cause it to be administered impartially; to leave to the subject the liberty to do good; to repress licentiousness and abuses; to respect and enforce respect for the laws of religion, without the sanction of which moral and human laws are worthless. They must also be careful only to confide public functions, responsibilities, and employments to men who are capable, worthy, honest, and virtuous; they must also make it their duty to reward merit, punish treason, shortcomings, and crimes; to patronise useful public institutions and establishments.

33. Whatever be the form of government of their country, *legislators* are guilty of sin if they make or vote laws contrary to the rights of religion and the

Church; or if they tolerate either the publication of pernicious writings that tend to endanger the faith or morals of the people, or licentious theatres and indecent spectacles where neither virtue nor the sanctity of marriage is respected. *Magistrates* sin if they are unfaithful to the duties of their office; if they do not show the firmness necessary for preventing or stopping abuses, injustice, or extortions on the part of their subordinates; or if from party spirit or interested motives they show themselves unjust towards any one under their jurisdiction. Many faults of this kind entail the obligation of restitution.

34. The duties of subjects towards the king and civil authorities are to honour, respect, and obey them according to the laws, so far as these are not contrary to the laws of God and the rights of the Church. St. Paul says: 'Let every soul be subject to higher powers; for there is no power but from God. And those that are, are ordained of God. Therefore he that resisteth the power resisteth the ordinance of God. The prince is God's minister for good' (Rom. xiii.).

35. *Masters* are bound to see that their servants observe the law of God, to instruct them or cause them to be instructed in the primary truths of faith, and to give them the necessary time for the fulfilment of their religious duties. They must remonstrate with servants if they do wrong, always, however, with kindness and charity, giving them good advice and good example; they must also pay their wages punctually. If a servant falls sick his master ought, out of charity at least, to procure for him the necessary and suitable remedies or help; and if the illness prove a serious one, the priest should be sent for in good time. A master would be gravely culpable if, instead of edifying his servant, he should scandalise him by his disorders, or by any actions contrary to morality or religion; and he would be still more guilty were he to command or propose to his

servant to do a thing that was unjust, immoral, or forbidden by the laws of the Church.

36. *Servants* and *domestics* owe respect, obedience, service, and fidelity to their masters. Fidelity consists in preserving and using the goods of a master carefully, without ever doing him any injustice or allowing it to be done to him. Obedience binds a servant in all that is just and reasonable, according to the nature of the service for which he was engaged. His obedience should be prompt, exact, and entire; and in order to render it meritorious, he should obey his master as if he obeyed God, as if he obeyed Christ Himself (Eph. vi. 5 seq.). A servant, however, must never execute the commands of a master when they are contrary to the law of God, justice, or morality; his obedience would then be criminal. It would be equally culpable if, for the prospect of reward or the fear of dismissal, he were to allow himself to be drawn into licentiousness, or lend himself to the intrigues and disorders of his master. As to the laws of the Church, a servant may do what is commanded contrary to those laws if he cannot resist the will of his master without serious results, without exposing himself, for instance, to the risk of dismissal, when he could not easily find another master who would allow him to fulfil his duties. The Church does not wish to oblige those who are placed in such a position.

37. Servants render themselves highly culpable by revealing certain family secrets which might compromise the honour, reputation, or interests of their masters. Backbiting and calumny on the part of a servant against his master are much more sinful than if directed against another, and the same is to be said of unfaithfulness, theft, or injustice.

38. Proprietors and the managers of workshops or factories should treat their workmen with Christian kindness, pay them a just salary, and see, above all, that religion and morals are respected amongst them.

On the other hand, workmen should respect their masters, serve them faithfully, and take an interest in their concerns.

39. *Officers in the army* should also treat the soldiers kindly, making them fulfil their religious duties, being themselves an example to them. On their side, soldiers should respect their officers, and obey them in all that concerns military service.

Fifth Commandment:
'Thou shalt not kill.'

1. This commandment has for its end the protection of the life of man, which constitutes the first and foremost of the goods he enjoys on earth; and this must be understood not only of the life of the body, but also of the life of grace, which is the spiritual life of the soul. A man's other possessions, such as his honour, reputation, and fortune, are equally protected by distinct commandments, as will be seen hereafter.

The fifth commandment forbids the murder of the body and the spiritual murder of the soul, which is scandal.

I. Homicide, or Murder.

2. Under this heading are included duelling, suicide, and everything which tends to injure the integrity of human life.

3. *Homicide,* which is forbidden by the fifth commandment, consists in taking away the life of a fellow-man without lawful authority.

No man, however powerful he may be, or whatever wrong he may have sustained, is allowed to kill or wound another without legitimate authority. Those who are legitimately authorised are the executioners of legal sentences, soldiers who fight in a just war, and persons who have no other means of protecting their own life against an unjust aggressor.

4. In the case of defending our own lives we are not allowed to go beyond the limits of a just defence; that is to say, we cannot do more evil to an aggressor than is necessary to avert evil from ourselves; nor is it allowed to strike him before or after the time of his attack. He must have first attacked or shown his intention of doing so before we have a right to wound him; for instance, if he were loading his pistol or drawing his sword, we should then be justified in defending ourselves.

In *every* case where we should be justified in killing an unjust assailant in self-defence it would also be right to do it in defence of another.

5. By a *duel* is meant a premeditated combat between two or more persons, who, on their own private authority, attack each other with murderous weapons in a manner and at a time and place previously agreed upon. However it may be sought to justify a duel, it must always remain a crime in the eyes of religion and sound morality, and a double crime, since we desire to kill another at the same time that we expose our own life. A duel cannot be permitted, either to redeem one's honour, to escape the imputation of cowardice, or under any other pretext. The Church even fulminates her excommunication both against duellists themselves and those who take part in their combat as witnesses or otherwise; she declares them to be infamous, which title they justly earn, since they are cowards in not having courage to forgive, they are bad citizens who violate the laws of society, and bad Christians who trample under foot the laws both ecclesiastical and divine. Those who fall in these barbarous conflicts are deprived of the prayers of the Church and also of Christian burial, the same as those who die by suicide.

6. It is never allowed to kill oneself. To do so is to usurp the rights of God, who is the author and arbitrator of our existence and those of society, whose

members we are. We have only received from God the use of our life, and no one is so far master of it as to be able to take it away when it pleases him. For this reason the law does not say 'Thou shalt not kill thy neighbour,' but in an absolute manner it commands: 'Thou shalt not kill.' The suicide violates this law by committing the most hideous of murders, and merits eternal damnation. It is not suicide to expose one's life to danger from necessity or for the public good. Those who, like the soldier, die rather than quit their post, or the dutiful son who gives to his father the bread he himself is in need of, or the charitable person who, though drowning himself, gives up to another the plank which is his only hope, cannot be held guilty of suicide.

7. Married people, above all, mothers and nurses, cannot ignore the fact that they are guilty of homicide if they expose an infant to perish through malice, or if by some grave imprudence or negligence they endanger the life of a child.

8. The fifth commandment forbids, besides formal homicide, all that is akin to it, or that tends in any way to destroy the integrity of human life; and this comprehends, (1) hatred, anger and revenge, evil wishes and desires of revenge, quarrels, angry blows or threats, all ill-treatment of one's neighbour and hardness towards the poor; (2) all that is hurtful to ourselves, intemperance, excesses that shorten life, and rash exposure of our lives without necessity.

II. Scandal.

9. *Scandal* is contrary to the fifth commandment, because it wounds and kills the soul of our neighbour. It is spiritual murder; for by scandal is meant all that may be the occasion of spiritual ruin to our neighbour. It is defined as a word, action, or omission, either apparently or really bad, that is an occasion of sin to another. Scandal is *direct* when he who is guilty of it has the

intention of leading another into sin ; such is the sin of scandal of him who incites another to a sin of impurity, theft, or perjury. Scandal is only *indirect* when, without intending to be the cause of another's sin, we give bad example, or say or do anything which is to that other the occasion of sin.

10. Those persons must be looked upon as seriously guilty of giving scandal, (1) who are in the habit of blaspheming; (2) who publish newspapers, pamphlets, or other productions contrary to religion or morality; (3) who sell such writings, or cause them to be read; (4) who compose, disseminate, or sing immoral songs; (5) who write or countenance plays or comedies in which there is an absence of all respect for religion, virtue, or the sanctity of marriage; (6) artists who paint or carve indecent pictures or statues ; (7) women who disregard the rules of decency and modesty in their dress.

11. It is a species of scandal to contribute to one's neighbour's sin by a *formal* coöperation, which is never allowed. *Material* coöperation is not the same. By this is meant an action indifferent in itself, which aids and abets the sin of another against the intention of the coöperator. Thus the sale of arms is lawful, notwithstanding the abuse to which they are frequently turned.

12. Real scandal is a great sin, condemned by our Lord in that terrible sentence, 'He that shall scandalise one of these little ones that believe in Me, it were better for him that a mill-stone should be hanged about his neck, and that he should be drowned in the depth of the sea. Woe to the world because of scandals! Woe to that man by whom the scandal cometh !' (Matt. xviii. 6, 7.)

What renders the scandals of the world ruinous to Christians, and more especially to the young, is the rashness with which, on the one hand, persons expose themselves to it, and on the other hand, the human respect which makes them follow bad example, and yield like cowards to doing as others do.

13. The fifth commandment, though prohibitory, also implicitly includes certain obligations. It obliges us, (1) to forgive those who have offended us; (2) to give good example; (3) to repair the evil we have done to soul and body; (4) to assist our neighbour in his spiritual and corporal necessities.

Sixth and Ninth Commandments:

'Thou shalt not commit adultery. Thou shalt not covet thy neighbour's wife.'

1. These two commandments forbid adultery, and whatever is contrary to the holy virtue of chastity. The *sixth* forbids, (1) all external acts of impurity, all conversations, looks, touches, or other actions contrary to the virtue of purity; (2) all occasions that lead to impurity, such as bad company, too free intercourse or familiarity between the sexes, dangerous dances, immodest fashions, indecent pictures or statues, and also plays, songs, newspapers, pamphlets, books, and novels of a licentious and immoral tendency.

The *ninth commandment* forbids interior sins, that is to say, thoughts and desires contrary to purity.

2. We sin by evil thoughts, (1) when we consent to them and desire their accomplishment; (2) when we take pleasure in them even when we have not the will to accomplish them; (3) when we wilfully neglect to put away such thoughts as soon as we perceive them.

There are three distinct parts of an evil thought: (1) the *suggestion*, or the simple idea of the evil which comes to the mind, and which in itself is not sin; (2) the *delectation*, or the sensual pleasure or agreeable impression which generally accompanies an evil thought; (3) the *consent*. If the will advertently and deliberately takes pleasure in the impression felt, there is mortal sin; but if the will gives only an imperfect advertence or a half consent, there is venial sin; if the will does not consent at all, there is no sin.

3. Every sin against holy purity is mortal when it receives full consent. The sin of impurity, disgraceful in the sight of men, and abominable before God, especially when committed by a Christian, is ruinous in its effects and terrible in its punishments.

The effects of impurity are relapse, bad habits, sacrilege caused by the shame of confessing this vice, scandals, and a multitude of other sins, incredulity, hardness of heart, and final impenitence.

The chastisements which follow it often, even in this life, are the loss of honour, goods, and health, and a premature death; and after death, the eternal flames of hell. St. Liguori says that the greater number of the lost owe their condemnation to this sin.

4. There are remedies for impurity, both for the healing of the wounds which the soul has already received, and for preserving it from future falls. Of these remedies some are positive, others negative. Positive means: (1) the love of chastity. This virtue, the beauty of which is extolled by the Scriptures, is the pearl of Christian virtues. It makes men like unto angels; it is the guardian of the heart's peace, and the fruitful source of other virtues and of all kinds of good works.

(2) Prayer, devotion to the Blessed Virgin, to St. Joseph, and to our angel guardian.

(3) The frequenting of the Sacraments.

(4) Fasting, mortification, and work.

(5) Modesty and the custody of the senses.

(6) Humility.

(7) The remembrance of the four last things and the presence of God.

(8) Respect for our dignity as Christians. We ought to preserve the purity of our souls and bodies, because they have been consecrated to God by baptism, by which they were made the members of Jesus Christ, and living temples of the Holy Ghost.

The negative means are: (1) avoiding the occasions

of sin, such as dangerous reading or companions, &c.;
(2) avoiding idleness; (3) avoiding intemperance.

Seventh and Tenth Commandments:
'Thou shalt not steal. Thou shalt not covet thy neighbour's goods.'

1. The seventh and tenth commandments forbid all injustice towards our neighbour with regard to his worldly goods. The *seventh* forbids the outward act of stealing; the *tenth* forbids the inward desire to steal, and all covetousness tending to the acquirement of temporal goods by unjust means. God forbids evil desires, because they are bad in themselves and are the roots of external sins.

In condemning theft, the divine law forbids us at the same time to cause any damage or harm to our neighbour, and commands us to restore what we possess unjustly, and to repair the evil we have done.

2. It is, then, forbidden to take, keep, or unjustly injure our neighbour's goods; to steal or assist in stealing; to buy or receive stolen property; to commit fraud in trade, by using false weights and measures, by passing off false coin or spurious merchandise; to give rise to unjust law-suits; to pass or provoke an unjust sentence; to damage our neighbour's goods unjustly; to prevent him from making a fair profit; to appropriate trust-money to ourselves; to neglect to pay our debts; to dissipate our property by gambling or debauchery, to the prejudice of our family and creditors; to exercise a public function without having the capacity for it. Judges, notaries, lawyers, doctors, &c., are bound by the seventh and tenth commandments to qualify themselves for following their profession properly, and to fulfil conscientiously the duties that relate to it.

3. Theft does not always constitute a mortal sin, because it may be modified by the slightness of the matter. A few pence or even a few shillings do not gene-

rally constitute a grave matter. St. Alphonsus Liguori, in the last century, when money was of much more value than it now is, laid down as a rule that the sum of three *écus*, or fifteen francs, always constituted matter for a mortal sin. But it is hardly possible to establish an absolute and invariable rule in this respect; the faithful must leave such decisions to the judgment of the confessor, who weighs all the circumstances of the case.

4. Small thefts and frauds, continually carried on with the intention of arriving at a considerable sum, are mortal sins, because each of these acts is committed with a gravely culpable intention.

5. Children sin when they steal from their parents, and at the same time they wrong their brothers and sisters, and often cause suspicions of theft to fall on innocent persons in the house.

6. Servants have no right to give alms from the property of their masters, or to pay themselves by secretly withholding or subtracting the amount of their wages.

7. We are bound in justice to restore what belongs to another, to repair any injury we may have caused him, and to pay our debts. We must do this as soon as we can, as far as we can, and to whom we can; that is to say, to the person himself to whom we owe the money, or, if he be dead, to his heirs; and if that is not possible, the sum must be spent in alms and good works. He who is in a position to make restitution is bound to do it himself, and cannot leave it to be done by his heirs.

8. The duty of making restitution, like that of paying debts, forms a part of the responsibility of inheritance, and passes on to the heirs, who share it in proportion to the amount of their inheritance. Their obligations do not, however, extend beyond their proportionate share.

9. The obligation of restitution may be cancelled by the consent of the creditor, and it is suspended by the inability of the debtor to discharge it.

When a person is unable to make immediate restitution, he must have the good-will to do so as soon as he is able; and if he be able to make partial restitution, he must do so without delay.

Urgent need exempts from the duty of restitution those who, by making it, would expose themselves to the danger of losing their position, provided that such position has been legitimately acquired, and not by unjust means. Any one, however, who possesses another man's property may restore it secretly, and without compromising himself.

Eighth Commandment:

'Thou shalt not bear false witness against thy neighbour.'

1. The eighth commandment forbids false witness, and under this head all the wrong that we may do to our neighbour by abusing the faculty of speech.

2. The sins contrary to this commandment are: (1) false testimony; (2) lying and hypocrisy; (3) backbiting and calumny; (4) evil reports; (5) injurious speaking; (6) violation of secrecy; besides (7) also rash judgments and unjust suspicions, which are like injurious words spoken in the heart.

3. (1) False testimony is a deposition made contrary to truth, and upon oath, in a court of justice. False testimony is a mortal sin, for it includes perjury, which does not admit lightness of matter.

4. (2) To tell a *lie* is to speak against one's conviction, to say what one believes to be false knowingly, and with the intention to deceive. There are three kinds of lies, namely, the *jocose* lie, which is told for the sake of merriment; the *officious* lie, which is told to excuse or to spare oneself or others some inconvenience; and the *pernicious* lie, told in order to injure

one's neighbour. There is no lie in words said in jest, the untruth of which is apparent; or in certain phrases which appear false, though their meaning is readily understood. A real lie is a sin, generally venial; but it becomes mortal when it causes a serious injury to the honour or goods of one's neighbour.

5. Hypocrisy is also a kind of lie. It consists in borrowing the appearance of virtue in order to gain the esteem of men.

6. (3) *Backbiting* is the injury done to the reputation of our neighbour, by unjustly revealing his hidden faults and defects. *Calumny* consists in imputing to our neighbour a crime which he has not committed, or in exaggerating a real fault. To constitute backbiting, what we reveal must not have been public before, and it must be *unjust* to reveal it; because Christian charity sometimes requires us to make known our neighbour's faults in order that he may be corrected, or hindered from perverting others, or in order to prevent some evil. In such cases the faults should only be made known to those who ought to be acquainted with them, such as parents, masters, and superiors. It is not backbiting to give disadvantageous, though correct, information concerning another, when we are consulted by persons interested in ascertaining it, when there is question of some projected alliance, or some other affair of importance.

7. Backbiting and calumny are called *detraction*. We may be guilty of detraction in several ways, namely, by attributing to our neighbour a fault which he has not committed, or a defect which he has not; by exaggerating his faults; by proclaiming as certain those which are uncertain; by making known those which before were hidden; by insinuating them; by causing suspicion by speeches such as the following: 'It is reported,' 'They say,' &c.; by putting an unfavourable interpretation on the good actions of our neighbour; by denying his good qualities and seeking to diminish

his merit; sometimes by praising him coldly, or by keeping silence when such silence is an approval of the evil which others are retailing, or a disavowal of the good which is spoken of our neighbour.

8. Detraction and defamation are not only committed by the tongue, but they may be committed in a still more disastrous way by the press, in newspapers and other publications.

9. It is no more allowed to defame a religious order, or any kind of community, than any individual person. Slander and calumny, all other things equal, are even more serious in the former than the latter case.

It is forbidden also to defame the dead, both because their memory should be respected, and also because by defaming them their parents and relations may be seriously injured.

10. It is never allowed to participate in detraction, or to listen to it with pleasure. We must, if possible, excuse our neighbour; or, if we have the authority to do so, we must impose silence on the detractors; if not, we must show by our own silence or serious looks that we disapprove of such conversation; or, according to circumstances, we should turn it adroitly to some other subject.

11. When by slander or calumny we have injured our neighbour in his reputation or possessions, we are bound to repair the wrong as far as possible, either by retracting the calumny or by speaking well of the person whom we have defamed by our slander.

12. (4) Evil report, which is called by theologians *susurration*, consists in repeating to another the unfavourable things we have heard concerning him from a third person. This detestable failing has the effect of sowing discord where peace reigned before, and of disturbing the good relations existing in families and between friends. It is a graver sin than the sin of detraction.

13. (5) Injurious words are offensive words spoken to our neighbour to his face; they may constitute a contempt and an affront which wound his honour. We are guilty of this sin by using hard words, reproaches, by speaking in insinuations, and by cutting raillery. There is, however, no sin in a simple joke amongst friends by way of recreation, unless we foresee that the object of it will be annoyed.

He who has done an injury to another must make reparation as soon as possible.

14. (6) We sin also by the abuse of the tongue when, without sufficient cause, we reveal a secret that has been confided to us. The following are cases where we are dispensed from keeping a secret: (1) when it has become notorious and public, for then it is no longer a secret; (2) when the revelation of the secret is judged necessary for the public good, or for some other very serious reason. We of course are speaking of natural secrecy, and not the sacramental secrecy of confession, from which nothing, under any circumstances, can dispense, and which is guarded by the seal of God Himself.

The law of secrecy not only forbids us to betray what has been confided to us; it also forbids us to extract the secrets of others; and in that is comprehended the breaking of the seals of letters that are not addressed to us, unless we act by legitimate authority, or for a sufficient reason. In this, as in all else that regards the law of justice and of charity, we must act on the grand principle of doing to others as we should reasonably wish they should do unto us.

15. (7) To judge rashly is to judge badly of another's actions without just cause.

When doubts or suspicions or derogatory judgments concerning our neighbour occur to our minds, we must not dwell on them, but rather disapprove and reject them as soon as ever we perceive them to be rash and unjust.

The doubts and suspicions of superiors, of masters, and of fathers of families are not unjust or blameworthy, for it is their duty to watch over their inferiors, and, to a certain degree, mistrust them, that so they may prevent them from doing wrong. They act in such cases from motives of prudence. We may consider the doubts which we form in order to avoid some harm, or to take precautions against the possible occurrence of evil that might happen, of a similar description. A person who receives a stranger into his house may prudently provide for the safety of his possessions, just as he would if the stranger were a person whose honesty he suspected.

16. In order to observe the eighth commandment well we should purify our hearts from all jealousy, envy, and hate, and ask God's help to enable us to govern our tongues, saying with the prophet: 'Set a watch, O Lord, before my mouth, and a door round about my lips. Incline not my heart to evil words, to make excuses in sins' (Ps. cxl.).

CHAPTER III.

COMMANDMENTS OF THE CHURCH.

1. To the ten commandments of God we must add the five *commandments* of the Church, so called because they were established by the Church, that is, by ecclesiastical superiors invested with the authority of Jesus Christ.

2. The commandments of the Church must be observed by all the faithful like the ten commandments of God. They cannot be broken without incurring the guilt of mortal sin and the penalty of eternal damnation. At the same time, being in their nature human laws, the precepts of the Church do not oblige when it is impossible or very difficult to observe them, and they admit of

dispensation. With these legitimate exceptions, we are bound to observe the precepts of the Church as the precepts of God Himself, because they are laid on us by the pastors who govern in His place, and to whom we owe the same obedience as we owe to God, according to the words of our Lord: 'He that heareth you heareth Me; and he that despiseth you despiseth Me' (St. Luke x. 16).

3. The commandments of the Church have for their end, (1) to help us to observe the commandments of God, and the things prescribed by our Lord Jesus Christ; (2) to make us practise the filial obedience, respect, and love that we owe to the Church, our Mother.

4. Among all ecclesiastical ordinances and laws,* there are five which in a special manner concern all the faithful; and these are called the *five commandments of the Church;* they are,

(1) To keep certain appointed days holy, with the obligation of resting from servile works.

(2) To hear Mass on all Sundays and holidays of obligation.

(3) To keep the days of fasting and abstinence appointed by the Church.

(4) To confess our sins to our pastors at least once a year.

(5) To receive the Blessed Sacrament at least once a year, and that at Easter or thereabouts.

First Commandment of the Church :†

To keep certain appointed days holy, with the obligation of resting from servile work.

I. Meaning of Holidays or *Feast*-days.

1. A *feast*-day, or festival, is a day of joy, a day of solemn assembly or public rejoicing, established either

* See above, chap. i. 'Laws,' second article, p. 275.
† See Translator's Preface.

in honour of some distinguished person, or in commemoration of some great event. There are civil festivals and religious festivals; it is of the latter only that we are here about to treat.

2. Religious festivals are days especially consecrated to divine worship. They are established, (1) in order to render to God the solemn homage due to Him; (2) for the spiritual welfare of men; (3) to enliven the days of our earthly pilgrimage with holy joy.

3. There have been festivals as long as there has been any public worship, that is to say, ever since the origin of the human race. The holy Scripture reveals to us this fact of these real festivals in the solemn invocations of the name of the Lord, established by Enos, in the time of our first father, Adam (Gen. iv. 26); then again in the holocausts offered by Noe and his family after the Deluge; and lastly in the celebrated sacrifices offered by Abraham and the other patriarchs on the altars which they had erected.

4. Formed into a nation, the family of the patriarchs received, together with the law of Moses, the institution of various solemn festivals. The chief of these were the Feasts of the Pasch and of Pentecost, which two solemnities were to endure to the end of time, and to be continued in later days, though under a more perfect form, in the Church of Jesus Christ.

5. The Church, in virtue of the power delegated to her by her divine Founder, to regulate all that concerns divine worship, has established festivals (1) in honour of the Blessed Trinity; (2) in honour of our Lord Jesus Christ; (3) in honour of the Blessed Virgin; and (4) in honour of the angels and the saints.

The end of all these festivals is not only to render fitting homage to God and His saints, and a just acknowledgment of their benefits, but likewise to obtain their protection, to inspire the faithful with holy joy, to encourage them, and to nourish their piety and devotion by putting vividly before them the mysteries of faith, and the example of Jesus Christ and His saints.

6. The Church orders that the festivals that are *commanded*, or of obligation, are to be kept holy like Sundays. For France and Belgium there are four of these, which may fall on other days than Sunday, namely, Christmas-day, Ascension-day, the Assumption, and All Saints'.*

7. Besides these feasts of obligation, there are others that are designated as *abolished feasts;* they are those festivals which, by virtue of an indult granted by Pius VII., on the 9th of April 1802, have ceased to be of obligation for France and Belgium, although the divine office is to be continued as before, because the Church desires that the faithful should continue to assist at it. Among these abolished feasts are the *patronal feasts*, that is, the feasts of the patrons of each diocese, parish, or country.

II. General View of the Liturgical Year.

8. This is not all. In addition to the festivals, properly so called, offices are daily celebrated in the Church, which, though of minor solemnity, give to each day a religious colouring, and make it a kind of festival in which the faithful may participate according to their leisure or devotion; so that, viewed as one magnificent whole, the ecclesiastical liturgy presents the aspect of a perpetual festival.

9. By the word *liturgy* is understood the order of religious ceremonies adopted by the Church; it may be said to be the compendium of the external worship prescribed and deposited by her in her official books, which are for that reason called *liturgical books*.

The principal of these books is that which is known to all, the Missal, which the priest uses in saying Mass, and in which the entire ecclesiastical year is unfolded,

* For England, add the Circumcision, the Epiphany, Corpus Christi, and SS. Peter and Paul.

from Advent to All Saints'—the beginning and end of it.

The liturgy is composed of a series of sacred offices relating to the various mysteries of religion, the periodical succession of which, extending over the entire year, is perpetuated through the course of ages.

In this liturgical cycle first appear the three great solemnities of Easter, Pentecost, and Christmas; next come the different feasts of the Blessed Virgin Mary, and those of the holy Apostles, Martyrs, Confessors, and Virgins; and finally the solemnity of All Saints, on which day we honour the whole multitude of the saints and blessed.

The few days that are not saints' days are, nevertheless, sanctified by offices proper to them, and are called *ferias*, from which name the Church would have her ministers to understand that, though they appear but ordinary days, they are given to them to be devoted to the praises of God.

10. We see, then, that the Church has fully made herself mistress of *the time* of the present life, which is the prelude to eternity. Knowing that time here below is only given to man as a pathway to lead him to his eternal country, she has divided this time into certain parts, as if into as many stages, broken by various festivals, to render the journey easier and more agreeable.

This division of time, marked by the ecclesiastical calendar, bears the impress of an admirable wisdom, and of the divine assistance of the Holy Ghost. It is based upon the division established by God Himself — the annual period and the weekly period.

11. The *hebdomadary period*, or the week, which is taken from the history of the creation of the world, represents the short duration of our mortal life—a life of labour and of sorrow—that will be followed by eternal rest in the house of the Lord. The Church sanctifies the days of the week by the holy day of Sunday. She

goes so far as even to impress each individual day with a sacred character; so that the attentive Christian may every week behold the principal mysteries of his faith unfolded to his view. Thus, Sunday is especially consecrated to the Resurrection of our Lord; Friday, to His Passion; Thursday, to the mystery of the Blessed Eucharist; Saturday, to the Blessed Virgin; Monday, to the Blessed Trinity; Tuesday, to the holy Angels; and Wednesday, to the holy Apostles. This is indicated by the rules of the Missal, which reveal to us the mind of the Church.

12. The *annual period*, which is called the ecclesiastical year, rests upon the feasts of Christmas, Easter, and Pentecost, the three greatest solemnities, of which the most important is that of Easter, the movable centre of the whole liturgical order. These three solemnities remind us of the Three Persons of the Adorable Trinity. Christmas is, as it were, the festival of the infinite love of God the Father, who gives His only Son to the world; Easter, the festival of the infinite love of the Son of God, who dies for us on the Cross; and Pentecost is the festival of the infinite love of the Holy Ghost, the Third Person of the Blessed Trinity, who communicates Himself to the Church.

The festivals of Christmas, Easter, and Pentecost are like three cardinal points in the ecclesiastical liturgy. To the festival of Christmas are linked the feasts of the Sacred Infancy and the hidden life of our Lord; to that of Easter, the mysteries of the public life, of the Passion and the Ascension; and with Pentecost are connected the mysteries of grace poured out by the Holy Ghost into the souls of men. The cycle of Pentecost is bound to that of Easter, and terminates with Advent.

During the period of about six months following the feast of Pentecost the eye of faith beholds the completion of the majestic construction of the Church, which, founded on the rock of truth, fructified by the blood of Christ, fortified by all the succours of grace and the helps of the Holy Spirit, constitutes, and will constitute to the end of time, the Ark of the New Covenant; that is to say, the ark of salvation for all who abandon themselves in a filial spirit to Providence within her pale.

13. The ecclesiastical year, then, we find is divided into three parts. The first of these comprises the four weeks of Advent preceding the nativity of our Lord Jesus Christ, and represents the four thousand years that preceded the coming of the Redeemer; the second part, from Christmas to the Ascension, retraces the mortal existence of our Lord when on earth; the third, namely, from Pentecost to All Saints'—or rather up to the Sunday which closes the ecclesiastical year—represents the entire duration of the Church militant on earth, until the consummation of ages.

To the final solemnity of All Saints' succeed the Commemoration of the Dead, the Dedication of Churches, and the feast of Holy Relics, which, in like manner, bear reference to eternal life and to heaven.

We see, then, that the liturgical order, which represents to us the history of the world and the whole life of Christianity past, present, and future, terminates in the festivals of heaven, because, for the Christian, all tends to that happy consummation. Heaven, to the eyes of faith, is the watchword of existence.

14. What words can describe the beauty of our festivals, their harmony with the seasons at which they are celebrated, with the mysteries they recall, and the needs of our hearts? Let us for a moment suppose the festivals no longer to exist. Life and joy would have disappeared together with them; a dull monotony would reign throughout the year; the succession of days and seasons would become wearisome and insipid; and life, especially the Christian life, would become as it were impossible.

The solemnities of the Catholic Church, giving to each season of the year its joys and Christian feelings, are a necessity. In winter our attention is fixed on the touching birth of the poor Babe of Bethlehem, the true light in darkness, the true joy of the family; in spring it is the resurrection of our Lord that captivates us, when nature is again springing into new life; then we have. Pentecost and Corpus Christi, coming like the triumph of Christianity in the splendour of the summer days; and lastly, in autumn, when nature seems to be failing and dying, the feast of All Saints gives us a glimpse of heaven, and we are lifted by faith to that other world, where death shall be no more.

Such is the character of the Church festivals. They instruct, rejoice, fortify, and encourage; and by causing us to regard the Church on earth as an image of the Church in heaven, and, as it were, as the vestibule of paradise, they shed over this valley of tears a few rays of heavenly joy, and make the Christian life a prelude to a blessed eternity.

Second Commandment of the Church:
To hear Mass on all Sundays and holidays of obligation.

1. As it has been said in the explanation of the third commandment of God, Holy Church obliges all the faithful who have come to the use of reason, and are not lawfully prevented, to assist devoutly at Mass on Sundays and holidays of obligation. When we cannot go to church on account of some obstacle, which, nevertheless, does not prevent us from being recollected at home —for example, taking care of an invalid—it is proper to supply for the Mass by saying prayers in union with the priest and the faithful who are in church.

2. To assist devoutly at the divine Sacrifice, at which the angels themselves assist with a holy awe, we must remember that the holy Mass is the unbloody renewal or continuation of the bloody Sacrifice which Jesus Christ

offered upon the Cross by immolating Himself for the salvation of the world; then to unite our intention with that of the priest, to follow attentively all that is done at the altar, and to redouble our fervour at the principal parts. At the priest's communion, if we have not the happiness of communicating sacramentally, it is a very holy practice to make a spiritual communion, which consists in the desire of a devout heart sighing to receive the Body of Jesus Christ really. Then, when the moment has arrived, we should say with all our heart, in union with the priest, the words of the centurion in the Gospel, 'Lord, I am not worthy that Thou shouldst enter under my roof; say but the word, and my soul shall be healed;' and at the same time we should have a holy and lively desire to receive our Lord in sacramental communion, saying, in our hearts and with our lips, 'Deign, O Lord, soon to nourish me with Thy life-giving flesh, that I may be filled with Thy life.'

3. During Mass we must pray with recollection and devotion. All prayers are good, and the Church has not prescribed any in particular. It is customary for the faithful to use those found in an approved book, or to say the Rosary, or meditate on the mysteries of the Passion, which the Mass recalls to mind.*

4. We call a *Parochial Mass* that which the parish priest celebrates for his parishioners in their own church, and at which he gives an instruction especially adapted to their wants. As a general rule it is well to assist at it; nevertheless there is no obligation to do so, and we are allowed to hear Mass in any other church, especially if it is more convenient, and we receive an instruction equally beneficial.

5. Although the Church only obliges her children

* The knowledge of the different parts and ceremonies of the Mass is very useful in increasing the devotion of the faithful. See the 'Dogmatic' Part, 'The Eucharist as a Sacrifice,' nos. 83, 84.

to hear Mass on Sundays and holidays of obligation, she desires, nevertheless, that they should also assist at Mass during the week. Nothing is more conformable to the Christian spirit than to hear Mass every day, when one has the time; and nothing draws down on a family more blessings from God than to be represented every day by some of its members at the holy Sacrifice.

Third Commandment of the Church:
To keep the days of fasting and abstinence appointed by the Church.

1. This commandment of the Church is one of Christian penance; it prescribes fasting and abstinence.

2. Penance in general is a law imposed on all mankind since the sin of Adam, and constitutes an absolutely indispensable means of salvation. Our Lord has expressly declared it in these words, 'Unless you do penance you shall all likewise perish' (Luke xiii. 3); and we may say that His doctrine is contained in the words which He used in His first sermon, 'Do penance, for the kingdom of heaven is at hand' (Matt. iv. 17). Christianity itself, represented by Jesus Christ on the Cross, is one great expiation, and the Christian law, a law of penance for the remission of sins.

3. This general law may be divided into two parts, namely, into *interior* penance, which consists in contrition for our sins; and *exterior* penance, which comprises all the sufferings and corporal mortifications which we practise in expiation for our sins.

4. The third commandment of the Church is like a particular or organic clause of the great law of penance. The Church prescribes the days of fasting as a corporal penance that all the faithful must practise, thus determining what every Christian is strictly obliged to perform in order to satisfy the divine law of penance. As this divine law obliges every one, even those who are not capable of observing the ecclesiastical precept of fasting, these latter

must endeavour to supply for their shortcomings in this respect by prayer, good works, and alms-deeds.

5. We might ask why, among corporal penances, has the Church chosen and prescribed for the faithful that of fasting and abstinence? For these reasons: (1) because this form of penance has most generally been practised by the saints of every age, and sanctioned by the example of Jesus Christ Himself; (2) fasting is the most easy for the greater number of the faithful; (3) because, in fine, it procures precious spiritual advantages. For, as the Church says in her Liturgy for Lent, the effects of fasting are, (1) to deaden the passions by subduing the rebellion of the flesh against the spirit, and by weakening the strength of our wicked inclinations; (2) to elevate the mind and dispose it to prayer; (3) to appease the anger of God, and to draw down His blessings upon us.

6. We are obliged to fast, (1) during the whole of Lent; (2) on the Ember-days—that is, the Wednesdays, Fridays, and Saturdays of four weeks in the year, namely, the third week in Advent, the first week in Lent, Whit week, and the week of which the Wednesday follows the 14th of September, the feast of the Exaltation of the Cross; lastly, on the following vigils, those of Christmas-day, Pentecost, the feast of SS. Peter and Paul,* the Assumption, and All Saints.† *Lent*, which is of apostolic tradition, is established to honour and imitate the fast of Jesus Christ in the desert. The *Ember-days* are instituted to consecrate to God all the seasons of the year, to draw down His blessings on the fruits of the earth, and to thank Him for those which He has given us; lastly, to ask of Him ministers worthy of His altars, and an abundant outpouring of graces on the ordinations that take place regularly at these times.

7. The ecclesiastical fast contains three elements,

---

* In Belgium and France the fasting day is on Saturday before the Sunday on which this feast is *solemnised*, instead of on the vigil.

† Add, for England, the Wednesdays and Fridays of Advent.

which are one meal, abstinence from flesh meat and white meats, and the hour of the repast. The one meal requires that we take only one meal in the day; this constitutes the main point in fasting. The Church, however, allows, besides the principal meal, a light collation. With regard to the hour of repast, it will vary according to the custom of different families.

8. The law of fasting is binding, under pain of mortal sin, upon all those who have completed their twenty-first year, unless they are dispensed from it. There are three causes for lawful exemption: dispensation, inability, and hard labour. Thus the following are excused from fasting: the sick and infirm; the aged, when their strength begins to fail, which happens generally about the age of sixty, though there is no fixed time; and all who cannot fast without danger of seriously injuring their health, or rendering them incapable of fulfilling their duties.

If we cannot fast, but are able to abstain, we are bound by this second law.

9. Abstinence *from flesh meat* is commanded, (1) on all Fridays throughout the year, excepting that on which Christmas-day may fall; (2) on all fasting days, excepting, in Belgium, the Mondays, Tuesdays, and Thursdays of Lent (Maundy Thursday excepted), by virtue of a dispensation.

Abstinence from *white meats* is prescribed, for most of the dioceses of Belgium, on Ash Wednesday and Good Friday; from *eggs* the following seven days of Lent: Ash Wednesday, the Ember-days, and the three last days of Holy Week. Finally, all details of the law of abstinence will be found in the Lenten dispensations for the different dioceses.

The Church has instituted abstinence on the Fridays and Saturdays throughout the year in memory of the death and burial of our Lord, and as a preparation for Sunday.

A dispensation has been granted in Belgium from

abstinence on Saturdays whenever that day is not also a fasting day.

10. The law of abstinence binds all the faithful who have come to the use of reason, unless they are lawfully dispensed by their ecclesiastical superiors, or exempted on account of moral or physical inability. He sins mortally who, without dispensation or exemption, eats food which is forbidden, or makes his children, servants, or labourers do so.

Children and servants who cannot obtain abstinence food from their parents or masters should consult their confessors, who will tell them what to do under the circumstances.

Fourth Commandment of the Church:

To confess our sins to our pastors at least once a year.

1. By this commandment the Church obliges all the faithful to approach the sacred tribunal of penance at least once a year. Children who have come to the use of reason are also bound by this precept; and it is incumbent on parents and masters to prepare them for this duty and send them to confession.

2. This law of annual confession dates from the fourth Council of Lateran, A.D. 1215. In the earlier times the faithful were in the habit of confessing and communicating frequently, and did not require to be stimulated by an express command; the general law established by Jesus Christ in the institution of the Sacrament of Penance, and their own fervour, were enough to bind them. But at the time of the above-named Council the laxity of a great number rendered this commandment necessary.

3. The Church, then, has ordered yearly confession as an act strictly necessary for fulfilling the divine precept regarding confession; and not by any means as a practice with which we are to be satisfied. It is to manifest her intention clearly that she makes use of the

words *at least,* thus showing her desire that her children should not content themselves with the annual confession; implying even that it may be necessary for them to confess oftener.

4. If it is asked why the Church desires the faithful to confess oftener, we reply that it is in order that they may avoid grave falls, and reap most precious benefits. (1) Those who only confess at Easter show but little zeal for their salvation; they deprive themselves of many graces, fall more easily into mortal sin, and expose themselves to the risk of dying in that miserable state. (2) Frequent confession, on the contrary, not only preserves us from mortal sin, but also helps us to avoid the slightest faults, and to acquire that purity of conscience which makes virtue take root and flourish in our souls.

5. Besides the precept of the Church to confess annually, there is also an obligation of divine right to confess when in danger of death; and in this case it cannot be put off. Besides, the love which we owe to God and to ourselves demands that we lose no time in making use of this salutary remedy, when we have had the misfortune to fall into mortal sin, (1) because we should be doubly ungrateful and culpable if, after having offended God, we continued to live under His displeasure; (2) because it is very prejudicial to live in a state of mortal sin, since by doing so we deprive ourselves of many graces, and all the good works done in that state are devoid of merit for heaven; (3) because it is very dangerous to remain in such a state, as we thus expose ourselves to fall into still greater and more numerous sins, and to die at enmity with God.

6. We satisfy the precept of annual confession only by a good confession. So, in order to make a confession not only valid, but also fruitful, according to the intention of the Divine Institutor, two conditions are requisite: (1) adequate instruction concerning this

Sacrament and its different parts; (2) a practical method for accomplishing properly the different acts which the Sacrament demands. There are acts to be performed before, during, and after confession.

Before.—We must (1) ask of God the grace to confess our sins with true repentance, as if it were for the last time in our lives; (2) we must examine our conscience; (3) we must excite ourselves to sorrow for our sins, and make a firm purpose of amendment; then recite with all our heart the acts of faith, hope, charity, and contrition.

During confession—that is to say, in the confessional—we must declare our sins with humble sincerity, and afterwards listen with respect to what the confessor says.

After confession, when we have received absolution, we must accomplish the penance imposed, and carefully put in practice the good advice which we have received from the priest.*

Fifth Commandment of the Church:

To receive the Blessed Sacrament at least once a year, and that at Easter or thereabouts.

1. Our Lord, speaking of the Holy Eucharist, says in the Gospel: 'Except you eat the Flesh of the Son of Man, and drink His Blood, you shall not have life in you' (John vi. 54). These words, according to the unanimous teaching of the doctors, contain a divine precept which obliges all the faithful to communicate, (1) from time to time during their lives; and (2) for the last time at the approach of death.

2. The Church, wishing to determine exactly what the faithful have to do, in order to fulfil this divine command of communion during life, has prescribed the yearly communion at Easter. This is the object of the

---

* See 'The Practice of Confession,' afterwards more fully explained, chap. vii. first article.

fifth commandment, which was established at the fourth Council of Lateran, A.D. 1215, at the same time as the law of annual confession, and for similar reasons and motives. In virtue of this precept all the faithful, who have attained the age of discretion, and are capable of sufficiently understanding the mystery of the Holy Eucharist, are obliged to communicate once a year, at Easter or thereabouts. The Council decrees a double penalty for those who neglect this duty, namely, that they shall be excluded from the Church during their lives, and deprived of Catholic burial at their deaths. These penalties, however, are comminatory; to incur them practically the bishop must pass the sentence. In issuing this celebrated decree the Council of Lateran had for its end, as we have stated above, to stimulate the devotion of a great number of Christians who no longer frequented the holy table as of old.

3. Why should the yearly communion be made during Easter time? Evidently because the feast of Easter is the greatest of all feasts; and it was at that time that our Lord, instituting the holy Eucharist, gave Himself in communion to His disciples. Those who are prevented from making their communion during Easter must, if they wish to act according to the spirit of the Church, do so as soon as they can afterwards.

4. To fulfil the Paschal obligation we must communicate worthily. It is evident, in fact, that one could not satisfy the precept of the Church by a communion made with a conscience stained with mortal sin, for to make such a communion would be to commit a fearful sacrilege, and to profane the Body and Blood of Jesus Christ. To communicate worthily we must, above all, be in a state of grace; this condition is essential. We must, moreover, before approaching the holy table, excite in ourselves sentiments of lively faith and devotion, as a fitting means of preparation; and after communion make at least a quarter of an hour's thanksgiving,

ovingly entertaining the Divine Guest whom we have received, or reciting devoutly the prayers to be found in the prayer-book.*

5. The Church in her precept does not say simply that we must communicate at Easter, but *at least* at Easter; to show that she by no means intends that the faithful should limit themselves to the one Paschal communion. On the contrary, she wishes her children to communicate several times a year, and even to approach frequently to the holy table, because frequent communion, always beneficial to souls, is sometimes even indispensable. Monthly communion is justly looked upon as a means generally necessary for leading a life of solid virtue. The faithful cannot be too strongly urged to communicate devoutly once a month; and if that is not always possible, at least at the principal feasts of the year. Weekly or even daily communion, equally conformable to the spirit of the Church, is very salutary to fervent souls, who, with the approbation of a prudent confessor, merit to partake so frequently of the divine banquet.

CHAPTER IV.

SIN.

HAVING seen the law, and the different commandments it comprises, we must now consider the violation of the law, or sin.

First Article: The Nature of Sin.

1. Sin is an offence against God committed by a rational creature. The word *sin* is used sometimes for *the act*, sometimes for the *state of sin*. The *act of sin*

* See further on, chap. vii. second article, ' Communion.'
† Chap. vii. second article, ' Frequent Communion.'

is the transitory action by which the offence against God is committed; the *state of sin* the permanent condition of a soul that has committed the offence against God. The soul remains guilty and stained until the sin is forgiven.

There are two kinds of sin: *original* sin, in which we are all born; and *personal* sin, which we commit by an act of our own will. It is of personal sin that we are going to treat here; we shall consider it particularly in the act that produces it, and which is called *actual sin*.

2. Sin is an act of disobedience to God, or a voluntary transgression of the law of God. It is defined more distinctly thus: Any thought, word, deed, or omission against the law of God. By the law of God is understood not only the commandments of the decalogue, but any precept whatsoever, given by lawful authority, which obliges in conscience like the commandments of God.

3. Sin is called a *voluntary* transgression of the law; that is to say, a transgression freely willed, and freely accepted by the will. Sin is committed in the following manner: (1) the forbidden object presents itself attractively to the senses or the imagination; (2) the intelligence perceives the malice; (3) the will, thus enlightened upon the wickedness of the object, and being free to resist, consents and accepts it.

This free acceptance of the will, which is called *voluntary*, properly constitutes sin, which is in its nature an irregularity of the will, a bad intention of the will.

'The will,' says St. Thomas, 'is the principle of sin.' Hence the maxim: 'The will has sinned, the will must repent.'

4. Thus, to make a sin, three conditions are necessary: advertence, liberty, and consent.

(1) Advertence consists in being aware of the

malice of the act. If this attention is wanting when we act, then there is inadvertence. Inadvertence excuses, but not always; because inadvertence itself may be culpable in its cause, through wilful ignorance, negligence, passion, a bad habit, or the thoughtlessness with which we give ourselves to an act of which we suspect the danger.

(2) Liberty is the power of the will either to do an action or not. There is no real sin when the will is powerless, as it happens sometimes in sleep or in an irresistible paroxysm, in the sudden frenzy of a passion which affects the reason.

(3) Consent is the free act of the will accepting, directly or indirectly, the forbidden object presented to it; an acceptance which does not imply a formal intention of committing sin or offending the Divine Majesty. Consent is *direct* when we desire the thing in itself; *indirect* when we desire it in its cause. The will can act, with regard to the proposed action, in three different ways, (1) by consenting positively—then there is sin; (2) by resisting positively—then there is no sin; (3) by remaining neutral, passive, without any positive act of resistance or consent—then we often expose ourselves to sin, even mortally, especially at times of delicate temptation.

Second Article : Distinction of Sins.

5. Sins are distinguished in many ways, on account of their gravity, their object, the manner in which they are committed, &c. Hence there are, (1) mortal sins and venial sins; (2) sins against God, our neighbour, and ourselves; (3) interior and exterior sins; (4) sins of thought, word, and deed; (5) sins of the same kind and sins of different kinds; (6) sins of weakness and sins of malice; (7) material sins and formal sins; (8) the deadly sins; (9) the sins against the Holy Ghost; (10)

the sins of others; (11) the sins crying to Heaven for vengeance.

6. (1) Looking to their gravity we distinguish mortal and venial sins. *Mortal* sin is so called because it deprives us of sanctifying grace, which is the life of the soul, and merits damnation, which is eternal death. *Venial* sin is that which does not destroy sanctifying grace or the friendship of God, yet weakens the fervour of charity and deserves temporal punishment.

7. Mortal sin is a transgression of the law of God or the Church in any matter of importance, with full advertence or knowledge of the evil, and full consent.

8. Thus, to constitute mortal sin, three conditions are requisite: (1) *gravity of matter*, which must be understood either in itself, the circumstances or effects, or the reason for which the law was made; (2) *full advertence* of the mind; (3) *free consent* of the will, which must be *full* and *perfect*.

9. Mortal sin is a crime infinitely displeasing to God and disastrous to ourselves in its effects. (1) With regard to God, it is a revolt, an outrage, a black ingratitude; (2) with regard to ourselves, it disfigures the image of God in us, it brings death to the soul, despoils it of its good works, renders it an enemy of God, a slave to the devil, and deserving of hell; it often draws down even temporal punishments on the head of the sinner. We obtain pardon of mortal sin by the Sacrament of Penance and by perfect contrition, accompanied by an earnest desire to confess our sin.

10. Sin, mortal *in itself*, may become venial in three ways: (1) when the matter is not grave; (2) when there is not perfect advertence; (3) when there is not full consent. Thus a slight detraction would only be a venial sin; if it were grave and likely to destroy a man's reputation, then it would be mortal.

There are commandments of God—for example, the sixth—which do not admit of unimportant matter.

11. Venial sin is an offence against God in slight matters, or else in a grave matter, but without full knowledge, or advertence, or full consent. Although venial sin does not deprive us of the friendship of God, it nevertheless weakens the fervour of charity, disposes the soul to mortal sin, and renders us deserving of purgatory and punishment in this world. We can obtain pardon of venial sins, not only by the Sacrament of Penance, but also by a sincere repentance, by prayers and good works performed with a contrite heart.

12. (2) We distinguish sins *with regard to God, to our neighbour, and to ourselves.* But in reality there is no sin which is not against God, since there is no sin which is not an offence against God, and transgression, more or less direct, of some law, either divine, natural, or positive.

13. (3) We call *interior* sins those which are committed in the soul by the will alone; *exterior* sins are those which begin with the will, and are consummated outwardly by word or action.

(4) According to the manner in which sins are committed, they are divided into sins of thought, word, deed, and omission.

14. (1) By *sins of thought* we mean the simple *thought* or imagination, the *desire* and the pleasure or complacency combined. It is a *sin* of simple *thought* when we take deliberate pleasure in bad imaginations; for instance, in imaginations of impurity or revenge. A wicked thought only becomes really sinful from the pleasure we take in it and the consent we give to it. It is a *sin of desire* when we wish to consummate the act of which a bad thought is the object. It is a *sin of complacency* when we take pleasure in the recollection of evil done.

The pleasure taken in hearing certain bad actions related is not always sinful, because we may be amused by the odd manner in which the thing has taken place, without consenting to the evil it has involved. For instance, in hearing of a robbery; the manner in which it has been effected has been so dexterous and clever that we may hear of it and relate it ourselves with satisfaction, without at all approving of the wrong done to our neighbour or of the offence against God. Or a witticism may escape from some one somewhat infringing on delicacy, and the tone of the speaker and his manner of turning the thing may strike one and provoke a smile. This pleasure that one takes has not the evil for its object, but the circumstances which are foreign to it; therefore it is excusable, and must not be confounded with the delectation of bad thoughts.

15. (2) We sin by *word* when we indulge in conversations against faith, religion, charity, justice, or purity; when, for example, we give way to blasphemy, backbiting, calumny, lying, perjury, or immodest discourse.

16. (3) We sin by *action* when we do what is forbidden, and by *omission* when we neglect to do what is commanded, though we are aware of the obligation, and could comply with it if we chose; for example, if we miss Mass on a Sunday without some lawful motive.

17. (5) Sins are of the *same kind* when they are opposed to the same virtues or commandments; *they differ in kind* when they are opposed to different virtues or commandments, or also if they are accompanied by circumstances that give them a new character of malice. Circumstances that change the nature of a sin must be mentioned in confession.

18. (6) *Sins of frailty* are those which are either committed through ignorance that does not altogether excuse, or by yielding to some strong temptation; *sins of malice* are those to which we consent with full knowledge, of our own accord, and by the pure choice of the will. Sins of frailty are not always venial; they

may be mortal, and are so, in fact, whenever we yield to temptation in a matter of weight.

19. (7) There is *material* sin when a bad act is committed through inadvertence or ignorance, for which we are not to blame, and without any participation of the free will; *formal* sin, when we act with knowledge and of our own free will. Formal sin only renders us guilty.

20. (8) There are seven capital sins—pride, covetousness, luxury, anger, gluttony, envy, and sloth. They are called *capital* sins, not because they are always mortal, but because every capital sin is the source of many other sins.

21. (1) *Pride* is an inordinate desire of our own elevation and a vain complacency in ourselves. It may be called a swelling out of the heart proceeding from a puffed-up mind, that is to say, from a too high idea a man has of himself and his own merit; it leads us to set ourselves up before others by despising them, and to self-glorification by referring things to ourselves, instead of glorifying God by referring everything to Him.

Almost all vices spring from pride as from their fountain-head; but there are some that flow more directly from it, and which are on that account called the offspring of pride. The chief of these are vainglory, boasting, display, pompousness, haughtiness, ambition, hypocrisy, presumption, obstinacy, disobedience, self-delusion with regard to our own defects.

22. (2) *Covetousness* is an inordinate love of money and the goods of this world. To seek a fortune for a good end, subordinate to one's duties and to salvation, is right and proper; but otherwise, there is a sin which is avarice. This vice separates us from God, because we cannot serve two masters—God and mammon. It produces neglect of salvation, selfishness, hardness towards the poor, craftiness, injustice, quarrels; to say

nothing of cares, anxieties, and murmurings against Providence.

23. (3) By *envy* is meant the sadness that springs from witnessing the spiritual or temporal good of another, because it seems to lessen our own, or our own merit. This vice engenders rash judgments, detraction, malicious joy at the faults or disgrace of our neighbour, hatred, and vexations of all kinds.

24. (4) *Luxury*, or the vice opposed to chastity, and forbidden by the sixth and ninth commandments, is the vile source of innumerable sins. Moreover, the criminal affection for carnal pleasures produces disgust for piety, darkness of the understanding, hardness of heart, the diminution and even extinction of faith. It destroys the health of the body and the noblest qualities of the soul, brings trouble and ruin upon families, and often leads to final impenitence.

25. (5) *Gluttony* is an inordinate love of eating and drinking, or the evil inclination that inclines men to the immoderate use of food or drink. The slaves of this degrading vice stoop so low as to make a god of their belly (Phil. iii.). Gluttony may be committed by indulging in food too expensive or delicate for one's condition in life, by eating at unsuitable hours, or by eating and drinking to excess. Gluttony produces drunkenness, impurity, outbursts of passion, blasphemies, angry quarrels, blows or threats, heaviness of soul, disgust for spiritual things, disregard of the laws of the Church for fasting and abstinence. When excess in drinking amounts to intoxication, and deprives a man of the use of his reason, it is a mortal sin.

26. (6) *Anger* is an emotion or inordinate transport of the soul, which causes us violently to reject what displeases us, and impels us to take revenge on those who contradict us. The effects of anger are hatred, revenge, imprecations, blasphemies, outrages, and sometimes duelling and murder. Anger becomes a mortal sin

when the emotion goes so far as to extinguish the love of God and our neighbour, and makes us blaspheme or commit other sins of serious gravity. There is a certain anger, a just and reasonable indignation, which is exempt from sin; it springs from true zeal and the pure love of justice.

27. (7) *Sloth* is an inordinate love of ease, a languor of the soul, and a disgust for the labour required for the fulfilment of our duties. Sloth becomes a mortal sin when through it we fail to fulfil a serious obligation. Sloth produces idleness, loss of time, negligence, ignorance, inconstancy in keeping good resolutions, tepidity, temptations of all kinds, and cowardice, which disposes us to yield to them.

28. (8) The virtues contrary to the capital or deadly sins are humility, which is opposed to pride; liberality, to covetousness; brotherly love, to envy; chastity, to luxury; temperance, to gluttony; patience, to anger; diligence and fervour, which are opposed to sloth.

29. (9) The sins classified as *sins against the Holy Ghost* are those of pure malice, which, being directly opposed to the mercy of God and the grace of the Holy Ghost, render conversion very difficult. They are six in number, namely:

(*a*) Despair of the grace of God or of salvation.

(*b*) Presumption of God's mercy to save us without good works.

(*c*) To impugn the truths of faith proposed by the Church.

(*d*) Envy at another's spiritual good.

(*e*) Obstinacy in sin in spite of the salutary exhortations, graces, lights, and warnings that God sends us.

(*f*) Contempt of doing penance for sin. To wish to die in impenitence is the height of obstinacy.

30. (10) The sins here called the *sins* of *others* are those committed by others, but in which we may participate in any of the following ways: by counsel; by

giving our protection or assistance; by command; by approval or praise; by partaking materially; by taking pleasure and giving our consent; by not speaking when we ought to speak to prevent sin; by not punishing sin; by screening the guilty from salutary reprehension.

31. There are some sins which, by their extraordinary malice, cry to Heaven for vengeance. They are the following: wilful murder; impure sins against nature; oppression of the poor, the widows and orphans; defrauding labourers of their wages.

32. The *formal* cause of sin is the will of him who commits it; but generally this will, without ceasing to be free, is actuated by other causes, which are called *impulsive;* these are *temptations.* By *temptations* we understand, in general, every attraction and internal or external force which induces us to sin. They are excited within us by our three spiritual enemies, namely, the world, the flesh, and the devil.

33. The *remedy* for sin may be viewed in relation to the past or to the future. As regards the past, namely, the sins which we have committed, we must apply the remedy of Christian penance, which derives its strength from the merits of Jesus Christ. This penance may be sacramental or non-sacramental; the first consists of the Sacrament of Penance, and the second in all the satisfaction and good works which we practise besides. As regards the future, the preservative against falling again into sin is the employing of means to avoid it.

34. There are four principal *means* to be employed to avoid sin: (1) the knowledge of God and meditation on His holy law; (2) prayer, combined with the remembrance of the eternal truths; (3) the frequentation of the Sacraments of Penance and the Holy Eucharist; (4) avoiding the occasions of sin.

We call *occasions of sin* certain exterior circumstances which lead us into evil, whether by their nature or our own weakness. The occasions, which in our days are the most common and dangerous, are:

(1) Seductive *persons* or *society*, which insinuate into our hearts the poison of voluptuousness and irreligion.

(2) Infidel and immoral *newspapers* and *books*, licentious *novels*, and other unhealthy and useless productions of the press.

(3) The *theatre*.—Though the drama is not bad in its nature, in point of fact it generally is so in our times. There are some plays so immoral, either in themselves or in their accessories, such as costumes, ballets, &c., that we cannot be present at them without rendering ourselves gravely culpable; and others which are called innocent are in reality only less bad, and are never without danger. We may say, then, that the theatre is not the place for a Christian. Apart from the case in which a person, by reason of his social position or other circumstances not depending on his will, is obliged to observe a legitimate condescension, to frequent the theatre is to give up a devout life, to expose oneself to fall into every vice, and even to lose the treasure of the faith.

(4) *Balls* and *dances*.—There are balls which are gravely licentious, either on account of immodest dances or of the costumes and dresses introduced at them. In these no one should take part. Even modest dances are rarely without danger, and a Christian should not frequent them from choice and of his own free will.

In cases of doubt in these delicate matters it is obviously our duty to seek the advice of a prudent confessor.

CHAPTER V.

VIRTUES AND GOOD WORKS.

1. IN the same way as sins are bad actions contrary to the law of God, and vices are the habits of these actions, so good works are actions conformable to the law of God and His divine will, and virtues are the habits of such actions or dispositions of the soul.

As the doctrine concerning virtues has been explained in the 'Dogmatic' Part of this book, it will suffice to add here the points which enter more particularly into the duties and practice of the faithful.

2. A *Christian* virtue is an abiding disposition of the soul which leads us to do good in a manner conformable to the doctrine of Jesus Christ and worthy of eternal life.

In infusing sanctifying grace into the soul, the Holy Ghost communicates to it at the same time the theological and all the other Christian virtues. But, generally, these virtues, infused into the soul, exist therein, at first only in a state of germ, or like young plants, which must grow up by our own coöperation. Practice, good works, prayer, and the Sacraments sustain the *infused* virtues, fortify them, and produce those *acquired* habits which constitute their perfection.

We will first speak of the theological virtues, and then of the moral virtues and of good works.

First Article : The Theological Virtues.

3. Amongst the Christian virtues there are three which are greater than all the others, and which we must learn to cultivate and increase in our hearts above all others. These are the three theological virtues— faith, hope, and charity.

I. Faith.

4. *Faith* is a supernatural virtue, by which we believe

firmly, because of the supreme truthfulness of God, all that He has revealed, and proposes, through His Church, to our belief.

5. Faith is absolutely necessary for salvation. Every one who is capable of actual faith is obliged to believe, at least implicity and in general, all that the Church believes and teaches. Moreover, he must believe *explicitly*, and consequently *know in particular*, certain points of Christian teaching.

Amongst these points some are necessary by *necessity of means* and others by *necessity of precept*. The first are those of which the knowledge is so indispensable that if an adult is ignorant of them, even though not through his own fault, he cannot receive the Sacraments or attain salvation. Regarding the second, it is so far of obligation to know them that an adult cannot, without sin, neglect to learn them; but an involuntary ignorance will not render him incapable of justification and salvation.

The four following points are *necessary by necessity of means* : (1) that there is one only God; (2) that there are Three Persons in God, namely, God the Father, God the Son, and God the Holy Ghost; (3) that God the Son, the Second Person of the Blessed Trinity, became man for us, was crucified, died, and rose again; (4) that God rewards good and punishes evil. The *six points* that follow are, as to their substance, of the necessity of precept: (1) the Lord's Prayer; (2) the Hail Mary; (3) the Apostles' Creed; (4) the Commandments of God and of the Church; (5) the Sacraments, or at least those which every Christian must receive; (6) the duties of each one's state of life.

6. We are obliged, not only to believe the articles of faith, by an interior act, but also to confess our faith exteriorly by the practices and worship which God demands. The Christian must make an act of faith as soon as he arrives at the age of reason; he must also

often repeat it during his life, and at the approach of death.

7. The sins which are essentially contrary to faith are infidelity, heresy, and apostasy.

8. *Infidelity* consists in not believing the Christian doctrine. It is *negative* in those who have never heard of it; *privative* in those who are ignorant through their own fault; *positive* or contradictory in those who reject it when it has been proposed to them. We commit a sin of infidelity as soon as we reject any point of faith, or wilfully doubt it.

9. We call by the name of *heresy* an obstinate error contrary to some article of faith and meriting the penalty of excommunication. In order to constitute heresy the article of faith must be denied; and to incur censure as well, the heresy must be at the same time both exterior and interior: it must be, as it is customary to say, an exterior and obstinate profession of an error contrary to faith.

10. *Apostasy* consists in renouncing Christianity. The impious, who, after having received baptism, profess deism, materialism, *free-thinking*, &c., must be ranked as apostates. We might say the same of those who, being indifferent in matters of religion, profess nothing, neither truth, nor error. All these, in fact, renounce the religion of Jesus Christ, which they embraced at baptism.

11. *Human respect*, which makes us ashamed of our faith, is contrary to the exterior confession which Jesus Christ demands of His disciples.

12. The virtue of faith obliges the faithful also to preserve this precious gift of God and to fly from the danger of losing it, which lies in infidel conversations, books, newspapers, &c., and in indifferent or irreligious schools.

II. Hope.

13. Hope is a supernatural virtue, by which we

expect of God eternal beatitude and the means of attaining it, because Jesus Christ has merited them for us, and God has promised them to us, and He is infinitely good, powerful, and faithful in His promises.

14. Hope is necessary to salvation. We are obliged, from time to time, to make an act of hope; and this obligation is especially urgent when we are tempted to despair, or are in danger of death.

15. We sin against hope by default or by excess; that is to say, by giving way to despair or to presumption. We give way to *despair* when we persuade ourselves that we cannot obtain pardon or subdue our passions, and in consequence abandon all prayer; also, when in adversity we allow ourselves to be so far cast down as to become disgusted with life, and to wish to hasten our death. We are guilty of *presumption* when, for example, we hope to obtain God's pardon as easily for ten sins as for five, and make use of this injurious confidence in God to continue in our sins. He who perseveres in sin, hoping one day to be converted, does not sin precisely against hope, but he sins against charity towards himself, because he obviously exposes himself to eternal damnation.

16. Besides Christian *hope*, in the strict sense of the word, of which we have been speaking, there is Christian *confidence*, or hope in a broader sense. It is that which rests in the providence of God, with a filial abandonment, amid all the events of life.

III. Charity.

17. Charity, which is the most excellent of the theological virtues, and the queen of all Christian virtues, presupposes faith and hope.

18. Charity is absolutely necessary to salvation; without it all the other virtues would be of no avail.

19. It is defined as a supernatural virtue, by which we love God for Himself above all things, and our

neighbours as ourselves for God. God, ourselves, and our neighbours constitute the material object of charity. The motive is God Himself, His infinite perfection and sovereign amiability.

20. There is only one virtue of charity, but there are two precepts of it: one regards God, the other our neighbours.

(1) *The precept of the love of God.*—Our Lord proclaims it in these words: ' Thou shalt love the Lord thy God with thy whole heart, with all thy soul, and with all thy mind. This is the greatest and the first commandment' (Matt. xxii. 37, 38). This precept obliges us to love God above all things, to prefer Him above all; to love creatures for God, because God wishes it, and because all the good which is in them comes from God.

21. We must love God, because He is the sovereign good; because He loved us first and gave us His only Son; because He loads us every day with His benefits; and lastly, because He commands us to love Him, and promises us the recompense of eternal beatitude.

22. To love God chiefly for His own sake, because He is infinitely good and amiable, is charity, properly so called; to love Him chiefly for His gifts and benefits is what is called the love of hope or of gratitude. This love is distinct from the love of charity, with which it must not be confounded, but it leads to that pure virtue; for if we love God because of His benefits, we shall soon love Him because of His infinite goodness manifested by His benefits, and this love is charity.

23. The love of God must be *sovereign;* that is to say, we must love God above all things, or, as the Scripture says, *with all our heart.* This shows the disposition in which we should be to sacrifice everything rather than commit mortal sin, which is essentially opposed to charity.

24. The precept of the love of God obliges us to

make acts of it from time to time during our lives, and also at the approach of death. Whoever devoutly recites the Lord's Prayer makes an act of the love of God in saying the words, 'Hallowed be Thy name, Thy will be done on earth as it is in heaven.'

25. We sin against the love of God, (1) indirectly, by every mortal sin; (2) directly, by hatred of God. This hatred is the most horrible of sins. It is that of the demons and of the damned, who hate God because He is just and is the avenger of their crimes.

26. *The precept of the love of our neighbour.*—The love of our neighbour is inseparable from the love of God: 'He who loveth God' shall 'love also his brother' (1 John 4). We must love our neighbour—that is to say, all men who live on the earth—(1) because God ordains it; (2) because Jesus Christ has taught us both by His words and example; (3) because all men are images of God, brothers of Jesus Christ, children of the Eternal Father, and called to the same heavenly inheritance.

'The second commandment is like to the first,' says our Saviour. 'Thou shalt love thy neighbour as thyself.' The sense of these words is this: As you love God for Himself, so you must love yourselves for God, and your neighbour as yourselves also for God.

27. The love of ourselves must be well regulated; and it will be so, if we submit our will to the will of God, if we do not seek our own good at the expense of our neighbour's, and if we love our souls better than our bodies.

28. We must love our neighbour as *ourselves*. This is the rule of Christian charity: it consists in doing for others what we should reasonably wish them to do for us, and in never doing to them what we should not wish them to do to us.

29. We satisfy the general obligation of fraternal charity, (1) by not wishing evil to any one; (2) by sincerely wishing to every one, without exception, every

spiritual and temporal good which we ought to wish, or can wish, for ourselves ; (3) by doing to others the good which we should reasonably expect them to do to us; (4) by praying for all.

30. There is a certain order to be followed in the accomplishment of the duties of charity. After God, whom we must love before all things and above all things, we must love ourselves, and ourselves more than all others in what relates to spiritual goods. With regard to our neighbour, we must observe the order of goods and the order of persons.

(1) With regard to goods, spiritual life is to be preferred to temporal life, temporal life to reputation, and reputation to riches. According to this principle, when our brethren are in extreme necessity, but only in that case, we ought to sacrifice our goods of the inferior order to fulfil the duty of charity towards them.

(2) With regard to the order of persons, in case of want, but not of extreme necessity, we must, in the first place, help our husband or wife; then our children; thirdly, our parents ; and then successively our brothers and sisters, kindred, servants, friends, benefactors, neighbours, fellow-citizens ; and lastly, all strangers without distinction. In case of extreme necessity we ought to help our parents before all others.

It follows, from what precedes, that we are grievously wanting in charity if we neglect our own salvation, or allow our parents or kindred to die without the Sacraments.

31. We have been speaking of the love of our neighbour *in general*. If we consider it *in particular* it involves three special obligations : *the love of our enemies, almsgiving,* and *fraternal correction*.

32. (1) We must love all our brethren, not excepting our enemies, with an interior as well as an exterior love. The love of our enemies is a special precept of

the Gospel, which obliges us sincerely to forgive those who have wronged us; to give them such signs of friendship as circumstances may require; and to become perfectly reconciled to them.

(*a*) To forgive sincerely is to banish from our hearts all rancour, vengeance, and ill-will towards our enemies; not to exclude them from our prayers; and to be willing to serve them in case of necessity. It is one thing, however, to forgive injuries, and another to renounce one's rights: this we are not obliged to do; and we may always claim them in a suitable manner.

(*b*) We should sin against charity by refusing to meet our enemy, unless it were because we feared not being able to restrain our feelings in his presence. It is also, according to circumstances, a more or less serious sin against charity to refuse to salute an enemy or to return his salutation, when such a refusal would be understood as an act of enmity or ill-feeling.

(*c*) Charity imposes the obligation of reconciliation with our enemies; and we sin against that virtue when we refuse to be reconciled or to meet them.

33. (2) Charity is not a barren virtue, but is manifested by works of mercy, both of the spiritual and temporal order, which are called the 'spiritual works of mercy' and the 'corporal works of mercy.' These will be spoken of further on. The corporal works of mercy are represented by alms-deeds.

Almsgiving, or the temporal succour given to the indigent, is of obligation for all who are in a position to fulfil the precept. Jesus Christ expressly declares that the reprobate will be condemned to everlasting fire for not having given alms to the poor.

34. Those who have more abundant goods than they require are bound, by the precept of charity, to help the indigent who are suffering from *serious and pressing necessity;* and, in order to do this, they ought to deny themselves all vain and frivolous expenditure which is

not requisite for the keeping up, in a Christian sense, of their position.

The precept of almsgiving is especially binding in times of public calamity; for instance, in time of famine or when the land has been ravaged by inundations, war, or other scourges.

35. The *ordinary necessity* of the poor, who have not the necessaries of life, and who cannot procure them by work, does not impose any obligation on those who possess only what is absolutely necessary for the keeping up of their position and rank in a proper way; but the rich should give the superfluity of their goods to this class of poor; and their obligation in this respect is a very serious one.

36. Though it is hard to determine the precise amount of alms which one is bound to bestow in times of public calamity, we may, however, say that we are not obliged to give to the poor the whole of our superfluous wealth, but we may reserve a part for the benefit of religion or the country, to augment our patrimony, or for the improvement of our own position or that of our children. On the other hand, it must be said that those who possess more than enough to keep up their rank, and who give nothing to the poor, but inhumanly repulse all beggars, and never bestow an alms on those who have no other means of living, are in a bad state, and unworthy of absolution.

37. When any one is in *extreme necessity* and in evident danger of perishing, we, if no one else comes forward, are bound, under pain of mortal sin, to assist him, not only with the goods not required for our rank, but also with those which are not required for our subsistence.

38. (3) Fraternal correction is a spiritual work of mercy, which consists in reprehending the faults and sins of our neighbour through a motive of charity. It is a precept, and is binding on every one, especially

on superiors. It is not, however, always obligatory, and to make it so for persons who are not superiors, several conditions are necessary: (1) that the sin be certain; (2) that it be grave; (3) that there be no others more capable of reprehending; (4) that there be reason to hope that the correction will have good effect; (5) that it can be given without serious inconvenience; (6) that the time be opportune and the opportunity favourable; (7) that it be probable that the sinner has not reformed, and that he will not reform of his own accord.

39. The principal sins against the love of our neighbour are hatred, envy, discord, and scandal. Scandal is the sin most opposed to the love of our neighbour; for it tends to give death to souls. It is spiritual homicide. This has been spoken of under the fifth commandment of God.

40. We are obliged to make acts of faith, hope, and charity, (1) when we arrive at the age of reason; (2) in times of severe temptations against these virtues; (3) at the hour of death; (4) often during the course of our life. It is highly beneficial to make acts of these virtues when we receive the Sacraments, especially Penance and the Holy Eucharist. It is also very proper that we should make these acts every day; fervent Christians never omit doing so.

We must add to the theological virtues the *moral virtues*, and those which are called the *gifts of the Holy Ghost* and the *fruits of the Holy Ghost*.

Second Article: Moral Virtues, Gifts, and Fruits of the Holy Ghost.

41. Those virtues are called *moral* which have for their direct and immediate object the regulation of our morals, differing from the theological virtues in that these latter exercise, it is true, a powerful influence over our morals; but it is in an indirect way, their direct

object being God Himself and His divine perfections. The moral virtues are the worthy and faithful companions of the theological virtues.

The moral virtues, in their nature and by themselves, are of the natural order, because God has sown the seeds of them in our nature, and has given us a certain aptitude for developing them within us. But they become supernatural in the Christian, (1) at the moment of justification, when they pass into the state of infused virtues; (2) in the exercise of them; for their acts are ennobled by the grace which accompanies them and by motives founded on faith.

42. There are numerous moral virtues, amongst which four are predominant over all the others, and are called *cardinal*, because they are, as it were, the centres round which the others are grouped and the pivots upon which they turn.

The four cardinal virtues are *prudence, justice, fortitude*, and *temperance*. A group of secondary or tributary virtues rallies round each one.

43. (1) Prudence is a virtue which points out and commands what is to be done in order that each of our actions be such as honesty and wisdom require.

It is called the *conductor of the virtues*. It holds the reins of all the others, and this is why it occupies the first place amidst the cardinal virtues.

Real and perfect *prudence* is that Christian prudence which is regulated by the faith and the principles of the Gospel. It directs man in all his actions towards his last end—that is to say, towards God, and salvation, which is in God. To Christian prudence is opposed *false prudence*, which is called the prudence of the *children of this world*, which is regulated by the false principles of the world, and directs the whole man towards the perishable goods of the earth.

To prudence belong the consideration of past events; the knowledge of things present; the forecasting of the future; docility in following the advice of wise and experienced persons; sagacity in choosing the right thing according to the occasion; circumspection, by which we examine all the circumstances of time, place, and persons; precautions against obstacles, dangers, and unpleasant events; discretion in keeping secrets; vigilance; and lastly, activity.

The vices opposed to prudence are precipitation, inconsiderateness, inconstancy, negligence, trickiness, fraud; prudence of the flesh, which makes all things subordinate to the gratification of pride and sensuality; and lastly, too great solicitude for temporal things.

44. (2) The word *justice* is often taken in a general sense for all the virtues which constitute Christian holiness. In this acceptation we say the *just* man in opposition to the *sinner*. But we here take the term justice in a restricted sense to signify the second of the cardinal virtues. It may be defined as a moral virtue which inclines our will to render exactly to each one that which is his due.

It is divided, (1) into justice towards God, towards ourselves, and towards others; (2) into legal, distributive, vindictive, and commutative justice.

To justice are attached the virtues of religion, piety, respect, obedience, gratitude, penance, veracity, friendship, affability, and liberality. In this group religion is distinguished above all the others, being the most excellent of the moral virtues, because it has for its object the worship of God.*

The vices opposed to justice are injustice, theft, impiety, sacrilege, contempt, disobedience, and ingratitude.

45. (3) The virtue of fortitude is that which leads us to face all perils and to undergo all labours in order to fulfil the duties which are imposed upon us by reason

* See 'First Commandment of God.'

or faith, whether they be towards God, our neighbour, or ourselves. The most heroic act of fortitude is martyrdom.

To this virtue are attached confidence and courage, firmness, patience, longanimity, perseverance, and magnanimity, which raises the feelings of man and his love of duty above honours and dignities.

To the virtue of fortitude are opposed, either by default or excess, rashness, audacity, presumption, ambition, obstinacy, impatience, cowardice, softness, pusillanimity, and inconstancy.

46. (4) Temperance is the fourth of the cardinal virtues, and is that which moderates and directs the desires of man in the use of sensible pleasures. The object of this virtue is the legitimate and proper use of what is calculated to flatter the senses.

The *rule* of temperance is not the appetite of our passions or a blind instinct, but the real wants of nature, which demand what is necessary for the preservation of life. By what is necessary is meant also that which is useful and proper.

To temperance are attached sobriety and abstinence, chastity, modesty, humility, meekness, and clemency.

The vices opposed are gluttony, drunkenness, impurity, immodesty, pride, anger, levity, dissipation, and in general all excess in things which are agreeable to the senses.

47. We call *gifts of the Holy Ghost* seven special virtues which the Holy Spirit communicates to the soul, especially in the Sacrament of Confirmation. These are the gifts of wisdom, understanding, counsel, fortitude, knowledge, piety, and the fear of the Lord.

The gift of *wisdom* makes us esteem, love, and relish the things of God.

The gift of *understanding* makes us comprehend and penetrate the truths of faith.

The gift of *counsel* makes us choose whatever contributes to the greater glory of God and our salvation; it includes the discernment of spirits.

The *gift of fortitude* inspires us with courage to overcome all obstacles in the way of salvation, especially human respect and persecutions.

The gift of *knowledge* makes us know what is necessary for salvation and perfection; it is the science of the saints.

The gift of *piety* makes us embrace with joy all that relates to the service of God; and it animates us with a filial affection for God, the Blessed Virgin, and the saints.

The gift of the *fear of the Lord* makes us fear, above everything, to displease God and lose His friendship by sin. It is the fear of the children of God, it is the horror of sin.

48. The virtues, which St. Paul (Gal. v. 12) calls the *fruits of the Holy Ghost,* because the Holy Ghost produces them in our souls, are charity, joy, peace, patience, longanimity, goodness, benignity, mildness, faith or fidelity, modesty, continency, and chastity.

Third Article : Good Works.

49. There are three kinds of *good works*, which include all the others, namely, *prayer, fasting,* and *almsdeeds.* These works, as the Catechism of the Council of Trent teaches, are three remedies for the three concupiscences. Moreover, by prayer we appease the justice of God, by alms-deeds we satisfy our neighbour, and by fasting we chastise ourselves. Good works are, (1) *meritorious* in the sight of God; they merit grace in this life and heavenly glory in the next. (2) *Satisfactory;* they make satisfaction for the temporal punishment due to our sins. (3) *Impetratory;* they obtain the pardon of our venial sins, and the graces of which we stand in need.

50. Works of mercy are divided into corporal and

spiritual. The *corporal works* of mercy are, (1) to feed the hungry; (2) to give drink to the thirsty; (3) to clothe the naked; (4) to harbour the harbourless; (5) to visit the sick; (6) to visit the imprisoned; (7) to bury the dead.

51. The *spiritual works* of mercy are, (1) to bring sinners to repentance; (2) to instruct the ignorant; (3) to counsel the doubtful; (4) to comfort the sorrowful; (5) to bear wrongs patiently; (6) to forgive injuries; (7) to pray for the living and the dead.

52. These works of mercy or of charity, which are more or less obligatory for all, are of strict obligation and justice for certain persons and in certain circumstances. Thus parents and superiors are obliged by duty and by justice to give good advice to their inferiors, to reprehend them if they do wrong, to instruct them, &c.

53. The eight *beatitudes* are eight special virtues, for which Jesus Christ has promised eternal beatitude, in the following terms:

(1) Blessed are the poor in spirit, for theirs is the kingdom of heaven.

(2) Blessed are the meek, for they shall possess the land.

(3) Blessed are those that mourn, for they shall be comforted.

(4) Blessed are they that hunger and thirst after justice, for they shall have their fill.

(5) Blessed are the merciful, for they shall obtain mercy.

(6) Blessed are the clean of heart, for they shall see God.

(7) Blessed are the peace-makers, for they shall be called the children of God.

(8) Blessed are they that suffer persecution for justice' sake, for theirs is the kingdom of heaven.

CHAPTER VI.

CHRISTIAN PERFECTION: EVANGELICAL COUNSELS, STATES OF LIFE, VOCATION.

1. THE evangelical law has degrees. It not only leads souls to justification, but to perfection.

2. Christian *justice* consists in the flight from evil and the practice of good; Christian *perfection* consists in the union of the soul with God by the bonds of perfect charity. This perfect charity requires that, free from every inordinate love of the world and of ourselves, we should love God alone in Himself and in our neighbours, and seek Him alone in all things.

The most efficacious means of arriving at this detachment and liberty of heart is the observance of the evangelical counsels, which, when confirmed by vows, constitute the religious state, called also the state of perfection.

3. The evangelical counsels of which we here speak consist in the practice of the three great virtues of voluntary poverty, perpetual chastity, and entire obedience. Our Lord proposes them as a more excellent way than the way of the commandments.

The Gospel shows us three ways of going to God. The first is that of the commandments, for all men must keep them to be saved; the second is that of the counsels, which consists in adding the evangelical counsels to the way of the commandments. Our Lord does not in any way make it obligatory, but He proposes it to generous souls who wish to consecrate their existence entirely to God. Such is religious life. The third way is that of celibacy, or of virginity, in the world.

4. We have thus three states of life—marriage, celibacy, and religious life. These states are all venerable and holy, but not equally perfect if considered in themselves, or as a means of salvation and sanctification.

Celibacy is more perfect than marriage, and the religious life the most perfect of the three.

5. The religious state is found in the Monastic Orders approved by the Church. The faithful who wish to join them must engage to live according to the rules, and to aim at perfection by the observance of the perpetual vows of poverty, chastity, and obedience.

By these sacred vows man not only offers to God all that he has and is, but he also removes the great obstacles to Christian perfection.

The religious state is in itself only of counsel, a gift offered to the free choice of those who have to decide on a state of life; but it may become an obligation in a case where a person cannot save his soul without employing this great means of salvation.

6. Nothing is more holy, more beautiful, or more meritorious than to follow the evangelical counsels and embrace the religious life, provided we are called to it by God. The divine *vocation* manifests itself ordinarily by the following signs: (1) a spiritual and constant attraction, founded on motives of reason and faith; (2) the qualities requisite for fulfilling the obligations which are to be contracted, and the dispositions for fulfilling them; (3) the moral possibility of quitting the world, or the absence of serious obstacles; (4) the consent of a prudent and wise director.

CHAPTER VII.

THE SACRAMENTS.

1. THE law of God, which we have so far explained, is the way of salvation traced out by Jesus Christ, the way in which the Christian must walk, by avoiding sin and practising virtue. To accomplish this, man, who is

in his nature weak, requires help and means; and an all-powerful help is offered to him, which is the grace of God. Means are placed at his disposal for obtaining grace, and these means are the Sacraments and prayer. That which relates to grace has been explained elsewhere; we have still to direct our attention to the Sacraments and to prayer. We will begin with the Sacraments.

The Sacraments of Baptism, Confirmation, and Extreme Unction do not require further explanation than that which has been already given in the 'Dogmatic' section. It will suffice to add here, that parents are obliged to procure the blessing of the two first for their children, and that, in case of sickness, the sick person himself, and those who have care of him, should think in time of the salutary Sacrament of Extreme Unction.

As to the other Sacraments—Confession, Communion, Holy Orders, and Marriage—we will complete the dogmatic doctrine already given concerning them by briefly explaining what concerns them from a practical point of view.

First Article : Confession.

2. The effects of the Sacrament of Penance are: (1) the remission of our sins, and reconciliation with God, by the infusion of sanctifying grace. (2) The remission of the eternal punishment and a part, at least, of the temporal punishment. (3) An increase of sanctifying grace, when the penitent is already in a state of grace. (4) Actual graces, to enable us worthily to expiate our sins, and to prevent our again falling into them. (5) The recovering of the merits of our good works, which we had lost by mortal sin, and which are revived by holy absolution.

3. Sacramental confession is rendered obligatory by the law of God and the law of the Church. All the

faithful who have arrived at the age of discretion are obliged to go to confession at least once a year during life, and a last time at the approach of death.*

4. The Sacrament of Penance as it concerns the penitent has three parts, contrition, confession, and satisfaction. The principal of the three is contrition.

5. (1) Contrition is a *sorrow* of the soul, a real regret for having offended God, and a detestation of the sins we have committed, joined to a firm purpose not to commit them for the future.

This *sorrow* must be *interior*, coming from the bottom of our heart; *supernatural*, excited in us by a movement of the Holy Ghost and by supernatural motives, that is to say, by the consideration of certain truths of faith such as these: that sin merits for us eternal death and makes us lose heaven; that it is a black ingratitude towards God, a revolt against His Supreme Majesty, &c. Contrition must also be *universal*, extending to all our sins, or at least to all our mortal sins; *sovereign*, causing us to detest sin as a sovereign evil. This sorrow need not be *sensible*, since it consists in the disposition of the *will*, which hates and detests sin. *The firm purpose* of amendment, or a resolution never to sin again for the future, must have similar qualities to those we have just enumerated for the sorrow; it must be *sincere, firm, universal, efficacious*, which means that the penitent must take the means which are judged necessary in order to avoid sin, and must above all shun the immediate occasions of it.

6. Contrition *for venial sins* must also be interior, supernatural, and sovereign, without which it is impossible to obtain pardon; but it is not necessary that it should be universal; for one venial sin can be remitted without the others we may have committed, which does not hold good with regard to mortal sin. As the forgiveness of mortal sin is a reconciliation with God, to

* See the 'Fourth Commandment of the Church.'

receive pardon of one mortal sin and not of all the others would be to reconcile ourselves to God and still remain His enemy.

7. *Perfect* contrition is founded on the love of God, *imperfect* contrition on the deformity of sin or the fear of hell. I have *perfect* contrition if I am sorry for having offended God because He is sovereignly amiable, good, and perfect in Himself, and because sin displeases Him. I have *imperfect* contrition if I repent of having offended God because by doing so I have merited His chastisements and forfeited heaven.

Though imperfect contrition is sufficient for confession we must nevertheless try to excite ourselves to perfect contrition, because it is more meritorious and more agreeable to God. Moreover, if we cannot confess to a priest, perfect contrition suffices in itself to efface sin and restore us to the grace of God without absolution, provided we have the desire to receive it.

8. (2) Confession is the *humble, sincere, candid,* and *entire* accusation of our sins made to a priest, in order to receive absolution. Confession is necessary, because Jesus Christ willed that it should form part of the Sacrament, and also because without the declaration of our sins the priest could not know whether to remit or retain them.

9. Confession, in order to be *sincere,* must be a declaration of our sins, such as we know them to be after a serious examination, without making them appear either greater or less, without either exaggeration or excuse. We must avoid naming third persons and telling unnecessary histories, and we must express ourselves in a becoming manner.

10. We must, in order to make our confession *entire,* accuse ourselves of all the mortal sins which we have committed since our last well-made confession. We must tell the exact number, or, if we cannot remember the exact number, the number as nearly as we can,

adding the words *more* or *less*. We must also declare the circumstances, (1) when they alter the kind of sin; for example, in a case of theft, where the stolen object is a sacred vessel; for in such case there is a double sin, namely, theft and sacrilege; (2) when they render mortal a sin which in its nature is venial, or venial a sin which is in its nature mortal. It is useful also to declare any *aggravating* circumstances, especially those which considerably augment the gravity of the sin.

11. If the confessor interrogates the penitent concerning his sins, he is bound to answer him sincerely.

12. A mortal sin involuntarily forgotten is remitted with the others; but if afterwards it recurs to the memory it must be confessed at least at the next confession.

13. It is not necessary, though it is very useful, to confess venial sins, especially those to which we are most attached.

14. A general confession is necessary if the preceding confessions have been null, either for want of sincerity or repentance. Sometimes, without being necessary, it is useful; for instance, when we are preparing to embrace a state of life. When properly made, a general confession has the advantage of inspiring us with a more lively contrition, of animating our courage to begin a new life, and of procuring us a greater peace of conscience.

15. (3) Sacramental satisfaction is the acceptation and accomplishment of the penance imposed upon us by our confessor in reparation for the injury done to God by sin. It must be accomplished with care, and without delay.

We must also make satisfaction to our neighbour by repairing as far as possible the wrongs we have caused him, and by being reconciled with him if we have offended him.

Not content with fulfilling our sacramental penance,

we should try to make entire satisfaction to God by offering Him prayers, mortifications, alms, works, and the troubles of life, and also by gaining indulgences.

16. An *indulgence* is the remission of the temporal punishment due to the divine justice for our sins, the guilt of which has been forgiven. The Church, by virtue of the power which she has received to this effect from Jesus Christ, grants indulgences in order to supply for the insufficiency of our satisfaction, and also to excite and encourage the faithful to the practice of good works, the frequentation of the Sacraments, and meditation on the sufferings of our Saviour. It is for the last reason that the richest indulgences have been attached to the beautiful devotion of the *Way of the Cross.*

To gain indulgences we must (1) be in a state of grace, (2) we must fulfil exactly all the conditions prescribed by the Church; and if we desire to gain a plenary indulgence we must, moreover, in order to gain it fully, be free from all affection to venial sin. We can apply indulgences to the souls in purgatory when the Church declares them to be applicable. This is an excellent work of charity.

17. In order to make *a good confession* we ought (1) to place ourselves in the presence of God, and beg His grace that we may make a fitting preparation for the Sacrament of Penance; that we may know our sins and sincerely repent of them. It is a pious practice to consider that the confession we are about to make may, perhaps, be the last of our lives, and that we are going to make it to Jesus Christ Himself in the person of His minister.

(2) We must carefully examine our conscience. This examination must be based upon the commandments of God and of the Church, on the duties of our state, on the capital sins, on our predominant passion and bad habits. We must also examine as to the scandal we

may have given, and our sins of omission; the sins of others, the occasions to which we have wilfully exposed ourselves, our interior sins, our wilful thoughts, and evil desires of revenge, injustice, impurity, &c. We should also call to mind in what places we have been, who have been our companions, and what our occupations.

(3) After the examination of conscience we must occupy ourselves with contrition by considering, (a) the enormity of mortal sin, by which we lose heaven and expose ourselves to hell-fire; (b) the innumerable benefits of God, and the ingratitude of the sinner towards Him; (c) Jesus nailed to the Cross for love of us; and lastly, a God infinitely good and amiable, whom we have offended by our sins. After these considerations, which should lead us to repent of and detest our sins, we must make a firm purpose never to commit them again, to avoid the occasions of them, and to serve God with love and fidelity.

(4) When we have prepared in this way we must make our confession to a priest, remembering that he holds the place of Jesus Christ. We should begin our accusation by the gravest sins, lest we should forget them, or be tempted to conceal them through shame. If we have only venial sins to confess it is good to add one or more of the sins of our past life, for which we have the most lively sorrow. If the confessor asks an explanation, we must answer him with sincerity and modesty; if he gives us advice, we must listen with docility; and if he should find it necessary to withhold absolution, we must submit to his judgment.

18. A confessor is obliged to withhold absolution, (1) from those who refuse to overcome their hatred of their neighbour. (2) From those who, being able, refuse to make restitution of another's goods, or to make reparation for the injury they have done to their neighbour's reputation. (3) From those who are in the immediate

occasions of mortal sin and will not leave them. By *immediate occasion* we mean a person, a society, a house, an amusement, &c., which generally makes us fall into mortal sin, or would probably make us fall into it soon. (4) From those who refuse to make public reparation for, or to put an end to, a grave scandal. (5) From those who are ignorant of the truths of faith, which we are bound to know. (6) And lastly, from those who do not show any sign of contrition.

19. After confession we should thank God for the blessing which we have received, and beg of Him the grace to follow faithfully the advice of our confessor; and after that we should perform our penance.

Second Article : Holy Communion.

20. Holy Communion is the sacramental reception of the Blessed Eucharist. Our Lord instituted the Blessed Eucharist under the form of bread and wine to show that He wished in this Sacrament to be the food of our souls, just as ordinary bread and wine are the food of our bodies.

21. Communion is necessary for adults by *necessity* of precept. A divine precept of Jesus Christ obliges Christians to go to Holy Communion from time to time during life, and in the particular case of a dangerous illness. Besides this, a commandment of the Church prescribes the Paschal Communion.*

22. In order to communicate worthily, certain conditions are requisite; some of them regard the soul, some the body. The dispositions of the soul are, (1) the state of grace, which is absolutely necessary in order to make a good communion; (2) lively sentiments of faith, hope, charity, humility, and repentance, and a sincere desire to be united to Jesus Christ. The dispositions of the body are—to be fasting, excepting in case of illness, when the Blessed Sacrament is received as

* See above, the 'Fifth Commandment of the Church.'

viaticum, or again afterwards out of devotion. We must observe a proper and modest demeanour, and show the exterior recollection and respect due to the august mysteries in which we are about to participate.

23. Holy Communion is a tree of life, the *fruits* of which are as precious as they are abundant; (1) it unites us closely to Jesus Christ and augments sanctifying grace; (2) it bestows on the soul actual graces, which nourish and strengthen it to resist evil and practise virtues, above all the virtues of chastity and charity; (3) it remits venial sin and preserves us from mortal sin; (4) it sanctifies our bodies, sows in us the seeds of a glorious resurrection, and gives us a pledge of eternal life.

24. Affection to venial sins, negligence in preparing, and lukewarmness diminish the fruits of communion. Christians who habitually communicate with indifference are those who do not take the trouble to avoid venial sins, who are unfaithful to their exercises of piety, and who do not labour to correct their faults.

25. When we wish to communicate, we must, after being purified from all mortal sin, take proper time to excite the sentiments of faith and devotion enumerated above. With this view, we must produce from our hearts corresponding acts, by using, if we choose to do so, a prayer-book in which such acts are expressed. After Holy Communion, we should make at least a quarter of an hour's thanksgiving, by entertaining ourselves familiarly with the Divine Guest, whom we have the happiness to possess, or by using the prayers after Holy Communion set down in our prayer-book.

26. A communion which is made with a conscience stained by mortal sin is an unworthy communion, a sacrilege, and a profanation of the Body and Blood of Jesus Christ. It is an enormous crime, which often produces blindness of the understanding, hardness of heart, and final impenitence.

27. *Frequent* communion, properly so called, is not

weekly communion, but communion several times in the week, or even every day. Weekly communion is sometimes necessary, or at least very useful, in helping us to resist temptation, to overcome our bad habits, and to preserve the life of grace. More frequent communion requires particular dispositions. We must be not only free from all mortal sin and all affection to venial sin, but, moreover, we must have overcome most of our evil inclinations, we must meditate daily, and derive solid fruits from so great a grace. This is the doctrine of theologians and masters of the spiritual life.

28. *A spiritual communion** consists in an earnest desire of sacramental communion, in sighing for the happiness of receiving at the holy table the Body and Blood of Jesus Christ, and accompanying the desire with acts of faith, humility, and contrition for our sins. This beautiful and pious practice cannot be too highly recommended. Nothing can be more advantageous to the soul nor more pleasing to Jesus Christ, especially during the Sacrifice of the Mass, or in our visits to the Blessed Sacrament.

Third Article: Holy Orders.

1. Holy Orders is a Sacrament instituted by Jesus Christ for the perpetuation in the Church of the priesthood which He conferred upon His Apostles.

2. If we look upon it as a state of life, we see at once that the priesthood is the most holy and most sublime state of Christian society. Placed in the world to be the mediator between God and men, to exercise the ministry of the altar, to console all those who are in sorrow and suffering, to make men happy by promoting the growth of virtue and religion in their souls, and thus to help them to attain to eternal blessedness, the priest is justly called a visible angel, a messenger from God, another Jesus Christ. He has received the most

---

* See above, 'Second Commandment of the Church.'

august of missions; his is the most beautiful of vocations.

He who embraces this holy state becomes at once the happiest and most venerable of men, provided he be called to it by God. Without a vocation he should never undertake it, because he would not have the abundance of the graces necessary for the fulfilment of his serious and important duties. Vocation to the priesthood manifests itself in an unmistakable manner and by special indications, namely, a solid piety, a love of Jesus Christ and His Church, an intelligent and judicious mind, a command over the passions, and a generous desire to consecrate one's life to the good of souls and the work of God upon earth.

3. The Sacrament of Holy Orders gives to the priest the power, (1) to consecrate the Body and Blood of Jesus Christ in the holy Sacrifice of the Mass; (2) to remit and to retain sins; (3) to administer several other Sacraments; (4) to preach the word of God; (5) to bless persons and things.

4. Holy Orders, once received, can never be lost. It imprints on the soul a sacred character which nothing can efface. A priest always preserves his character of priest, even though he dishonour it by an evil life, or desert his state by apostasy.

5. The faithful ought to honour priests as the ministers of Jesus Christ and the fathers of their souls. They should always respect their sacred character, show them that submission that is due to them, and evince great gratitude towards them for the spiritual services which they receive at their hands. Special consideration and love are due, (1) to the Sovereign Pontiff, because he is the head of the Church, the Vicar of Jesus Christ on earth, and the common pastor of all the faithful; (2) to the bishop who is the pastor of the diocese to which we belong—his flock are bound to respect his commands, and faithfully to obey and listen

to them; (3) to the parish priest, who has the care of our souls, and to the other priests who administer to us the helps of religion.

6. Those Christians who, whilst they pretend to respect the Church and religion, do not hesitate to indulge in falsehoods and railleries against her ministers, are guilty of hypocrisy, ingratitude, and impiety. Like unnatural children they outrage the Church, their mother, and despise Jesus Christ Himself, who has said, in speaking of His ministers: 'He that heareth you heareth Me, and he that despiseth you despiseth Me.'

Fourth Article : Matrimony.

1. We have already seen that our Lord raised the contract of matrimony to the dignity of a Sacrament, and that this Sacrament confers on those who receive it worthily the graces necessary to fulfil all the duties of Christian spouses and parents.*

By the Sacrament of Matrimony husbands and wives are established in a lasting state, *the married state*, which is a venerable and holy state, though it is inferior in dignity to that of celibacy or evangelical virginity.

2. As a sacramental sign, marriage represents the indissoluble union of Jesus Christ with His Church; hence the Apostle concludes that wives must be obedient to their husbands, as the Church is obedient to Jesus Christ; and that husbands must love their wives, as Jesus Christ loves the Church, even to delivering Himself up for her (Eph. v.).

3. For the valid contracting of marriage it is necessary to be free from any impediment of relationship or otherwise, or at least to have been legitimately dispensed therefrom; to enter into the contract before our own parish priest (or his delegate) and two witnesses.†

---

* 'Dogmatic' Part, 'On Marriage.'
† As to England, see Translator's Preface.

Without the presence of these three persons the marriage would be null. A marriage contracted solely before the civil authorities is not a real one in the eyes of God and the Church. Such pretended union, called a *civil marriage*, is nothing but a shameful concubinage in the sight of God.*

4. In order to contract a legitimate marriage we must conform to all the prescriptions of the Church concerning the banns, time, and persons.

The *banns*, or the *publications of marriage*, are announced in order to obtain prayers for those about to be married, and to discover any impediments to their marriage which might exist.

The *time*, or the day of marriage, must be chosen out of Advent and Lent.† The Church ordains this because Lent and Advent are times of penance and recollection, which are hardly compatible with nuptial rejoicings.

5. The *persons* who marry must be not only Christians and baptised, but, moreover, Catholics and true children of the Church. *Mixed marriages*—that is to say, those which Catholics contract with heretics or schismatics—are valid, but forbidden.

If the Church sometimes for grave reasons allows them by dispensation, it is only on the condition and formal promise that all the children shall be brought up in the Catholic religion. Marriage with Jews or infidels is null and void.

The Church is opposed to alliances with heretics because they are contrary to the dignity of the Sacrament, dangerous to salvation, and seldom happy. Almost as much might be said of marriages contracted with bad Christians. Deprived of the blessing of God,

---

* As to such marriages in England, see Translator's Preface.

† According to the Council of Trent, it is forbidden to solemnise marriage from the first Sunday of Advent till after the Epiphany, and from Ash Wednesday till after Low Sunday (sess. xxiv. cap. x.).

such marriages too often result in perversion, cruel disappointments, and irremediable miseries.

6. According to the custom approved by the Church, the betrothal takes place before the parish priest of the female party. Betrothal consists in the reciprocal promise of future marriage. Whether it be solemn or private, this promise binds in conscience under pain of mórtal sin; but it may be cancelled by the mutual consent of the parties, and for other reasons.

7. The ceremonies of the Sacrament of Marriage are extremely simple. The priest, having received the consent of both parties to the marriage, pronounces these words: ' And I, as minister of the Church, unite you in marriage in the name of the Father, and of the Son, and of the Holy Ghost.' Then he blesses the nuptial ring, and addresses some prayers to God to draw down His blessings and graces on the newly-married.

8. The ceremonies of marriage tend especially to mark the sacramental bond which henceforth unites the contracting parties. It is indissoluble, and can only be broken by the death of one of them. God Himself has united them, and it belongs not to man, says our Lord, ' to separate what God has joined together' (Matt. xix. 6). For weighty reasons, ecclesiastical authority sometimes allows the parties to separate, and not to live together; but the marriage always subsists before God and the Church, even when the civil authorities grant *a divorce according to the law*. To marry again after separation, and live together in that way, is to live in a state of perpetual sin.

9. The duties of husband and wife consist in having a sincere affection for each other, in mutually keeping conjugal faith, in assisting each other in every necessity, in accepting without murmuring the will of God, in bringing up children in the fear of God, instructing them in Christian doctrine, correcting them with firm-

ness, giving them good example, and keeping them away from bad companions and all that could lead them to evil.*

Infidelity in marriage violates the sacred bond of union, disturbs domestic peace, impedes the good education of children, commits a gross injustice, and exposes those who are guilty of it to the most terrible chastisements of God, who often punishes adultery even in this life.

10. In order to receive this Sacrament in a Christian manner we must, (1) pray earnestly to God that we may know if we be called to the state of marriage, and whether we shall be able to fulfil its duties; (2) we must put aside all bad intentions, and have in view God alone, and the salvation of our own souls; (3) we must use great prudence in the choice of a suitable person, and look to virtue and religious sentiments rather than to riches or other perishable gifts; (4) before coming to a decision we should ask the advice of our parents or other prudent persons; (5) we should apply in good time to our pastor, so as to receive his instructions, and have the betrothal celebrated; (6) we should carefully acquaint ourselves with all the duties of the married state, and all that concerns a Christian life, so as to be able to instruct our children; (7) from the time of betrothal to that of marriage we must carefully avoid every offence against God, multiply our prayers and good works, prepare in good time for confession and Holy Communion, and receive those Sacraments at least three days before that of the marriage; we should celebrate the marriage at the time fixed without delay, unless we are obliged to postpone it through necessity or for some lawful reason; (8) we should spend the marriage-day in Christian rejoicing and celebrating our nuptials, with the fear of the Lord before us; (9) we should annually sanctify the anniversary of marriage

* See 'The Fourth Commandment.'

by approaching the Sacraments on that day, or at least by hearing Mass, and renewing our resolution to fulfil the duties imposed by Christian matrimony.

11. Bad marriages, which are, alas, too frequent, are often accompanied by evils and troubles, which make the married state a hell upon earth. The general causes are, (1) the disorders of youth, unlawful associations, and the unchristian intentions with which this holy state is embraced; (2) the want of preparation for the Sacrament of Marriage, which some persons do not fear to profane, by receiving it in a state of mortal sin, as if they were ignorant that this crime brings down the vengeance of God, instead of His graces and blessings; (3) the guilty conduct of those who are married, which is sometimes so abominable in the eyes of God that it merits His most terrible chastisements. Those who receive this great Sacrament in the spirit of Jesus Christ escape all these evils, and find the peace of the Christian family.

CHAPTER VIII.

PRAYER.

1. BESIDES the Sacraments, we possess another great means of obtaining the grace of God, namely, that of *prayer*. Prayer is a raising of the soul to God, a communication with God to render Him our homage, and to beg Him to grant us His favours. By prayer we render to God *homage;* that is, adoration, praise, thanksgiving, and proofs of love and devotion. By prayer we also beg of God His *favours*, forgiveness of our sins, the graces necessary for us to lead a good life, and all the good things we stand in need of both for body and soul.

2. Prayer glorifies the perfections of God, His power, wisdom, and goodness; it unites us to God, elevates and sanctifies our thoughts; it strengthens us against evil, encourages us to good, consoles us in tribulation, obtains for us help in all our needs, and all graces, even the great gift of final perseverance.

3. Prayer is necessary by necessity of precept and necessity of means; or, in other words, it is at once obligatory and necessary for every Christian who has arrived at the use of reason. (1) Prayer is necessary by the *necessity of precept*, since God commands us to pray; (2) it is necessary by the *necessity of means*, since we could not observe the divine law without the help of grace, nor can we generally obtain grace except by means of prayer. Such is the disposition of Divine Providence, who generally bestows His gifts only on those who humbly implore them. For this reason Jesus Christ has earnestly recommended prayer both by His precept and example, and has gone so far as to say that we must 'pray *always*' and without ceasing (Luke xviii. 1.).

4. When must we pray? Our Lord says that we must pray always and without ceasing, which means that we must do so frequently, by raising our hearts to God and offering Him our occupations, sufferings, and joys. There are, however, days and periods which impose on us the duty of special prayer. These are Sundays and feast-days, times of affliction and temptation, critical circumstances, when, for example, there is question of choosing a state of life, or preparing for the near approach of death.

Moreover, a true Christian does not fail to pray morning and evening, and before and after meals.

5. *Morning* and *evening* prayer is a practice as ancient as Christianity, and one which is universally received in the Church. As these prayers need not be long, they are practicable for all. There is no one,

generally speaking, who cannot recite every morning and night at least the Our Father, the Hail Mary, and the Creed, and an Act of Contrition.

6. Prayers *before and after meals* have also been in use amongst the faithful from the earliest times, and every good Christian considers it a duty to preserve the custom. The Church, in her liturgy, has a formula for the blessing and grace before and after meals, just as she has prayers for morning and evening in the canonical hours.

7. We must pray for the living and for the dead, for ourselves and for others; that is to say, for our superiors, benefactors, friends, and even for our enemies. We must pray also for the Church and her august head; 'for kings, and for all that are in high stations' (1 Tim. ii.); for the conversion of sinners, the perseverance of the just, the propagation of the faith, and for the good of our country.

8. We must ask of God before all else the good of our souls, and all that concerns salvation. At the same time we are allowed also to pray for temporal goods, such as health and success in business; but we must ask for them in a Christian spirit; that is to say, for a good end, with the glory of God in view, and with submission to His divine will.

9. We must pray in the name and through the merits of Jesus Christ, our Advocate and supreme Mediator, and make our prayer with attention, humility, confidence, resignation, and perseverance. In order to fulfil these conditions we must recollect ourselves at the commencement of our prayer, and be penetrated with the thought of the presence of God. A lively faith in the divine presence is the key to prayer; and we must persevere in this holy practice in spite of the distractions which may supervene; for involuntary distractions do not detract from the merit or the value of our prayers.

10. Prayer is all-powerful; it can obtain everything from God, not only because it glorifies the divine perfections, but also because it rests on the promises of God and on the merits of Jesus Christ. We may expect all from God, who can do all, and who will grant us all through the merits of Jesus Christ.

11. If we do not always obtain what we ask for, the reason is either that we do not pray well, or that what we ask for would not be beneficial, or that we have not persevered long enough in our petition. God sometimes defers hearing our petition to try our faith, to punish our lukewarmness, or to make us more humble and vigilant. Sometimes, also, it happens that he who asks for one favour obtains another, better than the one he desired; as for example, instead of the cure of a malady God grants the grace to bear it in a Christian spirit.

12. The church, called the House of God, is, by excellence, the holy place, the place of prayer. 'It is written that My house is the house of prayer' (Luke xix. 46). Public prayer, which is said in common in the church, is of especial efficacy. Jesus Christ promised to be in a special manner in the midst of those who pray in common.

13. *Vocal* prayer is that which springs from the heart and finds utterance in words. Thus when we piously say the Lord's Prayer we pray vocally. *Mental* prayer is made interiorly, and does not seek external expression. It is generally called *prayer* or *meditation*. Meditation consists in a holy reflection made at the feet of God, in a manner calculated to excite in our hearts pious affections towards His Divine Majesty. We reflect on the truths of religion that we may know them better, that so we may love them, relish them, and obtain the grace to conform our life to them. Meditation produces the greatest fruit in the soul; it is necessary for all those who aspire to perfection.

14. We generally begin our prayers by the sign of

the Cross, which is called the sign of the Christian. This sign reminds us of the mysteries of the Blessed Trinity, the Incarnation, and the Redemption. When we make it with faith and devotion it drives away temptations, and draws down upon us the blessings of God, for which reasons it is good to use it very frequently.

15. The Lord's Prayer, or 'Our Father,' is the most excellent of prayers, (1) because Jesus Christ Himself is the Author of it; (2) because it is a summary of all that we can wish or ask for. We must know it from necessity of precept, because our Lord has expressly commanded us to recite it.

This divine prayer is composed of a preface and of seven petitions.

The *preface* is contained in these words : ' Our Father who art in heaven.' We call God 'our Father,' (1) because we owe to Him our life, all that we are, and all that we have; (2) because, having adopted us through Jesus Christ, He recognises us as the brethren of His only Son, He loves us as His children, and makes us heirs of His kingdom. We add, 'who art in heaven,' in order to raise our hearts to heaven, where we are called to abide with God our Father, and also to make us desire and ask for whatever may render us worthy of this happiness. The seven *petitions* then follow :

(1) 'Hallowed be Thy name.' By this, the first of the seven *petitions*, we pray, (1) that the name of God may never be blasphemed or profaned; (2) that God may be known, loved, served, and glorified by all men, and particularly by ourselves.

(2) 'Thy kingdom come.' Here we pray, (1) that God may reign in all hearts, but especially in our own, by His grace and His love; (2) that He may make us reign with Him one day in heaven; (3) that the kingdom of God, which is the Church, may be extended more and more over the whole earth.

(3) 'Thy will be done on earth, as it is in heaven.'

By this petition we pray for grace to accomplish the will of God on earth, to obey His commandments with as much love and fidelity—if that be possible—as the blessed do in heaven.

(4) 'Give us this day our daily bread.' These words signify, 'Give us each day that which is necessary both for the life of soul and body.' For the life of the soul, —the word of God, grace, and the Holy Eucharist; for that of the body,—food, clothing, and lodging. We say *give us*, and not *give me*, because we must not pray for ourselves only, but for all others; because we are all members of one family. The words 'this day' teach us that we must not be anxious about the morrow, but banish excessive solicitude, and trust in God to give us what is necessary for each day.

(5) 'Forgive us our trespasses, as we forgive them that trespass against us.' By these words we beg pardon for our sins and the grace of a sincere repentance; but as God only forgives us in proportion as we forgive others, we add that we do forgive them with all our heart.

(6) 'And lead us not into temptation;' that is to say, preserve us from temptations, or grant us the grace to overcome them. We call temptation everything that leads us to offend God by sin.

(7) 'But deliver us from evil.' By this must be understood all the evils which can come to us either in this world or in the next, but especially from the spiritual evils of sin and eternal damnation.

Amen or 'So be it.' This conclusion confirms and ratifies all the prayers which have gone before it, and expresses an earnest desire to be heard.

16. After the Lord's Prayer, the Church generally recites the Angelical Salutation, to offer her prayers to God through the intercession of the Blessed Virgin Mary.

The Angelical Salutation, or 'Hail Mary,' the most

excellent of all prayers after the 'Lord's Prayer,' is composed of three parts: (1) the words spoken by the angel Gabriel to Mary on the day of the Annunciation; (2) those of St. Elizabeth, the cousin of the Mother of God, on the day of the Visitation; (3) a concluding supplication, 'Holy Mary, Mother of God,' &c., which is added by the Church.

The words of this beautiful prayer include things the most sublime; they may be briefly explained by the help of the following paraphrase:

'Hail, Mary, full of grace.' I salute and congratulate thee, O Blessed Virgin. Thou hast received from God more abundant graces than have been bestowed on any other creature, and thou hast constantly added to them by thy perfect fidelity and the sanctity of thy life.

'The Lord is with thee' in an especial and most wonderful way. He was with thee from the time of thine Immaculate Conception, and still more so at His Incarnation, and during the remainder of thy mortal life. He is with thee now in eternal glory for all eternity.

'Blessed art thou amongst women,' because thou hast been chosen from amongst all women to be the mother of God; because, in becoming a mother, thou didst not cease to be a virgin; and because thou art raised in sanctity and in glory above all women and above all creatures.

'And blessed is the fruit of thy womb, Jesus.' Jesus Christ, thy Divine Son, who has saved us and loaded us with blessings, is Himself, together with the Father and the Holy Ghost, the object of all the blessings of angels and of men for all eternity.

'Holy Mary, Mother of God, pray for us;' obtain for us from God by thy powerful intercession the forgiveness of our sins, and the grace to live and die holily.

17. Every Christian must honour the Blessed Virgin above the saints and angels with a special devotion, (1) because she surpasses them all in sanctity, being *full*

of grace; (2) because she surpasses them all in dignity, being the Mother of God and the Queen of Heaven; (3) because we must honour and love in a special manner her whom Jesus Christ Himself so much honoured and loved on earth, and whom He still loves and honours more than all the saints in heaven; (4) because Jesus Christ gave us Mary to be our mother and protectress; (5) because we must testify great gratitude towards her for her benefits, and constantly have recourse with great confidence to her powerful help.

Our *confidence* in her is founded on her power with God, and on the maternal affection she bears towards each one of us. Her *power* she derives from Jesus Christ, her Divine Son, who, by honouring her as His Mother, has constituted her Queen of Heaven, of angels, and of men. Her affection towards us springs from her double quality of Mother of God and mother of men. Jesus Christ gave us to her, and she adopted us as her children at the foot of the Cross.

18. Our devotion towards the Blessed Virgin *must consist*, (1) in honouring, loving, and invoking her; (2) in meditating on her virtues in order that we may imitate them, and become like unto our Saviour Jesus Christ, after her example. The *fruits* of devotion to our good Mother are consolations and continual helps from her during life, and her assistance at the hour of death. The *practices* of devotion to the Blessed Virgin especially recommended by the Church are, to celebrate her feasts by approaching the Sacraments; to recite the Litany in her honour; to say the Angelus and the Rosary; to honour and invoke her Immaculate Heart; to join one of the confraternities or congregations established in her honour; to wear her scapular; and above all, to love and glorify her Divine Son in the holy Sacrament of the Altar.

CHAPTER IX.

FEASTS, CEREMONIES, AND RELIGIOUS PRACTICES OF THE CHURCH.

1. BESIDES the Sacraments and prayer, the Christian finds another powerful means of salvation and sanctification in the feasts, ceremonies, and religious practices of the Church.

Ever guided by the Spirit of her Divine Spouse, holy Church has instituted feasts and sacred ceremonies, (1) in order to render worship more solemn and more worthy of the Divine Majesty; (2) to instruct and edify the faithful by helping them to understand and love religion by these agreeable and easy means.

2. Christian ceremonies are external signs, sacred observances, and in general, all the outward forms with which the Church publicly honours the Divine Majesty. These ceremonies consist either in actions, such as genuflexions and signs of the Cross; in words, such as prayers, hymns, or melodious songs; or in objects which are presented to the sight, such as the sacred vestments and ornaments of the altar. The various ceremonies constituting one special whole are called a *rite;* for example, the rite of the Mass, the rite of Baptism; and the whole of the different rites of the Church constitutes public worship or the liturgy.

3. The celebration of feasts is marked by special ceremonies. Every feast has its particular character, its ceremonies, and its colour. There are five *liturgical colours* —white, red, green, purple, and black. White, which is symbolical of innocence, grace, and glory, is used at Easter, and the other feasts of our Lord, of His holy Mother, and the holy confessors and virgins; red, which is the colour of fire and blood, is reserved for Pentecost, and the feasts of the martyrs; green signifies hope; purple, penance; and black, mourning and the prayers for

the dead. The several colours which are thus set apart for the different solemnities, give to each an appropriate outward character.

4. As we have already seen in the explanation of the first commandment of the Church, the ecclesiastical year is like a chain of feasts, which presents in turn to the eye of the Christian the principal mysteries of his faith, and the most cherished objects of his love.

This series of feasts and solemnities commences with the holy season of Advent, at the end of the month of November. With Advent begins also the ecclesiastical year.

5. *Advent* is a period consecrated by the Church to the honour of the mystery of the Incarnation, with a view of preparing the faithful worthily to celebrate the birth in time of the Divine Word on Christmas-day. This period, which comprises the four weeks before Christmas, represents the four thousand years which elapsed from the time of Adam to the coming of Jesus Christ. It recalls to our minds the desires of the patriarchs and prophets who sighed for this coming. We may sanctify Advent by four excellent practices: (1) by adoring in spirit the Incarnate Word, and congratulating our Lady on her happiness; (2) by ardently begging that Jesus Christ would come and establish and strengthen His reign in our hearts; (3) by renewing our spirit of prayer, recollection, and mortification; (4) by devoutly approaching the Sacraments.

6. The eighth of December is set apart as the feast of the Immaculate Conception of the Blessed Virgin, the Mother of God. Mary was conceived without the stain of original sin, and preserved from it by the future merits of Jesus Christ, whose Mother she was destined to become. From the first moment of her existence she was enriched with the treasures of grace, and adorned with all the gifts of the Holy Ghost. This is the mystery which the Church celebrates on this day.

7. *Christmas-day* is the feast of the Birth of our Lord, Jesus Christ. On this day priests celebrate three Masses to honour the threefold birth of the Son of God: His birth in time in the stable of Bethlehem; His spiritual birth by faith and charity in the souls of the shepherds and the faithful; and lastly, His eternal birth or generation in the bosom of the Father. Though we are not bound to assist at the three Masses, fervent Catholics endeavour not to forego a practice which is so holy and so conformable with the spirit of the Church.

8. The first of January is the day on which is celebrated the Circumcision of our Lord. The Circumcision in the Old Law was a painful and humiliating ceremony prescribed to the Israelites as a sign of their alliance with God, and of their faith in the future Messiah. It was the distinguishing mark of the children of Abraham, and obliged them to observe the law of Moses, just as Baptism, of which it was the figure, obliges Christians to observe the law of Jesus Christ. The mystery of the Circumcision of our Lord teaches us that we must practise spiritual circumcision, which consists in casting out from our souls all sin and all irregular and even superfluous and useless desires.

On the day of the Circumcision, the Son of God made man received the name of *Jesus*, which signifies *Saviour;* an adorable name that should inspire us with sentiments of respect, confidence, and love.

9. Five days after is the feast of the *Epiphany*. The word *Epiphany* signifies *manifestation*. We celebrate on that day the three great mysteries by which Jesus Christ made Himself known, and manifested His glory to men: (1) the vocation of the Gentiles to the faith in the persons of the Magi, who, being led to Bethlehem by a miraculous star, believed in Jesus Christ; (2) the Baptism of our Saviour in the waters of the Jordan, when the Voice of the Heavenly Father was heard saying, 'This is My beloved Son, in whom I am

well pleased;' (3) the first miracle worked by Jesus Christ at the marriage-feast of Cana, when He changed water into wine, and thus began to manifest His power.

10. The *Purification,* or *Candlemas-day,* is at the same time a feast of the Mother of God and of her Divine Son. The law of Moses commanded that the first-born male children should be offered to God in thanksgiving for the favour granted formerly to the first-born of the Israelites in Egypt, when they were spared by the exterminating angel. This ceremony was performed forty days after the birth of the child. The law prescribed, moreover, that on the same day the mother, who had contracted a legal stain, should be purified in the temple by offering as sacrifices a lamb and a dove, or, if she were poor, a pair of turtle-doves. This was called the purification of the mother, and the presentation of the child in the Temple. It was in order to obey this law, by which, however, neither she nor the Divine Son was bound, that the Blessed Virgin went to be purified in the Temple of Jerusalem, and that she there presented her Divine Son to the Lord. At the same time, an old man called Simeon, being enlightened from heaven, recognised the infant Messiah; and taking Him in his arms with ineffable joy, he predicted that the God-Saviour would be a sign for the contradiction of men, and that the soul of His Mother would be pierced by a sword of sorrow.

11. On this feast candles are blessed, signifying, (1) that Jesus Christ is the true Light of the world by His doctrine and examples; (2) they also represent the lively faith and ardent charity with which we ought to attach ourselves to God in union with Jesus Christ. The blessed candles are carried in procession in honour of the journey of the Blessed Virgin, when she carried her Son Jesus to Jerusalem.

12. The devotion of the Forty Hours is one which was originally established to draw away the faithful

from the disorders of the Carnival, and to beg pardon of God for the sins and excesses which are committed in those days of disorder. It sometimes also takes place at other periods of the year, always having for its object to implore the mercy of God and to avert His chastisements. The devotion lasts for three days, during which the Blessed Sacrament is exposed for forty hours or thereabouts.

13. Septuagesima Sunday, which is the seventh before Passion Sunday and the third before Lent, forms a kind of preliminary to the holy time of Lent. From that day the Church withdraws her joyous 'Alleluias' from her Offices. She adopts purple vestments, in sign of penance, and begins to meditate on the sufferings of her Divine Spouse.

14. We call by the name of *Lent* the forty days of fasting and penance prescribed by the Church to her children before the feast of Easter. She established it, (1) to honour and imitate the fast of Jesus Christ in the desert; (2) to lead us to practise the penance required by our sins; (3) to dispose us to celebrate worthily the great feast of Easter.

15. On the first day of Lent, which is Wednesday, the priest puts blessed ashes on the foreheads of all the faithful, saying, 'Remember, man, that thou art dust, and unto dust thou shalt return.' The Church makes use of this ceremony, (1) to preserve the remembrance of her ancient discipline, according to which ashes were sprinkled on the heads of public penitents, to engage them to humble themselves and repent of their sins; (2) to exhort us to penance by the thought of death, which will reduce our bodies to dust.

16. The *Annunciation* is the day on which the Archangel Gabriel announced to the Blessed Virgin that she was to be the Mother of God, and on which the Divine Word was made flesh in her virginal womb. The Church therefore celebrates on this day a double feast—

the Annunciation of the Blessed Virgin and the Incarnation of the Son of God.

17. The last Sunday but one of Lent is called *Passion Sunday;* and the week which it ushers in, *Passion Week.* The Church on that day covers with a veil of mourning the images and pictures which are exposed for the veneration of the faithful, especially those of our Saviour crucified; and they are kept thus covered during the whole of Passiontide. This custom represents (1) the mourning that shrouds the Spouse of Christ during the period when His sufferings are being prepared and inflicted; (2) it reminds us of how our Lord hid His divinity during the time of His Passion; (3) it warns the faithful to withdraw at this time from all vain pleasures, so as to devote themselves as much as possible to exercises of piety and to meditation on the sufferings of their God dying for love of them.

18. The last week of Lent is called *Holy Week*, or the *Great Week,* because of the holiness and greatness of the mysteries which were accomplished by Jesus Christ during the week wherein he died, the memory of which time is celebrated by the Church at this period. These mysteries are the triumphal entry of our Saviour into Jerusalem; His last supper, when He instituted the Blessed Eucharist; His sorrowful passion and death upon the Cross; His descent into limbo, and His burial.

19. On Palm Sunday the Church honours the triumphal entry of Jesus Christ into Jerusalem five days before His death. This day is called *Palm Sunday*, because on that day branches of palm, olive, and box-wood are blessed. These are afterwards carried in procession, in memory of what the Hebrew people did to honour the entry of our Lord into Jerusalem.

20. The Matins of Holy Thursday, which are sung, like those of the two following days, on the eve, are called *Tenebræ,* because formerly they were sung during the night, and even some parts of them without lights.

It was on Maundy Thursday that the last supper took place, when the Sacrament of the Body and Blood of our Lord was instituted. The Church commemorates this mystery by the celebration of only a single Mass in each church on that day. The priest who officiates represents Jesus Christ instituting the Eucharistic Sacrifice; and the other priests, who come to receive communion at his hands, represent the Apostles who received communion from the Divine High-Priest. After Mass, the *Blessed Sacrament is removed* to a place which has been prepared for it and carefully decorated, and which is called a Sepulchre or an Altar of Repose. A covered chalice, containing a Consecrated Host, is there deposited, (1) to bring before us more strikingly the institution of the Blessed Eucharist; (2) to represent to us the laying of the Body of Jesus Christ in the tomb; (3) to enable the priest to receive communion on the next day, which is Good Friday, when the Sacrifice of the Mass is not offered. The office of the day is terminated by the *stripping of the altars*, in memory of Jesus Christ, who is represented by the altar, and who was stripped of His garments during His Passion. The altars, stripped of their ornaments, are washed and purified, so that they may be in some degree worthy of the Lamb without spot, who is to be immolated on them, and to show us with what purity of conscience we should participate in the mysteries of the Holy Eucharist.

21. In cathedral churches the bishop blesses the *holy oils* on Holy or Maundy Thursday. The day on which our Saviour instituted the Sacraments of the Holy Eucharist, Holy Orders, and, it may be, of Confirmation, appeared a fitting time for the blessing of the holy substances which are used for their administration.

22. The faithful *visit the churches* during the day of Maundy Thursday, (1) to thank Jesus Christ for the institution of the Blessed Eucharist; (2) to honour the sufferings which He endured during the different stages

of His dolorous Passion; (3) to adore Him in His tomb; and to make reparation, not only for all the outrages which were committed against Him in His Passion, but also for those which He daily receives in the adorable Sacrament of the Altar.

23. From Maundy Thursday till Holy Saturday no bells are rung, as a sign of the grief and desolation in which the Church is plunged by the death of our Saviour.

24. On the mournful day of Good Friday the Church recounts the sufferings and death of the God-Man, and, entirely covered in robes of mourning, she celebrates, in a manner, the obsequies of her Divine Spouse. One of the most beautiful ceremonies of this day is the *Adoration of the Cross*. The priest, taking off the veil which covered it, presents the crucifix to the eyes of the faithful; then, placing it on the ground, he kneels down and prostrates himself, in that image to adore God dying for us on the Cross. All the faithful are also invited to adore their Saviour and God in like manner. After they have adored Jesus Christ in His image, they adore Him in His Person under the veil of the Sacrament, which is taken back in procession from the sepulchre to the altar. The priest, having again ascended the steps of the altar, although wearing the sacrificial vestments, does not consecrate either bread or wine; he merely elevates the Host, which was consecrated on the previous day, and then receives it in Holy Communion. There is therefore, properly speaking, no Mass. The Church omits the unbloody sacrifice, in memory of the bloody sacrifice which the High-Priest of the New Law offered on this day on Mount Calvary.

25. On Holy Saturday we honour the burial of our Saviour and His descent into limbo. The principal ceremonies consist in the triple benediction of the new fire, the Paschal candle, and the baptismal font.

The *new fire*, which is produced from flint, represents Jesus Christ, who shall soon rise from the tomb and kindle in the world the fire of His divine love. The *Paschal candle* also signifies Jesus Christ, who, being the Joy and true Light of the world, takes new life at the moment of His glorious resurrection. The *five grains of incense*, which are inserted into the Paschal candle, signify the five wounds of our Saviour, and the perfumes which were used to embalm His Body. The *blessing of the baptismal font* also takes place on this day, because formerly Holy Saturday was especially set apart for the solemn administration of the Sacrament of Baptism. The same ceremony is performed, for the same reason, on the eve of Pentecost.

26. The feast of Easter, or of the resurrection of Jesus Christ, is the greatest solemnity of the year. In the Old Law also the *Pasch* was the greatest feast amongst the Jews. It was called the *Pasch*, or *Passover*, (1) because of the passage of the exterminating angel, who smote with death all the first-born of the Egyptians, but spared the houses of the Hebrews, which were marked with the blood of the lamb which they had immolated; (2) because by the Passover God released His people from a long and cruel captivity, and established them in a happy and prosperous freedom.

In the New Law the feast of the *Resurrection of our Saviour* is likewise called *Pasch*, or *Passover*, (1) because of the passage which Jesus Christ made on this day from death to life; (2) because by His resurrection He has made us pass from the death of sin to the life of grace; (3) because this feast should be the period of the Christian's passage to a new and more perfect life.

The resurrection of Jesus Christ is, (1) the foundation of our faith, because it proves the divinity of Jesus Christ, and consequently the truth of our religion; (2) the motive of our hope, because it is the pledge and model of the future resurrection of our bodies, when the members are to be reunited to their head, and our bodies to become conformable to the glorious Body of Jesus Christ.

27. The *Rogations* are public prayers, accompanied by processions, which take place on the three days before the feast of the Ascension. The Church prescribes abstinence from flesh-meat on these days.* The rogation days are instituted, (1) to appease the anger of God by our prayers and our penances, and to avert His chastisements; (2) to draw down the blessing of God on the fruits of the earth, which at this time are exposed to various accidents; (3) to implore the divine help in the various wants of the Church and State.

28. The feast of the *Ascension* celebrates the glorious mystery of our Saviour's ascending up into heaven, after having, from the time of His resurrection, spent forty days on the earth, conversing with the Apostles and speaking to them of the kingdom of God. Our Lord ascended into heaven, (1) to give to His sacred humanity the throne of glory which it had merited by its humiliation and death; (2) to prepare a place for His elect, and to inflame them with the desire of being reunited to Him in heaven; (3) that He might be their advocate and mediator before God the Father; (4) in order to send down the Holy Ghost from heaven upon His Apostles.

29. In the Old Testament *Pentecost* was celebrated in memory of the law given to Moses, and promulgated on Mount Sinai fifty days after the exodus from Egypt.

In the New Testament the feast of Pentecost is meant to honour the descent of the Holy Ghost on the Apostles and on the Church, fifty days after our Lord's resurrection.

30. All days of the year, but especially Sundays, are consecrated to the Blessed Trinity. The Church deemed it meet to establish, in addition, a special feast

* A dispensation is granted in Belgium.

for the celebration of this mystery on the first Sunday after Pentecost. This feast is meant to remind us vividly of the greatest of our mysteries, which is at the same time the foundation and epitome of our religion and the source of our justification. (1) The faithful should call to mind on *Trinity Sunday* that they have been baptised, confirmed, and sanctified in every way, in the name of the Father, the Son, and the Holy Ghost; that is to say, by virtue of the Blessed Trinity, that they have become living temples of the Blessed Trinity, and have been wholly consecrated to it. (2) They should renew this consecration of themselves to the honour and service of the Blessed Trinity. (3) They should, in union with the Church, adore and glorify the Divine Trinity, by devoutly making the sign of the Cross, and often repeating the doxology, 'Glory be to the Father, and to the Son, and to the Holy Ghost.'

31. As on Maundy Thursday the Church is chiefly occupied in mourning over her Divine Spouse, she can but imperfectly celebrate the feast of the Blessed Sacrament; therefore she has set apart another Thursday, that following Trinity Sunday, to honour the mystery of the Eucharist with all fitting solemnity. The day is rendered more marked by a solemn procession, in which the God of the Eucharist is carried in triumph, to receive our homage and praise, with all the splendour with which we can enhance them. The feast of *Corpus Christi* was instituted in 1264.

32. As the feast of the *Sacred Heart* is a completion of Corpus Christi, it is celebrated on the Friday which immediately follows the octave of the latter feast. The object of this feast is to kindle the love of our Lord Jesus Christ in the breasts of men, and to make reparation for the outrages which are committed against Him.

33. The feast of the *Visitation* is established in memory of the visit paid by the Blessed Virgin to her

cousin, St. Elizabeth, a visit which sanctified the house of Elizabeth, and called forth the wonderful words of Mary, in what is called the hymn of humility: ' My soul doth magnify the Lord !'

34. We celebrate on the *Assumption* the glorious entrance of the Blessed Virgin into heaven, whither, according to common tradition and the pious belief of the Church, she was transported, both in body and soul. In order to enter into the spirit of this feast we must rejoice in the happiness of the blessed Mother of God, excite in our souls great confidence in her powerful aid, and beg of her to obtain for us the grace to glorify her for all eternity.

35. The Church celebrates also the *Nativity*, or *birth*, of the Blessed Virgin by a special feast, (1) because this privileged creature came into the world not only exempt from sin, but already full of grace ; (2) because as the dawn heralds the rising of the sun, so did the birth of Mary herald the near approach of the Redeemer.

The Blessed Virgin's parents were St. Joachim and St. Anne, who were descendants of the family of David and the kings of Israel.

36. *Feasts of St. Michael and the Holy Angel Guardians.*—The Archangel Michael, the chief of the hierarchy of blessed spirits, remarkable for his zeal for the glory of God against Lucifer and his wicked angels, is the special protector of the Church ; it is he who conducts pure souls, who have left this life, into eternal light. Faith teaches that each one of us has an *angel guardian*, who prays for us, offers our prayers and actions to God, turns us away from evil, and excites us to good ; who protects us in danger of body and soul, and who helps us particularly at the hour of death.

37. On the first Sunday of October we celebrate the feast of the Holy Rosary. The Rosary is a prayer in

honour of the Blessed Virgin. It is composed of the Creed, followed by one Our Father, three Hail Marys, and one Glory be to the Father; and then of fifteen decades of Hail Marys, each decade preceded by an Our Father, and terminated by a Glory be to the Father, &c.

We honour the Blessed Virgin by reciting the Rosary and meditating, during the recitation of the fifteen decades, on the fifteen mysteries relating to her own life, or those of her Divine Son, connected with it. These mysteries are divided into three groups: the five *joyful* mysteries, the five *sorrowful* mysteries, and the five *glorious* mysteries. The chaplet, which is composed of five decades, represents five of these mysteries.

38. The Church has instituted the feast of *All Saints*, (1) to honour together in one solemnity all the saints and elect who are in heaven, the greater number of whom are unknown to us; (2) to excite us powerfully to virtue by so many examples; (3) to obtain for us more graces, by giving us a greater number of intercessors; (4) to help us to supply by this general feast for all our shortcomings in the honour we have rendered to the saints.

39. The Church has chosen the day following the feast of All Saints for the *commemoration of the dead*. On this day she offers solemn prayers to God for all the souls in purgatory, thus showing that the Church triumphant, the Church suffering, and the Church militant are united by the closest bonds of charity, and go to form but the one Church of Jesus Christ. In order to enter into the spirit of this day we must, (1) pray and obtain prayers, practise good works, and, above all, cause the Holy Sacrifice to be celebrated for the faithful departed; (2) we must conceive a great horror of venial sin, which is punished so rigorously in the next life; (3) we must try to make satisfaction in this world to the justice of an offended God.

D D

40. *Burial.*—A feeling of natural piety leads us to honour the mortal remains of man. In accordance with this we find amongst every people and in every age religious ceremonies set apart for the purpose of honouring the dead. The Jews prayed and celebrated a public office for the dead, and they called their cemeteries 'the houses of the living.' Christianity has its far more significant practices. Positive faith in the future life, in purgatory, and in the resurrection; the sentiment of the dignity of human nature and respect for the body which has been the temple of the Holy Ghost; charity for our deceased brethren, who implore the suffrages of our prayers,—have always inspired Christians with a pious solicitude for those who have fallen asleep in the Lord. The exalted and luminous idea which the Church cherishes of the next life, the special manner in which she looks on death, is visible in all her prayers, chants, symbols, and ceremonies for Catholic burial, which are all based on it.

41. The feast of *Dedication* was instituted in memory of the day on which a church was dedicated and solemnly consecrated to the divine worship. This consecration is performed by the bishop with imposing ceremonial and lengthy prayers, which relate to great mysteries and certain important instructions. The solemnity with which the dedication of churches is accompanied has for its aim to inspire respect for the holy places, which are truly the temples of God and the houses of prayer, for those sacred tabernacles in which Jesus Christ deigns to reside in His Sacred Humanity, in which the faithful assemble at His feet, in which God deigns in a special way to receive our homage, to listen to our petitions, and to communicate His graces to us. Churches should remind us that we also are the living temples of God.

42. The feast of the *Presentation of the Blessed Virgin* was established in honour of the oblation which the Blessed Virgin made of herself in the temple of

Jerusalem, by consecrating herself at the tenderest age to the service of the Lord by a vow of perpetual chastity. This consecration of Mary to her God was prompt, entire, and constant.

43. The *Ember-days* are days of fasting, instituted to sanctify the four seasons of the year, and to obtain worthy ministers of the altar, as has been said in the third commandment of the Church.

44. *Confraternities* are societies of pious Christians canonically established to honour some mystery or saint in a particular manner, and for the practice of certain acts of virtue or charity. The sodalities or congregations of the Blessed Virgin are a kind of confraternity. All these pious associations are meant to excite the faithful to good works, and to unite them by the bonds of Christian charity; and for this reason the Pope encourages them and enriches them with indulgences.

45. *Pilgrimages* are journeys, undertaken from devotion, to some holy place, some monument of our holy religion, where God and His saints are honoured with an especial worship, and where God is pleased to confer special favours and to work miracles. Pilgrimages are a great homage of respect rendered to God and the saints, and a powerful means of obtaining the graces of which we stand in need, of satisfying for our sins, and exciting us to piety by the sight of the sanctuaries privileged of God. The pastors of the Church are careful to prevent the abuses which might creep into these pious journeys.

46. A *procession* is a religious march of the clergy, followed by the people singing hymns, psalms, and prayers. Processions are made, (1) to honour the journeys which our Lord made during His mortal life, and particularly His painful journey to Jerusalem; (2) to remind us that our life is a journey, and that we are only wayfarers on this earth; (3) to appease the divine justice in times of public calamity, obtain some particular favour from

God, or to thank Him for some signal grace; (4) to render to God or to the Blessed Virgin a particular honour by reason of the mystery or the feast which is celebrated; (5) and lastly, to awake the piety of the faithful, to remind them of the blessings of God, to induce them to return thanks to Him, and to beg new favours from Him.

47. The *processions of the Blessed Sacrament* are especially intended, (1) to celebrate the victories of Jesus Christ over heretics and impious men who have assailed this mystery; (2) to repair the outrages which have been committed against this Sacrament of love; (3) to make public profession of our faith in His real presence; (4) to obtain His blessings on all the places and parishes through which He is carried in triumph.

48. We give the name of *Sacramentals* to certain ceremonies or objects in use in the Church, and which bear some analogy to the Sacraments, though their nature is entirely different. They do not produce any grace by their own virtue; but, by virtue of the prayers of the Church, they can obtain particular graces, and even the remission of venial sins, for those who make use of them in a spirit of faith and repentance. Under the category of Sacramentals come, (1) all that the Church blesses for her own and for our use, such as holy water, candles, bread, salt, &c.; (2) exorcisms and various prayers, which are called blessings.

The Church, making use of the power which Jesus Christ has given to her, blesses all that is intended for her use, such as altar-linen, the sacerdotal vestments, sacred vessels, crosses, statues, and objects of piety. They are blessed to make them holy, and to consecrate them to the divine service, and to render them advantageous and worthy of our veneration. The Church also blesses persons, new houses and ships, arms and standards. In particular she blesses churches and cemeteries, which she converts into holy places: to profane them would constitute a sacrilege.

After the example of Jesus Christ the Church blesses

bread, wine, and the fruits of the earth, so that all things may contribute to the welfare of those who love God, and that the blessing of the Lord may extend over all His creatures.

By using objects that are blessed we participate in the prayers and benedictions which the Church has pronounced over them, and from which they derive a very special virtue. This good and tender mother generally prays in her benedictions that the Lord would deign to turn away the scourge of His anger, that He would defend us from our enemies, and that He would grant us peace and happiness both of body and soul.

49. Amongst Sacramentals *holy water* is that most frequently used. Holy water is only common water mixed with a little salt, and sanctified by the prayers of the Church. By virtue of these prayers holy water procures for us grace, which disposes us to contrition and the remission of our sins. When used with faith and devotion it chases away the devil, averts sickness and other troublesome accidents, and even remits venial sin when properly used to those who repent of it, and who are also in a state of grace.

A true Christian takes holy water in the Church and in his house. He takes it with devotion, begging of God to purify him more and more by the Blood of Jesus Christ, and to deliver him from all dangers. When he falls sick, his bed is sprinkled with it; and when he comes to die, his mortal remains receive it upon them; so also does the grave in which his body rests in hope, awaiting the awakening of the glorious resurrection.

THE END.

www.ingramcontent.com/pod-product-compliance
Lightning Source LLC
Chambersburg PA
CBHW030558300426
44111CB00009B/1031